STREET ATLAS
Bristol and Avon

Contents

III *Key to map symbols*

IV *Key to map pages*

VI *Administrative boundaries*

1 *Street maps*

140 *Index explanation and abbreviations*

141 *Index of towns, villages and rural localities*

142 *Index of street names*

PHILIP'S

First edition published 1995
Reprinted 1999, 2000 by

George Philip Ltd, a division of
Octopus Publishing Group Ltd
2-4 Heron Quays, London E14 4JP

ISBN 0-540-06142-5 (pocket)

To the best of the Publishers' knowledge, the infor-
mation in this atlas was correct at the time of going
to press. No responsibility can be accepted for any
errors or their consequences.

The representation in this atlas of a road, track or
path is no evidence of the existence of a right of way.

Printed and bound in Great Britain
by Cox & Wyman Ltd, Reading, Berkshire

Key to map symbols

⇌	**British Rail station**
🚂	**Private railway station**
⬤	**Bus or coach station**
Ⓗ	**Heliport**
◆	**Police station** (may not be open 24 hours)
✚	**Hospital with casualty facilities** (may not be open 24 hours)
▢	**Post office**
+	**Place of worship**
◣	**Important building**
P	**Parking**
174	**Adjoining page indicator**
✕	**No adjoining page**
▬▬	**Motorway**
▬▬	**Dual carriageway**
▭	**Main or through road**
A27(T)	**Road numbers** (Department of Transport)
⊤	**Gate or obstruction to traffic** (restrictions may not apply at all times or to all vehicles)
- - - -	**Path, bridleway, byway open to all traffic, road used as public path, dismantled railway etc.**
═══	**Track**

The representation in this atlas of a road, track or path is no evidence of the existence of a right of way

Amb Sta	**Ambulance station**	LC	**Level crossing**
Coll	**College**	Liby	**Library**
FB	**Footbridge**	Mus	**Museum**
F Sta	**Fire station**	Sch	**School**
Hospl	**Hospital**	TH	**Town hall**

0	¼	½	¾	1 mile
0	250m	500m	750m	1 Kilometre

The scale of the maps is approximately 2½ inches to 1 mile (1:25497)

The small numbers around the edges of the maps identify the 1 kilometre National Grid lines

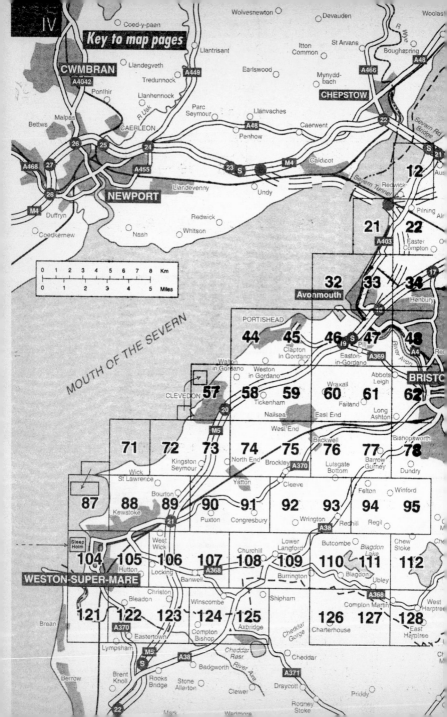

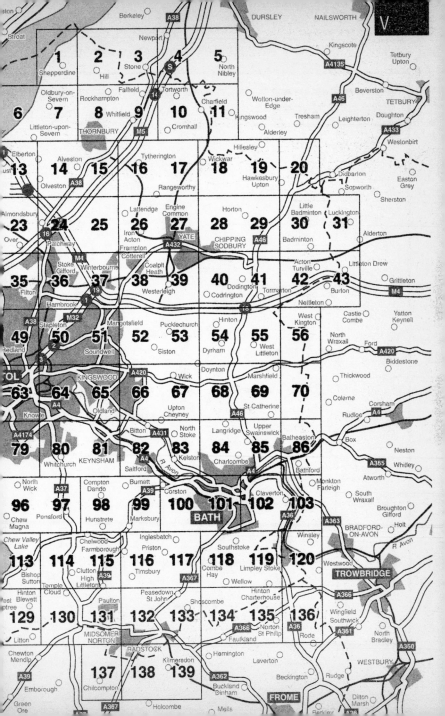

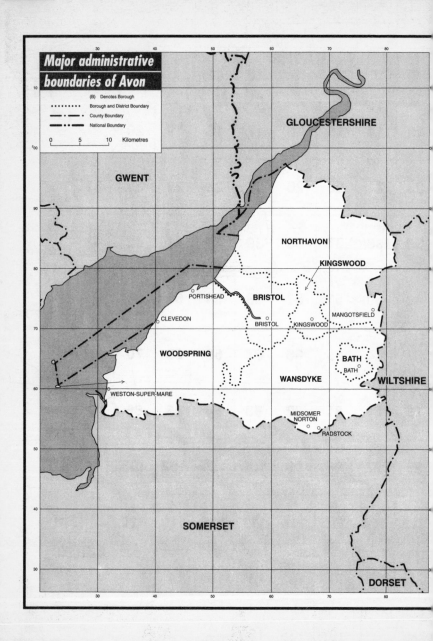

Major administrative boundaries of Avon

(B) Denotes Borough

········· Borough and District Boundary

—··—··— County Boundary

—··—··— National Boundary

0   5   10   Kilometres

GLOUCESTERSHIRE

GWENT

NORTHAVON

KINGSWOOD

BRISTOL

PORTISHEAD

CLEVEDON

BRISTOL

KINGSWOOD

MANGOTSFIELD

WOODSPRING

BATH

BATH

WILTSHIRE

WANSDYKE

WESTON-SUPER-MARE

MIDSOMER
NORTON

RADSTOCK

SOMERSET

DORSET

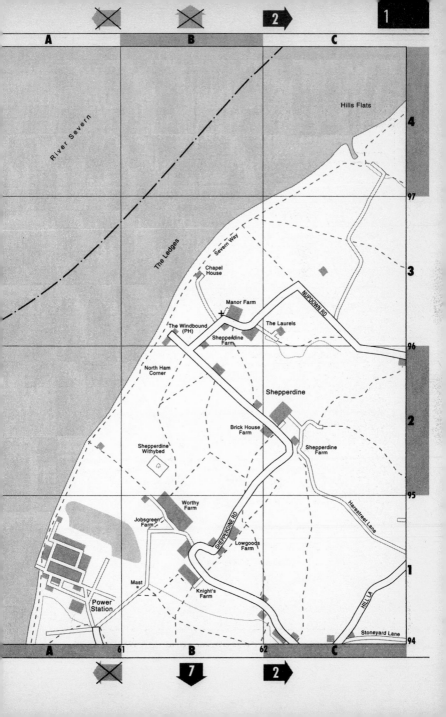

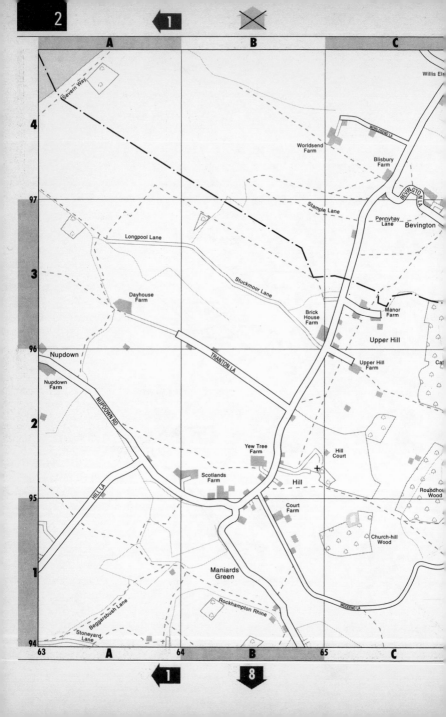

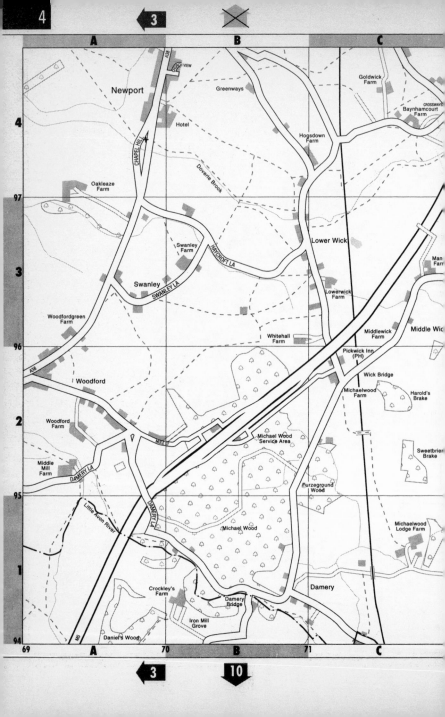

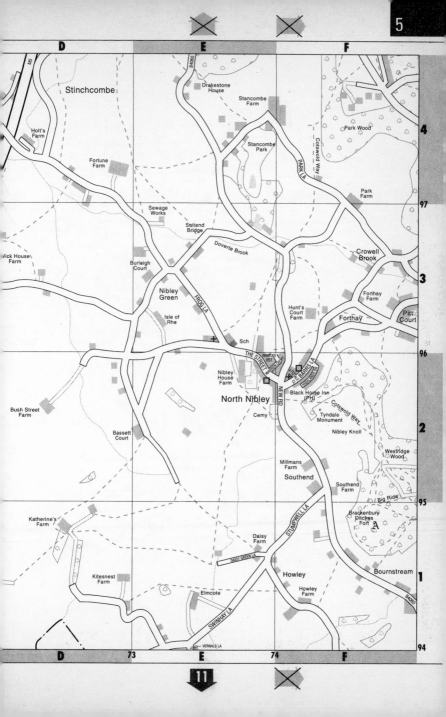

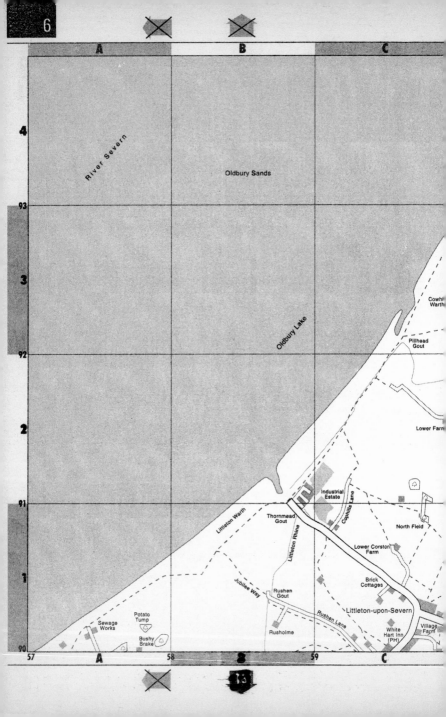

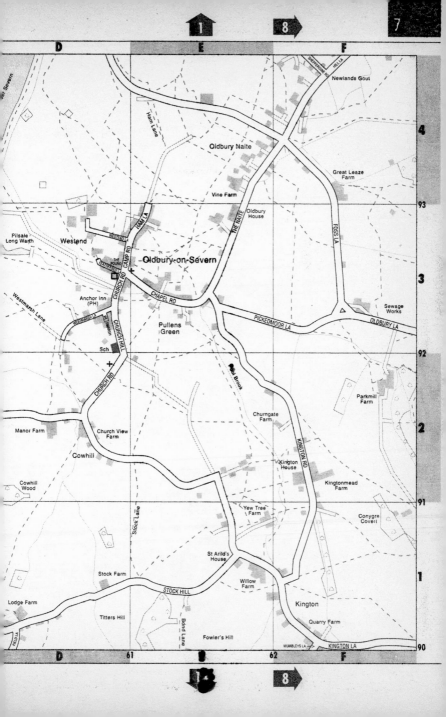

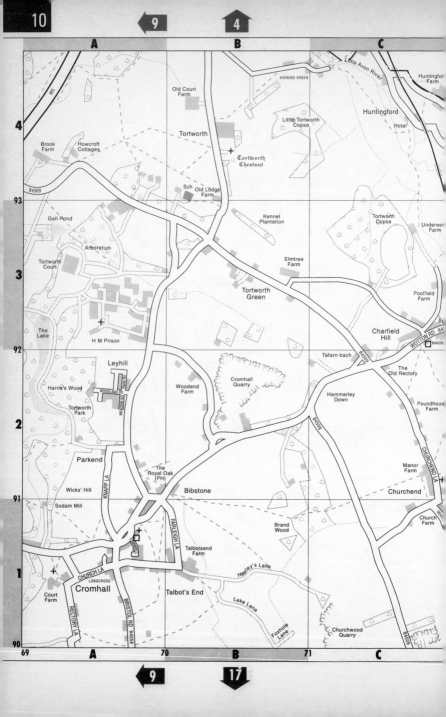

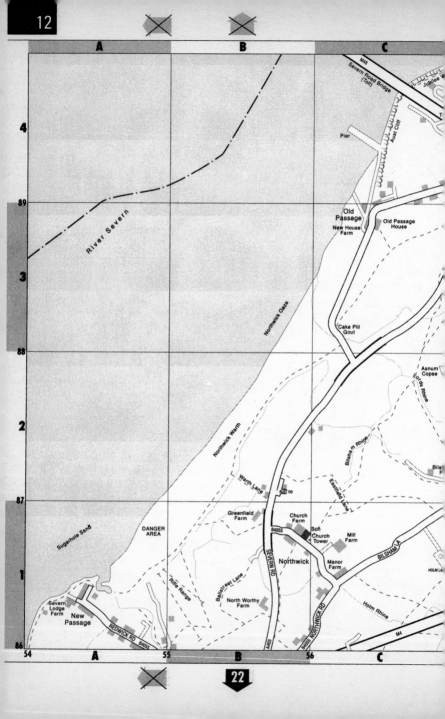

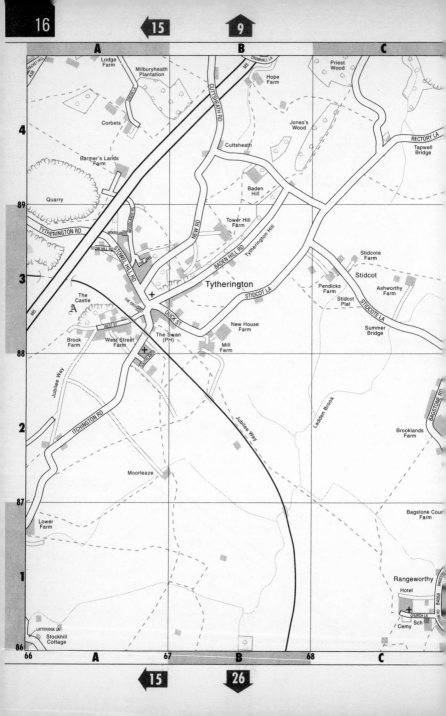

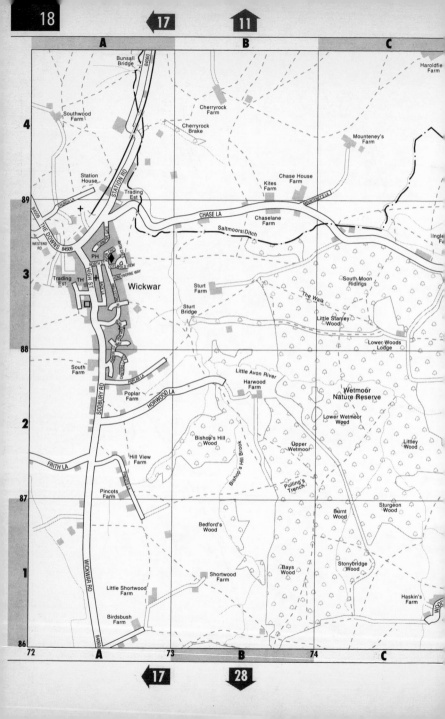

M4

English
Lake

Salmon
Pool

English Stones

The Binn Wall

4

BEACH
AVE

85

3

84

A403

2

New Pill
Gout

Works

83

Chittening Warth

SEVERN RD

Red Rhine

Works

Tanks

1

A403

Crook's Marsh

82

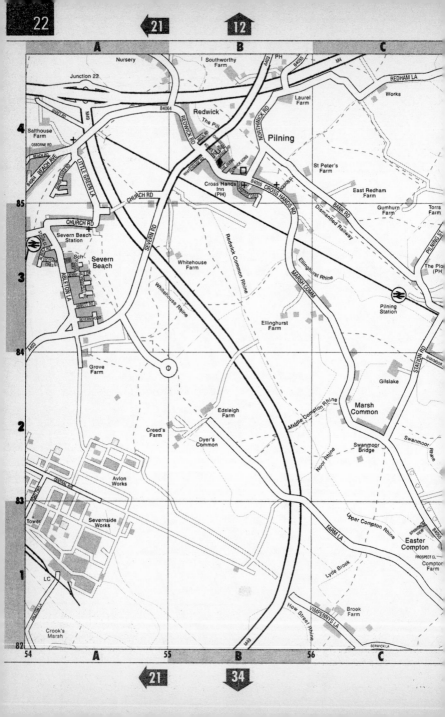

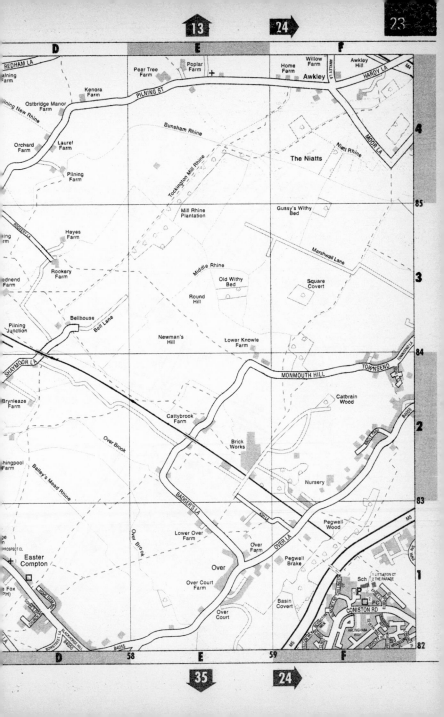

REDHAM LA

Pilning
Pilning New Rhine

Ostbridge Manor
Farm

Kenora
Farm

Pear Tree
Farm

Poplar
Farm

Home
Farm

Willow
Farm

Awkley
Hill

AWKLEY LA

HARDY LA

M4

MOOR LA

Awkley

PILNING ST

Orchard
Farm

Laurel
Farm

Pilning
Farm

Bunsham Rhine

Niatt Rhine

The Niatts

4

85

Hayes
Farm

Mill Rhine
Plantation

Gussy's Withy
Bed

Marshwall Lane

Rookery
Farm

Tockington Mill Rhine

Middle Rhine

Old Withy
Bed

Square
Covert

3

Headnend
Farm

Round
Hill

Bellhouse

Pilning
Junction

Bell Lane

Newman's
Hill

Lower Knowle
Farm

84

SHAYMOOR LA

MONMOUTH HILL

TOWNSEND

Catbrain
Wood

B4055

Brynleaze
Farm

Cattybrook
Farm

Brick
Works

2

Over Brook

Bailey's Mead Rhine

Nursery

83

Ishingpool
Farm

BADGER'S LA

Over Brook

Lower Over
Farm

Over
Farm

Pegwell
Wood

M5

OVER LA

Pegwell
Brake

PROSPECT CL

Easter
Compton

Over

Over Court
Farm

Sch

1 LITTLETON CT
2 THE PARADE

1

The Fox
(PH)

Over
Court

Basin
Covert

P PO
PC

CONISTON RD

ARLINGHAM
Way

B4055

58

59

82

D E F

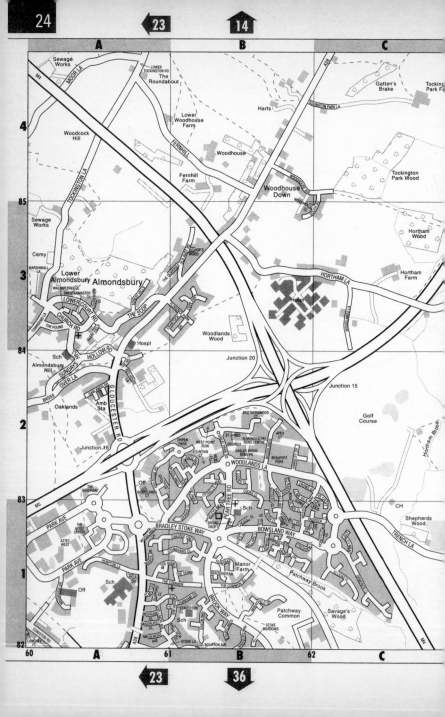

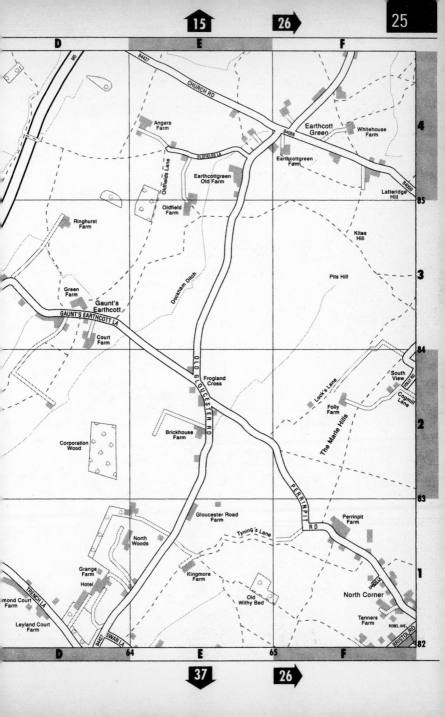

D
E
F

M5

B4427

CHURCH RD

Angers
Farm

Earthcott
Green

B4059

Whitehouse
Farm

4

OLDFIELDS LA

Oldfields Lane

Earthcottgreen
Farm

Earthcottgreen
Old Farm

Latteridge
Hill

B4059

85

Oldfield
Farm

Ringhurst
Farm

Kites
Hill

Dockham Ditch

Pits Hill

3

Green
Farm

Gaunt's
Earthcott

GAUNT'S EARTHCOTT LA

Court
Farm

OLD GLOUCESTER RD

84

Frogland
Cross

Lock's Lane

South
View

KELLY RD

Cogmill
Lane

Folly
Farm

The Marle Hills

2

Corporation
Wood

Brickhouse
Farm

PERRINPIT RD

83

Gloucester Road
Farm

Perrinpit
Farm

Tyning's Lane

North
Woods

TRENCH LA

Grange
Farm

Kingmore
Farm

SANDS LA

1

Hotel

-mond Court
Farm

North Corner

Old
Withy Bed

Leyland Court
Farm

Tanners
Farm

ROBEL AVE

BRISTOL RD

B4427 SWAN LA

D
64
E
65
F
82

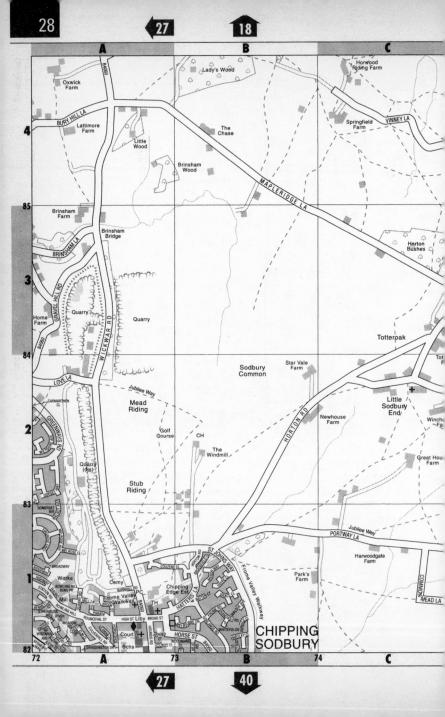

A   B   C

Oxwick
Farm

BURY HILL LA
Lattimore
Farm

Lady's Wood

Horwood
Riding Farm

Springfield
Farm

VINNEY LA

4

The Chase

Little
Wood

Brinsham
Wood

MAPLERIDGE LA

85

Brinsham
Farm

Brinsham
Bridge

Horton
Bushes

BRINSHAM LA

3

GRAVEL HILL RD

Home
Farm

Quarry

Quarry

WICKWAR RD

Totterpak

84

LOVE LA

Sodbury
Common

Star Vale
Farm

Tot
P

Little
Sodbury
End

CARMARTHEN CL

Jubilee Way

Mead
Riding

Wincha
Fa

2

GREENWAYS RD

Golf
Course

CH

HORTON RD

Newhouse
Farm

Great Hou
Farm

Quarry
(dis)

The
Windmill

SOMERSET AVE

Stub
Riding

83

Jubilee Way

PORTWAY LA

Harwoodgate
Farm

MELROSE CL

BROADWAY

Works

ST JOHNS WAY

Frome Valley Walkway

Park's
Farm

COMMON MEAD LA

1

Bowling Hill
BSNS PK

Cemy

Frome Valley
Walkway

HATTERS LA

Chipping
Edge Est

Mill

Bowling Hill

PARADY

PC

CHIPPING
SODBURY

HIGH ST Liby BROAD ST

HORSE ST

WISTARIA
AVE

Court
Schs

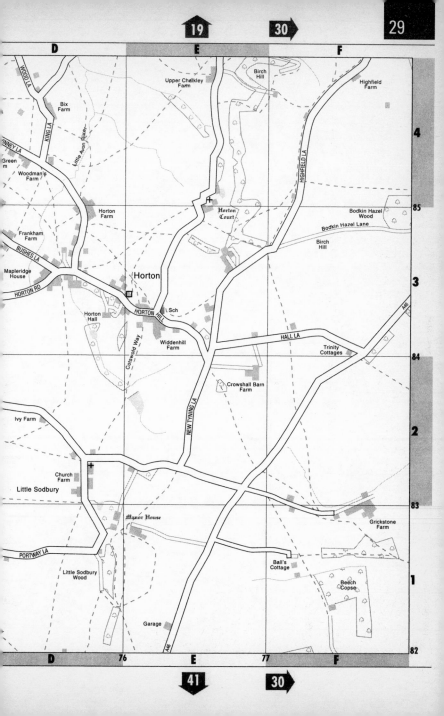

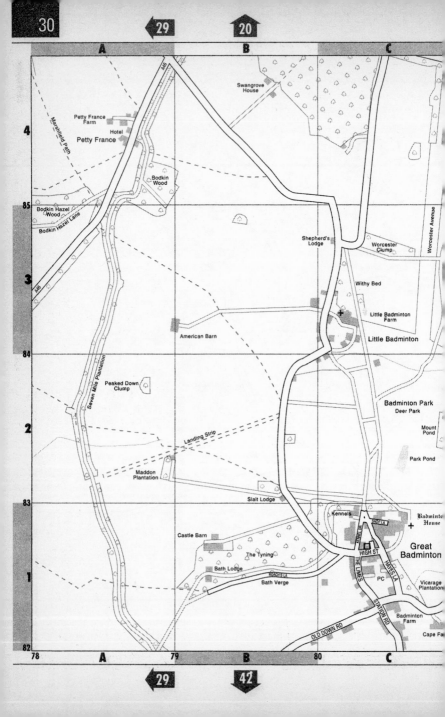

29
20

A   B   C

Swangrove
House

Petty France
Farm

Hotel

Petty France

Bodkin
Wood

85

Bodkin Hazel
Wood

Bodkin Hazel Lane

A46

3

Shepherd's
Lodge

Worcester
Clump

Worcester Avenue

Withy Bed

Little Badminton
Farm

Little Badminton

American Barn

84

Seven Mile Plantation

Peaked Down
Clump

Badminton Park

Deer Park

Mount
Pond

2

Landing Strip

Park Pond

Maddon
Plantation

Slait Lodge

83

Kennels

Badminton
House

Castle Barn

The Tyning

Great
Badminton

Bath Lodge

HIGH ST

THE LIMES

HAYES LA

PC

Vicarage
Plantation

Bath Verge

STATION RD

82

Badminton
Farm

Cape Fa

OLD DOWN RD

78 79 80

A   B   C

29
42

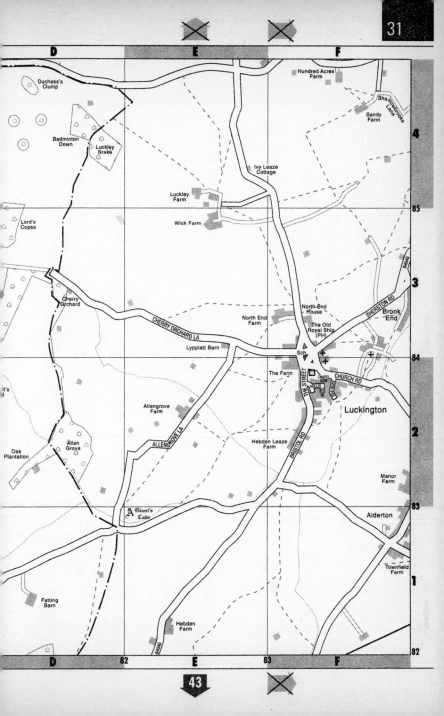

D   E   F

Duchess's
Clump

Hundred Acres
Farm

Shallowfords Lane

Sandy
Farm

Badminton
Down

Luckley
Brake

Ivy Leaze
Cottage

4

Luckley
Farm

85

Lord's
Copse

Wick Farm

B4040

CHERRY ORCHARD LA

Cherry
Orchard

North End
Farm

North End
House

SHERSTON RD

Brook
End

The Old
Royal Ship
(PH)

3

Lyppiatt Barn

Sch

CHURCH RD

84

it's
d

The Farm

CHAPEL
ROW

HOLLIS

THE STREET

Luckington

Allengrove
Farm

ALLENGROVE LA

Allen
Grove

Oak
Plantation

Hebden Leaze
Farm

BRISTOL RD

2

Manor
Farm

83

Giant's
Cave

Alderton

Townfield
Farm

1

Fatting
Barn

Hebden
Farm

B4040

82

D   82   E   83   F   82

4

81

3

80

2

Jetty
(dis)

Fuel S
Dep

79

Piers

1

King Road

East Pier

River Avon
Swash Channel

Resr

West Pier

78

48   A   49   B   50   C

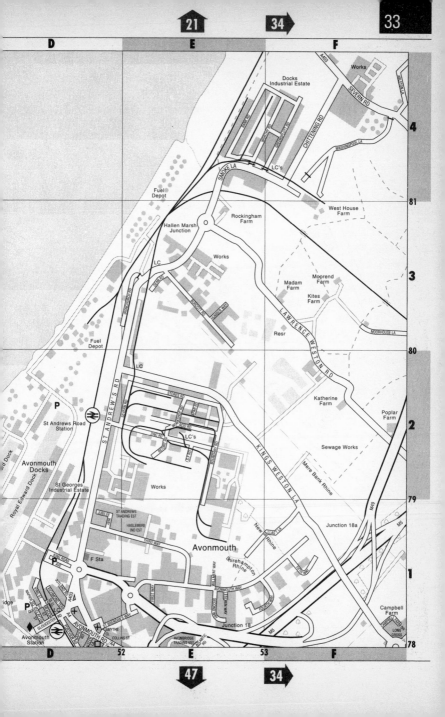

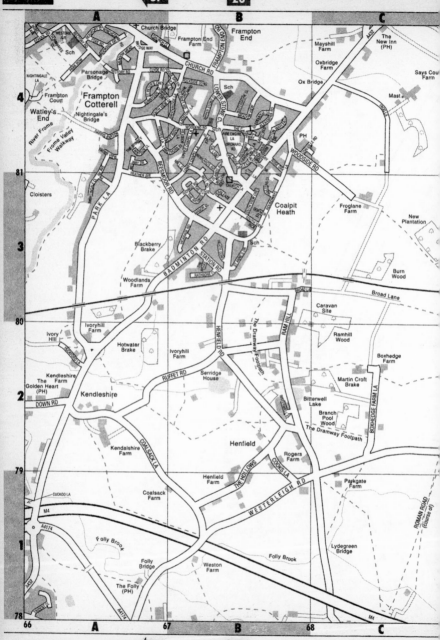

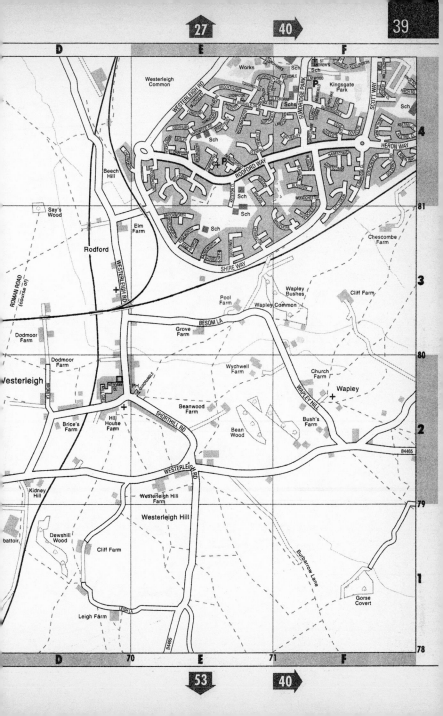

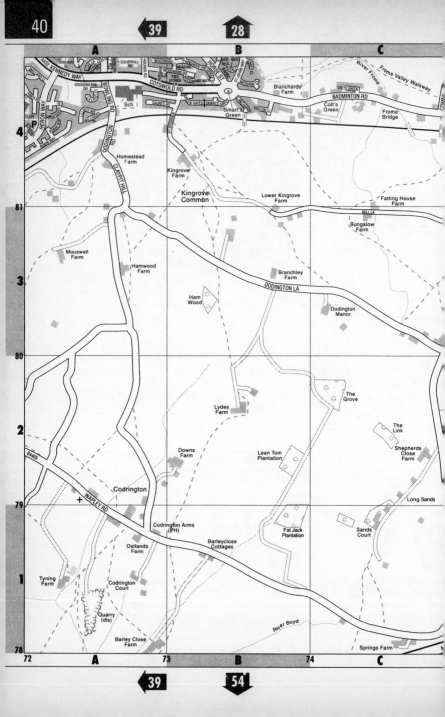

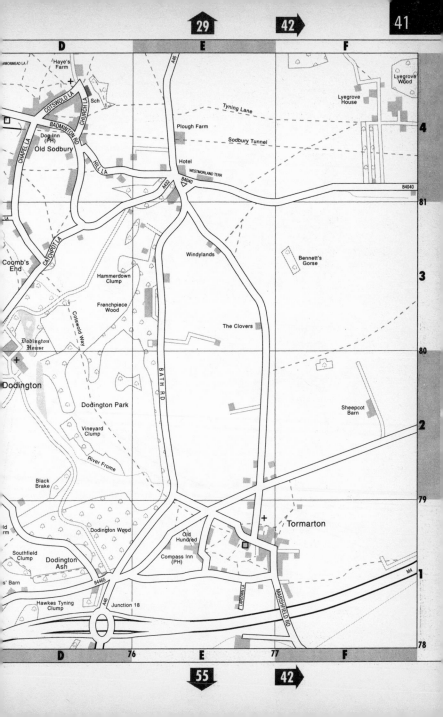

Black Nore

SEVERNMEADOWS

FEDDEN VILLAGE

NORE RD

Hang Rock

Redcliff Bay

Mast

DOWN RD

Redcliff Bay

Nightingale Valley

Caravan Park
Mast PH

Manor Farm

Charlcombe Bay

Charlcombe Wood

VALLEY RD

Weston Down

Black Rock Quarry (dis)

Walton Bay

Black Strip

The Ripple

Weston Lodge

Seven Acre Wood

Weston in Gordano

Culver Cliff

Common Hill Wood

Weston Wood

The Conygar

White Hart (PH)

Pigeon House Bay

Signal Station

Farley

Walton Down

Canon's Wood

B3124

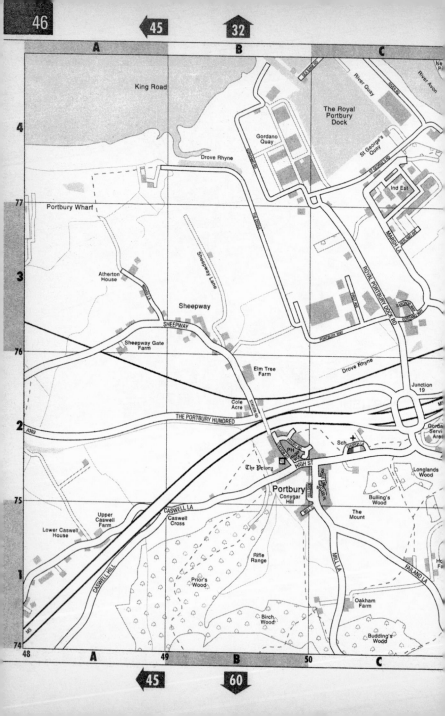

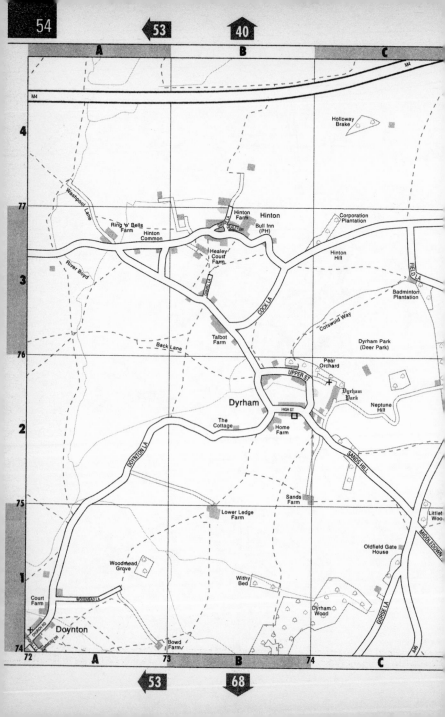

A B C

M4

4

Holloway
Brake

77

Hinton
Farm

Hinton

Bull Inn
(PH)

Corporation
Plantation

Ring 'o' Bells
Farm

Hinton
Common

Healey
Court
Farm

Hinton
Hill

FIELD LA

River Boyd

3

Badminton
Plantation

COCK LA

Cotswold Way

Back Lane

Talbot
Farm

Dyrham Park
(Deer Park)

76

Pear
Orchard

UPPER ST

Dyrham
Park

Dyrham

HIGH ST

Neptune
Hill

2

The
Cottage

Home
Farm

DOYNTON LA

SANDS HILL

75

Sands
Farm

Lower Ledge
Farm

Littlet
Woo

MIDDLEDOWN

Oldfield Gate
House

1

Woodmead
Grove

Withy
Bed

GORSE LA

Court
Farm

WOODLEAZE LA

Dyrham
Wood

A46

Doynton

74

Bowd
Farm

72 A 73 B 74 C

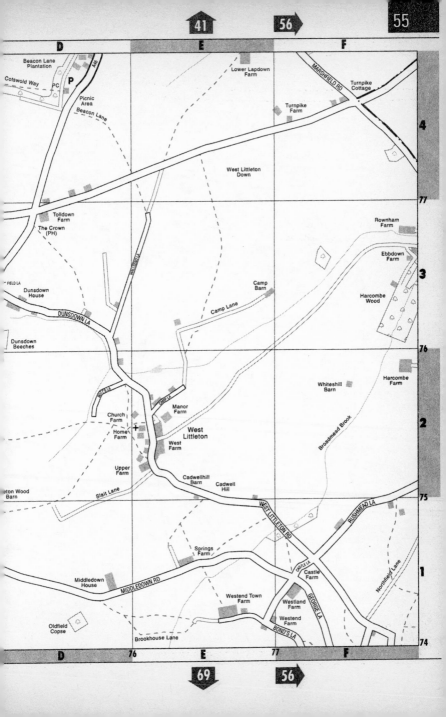

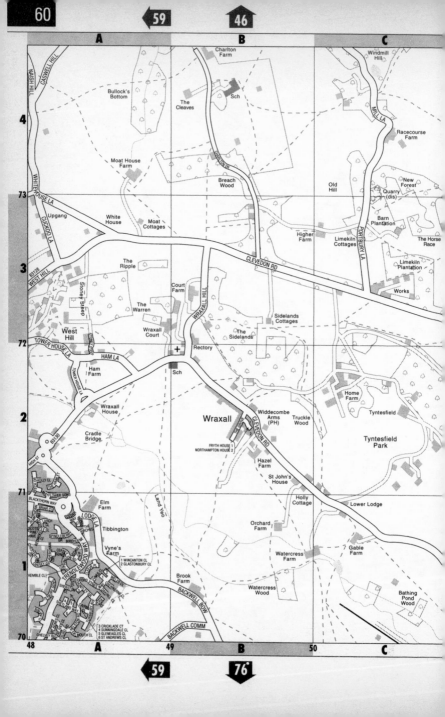

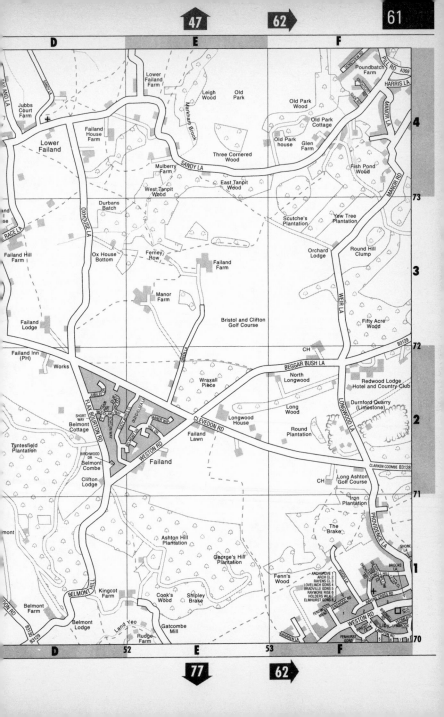

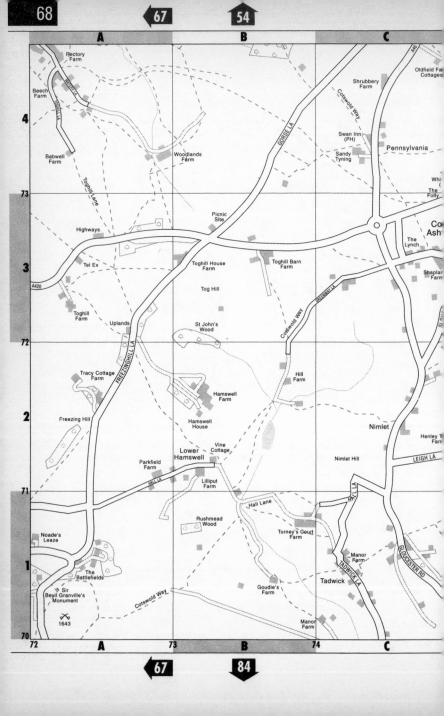

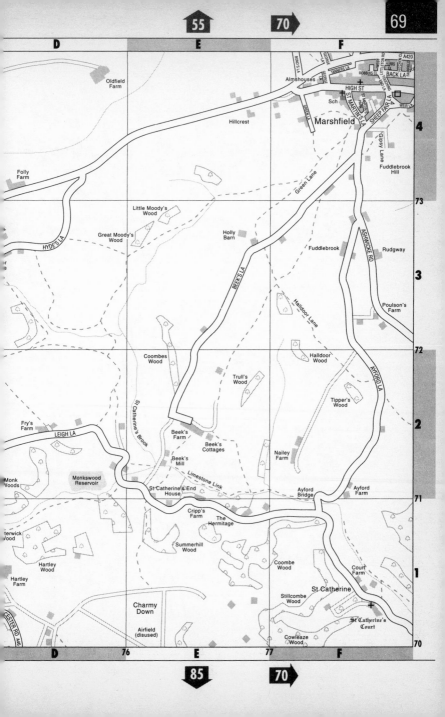

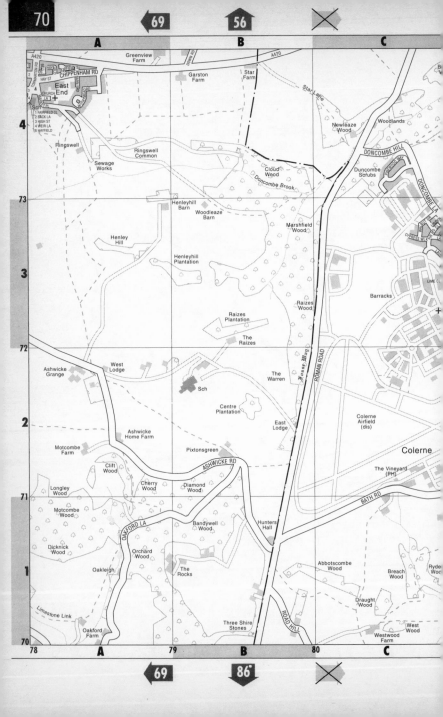

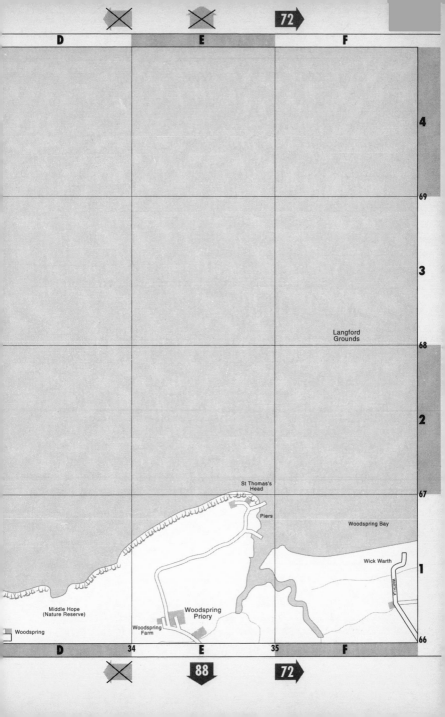

4

69

3

Langford
Grounds

68

2

St Thomas's
Head

67

Piers

Woodspring Bay

Wick Warth

1

Middle Hope
(Nature Reserve)

Woodspring

Woodspring
Farm

Woodspring
Priory

66

4

69

3

68

2

67

1

66

Dowlais Ditch

Kingston Pill

Hook's Ear

Sea Wall Farm

Treble House Farm

Channel View Farm

MIDDLE LA

Broadstone Rhyne

BROADSTONE LA

Broadstone Farm

HAM LA

Wharf Farm

Ham Farm

Pool Farm

Ham Rhyne

Sewage Works

Mendip View Farm

YEO BANK LA

Yeo Bank Farm

Muddy Lane

Tutshill

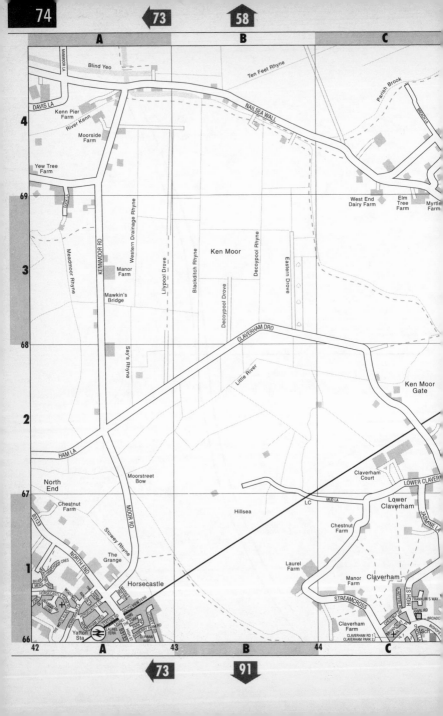

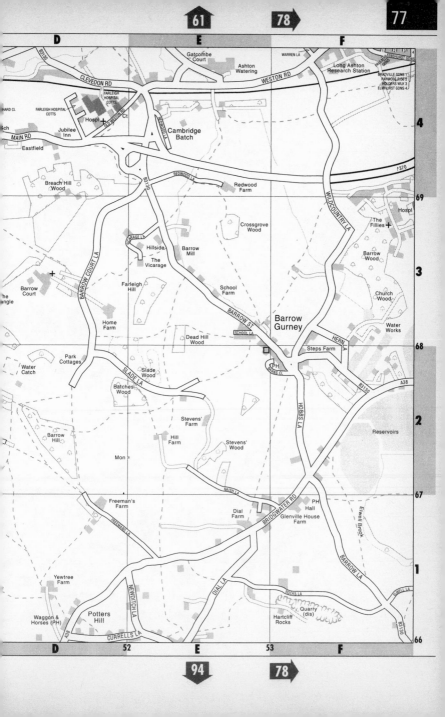

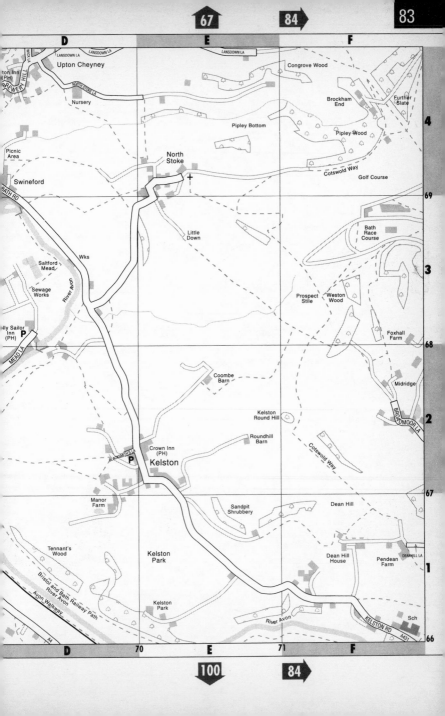

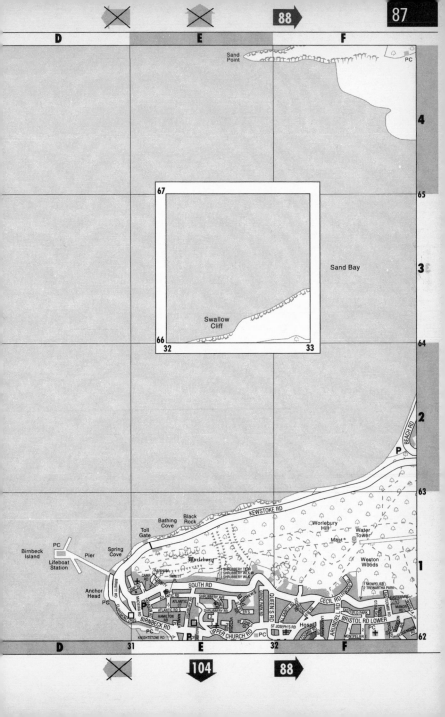

Sand Point

PC

4

67

65

66

32   33

64

Sand Bay

3

Swallow
Cliff

Worlebury

BEACH RD

P

2

63

KEWSTOKE RD

Worlebury
Hill

Water
Tower

Mast

Weston
Woods

1

Birnbeck
Island

PC

Lifeboat
Station

Pier

Spring
Cove

Toll
Gate

Bathing
Cove

Black
Rock

Worlebury

1 SHRUBBERY TERR
2 SHRUBBERY WLK N
3 SHRUBBERY WLK

1 MONPELISE
2 TREWARTHA PARK

CAMP RD

TRINITY

SOUTH RD

SHRUBBERY AVE

GROVE PARK RD

QUEEN'S RD

CECIL RD

Anchor
Head

PC

BIRNETT RD

MADEIRA RD

ATLANTIC RD S

ATLANTIC
RD

HAMILTON
RD

SHRUBBERY RD

MATTHEW'S RD

TER S

ALBERT
RD

CASTLE RD

ARUNDELL RD

BRISTOL RD LOWER

EASTFIELD PARK

EASTCOMBE
RD

MANOR
RD

P

BIRNBECK RD

CLEVEDON RD

KNIGHTSTONE RD

UPPER CHURCH RD

PC

ST JOSEPH'S RD

PC

Hosp

MONTPELIER

P

PC

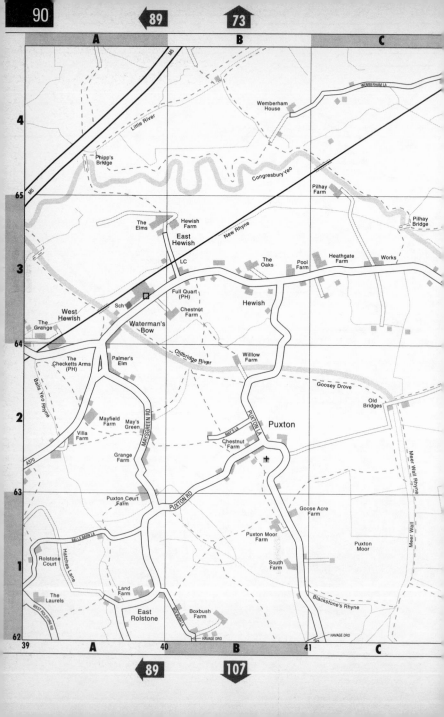

D E F

The Batch

Yatton

ASHLEIGH
THE GLEBE

Stowey Rhyne

HIGH ST

Sch
Sch

4

Le Street Rhyne

HUTT'S LA
STREAMCROSS
CLAVERHAM

BISHOPS RD
Sch

Bishops
Farm

CLAVERHAM RD

Henley
Farm

A370

65

Binhay Rhyne

Cadbury
Farm

Land
Farm

Frost Hill

MITFORD-SLADE
CT

Frost Hill

Fire
Sta

FROST HILL

HENLEY LA

Cadbury
Hill

RHODYATE HILL

PH

3

New Rhyne

Congresbury
Moor

SMALLWAY

WOOD HILL

The
Woodlands

WRINGTON LA

WRINGTON RD

Sharpham
Cottage

64

Stepstones
Farm

WESTON RD

Congresbury Yeo

Oak
Farm

Prince of
Wales
(PH)

STATION RD

GLEN YEO TERR

Schs

Dismantled Railway

HIGH ST

BRISTON RD

B3133

KENT RD

HILL PARK

ASLANDS WAY

SOUTH SIDE

PC

Congresbury
Bridge

Congresbury

Urchinwood
Manor

PH

Two Rivers Way

2

Little Wall Drove

Dolemoor Lane

Dismantled Railway

DOLEMOOR LA

Rookery
Farm

MILL LA

PARK RD

Park
Farm

63

Crookwell Rhyne

Crookwell Drove

Moor Drove

SILVER ST

BRINSEA RD

VENUS ST

BRINSEA BATCH

Brinsea Batch
Farm

BRINSEA LA

Poplar
Farm

STOCK LA

B3133

1

62

Cardich Drove

D 43 E 44 F

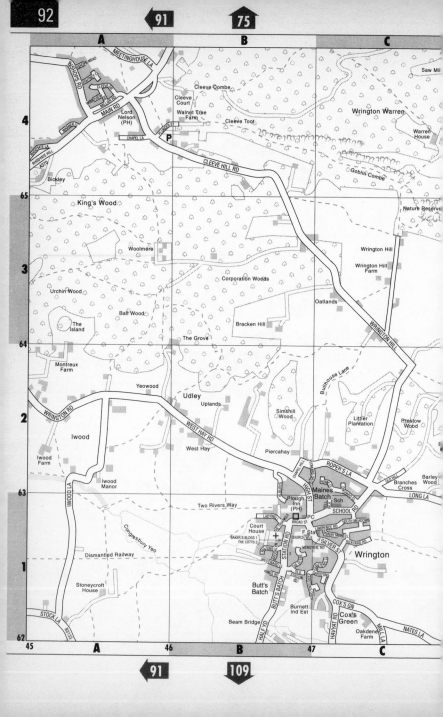

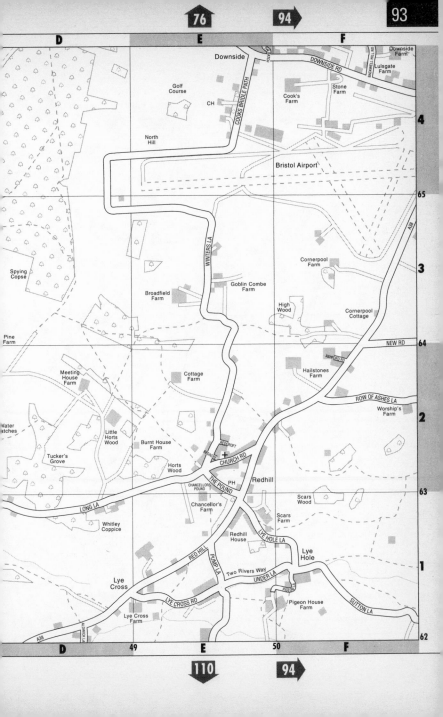

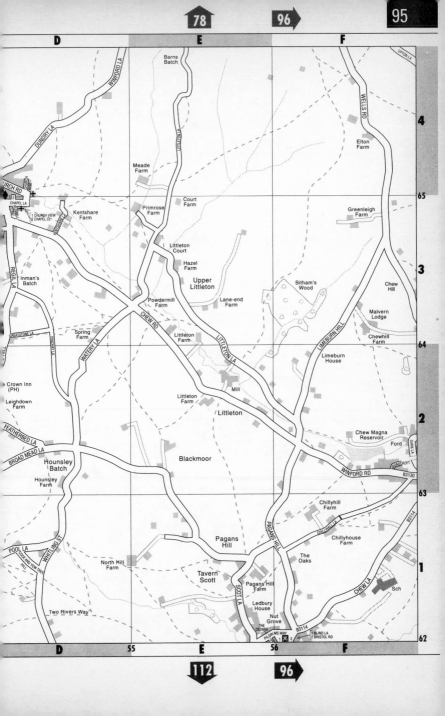

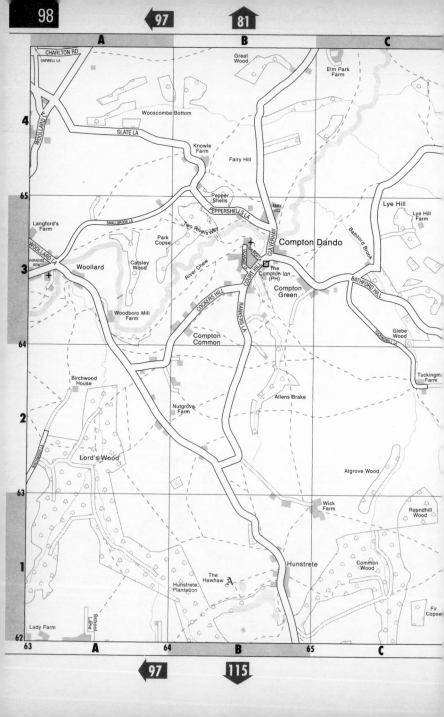

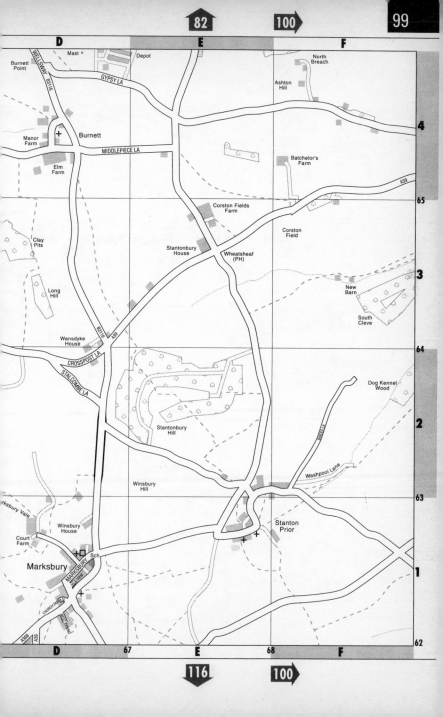

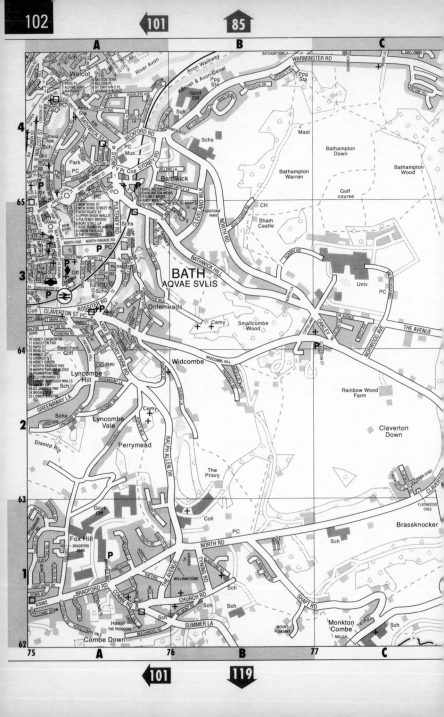

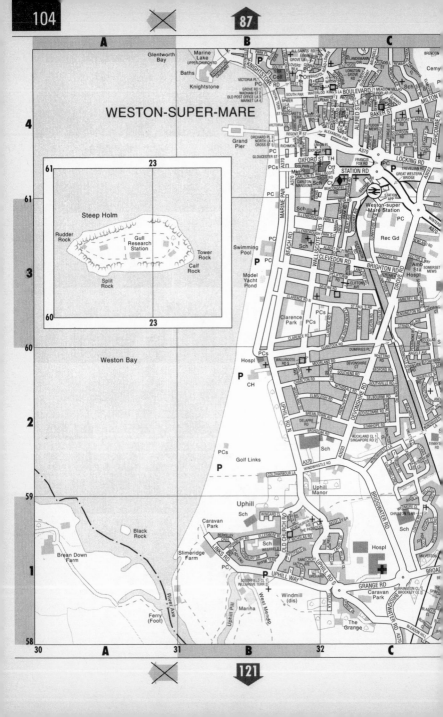

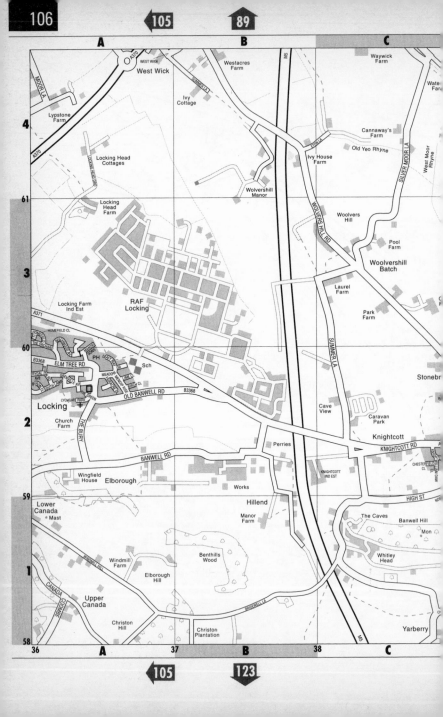

D
E
F

The Homestead
The Poplars
WEST ROLSTONE RD
PUXTON RD
Laurel Farm
Gout House Farm
Rockers Rhyne
PUXTON LA
Nye
Nye Farm
4
Lower Gout Farm
Moor Dairy
Nye Drove
Rookery Farm
Downend Farm
Liddy Yeo
or Rhyne
Court Farm
River Banwell Blind Ditch
MOOR RD
RIVERSIDE
Nye Drove
61
Hardmead Rhyne
Droveway Bridge
3
Droveway Farm
Moorland Farm
NYE RD
DROVE WAY
Mead Farm
60
West-Lea Farm
Towerhead Brook
Railway Inn (PH)
A368
WOLVERSHILL RD
Elmcroft Farm
STATION RD
Golling
Towerhead
2
WOLVERSHILL PARK
Dismantled Railway
HTCOTT RD
WEST GARSTON
CLEEVE DR
ORCHARD CL
P
TOWERHEAD RD
HILL RD
FIELD RD THOMAS CL WE
THE GABLES
ORCHARD CL
QUARRY RD
STATION RD DERBUS WAY
WEST ST PC
Sch
EAST ST
Liby
F Sta
59
Banwell
HIGH ST
THE SQUARE
A368
Banwell Plain
Sandford Batch
DARK LA
Banwell Wood
1 SMALL DOWN END
2 COPSE END
SOUTH CROFT
Works
CASTLE HILL
Banwell Castle
Nursery
LEX WAY
SHIPHAM LA
1
WNT HILL
THE RHYNE
Cemy
SANDFORD RD
Winthill House
Winthill Farm
Rhodyate Farm
MOORHAM RD
CHRISTON RD
MAX MILL LA
BANWELL RD A371
EVERGREEN CL
58

D
40
E
41
F

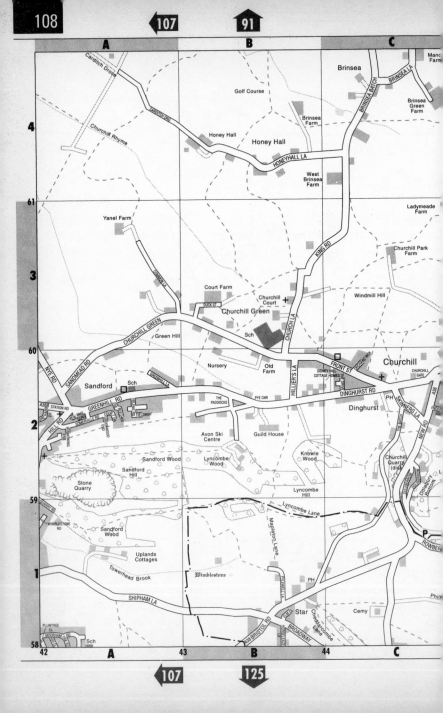

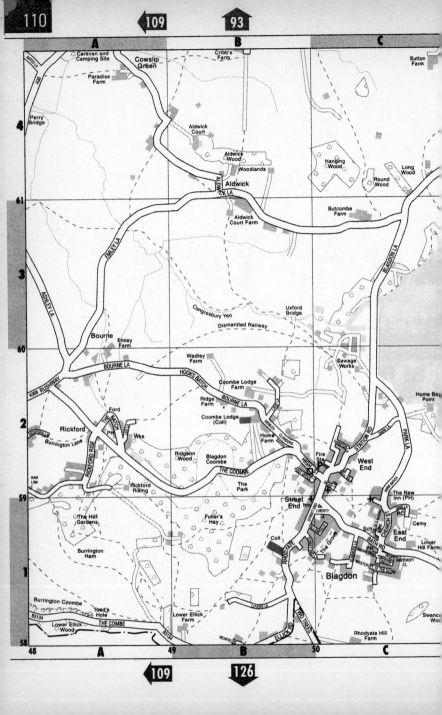

109
93

A   B   C

Caravan and
Camping Site

Cowslip
Green

Cribb's
Farm

Sutton
Farm

Paradise
Farm

4

Perry
Bridge

Aldwick
Court

Aldwick
Wood

Woodlands

Hanging
Wood

Long
Wood

Round
Wood

Aldwick

ALDWICK LA

61

Aldwick
Court Farm

Butcombe
Farm

EMLEY LA

3

ASHLEY LA

Congresbury Yeo

Uxford
Bridge

BLAGDON LA

Dismantled Railway

Bourne

Emley
Farm

Wadley
Farm

Sewage
Works

60

BOURNE LA

HOOKS BATCH

Coombe Lodge
Farm

Home Bay
Point

A368 RUSHWAY

Ridge
Farm

BOURNE LA

THE BATCH

Ford

Coombe Lodge
(Coll)

Rickford

PH

Wks

Home
Farm

NEWLY
CLIMBERS
BATCH

STATION RD

PARK LA

West
End

BATCH

2

Burrington Lane

RICKFORD RISE

Ridgeon
Wood

Blagdon
Coombe

HIGH ST

Fire
Sta

The New
Inn (PH)

HAM
LINK

Rickford
Rising

THE COOMBE

The
Park

Street
End

PC

Cemy

East
End

59

The Hill
Gardens

Fuller's
Hay

RHODYATE

Coll

The Grove

School

Lower
Hill Farm

BATH RD

EASTCROFT
CL.

Burrington
Ham

1

Blagdon

Burrington Coombe

Toad's
Hole

Lower Ellick
Farm

LOVERS LA

TWO TREES

Swance
Wood

B3134

THE COMBE

B3134

ELLICK RD

Rhodyate Hill
Farm

Lower Ellick
Wood

NEWFIELDS

58

48   A   49   B   50   C

109
126

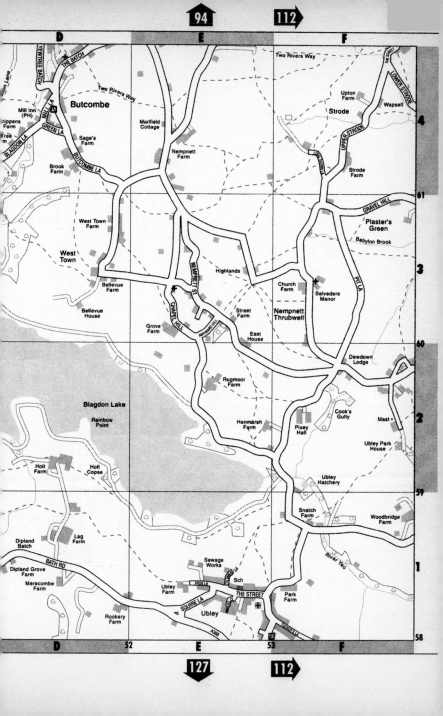

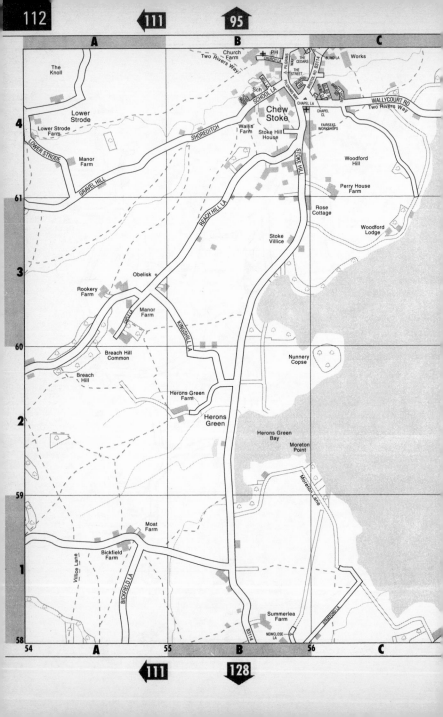

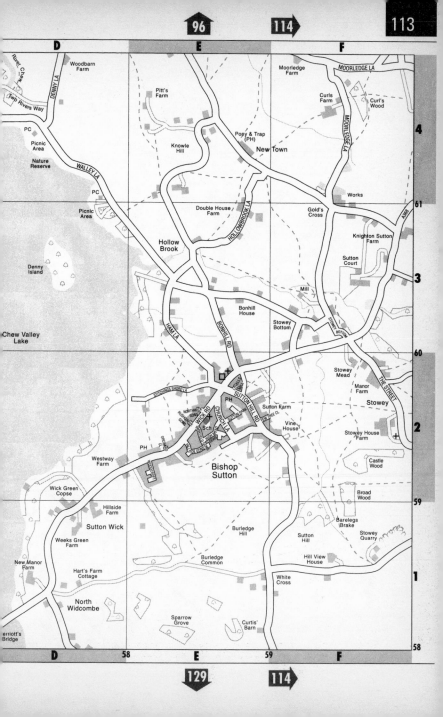

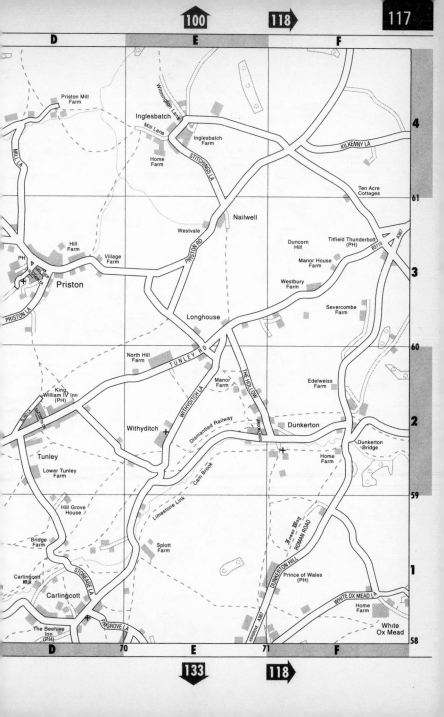

D E F

4

61

Priston Mill Farm

Winnington Lane

Inglesbatch

Mill Lane

Inglesbatch Farm

Home Farm

STITCHINGS LA

KILKENNY LA

Ten Acre Cottages

Nailwell

Westvale

PRISTON RD

Duncorn Hill

Titfield Thunderbolt (PH)

A367

Hill Farm

PH

Village Farm

HILL VIEW TERRACE

Priston

Manor House Farm

Westbury Farm

Severcombe Farm

B3115

PRISTON LA

Longhouse

3

60

North Hill Farm

TUNLEY RD

Manor Farm

THE HOLLOW

Edelweiss Farm

King William IV Inn (PH)

MAZE HILL DR

WITHYDITCH LA

Withyditch

Dismantled Railway

Dunkerton

Dunkerton Bridge

2

Tunley

Lower Tunley Farm

Cam Brook

HIGH STREET

Home Farm

59

Hill Grove House

Limestone Link

Splott Farm

Forge Way

ROMAN ROAD

Bridge Farm

Carlingcott Mill

STONEAGE LA

DUNKERTON HILL

Prince of Wales (PH)

1

Carlingcott

The Beehive Inn (PH)

FRY GROVE LA

ASHGROVE A367

WHITE OX MEAD LA

Home Farm

White Ox Mead

58

D 70 E 71 F

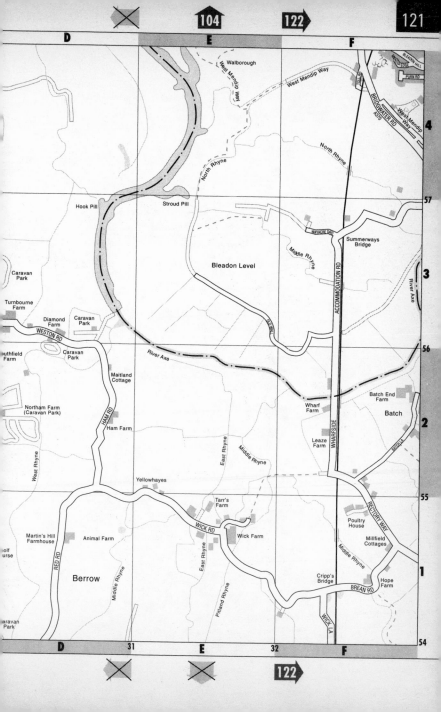

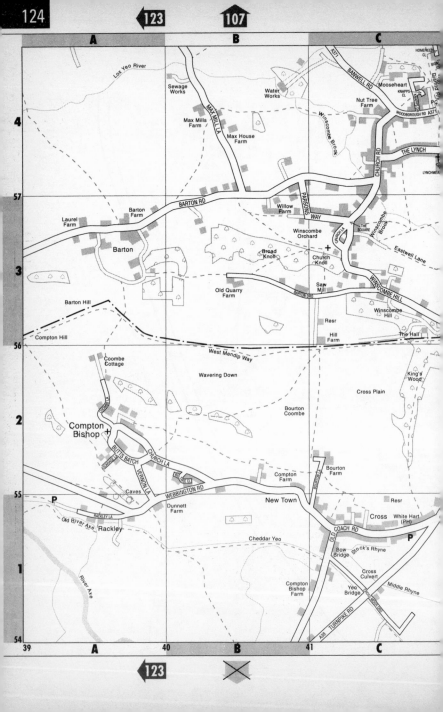

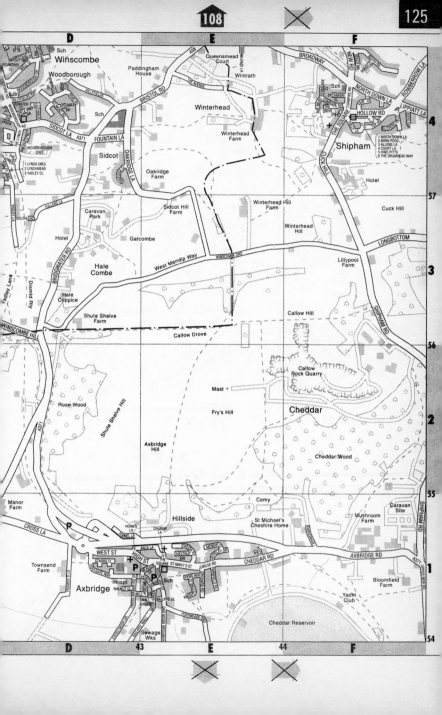

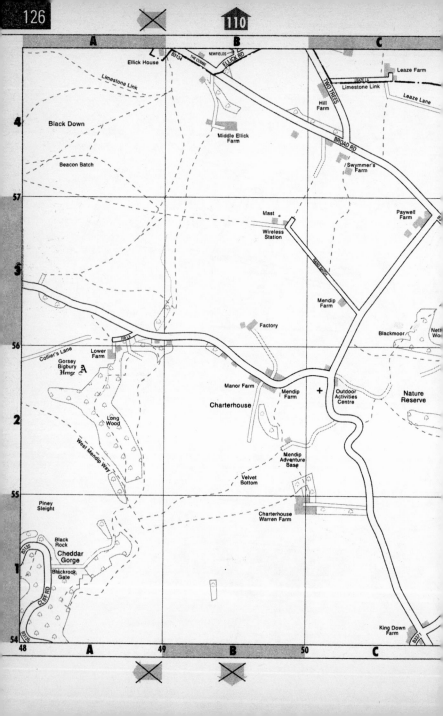

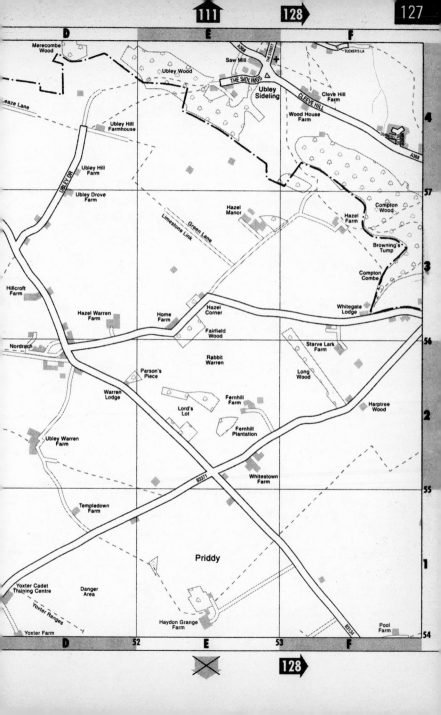

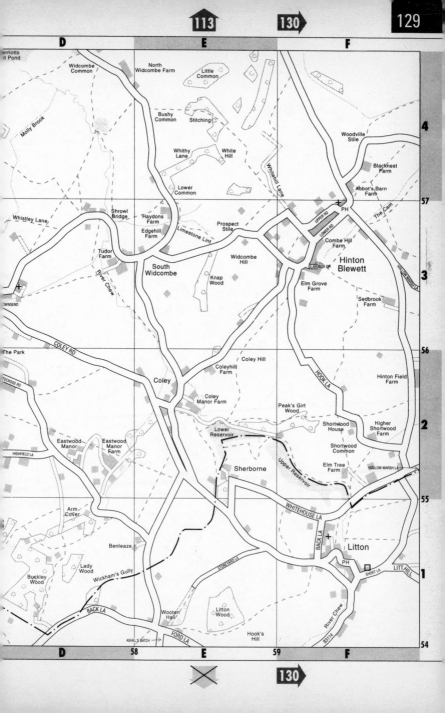

D   E   F

Highbury Hill
ASP
Rosewell Farm
Stephen's Hill
Factory
MARSH LA
LANGFORDS LA
GOOSARD LA
BROOM HILL LA
Goosard Bridge
Withy Mills Farm

Southside House
Limestone Link
Sewage Works
Hanham House

HARTS LA
The Court
Hallatrow Bridge
Haflatrow
PAULTON RD
Allard's Farm
BRISTOL RD
Plummer's Hill
BATH RD

4

WELLS RD
B3355
HALLATROW RD
Works
VICTORIA TERR
Cemy
Brittens
BRITTEN'S HILL
HILLSIDE CL
PAULTO' HILL

57

Old Station Inn (PH)
White Cross Farm
Butt's Lane
SPRINGHILL CL
PCs CHURCH LA
CHURCH ST
PITHAY
HIGH ST
Alexandra Terr
HAM LA
Paulton

3

New Town
FARRINGTON RD
VICTORIA PK
PARK VIEW RD
LILLAM TERR
Schs
Ham
Sch
Manor House
CHURCH LA
Dismantled Railway
Ruett Lane
PAULTON RD
TENNIS COURT RD
GREENVALE RD
UMPIRE
BROADWAY RD
Towns End
ALPINE CL
CLANDOWN RD
Salisbury
Amb Sta

56

THE CRESCENT
HILL VIEW
Farrington Gurney
FARMHILL FIELDS
OLD MILLS LA
SALISBURY RD
Hospl
PHILLIS HILL
MONGER LA
B3355

2

Farrington Golf Club
Langley Down Lane
Hillier's Down Wood
Hillier's Down
LANGLEY'S LA
Old Mills
SPRINGFIELD BLDGS
OLD MILLS
Superstore
ROXBURY HILL
WEST RD
A362
Thicketmead Bridge
Thicket Mead
VIVIAN AVE

55

NORTHMEAD
NORTHMEAD AVE
NORTHMEAD RD
UNDERHILL LA
Underhill Wood
Underhill Farm
ORCHARD AVE
NORTH RD
B3355

1

Wellow Brook
White Bridge
CLAPTON RD
Bull's Wood
WOODSIDE
PINEWOOD
Providence Place
Sch
PAULTON RD

54

D   64   E   65   F

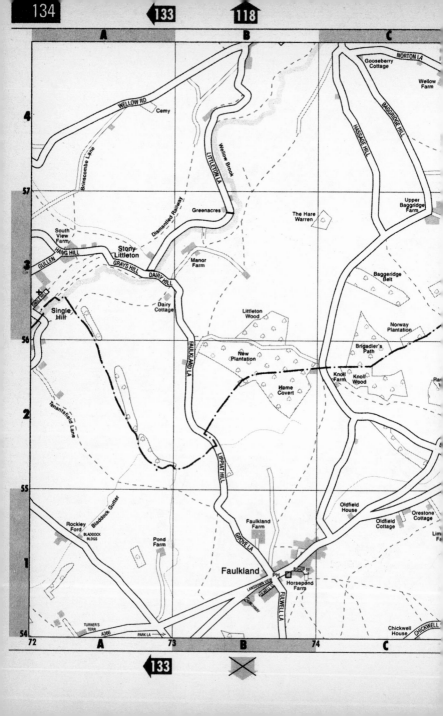

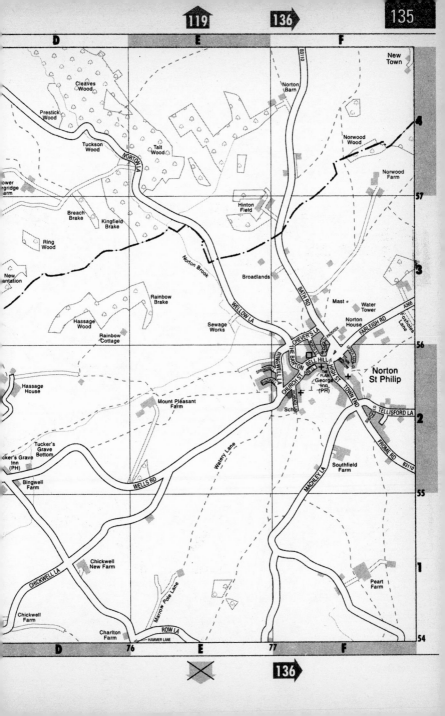

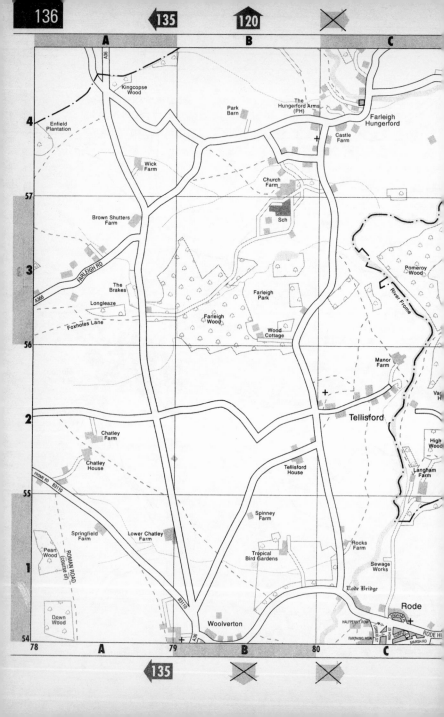

D E F

laydon Farm

Huish House

GREEN PARLOUR RD

Peak's Wood

Haywood Farm

A366

KNOBSBURY LA

TERRY HILL

FROME RD

A362

Upper Lentney Farm Cottage

Upper Lentney Farm

Upper Knobsbury

AMMERDOWN TERR

B3139

A366

4

Lentney Farm

KNOBSBURY HILL

Terry Hill Plantation

New Tyning Farm

Lower Knobsbury

Nap Wood

A362

53

Sch

Home Farm

Gagman Coppice

Ammerdown House

Sewage Works

Ammerdown Park

Coldbath Plantation

MERSDON HILL

Ammerdown Bridge

The Column

3

Manor Farm

SILVER ST

Kilmersdon

Wedingham Coppice

Hatchet Hill Coppice

52

Walton Farm

Beatle's Wood

Babington Wood

Batch Farm

NEW RD

HATCHET HILL

HOARE'S LA

SOUTH VIEW

Upton's Piece

Kingsdown Wood

2

Lowerfield Farm

Mells Down Farm

CORNISH'S GRAVE

Babington Park

Babington House

Works

Jericho Bridge

51

Babington

Lodge

Cherry Garden Farm

LUCKINGTON CROSS

Dismantled Railway

Edney's Farm

1

Newbury House

CHARITY LA

White Cottage

DARK LA

Newbury

TINKER'S LA

Newbury Farm

Luckington Manor Farm

PORK'S LA

Works

50

D 70 E 71 F

EXPLANATION OF THE STREET INDEX REFERENCE SYSTEM

Street names are listed alphabetically and show the locality, the page number and a reference to the square in which the name falls on the map page.

Example: Hill View Rd. Puck...53 E3

Hill View Rd   This is the full street name, which may have been abbreviated on the map.

Puck   This is the abbreviation for the town, village or locality in which the street falls.

53   This is the page number of the map on which the street name appears.

E3   The letter and figure indicate the square on the map in which the centre of the street falls. The square can be found at the junction of the vertical column carrying the appropriate letter and the horizontal row carrying the appropriate figure.

ABBREVIATIONS USED IN THE INDEX
Road Names

Approach	App	Grove	Gr
Arcade	Arc	Heights	Hts
Avenue	Ave	Industrial Estate	Ind Est
Boulevard	Bvd	Junction	Junc
Buildings	Bldgs	Lane	La
Business Park	Bsns Pk	North	N
Broadway	Bwy	Orchard	Orch
By-Pass	By-Ps	Parade	Par
Causeway	Cswy	Passage	Pas
Circle	Circ	Place	Pl
Circus	Cir	Pleasant	Plea
Close	Cl	Precinct	Prec
Common	Comm	Promenade	Prom
Corner	Cnr	Road	Rd
Cottages	Cotts	South	S
Court	Ct	Square	Sq
Courtyard	Ctyd	Stairs	Strs
Crescent	Cres	Steps	Stps
Drive	Dri	Street,Saint	St
Drove	Dro	Terrace	Terr
East	E	Walk	Wlk
Embankment	Emb	West	W
Esplanade	Espl	Yard	Yd
Gardens	Gdns		

Key to abbreviations of Town, Village and Rural locality names used in the index of street names.

ts Leigh	Ab Lei	62	A4
n Turville	A Tur	42	C3
ondsbury	Alm	24	A3
ston	Alve	15	D2
	Aust	13	D3
imouth	Avon	33	E1
idge	Axb	125	D1
well	Back	76	A3
gworth	Badg	123	F1
well	Ban	107	D1
ow Gurney	Ba Gu	77	F3
	Bath	102	B3
easton	Bathe	85	F2
ford	Bathf	86	B1
ow	Berr	121	D1
op Sutton	Bi Sut	113	E2
n	Bitt	82	C4
idon	Blag	110	C1
idon	Blea	122	B3
	Box	86	C2
iol	Bris	63	E3
kley	Brock	75	E1
on	Burt	43	D2
ombe	But	111	D4
field	Char	11	D3
tcombe	Charl	84	C2
iddar	Ched	125	F2
w Magna	Ch Mag	96	B2
w Stoke	Ch St	112	B4
rompton	Chil	137	E2
ping Sodbury	Ch Sod	28	B1
rchill	Chur	108	C2
redon	Cleve	57	D2

Clutton	Clut	114	C2
Cold Ashton	Co Ash	68	C3
Colerne	Col	70	C2
Compton Bishop	Co Bi	124	A2
Compton Dando	Co Dan	98	B3
Compton Martin	Co Mar	128	A3
Congresbury	Cong	91	F2
Corston	Cor	100	A4
Cromhall	Crom	10	A1
Didmarton	Did	20	C3
Dodington	Dod	41	D2
Doynton	Doyn	54	A1
Dundry	Dun	78	B1
Dyrham	Dyrh	54	B2
East Harptree	E Harp	128	C2
Easton in Gordano	E in G	47	D2
Englishcombe	Engl	100	C1
Falfield	Falf	9	F4
Farmborough	Farm	116	A3
Faulkland	Faulk	134	B1
Frampton Cotterell	Fr Cot	38	A4
Great Badminton	Gr Bad	30	C1
Grittleton	Grit	43	F3
Hawkesbury Upton	H Up	20	A1
Hillesley	Hill	19	E4
Hinton Blewett	Hin Ble	129	F3
Hinton			
Charterhouse	Hin Cha	119	F1
Holcombe	Hol	138	B1
Horton	Hort	29	E3
Iron Acton	Ir Act	26	B2
Kelston	Kel	83	E2
Keynsham	Keyn	81	F2

Kilmersdon	Kilm	139	D3
Kingston Seymour	K Sey	73	E1
Kingswood	Kings	11	F2
Kingswood	Kingsw	65	E4
Limpley Stoke	Li St	119	F4
Litton	Litt	129	F1
Locking	Lock	106	A2
Long Ashton	Lo Ash	62	A1
Luckington	Luck	31	F2
Lympsham	Lymp	122	A1
Mangotsfield	Mang	51	F4
Marksbury	Marks	99	D1
Marshfield	Marsh	69	F4
Midsomer Norton	Mid No	132	A2
Monkton Farleigh	Mon Far	103	F4
Nailsea	Nail	59	E2
Newport	Newp	4	A4
North Nibley	N Nib	5	E2
North Wraxall	N Wrax	56	C2
Norton St Philip	N St P	135	F2
Oldbury-on-Severn	O-on-S	7	E3
Olveston	Olve	14	A2
Paulton	Paul	131	F3
Peasedown St John	P St J	133	E4
Pensford	Pens	97	F2
Pilning	Piln	22	B4
Portbury	Portb	46	B2
Portishead	Portis	45	D2
Priddy	Priddy	127	E1
Priston	Pris	117	D3
Pucklechurch	Puck	53	D3
Puxton	Pux	90	B2
Radstock	Rad	132	C1

Rockhampton	Rock	8	C4
Rode	Rode	136	C1
Shipham	Ship	125	F4
Siston	Sist	52	C2
Southstoke	Sosto	118	C4
Stinchcombe	Stin	5	D4
Stoke Gifford	St Gif	36	C2
Ston Easton	Ston E	130	C1
Stone	Stone	3	F2
Tellisford	Tell	136	C2
Thornbury	Thorn	8	C1
Timsbury	Tims	116	A1
Tormarton	Tor	41	F1
Tytherington	Tyth	16	B3
Wellow	Well	118	B1
Westerleigh	West	39	D2
Weston in Gordano	W in G	44	C1
Weston-Super-Mare	W-S-M	104	B4
Westwood	Westw	120	C2
Whitchurch	Whit	80	B2
Wick	Wick	67	E3
Wick St Lawrence	W St L	89	D4
Wickwar	Wickw	18	A3
Winford	Win	94	C4
Winscombe	Winsc	125	D4
Winsley	Winsl	120	C4
Winterbourne	Wint	37	F3
Wotton-under-Edge	W-u-E	11	F4
Wraxall	Wrax	60	B2
Wrington	Wring	92	C1
Yate	Yate	27	E1
Yatton	Yatt	91	E4

5c Bsns Centre. Cleve 57 D1
Abbey Church Yd. Bath ... 102 A3
Abbey Cl. Keyn ... 81 F3
Abbey Green. Bath ... 102 A3
Abbey La. Hi Cha ... 120 A2
Abbey Park. Keyn ... 81 F3
Abbey Rd. Bris ... 64 C4
Abbey Rd. Chil ... 137 E1
Abbey Rd. Chil ... 137 F1
Abbey St. Bath ... 102 A3
Abbey St. Kings ... 11 F3
Abbey View Gdns. Bath ... 102 A3
Abbey View. Bath ... 102 A3
Abbey View. Mid No ... 133 D2
Abbeydale. Wint ... 37 F3
Abbeygate St. Bath ... 102 A3
Abbeywood Dr. Bris ... 48 B3
Abbot's Cl. W-S-M ... 89 D2
Abbots Ave. Kingsw ... 65 E2
Abbots Cl. Bris ... 80 A2
Abbots Horn. Nail ... 59 E1
Abbots Leigh Rd. Ab Lei ... 62 B4
Abbots Leigh Rd. Lo Leh ... 62 B4
Abbots Rd. Kingsw ... 65 E1
Abbots Way. Bris ... 49 E4
Abbotsbury Rd. Nail ... 59 E1
Abbotsford Rd. Bris ... 49 F2
Abbotswood. Kingsw ... 65 F3
Abbotswood. Yate ... 39 E4
Abbott Rd. Piln ... 22 A3
Abbotts Farm Cl. Paul ... 131 E3
Aberdeen Rd. Bris ... 63 D4
Abingdon Gdns. Bath ... 118 B4
Abingdon Rd. Bris ... 51 D2
Ableton La. Avon ... 33 F4
Ableton La. Pln ... 22 A3
Ableton Wlk. Bris ... 48 B3
Abon Rd. Wick ... 53 E2
Abson Rd. Wick ... 53 E2
Acacia Ave. Kingsw ... 51 E2
Acacia Cl. Kingsw ... 51 E2
Acacia Cl. Keyn ... 81 E2
Acacia Gr. Bath ... 101 E2
Acacia Rd. Kingsw ... 51 E2
Acacia Rd. Rad ... 132 C1
Accommodation Rd. Blea . 121 F3
Acid Rd. Avon ... 33 E2
Acorn Gr. Bris ... 78 C3
Acramans's Rd. Bris ... 63 E2
Acrebush Cl. Bris ... 79 D3
Acton Rd. Bris ... 51 D2
Adams Cl. P St J ... 133 E4
Addicot Rd. W-S-M ... 104 C3
Addiscombe Rd. Bris ... 80 A3
Addiscombe Rd. W-S-M ... 104 C2
Addison Rd. Bris ... 63 F2
Adelaide Pl. Bris ... 50 C2
Adelaide Pl. Bris ... 64 A4
Admiral's Wlk. Portis ... 45 D3
Agate St. Bris ... 63 D2
Aiken St. Bris ... 64 A4
Ainslie's Belvedere. Bath . 101 F4
Aintree Dr. Mang ... 37 F1
Air Balloon Rd. Bris ... 65 D3
Airport Rd. Bris ... 80 A4
Aisecombe Way. W-S-M .. 105 E3
Akeman Way. Avon ... 47 E4
Alard Rd. Bris ... 79 F4
Albany Gate. St Gif ... 36 C3
Albany Rd. Bath ... 101 E3
Albany Rd. Bris ... 49 F1
Albany St. Bris ... 65 E4
Albany Way. Kingsw ... 66 B3
Albemarle Row. Bris ... 62 C3
Albert Ave. P St J ... 133 E4
Albert Ave. W-S-M ... 104 C3
Albert Cres. Bris ... 64 A3
Albert Gr. Bris ... 64 C4
Albert Par. Bris ... 64 B4
Albert Park Pl. Bris ... 49 E4
Albert Park. Bris ... 49 F1
Albert Pl. Bris ... 49 E4
Albert Pl. Bris ... 62 C1
Albert Quadrant. W-S-M .. 104 C4
Albert Rd. Bris ... 64 A4
Albert Rd. Clave ... 57 E2
Albert Rd. Keyn ... 81 F3
Albert Rd. Kingsw ... 65 E3
Albert Rd. Mang ... 51 F2
Albert Rd. Piln ... 22 A3
Albert Rd. Portis ... 45 E3
Albert Rd. W-S-M ... 104 C3
Albert St. Bris ... 64 B4
Albert Terr. Bath ... 101 E3
Albert Terr. Bris ... 50 C2
Alberton Rd. Bris ... 50 C4
Albion Cl. Mang ... 51 F3
Albion Pl. Bris ... 50 A1
Albion St. Bris ... 64 B4
Alburys. Wring ... 92 B2
Alcove Rd. Bris ... 50 C2
Alder Dr. Bris ... 50 C1
Alder Terr. Rad ... 132 C1
Aldercombe Rd. Bris ... 48 B4
Alderdown Cl. Bris ... 48 A4
Alderley Rd. Bath ... 101 D2

Alderley Rd. Hill ... 19 E4
Aldermoor Way. Kingsw .. 65 F2
Aldernay Ave. Bris ... 64 C2
Alders The. Bris ... 37 D1
Alderton Rd. Grit ... 43 E3
Alderton Rd. Bris ... 49 F4
Aldertown Rd. Bris ... 79 E2
Aldwick La. Blag ... 110 B4
Aldwick La. Bul ... 110 B4
Aldwick La. Wring ... 110 B4
Alex Ricketts Cl. Bath ... 100 C3
Alexander Way. Yatt ... 91 D4
Alexandra Cl. Kingsw ... 51 E2
Alexandra Gdns. Kingsw .. 51 E2
Alexandra Par. W-S-M 104 C4
Alexandra Park. Bris ... 49 E1
Alexandra Park. Paul ... 131 F3
Alexandra Rd. Bath ... 102 A3
Alexandra Rd. Bris ... 63 D4
Alexandra Rd. Bris ... 76 C4
Alexandra Rd. Cleve ... 57 E2
Alexandra Rd. Fr Crot ... 38 B4
Alexandra Rd. Paul ... 131 F3
Alexandra Terr. Paul ... 131 F4
Alexandra Way. Thorn ... 8 A2
Alford Rd. Bris ... 64 B1
Alfred Hill. Bris ... 63 E4
Alfred Lovell Gdns. Kingsw . 66 A2
Alfred Pl. Bris ... 63 E4
Alfred Rd. Bris ... 49 D2
Alfred Rd. Bris ... 63 E2
Alfred St. Bath ... 101 F4
Alfred St. Bris ... 64 A3
Alfred St. Bris ... 64 B4
Alfred St. W-S-M ... 104 C4
Algars Dr. Ir Act ... 26 C2
Algiers St. Bris ... 63 E2
Alison Gdns. Back ... 76 A4
All Hallows Rd. Bris ... 64 A4
All Saints La. Cleve ... 57 E2
All Saints' La. Bris ... 63 E3
All Saints' Rd. Bath ... 101 F4
All Saints' Rd. Bris ... 49 D1
All Saints' St. Bris ... 63 E4
Allanmead Rd. Bris ... 80 A4
Allengrove La. Luck ... 31 E2
Allens La. Wins ... 125 F4
Aller Par. W-S-M ... 105 D1
Aller. W-S-M ... 105 D1
Aller Rd. Bris ... 80 A3
Allerton Gdns. Bris ... 80 A3
Allerton Rd. Bris ... 80 A2
Allfoxton Rd. Bris ... 64 A1
All Saints' St. Bris ... 63 E4
Allington Dr. Kingsw ... 65 F2
Allington Rd. Bris ... 63 E3
Allington Rd. Bris ... 75 E4
Allison Ave. Bris ... 64 C2
Allison Rd. Bris ... 64 C2
Alma Cl. Kingsw ... 65 F4
Alma Pl. Well ... 118 B1
Alma Rd. Bris ... 63 D4
Alma Rd. Kingsw ... 51 F1
Alma Road Ave. Bris ... 63 D4
Alma St. Bris ... 49 D1
Alma St. W-S-M ... 104 C4
Alma Vale Rd. Bris ... 63 D4
Almeda Rd. Bris ... 65 D3
Almond Cl. W-S-M ... 89 D1
Almond Way. Mang ... 51 F3
Almondsbury Bsns Centre.
Gil ... 24 B2
Almorah Rd. Bris ... 63 E2
Alpha Centre The. Yate ... 27 E2
Alpha Rd. Bris ... 63 E2
Alpine Gdns. Bath ... 102 A4
Alpine Rd. Bris ... 50 B1
Alpine Rd. Paul ... 131 F2
Alsop Rd. Kingsw ... 51 E1
Alton Rd. Bris ... 49 F3
Altringham Rd. Bris ... 64 B4
Alverstoke. Bris ... 79 F4
Alveston Hill. Thorn ... 15 D3
Alveston Rd. Olve ... 14 B2
Alveston Wlk. Bris ... 48 A4
Alwins Ct. Kingsw ... 65 F2
Amberey Rd. W-S-M ... 104 C3
Amberlands Cl. Back ... 76 A4
Amberley Cl. Keyn ... 81 F2
Amberley Cl. Mang ... 51 E4
Amberley Gdns. Nail ... 59 E1
Amberley Rd. Mang ... 51 E4
Amberley Rd. St Gif ... 36 A4
Amberley Way. Wickw 18 A2
Amble Cl. Kingsw ... 66 A3
Ambleside Ave. Bris ... 35 D1
Ambleside Rd. Bath ... 101 E1
Ambra Vale E. Bris ... 63 D3
Ambra Vale S. Bris ... 63 D3
Ambra Vale W. Bris ... 63 D3
Ambra Vale. Bris ... 63 D3
Ambrose Rd. Bris ... 63 D3
Ambury. Bath ... 101 F3

Amercombe Wlk. Bris ... 80 B4
Amery La. Bath ... 102 A3
Ames La. Kilm ... 139 D3
Amesbury Dr. Blea ... 122 A3
Ammerdown Terr. Faulk .. 139 F4
Anchor La. Bris ... 63 E3
Anchor Rd. Bath ... 84 A1
Anchor Rd. Bris ... 63 E3
Anchor Rd. Kingsw ... 52 A1
Anchor Way. E in G ... 47 E2
Andereach Cl. Bris ... 80 A4
Andover Rd. Bris ... 63 F1
Andrues Dr. Dun ... 73 F4
Angers Rd. Bris ... 64 A2
Anglesea Pl. Bris ... 49 D1
Annandale Ave. W-S-M ... 88 C1
Anson Cl. Keyn ... 81 F4
Anstey St. Bris ... 50 B1
Anstey's Rd. Kingsw ... 65 E3
Anthea Rd. Bris ... 50 C1
Antona Cl. Bris ... 47 E4
Antona Dr. Bris ... 47 E4
Antrim Rd. Bris ... 49 D2
Anvil Rd. Yatt ... 74 C1
Anvil St. Bris ... 63 F3
Apex Cl. St Gif ... 24 B2
Apperley Cl. Yate ... 39 E4
Apple Tree Dr. Wins ... 125 D4
Appleby Wlk. Bris ... 79 E4
Applecroft. Well ... 133 F3
Appledore Cl. Bris ... 80 A4
Applegate. Bris ... 35 D2
Appletree Ct. W-S-M ... 89 D1
Apseleys Mead. St Gif ... 24 B1
Apsley Cl. W-S-M ... 88 B1
Apsley Rd. Bris ... 49 D1
Apsley Rd. Bris ... 50 B2
Arbutus Dr. Bris ... 48 B4
Arcade The. Bris ... 63 F4
Arch Cl. Lo Ash ... 61 F1
Archer Cl. Kingsw ... 65 F2
Archer Wlk. Bris ... 80 C3
Archfield Rd. Bris ... 49 E1
Archgrove. Lo Ash ... 61 F1
Archway St. Bath ... 102 A3
Arden Cl. St Gif ... 36 C3
Arden Cl. W-S-M ... 88 C2
Ardenton Wlk. Bris ... 35 D2
Ardern Cl. Bris ... 48 A4
Argus Rd. Bris ... 63 E1
Argyle Ave. Bris ... 50 B1
Argyle Pl. W-S-M ... 104 C2
Argyle Dr. Yate ... 27 F2
Argyle Pl. Bris ... 63 D3
Argyle Rd. Bris ... 50 B1
Argyle Rd. Bris ... 63 F4
Argyle Rd. Cleve ... 57 E3
Argyle St. Bath ... 102 A3
Argyle St. Bris ... 50 B1
Argyle St. Bris ... 63 F4
Argyle Terr. Bath ... 101 E3
Arley Cotts. Bris ... 49 E1
Arley Hill. Bris ... 49 E1
Arley Park. Bris ... 49 E1
Arley Terr. Bris ... 50 C1
Arlingham Way. Bris ... 23 E3
Arlington Rd. Bath ... 101 E3
Arlington Rd. Bris ... 64 B3
Arlington Villas. Bris ... 63 D4
Armada Pl. Bris ... 49 F1
Armes Cl. Bath ... 102 A3
Armidale Ave. Bris ... 49 F1
Armoury Sq. Bris ... 64 A4
Armstrong Cl. Yate ... 27 E2
Armstrong Way. Yate ... 27 D2
Arnall Dr. Bris ... 34 C1
Arneside Rd. Bris ... 35 E1
Arno's St. Bris ... 64 A2
Arnold Ct. Ch Sod ... 28 A1
Arnor Cl. W-S-M ... 89 D2
Arrowfield Cl. Bris ... 80 A1
Arthur Skemp Cl. Bris ... 64 A4
Arthur St. Bris ... 64 A3
Arthur St. Bris ... 64 B4
Arthurswood Rd. Bris ... 79 D2
Arundel Cl. Bris ... 79 D3
Arundel Rd. Bath ... 101 E4
Arundel Rd. Bris ... 49 E2
Arundel Rd. Cleve ... 57 E2
Arundel Wlk. Keyn ... 81 E3
Arundell Ct. W-S-M ... 104 C4
Arundell Rd. W-S-M ... 87 F1
Ascot Cl. Bris ... 35 F1
Ascot Cl. Mang ... 37 F1
Ash Cl. St Gif ... 36 B4
Ash Cl. W-S-M ... 89 D2
Ash Cl. Wins ... 108 A1
Ash Cl. Yate ... 27 F1
Ash Gr. Bath ... 101 E2
Ash Gr. Bris ... 51 E2
Ash Gr. Cleve ... 57 F2
Ash Gr. W-S-M ... 104 C1
Ash Hayes Dr. Nail ... 59 F1
Ash Hayes Rd. Nail ... 59 F1
Ash La. Alm ... 23 E1
Ash Rd. Bris ... 49 F3
Ash Ridge Rd. St Gif ... 24 A2
Ash Tree Cl. Blea ... 122 B3
Ash Tree Ct. Rad ... 132 C1

Ash Wlk. Bris ... 35 D2
Ashbourne Cl. Kingsw ... 66 B3
Ashburton Rd. Bris ... 35 E1
Ashbury Dr. W-S-M ... 88 A1
Ashcombe Cres. Kingsw .. 66 B3
Ashcombe Gdns. W-S-M . 105 D4
Ashcombe Park Rd. W-S-M 88 A1
Ashcombe Rd. W-S-M ... 104 C4
Ashcott. Bris ... 79 F4
Ashcroft Ave. Keyn ... 81 E3
Ashcroft Rd. Bris ... 48 B4
Ashcroft. W-S-M ... 105 D1
Ashdene Ave. Bris ... 50 C3
Ashdene Rd. W-S-M ... 105 D4
Ashdown Rd. Portis ... 45 D3
Ashel's Batch. Litt ... 129 E1
Asher La. Bris ... 63 F4
Ashes La. Hi Cha ... 120 A2
Ashfield Pl. Bris ... 49 F1
Ashfield Rd. Bris ... 63 D2
Ashford Dr. W-S-M ... 105 D1
Ashford Rd. Bath ... 101 E2
Ashford Rd. Bris ... 36 A4
Ashford Rd. Wrng ... 93 F2
Ashford Way. Kingsw ... 66 A4
Ashgrove Ave. Ab Lei ... 62 A4
Ashgrove Ave. Bris ... 49 F2
Ashgrove Rd. Bris ... 49 F2
Ashgrove Rd. Bris ... 49 F2
Ashgrove Rd. Bris ... 63 D2
Ashgrove. P St J ... 133 E4
Ashgrove. Thorn ... 8 B1
Ashland Rd. Bris ... 79 D2
Ashleigh Cl. Paul ... 131 F3
Ashleigh Cl. W-S-M ... 105 D4
Ashleigh Cres. Yatt ... 91 D4
Ashleigh Rd. W-S-M ... 105 D4
Ashleigh Rd. Yatt ... 91 D4
Ashley Ave. Bath ... 101 E4
Ashley Cl. Bris ... 49 F2
Ashley Court Rd. Bris ... 49 F1
Ashley Down Rd. Bris ... 49 F2
Ashley Grove Rd. Bris ... 49 F1
Ashley Grove Rd. Bris ... 50 A1
Ashley Hill. Bris ... 49 F2
Ashley La. Blag ... 110 A3
Ashley La. Winsl ... 120 C4
Ashley La. Wring ... 110 A3
Ashley Par. Bris ... 49 F1
Ashley Rd. Bath ... 86 B1
Ashley Rd. Bris ... 49 F1
Ashley Rd. Bris ... 50 A1
Ashley Trading Est. Bris .. 49 F1
Ashley. Kingsw ... 65 F2
Ashman Cl. Bris ... 64 A4
Ashmans Gate. Paul ... 131 F3
Ashmead Rd Ind Est. Keyn . 82 A3
Ashmead Rd. Keyn ... 82 A3
Ashmead Way. Bris ... 63 D3
Ashmead. Clut ... 114 C1
Ashton Ave. Bris ... 63 D3
Ashton Cres. Nail ... 59 E1
Ashton Dr. Bris ... 62 C1
Ashton Gate Rd. Bris ... 63 D2
Ashton Gate Terr. Bris ... 63 D2
Ashton Rd. Bris ... 62 C2
Ashton Rd. Lo Ash ... 62 C2
Ashton Vale Rd. Bris ... 62 C2
Ashton Way. Keyn ... 81 F3
Ashton. Bris ... 37 E1
Ashvale Cl. Nail ... 60 A1
Ashville Rd. Bris ... 63 D2
Ashwell Cl. Bris ... 80 C3
Ashwicke Rd. Marsh ... 97 E1
Ashwicke. Bris ... 80 A3
Ashwood. E Harp ... 128 C2
Aspen Cl. Col ... 70 C3
Aspley Cl. Bath ... 101 D4
Aspley Rd. Bath ... 101 D4
Assembly Rooms La. Bris . 63 E3
Aston Gate Underpass. Bris 62 C2
Astry Cl. Bris ... 34 A1
Atchley St. Bris ... 64 A4
Atherston. Kingsw ... 66 B3
Athlone Wlk. Bris ... 63 F1
Atholl Cl. W-S-M ... 88 C2
Atkins Cl. Bris ... 80 C3
Atlantic Cl. W-S-M ... 87 E1
Atlantic Rd S. W-S-M ... 87 E1
Atlantic Rd. Avon ... 47 E4
Atlantic Rd. W-S-M ... 87 E1
Atlas Cl. Bris ... 51 D1
Atlas Rd. Bris ... 63 F2
Atlas St. Bris ... 64 A3
Atwell Dr. St Gif ... 24 A1
Atwood Dr. Bris ... 34 A1
Aubrey Meads. Bitt ... 82 C4
Aubrey Rd. Bris ... 63 D2
Auburn Ave. Kingsw ... 66 A2
Auburn Rd. Bris ... 49 D1
Auckland Cl. W-S-M ... 104 C2
Audley Ave. Bath ... 101 E4
Audley Cl. Bath ... 101 E4
Audley Gr. Bath ... 101 E4
Audley Park Rd. Bath ... 101 E4

Audrey Wlk. Bris ... 49 [F?]
Aust Rd. Aust ...
Aust Rd. Cleve ... 13 [?]
Aust Rd. Piln ... 12 [?]
Austen Dr. W-S-M ... 89 [?]
Austen Gr. Bris ... 50 [?]
Avalon Cl. Yatt ... 74 [?]
Avalon House. Nail ...
Avalon Rd. Bris ... 65 [?]
Avebury Rd. Bris ... 62 [?]
Avening Cl. Nail ...
Avening Green. Char ... 1 [?]
Avenue The. Bath ...
Avenue The. Back ... 76 [?]
Avenue The. Bath ... 102 [?]
Avenue The. Bris ... 64 [?]
Avenue The. Bris ... 48 [?]
Avenue The. Bris ...
Avenue The. Bris ... 64 [?]
Avenue The. Cleve ... 57 [?]
Avenue The. Keyn ... 81 [?]
Avenue The. St Gif ... 2 [?]
Avenue The. Tims ... 116 [?]
Avenue The. Wins ... 125 [?]
Avenue The. Yatt ... 74 [?]
Averay Rd. Bris ... 50 [?]
Avon Bsns Pk. Bris ... 51 [?]
Avon Cl. Keyn ... 82 [?]
Avon Cl. W-S-M ... 104 [?]
Avon Cres. Bris ... 63 [?]
Avon Cres. Wickw ... 18 [?]
Avon Ct. Bathe ... 96 [?]
Avon Gorge Ind Est. Avon . 47 [?]
Avon Gr. Bris ... 48 [?]
Avon La. Keyn ... 82 [?]
Avon Mill La. Keyn ... 81 [?]
Avon Park. Bath ... 101 [?]
Avon Park. Bris ... 64 [?]
Avon Rd. Char ... 11 [?]
Avon Rd. E in G ... 47 [?]
Avon Rd. Keyn ... 81 [?]
Avon Rise. Luck ... 31 [?]
Avon Riverside Est. Avon . 47 [?]
Avon St. Bath ... 101 [?]
Avon St. Bris ... 63 [?]
Avon Trading Est. Bris ... 64 [?]
Avon Vale. Bris ... 48 [?]
Avon Valley Bsns Pk. Bris . 64 [?]
Avon View. Kingsw ... 65 [?]
Avon Way. Bris ... 48 [?]
Avon Way. Portis ... 45 [?]
Avon Way. Bris ... 79 [?]
Avonbank Ind Centre. Avon 47 [?]
Avonbridge Trading Est.
Avon ... 33 [?]
Avondale Bldgs. Bath ... 85 [?]
Avondale Pl. Bathe ... 85 [?]
Avondale Rd. Bath ... 101 [?]
Avondown Cl. Bris ... 35 [?]
Avondown Ct. Bris ... 63 [?]
Avonlea. Kingsw ... 65 [?]
Avonleaze. Bris ... 48 [?]
Avonleigh Ct. Bris ... 63 [?]
Avonleigh Rd. Bris ... 63 [?]
Avonmouth Rd. Avon ... 33 [?]
Avonmouth Way. Avon ... 33 [?]
Avonmouth Way. Bris ... 34 [?]
Avonside Rd. Bris ... 64 [?]
Avonside Way. Bris ... 64 [?]
Avonsmere Residential Pk.
Bris ... 36 [?]
Avonwood Cl. Bris ... 47 [?]
Awdelett Cl. Bris ... 34 [?]
Awkley La. Olve ... 13 [?]
Awkward Hill. Bur ... 111 [?]
Axbridge Cl. Nail ... 75 [?]
Axbridge Moor Dro. Axb .. 125 [?]
Axbridge Rd. Bath ... 101 [?]
Axbridge Rd. Bris ... 80 [?]
Axbridge Rd. Ched ... 125 [?]
Axe Cl. W-S-M ... 105 [?]
Axe Way. P St J ... 133 [?]
Axis. Bris ... 79 [?]
Aycote Cl. W-S-M ... 88 [?]
Ayford La. Marsh ... 69 [?]
Aylesbury Cres. Bris ... 79 [?]
Aylesbury Rd. Bris ... 79 [?]
Aylmer Cres. Bris ... 80 [?]
Aylminton Wlk. Bris ... 34 [?]
Ayr St. Bath ... 101 [?]
Aztec Centre The. St Gif .. 24 [?]
Aztec West. St Gif ... 24 [?]

Back La. Axb ... 125 [?]
Back La. E in G ... 47 [?]
Back La. K Sey ... 73 [?]
Back La. Litt ... 129 [?]
Back La. Marsh ... 69 [?]
Back La. Wickw ... 34 [?]
Back Of Kingsdown Par. Bris 63
Back Rd. Bris ... 63 [?]
Back St. H Up ...

k St. W-S-M 104 C4
k Stoke La. Bris 48 C3
kfields La. Bris 63 F4
kfields. Bris 63 F4
kwell Bow. Back 60 B1
kwell Comm. Back 76 A4
kwell Rd. Back 76 C2
kwell Wlk. Bris 78 C4
en Hill Rd. Tyth 16 B3
en Rd. Bris 64 B4
en Rd.-Kingsw 66 A4
enham Gr. Bris 47 F4
enham Ct. Yate 27 E2
ger's La. Alm 23 E1
gers Ct. St Gif 24 B2
gers Rise. Portis 44 C2
gers Wlk. Bris 64 B1
geworth. Yate 39 E3
minton Centre The. Yate 27 E1
minton Cl. Yate 27 E1
minton Gdns. Bath ... 101 E4
minton Rd. Bris 49 F1
minton Rd. Ch Sod ... 40 C4
minton Rd. Fr Cot 38 B3
minton Rd. Mang 51 F4
minton Rd. West 38 B3
minton Wlk. Mang 51 F4
minton. Bris 37 E3
bridge Hill. Well 134 C4
ave. Kingsw 51 F2
ell Cl. Bris 80 C3
ell Rd. Bris 80 C3
stone Rd. Wicke 16 C2
rook Gr. Bath 85 E2
rook La. Bath 85 E2
on Cres. W-S-M 105 D2
on Ct. W-S-M 104 C2
on Rd. W-S-M 105 D2
rs Court Rd. St Gif ... 36 C3
rs Ct Rd. St Gif 37 D3
rs Ct. St Gif 36 C3
s Cl. Axb 125 E1
s' Wall. Axb 125 E1
View. Wint 137 F1
Cl. Cleve 73 D4
. W-S-M 104 C4
's Bldgs. Wring 92 B1
s Par Tims 116 A1
s La. Chil 137 E2
s La. Wring 109 E4
sfield. Kingsw 66 A2
ava Rd. Bris 50 C3
n St. Bris 63 E3
ar Rd. Bris 63 D2
ce St. Bath 101 F4
el La. Avon 33 F1
Barn La. Ban 90 A1
in St. Bris 64 A2
vral Cl. St Gif 36 B2
vral Ct. Mang 52 A3
vral Rd. Bris 49 F1
vral Rd. Keyn 81 F2
vral Rd. Kingsw 65 F1
vral Way. W-S-M 88 B1
PL E in G 47 E2
eld. Bris 80 A3
ton Cl. Bris 79 D4
nton. W-S-M 88 C1
I Cl. Bris 64 A4
ove Wlk. Bris 47 F4
r Gr. Bris 79 E4
ove Rd. W-S-M 47 E2
Rd. Avon 33 D2
Rd. Kingsw 65 E4
Rd. Pin 22 C3
Cl. Cleve 73 E4
de Rd. Bris 64 B2
de. Mang 51 F2
Rd. Bris 49 F1
rdown Cl. Bathe 86 A2
rdown Dr. Bathe 86 A2
rdown Rd. Bathe 86 B3
eigh La. Lo Ash 62 C3
eigh Rd. Lo Ash 62 C3
erman Rd. Bris 64 A4
tts Tree Cres. Alve ... 15 D3
k Cl. Bris 79 E3
Rd. Bris 79 D4
Cl. Bris 64 B1
yson Cl. Bath 82 A1
l Rd. Ban 123 F4
l Rd. Bath 118 B4
l Rd. Bris 80 A3
l Rd. Lock 106 A2
l Rd. Wins 123 F4
l Rd. Wins 124 C4
St. Bris 50 A1
ry Farm Rd. Yatt 74 A1
r Gdns. Bris 79 E2
l Cr. Bris 79 F2
t Cl. Bris 50 A1
Wlk. Bris 50 A1
Cl. Fr Cot 38 B4
Cl. Mang 52 A3
Croft. Bris 48 C3

Barn End. Marsh 70 A4
Barn Hill. Well 133 F3
Barn La. Pens 115 D4
Barn Owl Way. St Gif . 36 C3
Barn Pool. Ship 125 F4
Barnabas St. Bris 49 F1
Barnaby Cl. Mid No ... 132 A1
Barnack Trading Est. Bris 63 E1
Barnard Wlk. Keyn 81 E2
Barnard's Ct. Yatt 91 E4
Barnes St. Bris 64 B4
Barnfield Way. Bathe . 86 A2
Barnhill Rd. Ch Sod .. 28 A1
Barns Cl. Ba Gu 77 F2
Barns Cl. Nail 63 A3
Barnstaple House. Bris 63 F4
Barnstaple Rd. Bris ... 79 F4
Barnstaple Wlk. Bris .. 79 F4
Barnwood Rd. Yate ... 39 E4
Barossa Pl. Bris 63 A3
Barrack's La. Bris 63 E3
Barratt St. Bris 50 B1
Barrington Cl. Kingsw . 51 F1
Barrington Ct. Bris ... 63 F2
Barrington Cl. Kingsw . 51 F1
Barrow Court La. Ba Gu 77 D3
Barrow Court La. Back . 77 D3
Barrow Hill Cres. Bris . 47 E4
Barrow Hill Rd. Bris .. 47 E3
Barrow Hill. Wick 67 D3
Barrow La. Ba Gu 77 F1
Barrow La. Win 94 C4
Barrow Rd. Bath 101 E1
Barrow St. Ba Gu 77 F2
Barrow St. Lo Ash 77 E3
Barrowmead Dr. Bris . 47 F4
Barrows The. Bris 79 D2
Barrows The. W-S-M .. 105 E4
Barrs Court Ave. Kingsw 66 A3
Barrs Court Rd. Kingsw 66 A3
Barrs La. N Ib 5 F2
Barry Cl. Kingsw 66 B1
Barry Cl. W-S-M 105 D1
Bartlett St. Bath 101 F4
Bartlett's Rd. Bris 63 E2
Bartley St. Bris 63 E2
Barton Cl. Alve 15 D3
Barton Cl. Bris 64 A4
Barton Cl. Wint 37 F3
Barton Dro. Wins 124 B3
Barton Green. Bris 64 A4
Barton Hill Rd. Bris .. 64 A4
Barton Manor. Bris ... 64 A4
Barton Rd. .... 124 —
Barton Rd. Bris 63 F3
Barton Rd. Co Bi 123 F3
Barton St. Bris 63 E4
Barton The. Blea 122 B3
Barton The. Cor 94 A3
Barton The. Kingsw ... 65 E2
Barton The. N St P ... 135 F2
Barton Vale. Bris 63 F3
Bartonia Gr. Bris 64 B1
Barwood Cl. Kingsw .. 65 F4
Batch La. Lympy 121 F2
Batch The. Blag 110 A2
Batch The. But 111 D4
Batch The. Ch Mag ... 96 A2
Batch The. Chur 108 C2
Batch The. Co Mar ... 128 A3
Batch The. Farm 116 A3
Batch The. Hin Cha .. 119 F1
Batch The. Wring 93 E4
Batch The. Yat 91 D1
Batches The. Bris 63 D1
Batchfield La. West ... 53 E4
Bates Cl. Bris 64 A4
Bath Bldgs. Bris 49 F1
Bath Hill. Well 118 B1
Bath New Rd. Mid No . 132 C2
Bath Old Rd. Mid No . 132 C2
Bath Rd. Bitt 82 B4
Bath Rd. Blag 109 E2
Bath Rd. Blag 110 C1
Bath Rd. Box 86 C3
Bath Rd. Bris 64 B2
Bath Rd. Ch Sod 41 E2
Bath Rd. Chur 109 E2
Bath Rd. Corn 107 E2
Bath Rd. Doyn 42 A2
Bath Rd. Farm 115 F3
Bath Rd. Keyn 82 B2
Bath Rd. Kingsw 65 F2
Bath Rd. Kingsw 66 B3
Bath Rd. N St P 135 E4
Bath Rd. Paul 131 F3
Bath Rd. Sist 66 B3
Bath Rd. Thom 55 F4
Bath Rd. Tor 41 E2
Bath Rd. Wick 66 C4
Bath Riverside Bsns Park.

Bath 101 F3
Bath St. Bath 101 F3
Bath St. Bris 63 D3
Bath St. Bris 63 F3
Bath St. Kingsw 65 F2
Bath View. Chil 137 F1
Bathampton La. Bath .. 85 F1
Bathford Hill. Bathf ... 86 A1
Bathford Hill. Co Dan . 98 C3
Bathurst Par. Bris 63 E3
Bathurst Rd. W-S-M .. 105 E4
Bathwell Rd. Bris 64 A2
Bathwick Hill. Bath ... 102 B3
Bathwick Rise. Bath .. 102 A4
Bathwick St. Bath 102 A4
Batley Cl. Kingsw 66 B2
Batstone Cl. Bath 85 D1
Batten Ct. Ch Sod 28 A1
Batten's La. Bris 65 D3
Battenburg Rd. Bris .. 65 D4
Battens Rd. Bris 65 D4
Battersby Way. Bris .. 34 C1
Battersea Rd. Bris 64 B4
Battery La. Portis 45 D4
Battery Rd. Portis 45 E3
Battle La. Ch Mag 96 A2
Batton Rd. Bris 80 C2
Baugh Gdns. Mang ... 52 A1
Baugh Rd. Mang 37 F1
Bay Gdns. Bris 50 B1
Bay Rd. Cleve 57 E3
Bay Tree Cl. Bris 35 F4
Bay Tree Rd. Bath ... 85 D2
Bay Tree Rd. Cleve .. 57 F1
Bayleys Dr. Kingsw .. 65 E3
Baynham Ct. Kingsw .. 65 D3
Baynton Rd. Bris 63 A2
Bayswater Ave. Bris .. 49 D2
Bayswater Rd. Bris ... 49 F4
Baytree Rd. W-S-M .. 88 B1
Baytree View. W-S-M 88 B1
Beach Ave. Cleve 57 E1
Beach Ave. Pin 22 A4
Beach End Rd. W-S-M 104 B1
Beach Hill. Bitt 66 C2
Beach Hill. Portis 45 E3
Beach La. Bath 67 E1
Beach Rd E. Portis .. 45 E3
Beach Rd W. Portis .. 45 E3
Beach Rd. Piln 21 F4
Beach Rd. W St L 88 A3
Beach Rd. W-S-M 88 A2
Beachcroft. Bris 80 C2
Beachgrove Gdns. Bris 51 E2
Beachgrove Rd. Bris .. 51 D2
Beachley Wlk. Bris ... 47 E4
Beacon La. Wint 37 E3
Beacon Rd. Bath 85 D1
Beaconlea. Kingsw ... 65 F3
Beaconsfield Rd. Bris . 49 D1
Beaconsfield Rd. Bris . 64 A2
Beaconsfield Rd. Bris . 64 C4
Beaconsfield Rd. Cleve 57 F2
Beaconsfield Rd. W-S-M 104 C4
Beaconsfield St. Bris .. 64 A3
Beale Cl. Bris 80 C3
Beam St. Bris 64 B4
Bean Acre The. Bris .. 47 E4
Bean St. Bris 50 A1
Beanhill Cres. Alve ... 15 D3
Bearbridge Rd. Bris .. 78 C2
Beau St. Bath 101 F3
Beauchamp Rd. Bris .. 49 E2
Beauchamps Dr. Chil . 138 A3
Beauford Sq. Bath 101 F3
Beaufort Ave. Mid No . 132 A1
Beaufort Ave. Yate ... 27 E4
Beaufort Cl. Bris 64 B4
Beaufort Cres. St Gif . 36 C2
Beaufort Ct. Mang ... 52 A4
Beaufort East. Bath .. 85 E1
Beaufort Gdns. Nail .. 59 E1
Beaufort Hts. Bris 64 C4
Beaufort Park. St Gif . 24 B2
Beaufort Pl. Bath 85 E1
Beaufort Pl. Bris 37 D1
Beaufort Rd. Bris 64 A4
Beaufort Rd. Bris 49 D1
Beaufort Rd. Bris 49 F3
Beaufort Rd. Bris 51 E1
Beaufort Rd. Bris 64 C4
Beaufort Rd. Mang ... 51 F3
Beaufort Rd. Mang ... 52 A4
Beaufort Rd. W-S-M .. 104 C4
Beaufort St. Bris 63 E3
Beaufort St. Bris 64 A4
Beaufort Vs. Bath 37 E1
Beauley Rd. Bris 63 D2
Beaumont Cl. Kingsw . 66 A2
Beaumont Cl. W-S-M . 104 B4
Beaumont St. Bris ... 64 A4
Beaumont Terr. Bris .. 64 A4
Beaver Cl. Wint 37 F4
Beazer Cl. Kingsw ... 51 E2
Beck Cl. Puck 53 D3
Becket Dr. W-S-M 89 D2

Becket Rd. W-S-M 89 D2
Becket's La. Nail 75 F4
Beckford Gdns. Bath .. 102 A4
Beckford Gdns. Bris .. 80 A2
Beckford Rd. Bath 102 A4
Beckhampton Rd. Bath 101 E3
Beckington Rd. Bris ... 63 F1
Beckington Wlk. Bris . 63 F1
Beckspool Rd. Bris ... 105 D1
Beckspool Rd. Bris ... 51 E4
Bedford Cres. Bris 49 F3
Bedford Rd. W-S-M .. 104 C2
Bedford St. Bath 102 A4
Bedminster Down Rd. Bris 63 D1
Bedminster Par. Bris .. 63 E2
Bedminster Pl. Bris ... 63 E2
Bedminster Rd. Bris .. 63 E1
Bedwin Cl. Portis 44 C2
Beech Ave. Bath 102 C3
Beech Cl. Alve 15 D3
Beech Cl. Kingsw 66 A3
Beech Cl. Ship 125 F4
Beech Dr. Nail 60 A2
Beech Gr. Bath 125 F4
Beech Gr. Bath 101 E2
Beech Leaze. Alve 15 D3
Beech Rd. Bris 49 F3
Beech Rd. Keyn 82 C2
Beech Rd. Ship 125 F4
Beech Rd. Yatt 91 E4
Beech Terr. Rad 132 B1
Beech Cl. Ship 125 F4
Beechcroft. Dun 78 B1
Beechen Cliff Rd. Bath 101 F3
Beechen Dr. Bris 51 D2
Beeches Gr. Bris 64 B4
Beeches Ind Est. Ir Act 27 D1
Beeches The. Bath ... 101 E1
Beeches The. Kingsw .. 66 B1
Beeches The. Wins ... 108 A2
Beechfield Cl. Lo Ash . 62 B1
Beechmont Cl. W-S-M . 105 D1
Beechmont Gr. Bris ... 80 A4
Beechmount Dr. Bris .. 80 A4
Beechwood Ave. Kingsw 65 E3
Beechwood Ave. Lock . 106 A2
Beechwood Cl. Bris ... 80 B4
Beechwood Dr. Portis . 44 C3
Beechwood Rd. Bath .. 102 A1
Beechwood Rd. E in G . 47 D2
Beechwood Rd. Nail .. 59 E1
Beechwood Rd. Portis . 44 C3
Beehive Yd. Bath 102 A4
Beek's La. Marsh .....
Beesmoor Rd. Fr Cot . 38 A3
Begbrook Dr. Bris 50 C3
Begbrook La. Bris 50 C3
Begbrook Park. Bris .. 51 D4
Beggar Bush La. Lo Ash 61 F2
Beggar Bush La. Wrax . 61 F2
Beggars Bush La. Ab Lei 62 A3
Beggarswell Cl. Bris .. 63 F4
Belfast Wlk. Bris 79 F4
Belfry Ave. Bris 65 E4
Belfry. Kingsw 66 A3
Belgrave Cres. Bath .. 85 D1
Belgrave Hill. Bris 49 D1
Belgrave Pl. Bris 63 D4
Belgrave Rd. Bath 85 D1
Belgrave Rd. Bris 49 D1
Belgrave Rd. W-S-M .. 105 D4
Bell Barn Rd. Bris 48 B3
Bell Ct. Farm 115 F3
Bell Hill Rd. Bris 65 D4
Bell Hill. Bris 50 B2
Bell La. Bris 63 E4
Bell La. Fr Cot 38 B3
Bell Sq. Blag 110 C2
Bell Wlk. Wring 92 C1
Bella Vista Rd. Bath .. 101 F4
Bellamy Ave. Bris 79 E2
Bellamy Cl. Kingsw ... 65 D3
Belland Dr. Bris 79 F2
Belle Vue Rd. Bris ... 50 B1
B.llevue Cl. Kingsw ... 65 F4
Bellevue Cres. Bris ... 63 D3
Bellevue Cotts. Bris .. 63 D3
Bellevue Pk. Bris 64 B1
Bellevue Rd. Bris 50 B2
Bellevue Rd. Bris 51 E1
Bellevue Rd. Cleve .. 57 E2
Bellevue Rd. Kingsw . 65 F4
Bellevue Terr. Bris ... 63 D2
Bellevue Terr. Bris ... 63 E4
Bellevue. Bris 63 D3
Bellhorse La. E Harp . 128 B3
Bellhouse Wlk. Bris .. 34 A1
Bellifants. Farm 116 A3
Bellotts Rd. Bath 101 E3
Belluton La. Pens 97 E3
Belluton Rd. Bris 64 A2
Belmont Dr. St Gif ... 36 C3
Belmont Dr. Wrax 61 D2
Belmont Hill. Wrax ... 61 D1

Belmont Rd. Bath 102 B3
Belmont Rd. Bris 49 F2
Belmont Rd. Bris 64 B2
Belmont Rd. Wins ... 125 D4
Belmont St. Bris 50 A1
Belmore Gdns. Bath .. 101 D2
Beloe Rd. Bris 49 F3
Belroyal Ave. Bris 64 C2
Belstone Wlk. Bris ... 79 E4
Belton Ct. Bath 84 A1
Belton Rd. Bris 64 A4
Belton Rd. Portis 45 D3
Belvedere Cres. W-S-M 88 B1
Belvedere Rd. Bris ... 49 D2
Belvoir Rd. Bath 101 E3
Belvoir Rd. Bris 49 F1
Benches La. But .....
Benford Cl. Bris 51 E3
Bennell Batch. Chil .. 137 F2
Bennell Cl. Chil 137 F2
Bennell Cotts. Chil .. 137 F2
Bennett La. Bath 85 D1
Bennett Rd. Bris 64 C4
Bennett St. Bath 101 F4
Bennett Way. Bris ... 62 C3
Bennett's Ct. Yate ... 28 A1
Bennett's Rd. Bath ... 85 E1
Bennetts Way. Cleve . 57 F3
Bensaunt Gr. Bris 35 E2
Bentley Cl. Bris 79 F2
Bentley Rd. W-S-M .. 89 D2
Benville Ave. Bris 48 B4
Berenda Dr. Longw .. 66 A2
Beresford Cl. Keyn ... 82 C1
Beresford Gdns. Bath . 84 A2
Berkeley Ave. Bris ... 63 D4
Berkeley Ave. Bris ... 63 E4
Berkeley Ave. Mid No . 132 A1
Berkeley Cl. Char 1 D1
Berkeley Cl. Mang ... 52 A4
Berkeley Cres. W-S-M 104 B1
Berkeley Gr. Bris 81 F1
Berkeley Gr. Bris 50 B1
Berkeley Green Rd. Bris 50 C1
Berkeley Green. Bris . 37 D1
Berkeley Mead. St Gif 37 D3
Berkeley Pl. Bris 63 D4
Berkeley Rd. Bris 49 D1
Berkeley Rd. Bris 49 E2
Berkeley Rd. Bris 51 D1
Berkeley Rd. Kingsw . 65 E4
Berkeley Rd. Mang ... 51 E3
Berkeley Sq. Bris ... 63 D4
Berkeley St. Bris ... 50 B2
Berkshire Rd. Bris ... 49 E4
Berlington Cl. Bris ... 63 F3
Berners Cl. Bris 79 E4
Berrow Wlk. Bris 63 F1
Berrows Mead. Wickw 27 D4
Berry La. Bris 49 F3
Berwick La. Alm 34 B4
Berwick Rd. Bris 50 A1
Beryl Gr. Bris 80 B4
Beryl Rd. Bris 63 D2
Besom La. West 39 E3
Bethel Rd. Bris 64 C4
Betjeman Ct. Kingsw . 66 A3
Bevan Ct. Bris 35 F1
Beverley Ave. Mang . 37 F1
Beverley Cl. Bris 65 D3
Beverley Gdns. Bris .. 48 B4
Beverley Rd. Bris 49 F4
Beverston Gdns. Bris . 34 A1
Beverstone. Kingsw .. 65 D4
Beverston Kingsw 65 D4
Bevington Cl. Bris ... 35 F2
Bevington La. Stone .. 2 C4
Bevington Wlk. Bris .. 35 F2
Bewdley Rd. Bath ... 102 A3
Bexley Rd. Bris 51 D2
Bibstone. Kingsw 66 A4
Bibury Ave. St Gif ... 36 A4
Bibury Cl. Bris 62 A4
Bibury Cl. Nail 60 A1
Bibury Cres. Bris 49 E4
Bibury Cres. Kingsw . 65 E4
Bickerton Cl. Bris ... 34 C2
Bickfield La. Co Mar . 128 A3
Bickford Cl. Kingsw .. 66 A3
Bickley Cl. Kingsw ... 65 E1
Biddeston Rd. Bris ... 48 A3
Biddisham Cl. Nail ... 59 F1
Biddisham La. Bidd ... 123 F1
Biddle St. Yatt 91 D4
Bideford Cres. Bris .. 79 F4
Bideford Rd. W-S-M .. 88 C1
Bidwell Cl. Bris 35 D2
Bifield Cl. Bris 66 C3
Bifield Gdns. Bris ... 66 C3
Bifield Rd. Bris 66 C3
Big Tree Cl. Co Bi ... 124 B2
Bignell Cl. Wins 124 C4
Bigwood La. Bris 63 D3
Bilberry Cl. Bris 48 B2
Bilbie Cl. Bris 49 F4
Bilbie Cl. Ch St 112 C4
Bilbie Rd. Ch St 112 C4
Bilbie Rd. Chew 89 D2
Bilbury La. Bath 101 F3

144

Billand Cl. Bris. Brockley Rd. Key

Billand Cl. Bris 78 C2
Bilsham La. Piln 12 C1
Bince's Lodge La. Mid No . 132 A2
Binces La. Marks 99 F2
Bindon Dr. Bris 35 E2
Binhay Rd. Yatt 11 E4
Binley Gr. Bris 80 B2
Binmead Gdns. Bris 79 D2
Birbeck Rd. Bris 48 C3
Birch Ave. Blea 122 B3
Birch Ave. Cleve 57 F2
Birch Cl. Bris 35 F4
Birch Cl. Lock 106 A2
Birch Dr. Alve 14 C2
Birch Dr. Chur 109 D3
Birch Dr. Puck 53 D3
Birch Gr. Portis 45 E2
Birch Rd. Bris 63 D2
Birch Rd. Kingsw 51 F2
Birch Rd. Rad 132 A4
Birch Rd. Yate 27 E1
Birchall Rd. Bris 49 E2
Birchdale Rd. Bris 80 A4
Birchdene. Nail 60 A1
Birches The. Nail 60 A1
Birchwood Ave. W-S-M ... 105 D4
Birchwood Dr. Wrax 61 D2
Birchwood La. Pens 97 F1
Birchwood Rd. Bris 64 C2
Birdale Cl. Bris 34 C2
Birdcombe Cl. Nail 59 F2
Birdlip Cl. Nail 76 A4
Birdwell La. Lo Ash 61 F1
Birdwell Rd. Lo Ash 61 F1
Birdwood. Kingsw 65 E3
Birgage Rd. H Up 19 F1
Birkdale. Kingsw 66 A3
Birkdale. Yate 39 F4
Birkett Rd. W-S-M 87 D1
Birkin St. Bris 64 A3
Birnbeck Rd. W-S-M 87 B1
Bisdee Rd. Lock 105 E1
Bishop Ave. W-S-M 89 D2
Bishop Manor Rd. Bris 49 E4
Bishop Rd. Bris 49 E2
Bishop St. Bris 63 F4
Bishop's Cl. Nail 134 B1
Bishop's Wood. Alm 24 B3
Bishops Cl. Bris 48 C2
Bishops Cove. Bris 78 C3
Bishops Mead. Brock 92 A4
Bishops Rd. Brock 92 A4
Bishopsworth Rd. Bris 79 D4
Bishopthorpe Rd. Bris 49 F4
Bishport Ave. Bris 79 E2
Bishport Cl. Bris 79 D2
Bisley. Yate 39 C4
Bitten Cl. W-S-M 88 C4
Bitterwell Cl. West 38 B2
Bittlemead. Bris 79 F2
Black Boy Hill. Bris 49 D1
Blackacre. Wint 80 B2
Blackberry Ave. Bris 50 C2
Blackberry Dr. W-S-M 89 D1
Blackberry Hill. Bris 50 C3
Blackberry La. Winsl 120 B4
Blackbird Cl. Rod 138 A4
Blackdown Cl. P. Bris 80 A3
Blackdown Rd. Portis 45 D3
Blackfriars. Bris 63 E4
Blackfriars Rd. Nail 59 D1
Blackfriars. Bris 63 E4
Blackhorse Hill. Alm 35 D4
Blackhorse La. Mang 52 A4
Blackhorse Pl. Mang 52 A3
Blackhorse Rd. Kingsw 65 C4
Blackhorse Rd. Mang 52 A4
Blackmoor Cl. Chur 109 D3
Blackmoor Rd. Ab Le 47 F1
Blackmoor. Chur 109 E3
Blackmoor. Cleve 57 E1
Blackmoor. W-S-M 88 C1
Blackmoors La. Bris 62 C2
Blackmore Dr. Bath 101 E3
Blackrock La. Pens 97 F4
Blacksmith La. Bathe 85 D2
Blacksmith's La. Kel 83 D2
Blackswarth Rd. Bris 64 B4
Blackthorn Cl. Bris 49 E4
Blackthorn Dr. St Gif 36 A4
Blackthorn Gdns. W-S-M 89 D1
Blackthorn Rd. Bris 79 E3
Blackthorn Terr. W-S-M 89 D1
Blackthorn Wlk. Kingsw 51 E1
Blackthorn Wlk. Kingsw 60 A1
Bladdock Bldgs. Faulk 134 A1
Bladen Cl. Portis 45 F2
Blagdon Cl. Bris 63 F1
Blagdon Cl. W-S-M 104 C1
Blagdon La. Blag 110 A2
Blagdon La. But 110 C3
Blagdon Park. Bath 101 D2
Blagrove Cl. Bris 79 E2
Blagrove Cres. Bris 79 E2
Blaisdon Cl. Bris 34 C1
Blaisdon. Yate 39 F4

Blaise Hamlet. Bris 34 B1
Blaise Wlk. Bris 48 B4
Blake End. W-S-M 88 C2
Blake Rd. Bris 50 A3
Blakeney Gr. Nail 75 E4
Blakeney Mills. Yate 27 E1
Blakeney Rd. Bris 23 F1
Blakeney Rd. Bris 50 A4
Blakes Rd. Thorn 8 A1
Blanchards. Ch Sod 40 B4
Blandford Cl. Bris 49 D3
Blandford Cl. Nail 59 F1
Bleadon Hill. W-S-M 122 A4
Bleadon Rd. Blea 122 A3
Blenheim Cl. P St J 133 E4
Blenheim Ct. W-S-M 89 D1
Blenheim Dr. Bris 36 A2
Blenheim Dr. Yate 27 E2
Blenheim Gdns. Bath 85 D1
Blenheim St. Bris 50 A1
Blenheim Way. Portis 45 F3
Blenman Rd. Bris 49 D2
Blenman Cl. Bris 51 D4
Blind La. Bath 84 B1
Blind La. Ch St 112 C4
Blind La. Cong 91 F3
Blind La. Prey 117 D2
Bloomfield Ave. Bath 101 F2
Bloomfield Ave. Tims 116 A2
Bloomfield Cl. Tims 116 A2
Bloomfield Cres. Bath 101 E1
Bloomfield Dr. Bath 101 F2
Bloomfield Gr. Bath 101 F2
Bloomfield La. Paul 131 E3
Bloomfield Park Rd. Tims 116 A2
Bloomfield Park. Bath 101 F2
Bloomfield Rd. Bath 101 F2
Bloomfield Rd. Bris 64 B2
Bloomfield Rd. Tims 116 A2
Bloomfield Rise. Bath 101 E1
Bloomfield Rise. Bath 101 E1
Bloomfield Terr. P St J 133 E4
Bloomfield. W-S-M 105 D1
Bly St. Bris 50 B1
Bluebell Cl. Thorn 8 B1
Bluebells The. St Gif 36 C4
Blueberry Way. W-S-M 88 C1
Blythe Gdns. W-S-M 89 D2
Boat La. Lymp 122 B2
Boat Stall La. Bath 102 A3
Bobbin La. Westw 120 C2
Bobbin Parr. Westw 120 C2
Bockenem Cl. Thorn 15 E4
Bodey Cl. Kingsw 66 A3
Bodmin Wlk. Bris 79 F4
Bodyce Rd. Alve 15 D3
Boiling Wells La. Bris 50 A2
Bolton Rd. Bris 49 F2
Bond St. Bris 63 F4
Bond's La. Marsh 55 F1
Bonhill Rd. Bi Sut 113 E3
Bonnington Wlk. Bris 50 A4
Boot La. Bris 63 E2
Booth Rd. Bris 63 E2
Bordesley Rd. Bris 80 A2
Borgie Pl. W-S-M 88 C2
Borleyton Wlk. Bris 78 C2
Borver Gr. Bris 79 D2
Boscombe Cres. Mang 51 F4
Boston Rd. Bris 49 F4
Boswell Rd. Westw 120 C2
Boswell St. Bris 50 B1
Botham Cl. W-S-M 89 D2
Botham Dr. Bris 64 B1
Boucher Pl. Bris 50 A1
Boulevard. W-S-M 104 C4
Boulters Rd. Bris 79 E2
Boulton's La. Bris 65 E4
Boulton's Rd. Kingsw 65 D3
Bourne Cl. Bris 65 D2
Bourne Cl. Wint 37 F4
Bourne La. Blag 110 A2
Bourne La. Bris 50 A1
Bourne Rd. Bris 65 D2
Bourneville Bsns Centre.
  Bris 64 C1
Bourneville Rd. Bris 64 C1
Bournville Cl. Bris 64 C1
Bournville Rd. W-S-M 104 C2
Bourtsland Ct. St Gif 24 B1
Bourton Ave. St Gif 36 B4
Bourton Cl. St Gif 36 B4
Bourton Combe. Back 76 C4
Bourton La. Co Bi 124 C2
Bourton La. Lock 107 E3
Bourton Mead. Back 76 C4
Bourton Mead. Lo Ash 62 A1
Bourton Wlk. Bris 79 D4
Bouverie St. Bris 64 A4
Boverton Rd. Bris 36 A2
Bowden Cl. Bris 48 B4
Bowden Hill. Chil 137 D2

Bowden Pl. Mang 51 F4
Bowden Rd. Bris 64 C4
Bowden Way. Wrax 61 D2
Bower Rd. Bris 63 D2
Bower Wlk. Bris 63 F2
Bowerleaze. Bris 48 B3
Bowldich La. Mid No 132 A2
Bowling Hill Bsns Pk.
  Ch Sod 28 A1
Bowling Hill. Ch Sod 28 A1
Bowling Hill. Ch Sod 40 A4
Bowood. Bris 37 E1
Bowring Cl. Bris 79 E2
Bowsland Way. St Gif 24 B3
Bowstreet La. Alm 35 D4
Box Bush La. Ban 90 B1
Box Rd. Bathe 86 B2
Box Rd. Bathf 86 B2
Box Wlk. Keyn 81 E2
Boxbury Hill. Paul 131 F2
Boxhedge Farm La. West 38 C2
Boyce Dr. Bris 50 A1
Boyce's Ave. Bris 63 D4
Boyd Cl. Wick 67 F2
Boyd Rd. Keyn 82 B2
Brabazon Rd. Bris 36 A1
Bracewell Gdns. Bris 35 E2
Bracey Dr. Bris 51 E3
Brackenbury Dr. St Gif 36 C3
Brackendean. St Gif 24 B1
Brackenwood Rd. Cleve 57 F3
Bracton Dr. Bris 80 A3
Bradeston Gr. Bris 51 D4
Bradford Cl. Cleve 57 E1
Bradford Park. Bath 102 A1
Bradford Rd. Bath 102 A1
Bradford Rd. Bathf 86 A1
Bradford Rd. Winsl 120 C4
Bradhurst St. Bris 64 A3
Bradley Ave. Wint 37 F3
Bradley Cres. Bris 47 F3
Bradley Pk. Bris 23 F1
Bradley Stoke Way. St Gif 24 B1
Bradley Stoke Way. St Gif 37 D3
Bradstone Rd. Wint 37 E3
Bradville Gdns. Lo Ash 77 F4
Bradwell Gr. Bris 49 E4
Brae Cl. Nail 125 D4
Brae Rise. Wins 125 D4
Braemar Ave. Bris 35 F1
Braemar Cres. Bris 35 F1
Bragg's La. Bris 63 F4
Braikenridge Cl. Cleve 57 E1
Braikenridge Rd. Bris 64 B2
Brainsfield. Bris 48 C3
Brake Cl. Kingsw 65 F2
Brake Cl. St Gif 36 C3
Brake The. Fr Cot 38 B4
Brake The. Yate 27 F3
Brakewell Gdns. Bris 80 A2
Bramble Dr. Bris 48 B2
Bramble La. Bris 48 B2
Bramble Rd. W-S-M 88 C1
Bramble Way. Bath 102 A1
Brambles The. Keyn 81 E2
Brambling Wlk. Bris 50 C1
Bramley Cl. E in G 47 E2
Bramley Cl. Kings 11 F1
Bramley Ct. Olve 14 A2
Bramley Cl. P St J 133 E4
Bramley Cl. Yatt 91 D4
Bramley Ct. Kingsw 65 F2
Bramley Dr. Back 76 A3
Bramley Sq. Cong 91 F3
Bramleys The. Nail 75 D4
Brampton Way. Portis 45 F2
Bramshill Dr. W-S-M 88 C2
Branch Rd. Hin Cha 119 F1
Branche Gr. Bris 79 E2
Brandash Rd. Ch Sod 28 A1
Brandon Steep. Bris 63 E3
Brangwyn Gr. Bris 50 C3
Brangwyn Sq. W-S-M 88 C1
Branksome Cres. Bris 36 A2
Branksome Dr. Bris 36 A2
Branksome Dr. Wint 37 F3
Branksome Rd. Bris 49 D2
Branscombe Way. Portis 44 C2
Branscombe Wlk. Portis 44 C2
Branwhite Cl. Bris 50 A4
Brassknocker Hill. Bath 102 C1
Brassmill La. Bath 101 D4
Bratton Rd. Bris 79 F3
Braunton Rd. Bris 63 E2
Braydon Ave. St Gif 36 B4
Brayne Ct. Kingsw 65 E3
Braysdown Cl. P St J 133 D3
Braysdown La. P St J 133 E3
Braysdown La. Paul 133 E4
Breach La. Nail 74 C4
Breach Rd. Bris 63 D2
Breaches Gate. St Gif 36 C3
Breaches La. Keyn 82 A2
Breaches The. E in G 47 D3
Bream Down Ave. Bris 49 D3

Brean Down Ave. W-S-M 104 B2
Brean Rd. Lymp 121 F1
Brecknock Rd. Bris 64 A2
Brecon Rd. Bris 49 D3
Brecon View. W-S-M 105 D1
Bredon Cl. Kingsw 65 F4
Bredon Nook Rd. Bris 49 E4
Bredon. Yate 39 E4
Bree Cl. W-S-M 89 D2
Brendon Ave. W-S-M 104 C4
Brendon Cl. Kingsw 66 B2
Brendon Gdns. Nail 59 F1
Brendon Rd. Bris 63 E2
Brendon Rd. Portis 45 D3
Brenner St. Bris 50 A1
Brent Cl. W-S-M 105 D1
Brent Rd. Bris 49 F3
Brentry Ave. Bris 64 A4
Brentry Hill. Bris 35 D1
Brentry La. Bris 35 D2
Brentry Rd. Bris 50 C2
Brereton Way. Kingsw 66 A2
Brewerton Cl. Bris 35 E2
Brewery Hill. Bath 82 C4
Brewery La. Hol 138 B1
Briar Cl. Nail 60 A1
Briar Cl. Rod 138 B4
Briar Mead. Yatt 74 A1
Briar Rd. Lock 105 F2
Briar Way. Bris 51 E2
Briar Wlk. Bris 51 E2
Briarfield Ave. Kingsw 65 E3
Briarleaze. Alve 14 C1
Briars The. Back 75 F4
Briarside Rd. Bris 35 E2
Briarwood. Bris 48 C3
Briary Rd. Portis 45 E3
Briavels Gr. Bris 49 F1
Brick St. Bris 63 F4
Bridewell La. Bath 101 F3
Bridewell La. Lock 106 B1
Bridewell St. Bris 63 E4
Bridge Cl. Bris 80 B2
Bridge Farm Cl. Bris 80 A2
Bridge Farm Sq. Cong 91 E2
Bridge Place Rd. Tims 132 C4
Bridge Rd. Bath 101 F3
Bridge Rd. Blea 122 A3
Bridge Rd. Bris 50 A2
Bridge Rd. Ir Act 27 D1
Bridge Rd. Kingsw 52 A2
Bridge Rd. Lo Ash 62 B2
Bridge Rd. St Gif 52 B2
Bridge St. Bath 102 A3
Bridge St. Bris 63 F4
Bridge St. Bris 50 B1
Bridge Valley Rd. Bris 62 C4
Bridge Way. Fr Cot 38 A4
Bridge Wlk. Bris 50 A4
Bridgeleap Rd. Mang 51 F4
Bridgman Dr. Bris 36 A2
Bridgwater Ct. W-S-M 105 D2
Bridgwater Rd. Ba Gu 77 F1
Bridgwater Rd. Blea 122 B2
Bridgwater Rd. Bris 78 B3
Bridgwater Rd. Dun 78 B3
Bridgwater Rd. Lymp 122 B2
Bridgwater Rd. W-S-M 104 C1
Bridgwater Rd. Wins 125 D3
Bridle Way. Alve 14 C2
Brierclife Rd. Bris 48 B4
Brierly Furlong. St Gif 36 C2
Briery Leaze Rd. Bris 80 A3
Bright St. Bris 64 A4
Bright St. Kingsw 65 E4
Brighton Cres. Bris 63 E1
Brighton Mews. Bris 63 D4
Brighton Pl. Kingsw 51 E1
Brighton Rd. Bris 35 F4
Brighton Rd. Bris 49 E1
Brighton Rd. W-S-M 104 C3
Brighton St. Bris 63 F4
Brighton Terr. Bris 63 F1
Brigstocke Rd. Bris 63 F4
Brimbles. Bris 36 A1
Brimbleworth La. Lock 89 E2
Brimridge Rd. Wins 125 D4
Brinkmarsh La. Falf 9 E1
Brinkworthy Rd. Bris 50 B1
Brinmead Wlk. Bris 78 C2
Brins Cl. St Gif 36 C2
Brinsea Batch. Cong 108 C4
Brinsea La. Cong 108 C4
Brinsea La. Cong 91 F1
Brinsham La. Yate 28 A3
Briscoes Ave. Bris 79 E2
Brislington Hill. Bris 64 C1
Brislington Trading Est. Bris .. 64 C1
Bristol And Exeter Mews.
  Bris 63 F3
Bristol Gate. Bris 62 C3
Bristol Hill. Bris 64 B1
Bristol Phoenix. Bris 63 F4
Bristol Rd Lower. W-S-M 87 F1
Bristol Rd. Bris 37 D1
Bristol Rd. Bris 80 C4
Bristol Rd. Ch St 112 C4

Bristol Rd. Chur 109
Bristol Rd. Co Dan 81
Bristol Rd. Cong 91
Bristol Rd. Cor 100
Bristol Rd. Crom 17
Bristol Rd. Fr Cot 26
Bristol Rd. Ir Act 26
Bristol Rd. Lock 89
Bristol Rd. Luck 30
Bristol Rd. Mid No 132
Bristol Rd. Paul 130
Bristol Rd. Nail 131
Bristol Rd. Pens 97
Bristol Rd. Portis 45
Bristol Rd. Ship 108
Bristol Rd. Thorn 15
Bristol Rd. Wint 80
Bristol Rd. Wins 125
Bristol Rd. Wint 37
Bristol Rd. Wint 37
Bristol Vale Centre For Industry.
  Bris 63
Bristol View. Bath 118
Bristowe House. Bris 51
Britannia Cl. Chil 137
Britannia Cres. St Gif 36
Britannia Rd. Bris 35
Britannia Rd. Bris 50
Britannia Rd. Bris 65
Britannia Rd. Kingsw 65
Britannia Way. Cleve 58
Britten Rd. Bris 63
British Pl. Bris 46
Britten Pl. Portis 46
Britten Cl. Kingsw 65
Britten's Cl. Paul 131
Britten's Hill. Paul 131
Brixham Rd. Bris 63
Brixton Rd. Bris 64
Broad Croft. St Gif 24
Broad La. West 38
Broad La. West 39
Broad La. Yate 27
Broad Mead La. Win 95
Oak Oak Rd. Bris 78
Broad Oaks. Lo Ash 62
Broad Plain. Bris 63
Broad Quay. Bath 101
Broad Quay. Bris 63
Broad Rd. Bris 51
Broad Rd. Priddy 126
Broad St. Bris 102
Broad St. Cong 91
Broad St. Kingsw 51
Broad St. Mang 52
Broad St. Wring 92
Broad Street Pl. Bath 102
Broad Weir. Bris 63
Broad Wlk. Bris 64
Bradbury Rd. Bris 79
Broadcroft Ave. Yatt 74
Broadcroft. Yatt 74
Broadcroft. Ch Mag 95
Broadfield Ave. Bris 51
Broadfield Rd. Bris 64
Broadlands Ave. Keyn 81
Broadlands Dr. Bris 34
Broadlands. Cleve 57
Broadleas. Bris 79
Broadleaze Way. Winsc 107
Broadleys Ave. Bris 49
Broadmead La. Keyn 82
Broadmead. Bris 63
Broadmoor La. Bath 84
Broadmoor La. Chart 24
Broadmoor Park. Bath 84
Broadmoor Vale. Bath 84
Broadoak Hill. Bris 78
Broadoak Rd. Chur 109
Broadoak Rd. W-S-M 104
Broadoak Wlk. Bris 51
Broadstone La. K Sey 72
Broadstone Wlk. Bris 79
Broadstones. Mon Far 85
Broadway Ave. Bris 49
Broadway Cl. Char 24
Broadway Ct. Paul 137
Broadway La. Paul 132
Broadway Rd. Bris 49
Broadway Rd. Bris 78
Broadway. Bath 102
Broadway. Bris 102
Broadway. Chew 125
Broadway. W-S-M 105
Broadway. Yate 27
Broadways Dr. Bris 44
Brock End. Portis 44
Brock St. Bath 101
Brockhurst Gdns. Bris 65
Brockhurst Rd. Bris 65
Brockley Cl. St Gif 36
Brockley Cl. W-S-M 104
Brockley Combe Rd. Brock . 76
Brockley Cres. W-S-M 104
Brockley La. Brock 75
Brockley Rd. Keyn 82

ckley Way. Bris 75 D2
ckley Way. Yatt 75 D2
ckley Wlk. Bris 79 D4
ckridge La. Fr Cot 38 B4
cka La. Lo Ash 61 F1
cks Rd. Bris 79 E2
ckway. Nail 59 F1
ckwood. Winsl 120 C4
ckworth Cres. Bris 50 C3
ckworth. Yate 39 E3
mley Dr. Mang 51 E4
mley Heath Ave. Mang 51 E4
mley Heath Rd. Mang 37 E1
mley Heath Rd. Mang 51 E4
mley Rd. Bris 49 F3
mpton Rd. W-S-M 105 D1
mpton Cl. Kingsw 66 A4
mpton Rd. Pens 96 C1
ncksea Rd. Bris 35 F1
ok Cl. Lo Ash 62 A4
ok Gate. Bris 62 C1
ok Hill. Bris 49 F1
ok La. Bris 49 F1
ok La. Bris 50 C3
ok Lintons. Bris 64 A2
ok Rd. Bath 101 E3
ok Rd. Bris 49 F1
ok Rd. Bris 50 C1
ok Rd. Bris 51 D2
ok Rd. Bris 63 E2
ok Rd. Kingsw 66 A1
ok Rd. Mang 51 F3
ok St. Bris 64 B4
ok St. Ch Sod 28 A1
ok Way. St Gif 36 B4
okcote Dr. St Gif 36 B3
okdale Rd. Bris 79 D3
okfield Ave. Bris 49 E2
okfield Cl. Ch Sod 28 A1
okfield La. Bris 49 E1
okfield Park. Bath 84 A1
okfield Rd. Bris 49 E1
okfield Rd. St Gif 36 A4
okfield Wlk. Cleve 57 F2
okfield Wlk. Kingsw 66 B2
okland Rd. Bris 49 E3
okland Rd. W-S-M 105 D1
oklands. Pris 117 E2
oklea. Kingsw 66 A2
oklea Bldgs. Bath 85 D1
okleaze. Bris 48 B3
oklyn Rd. Bath 85 F1
oklyn Rd. Bris 79 D4
oklyn. Wring 92 B1
okmead. Thorn 15 E4
okside Cl. Bathe 85 F3
okside Cl. Paul 131 F3
okside Dr. Farm 115 F3
okside Dr. Fr Cot 38 A4
okside House. Bath 84 A4
okside Rd. Bris 64 C1
okside. E in G 47 E2
okside. Paul 131 F3
okside. Winsl 94 C4
okthorpe Ave. Bris 34 A1
okthorpe. Yate 39 E4
okview Wlk. Bris 79 D4
om Farm Cl. Nail 75 F4
om Hill. Bris 131 F4
om Hill. Bris 59 D1
omground. Winsl 120 C4
mla. Clut 114 C2
erswood Ct. St Gif 24 B2
gham Hayes. Bath 101 E3
Hill. Bathe 85 F2
. The Bath 101 D3
nling Ct. Bris 50 C2
nlow Rd. W-S-M 104 C2
Ave. Bris 50 B1
Rd. Bris 50 B1
rnel Way. Paul 131 E3
al Cl. W-S-M 104 C2
al Cl. Yate 27 E1
ol Lock Rd. Bris 62 C3
al Rd. Bris 62 C3
al Rd. Bris 59 D1
al Way. Thorn 15 D4
nwick Pl. Bris 63 D2
wick Sq. Bris 63 D1
wick St. Bath 102 A4
wick St. Bris 63 D1
wick St. Bris 64 B4
n Ave. Bath 101 F2
n Ave. Portis 45 D3
n Cl. Nail 75 F4
n. W-S-M 105 D1
sons Cl. Bris 50 B3
t Gdns. Cleve 57 E1
t's Hill. Bris 65 D3
ts Cl. Bris 37 E1
sd Ave. Bris 49 F2
Pk The. Bris 79 F2
ngham Dr. St Gif 36 B3
gham Gdns. Mang 51 F3
ngham Pl. Bris 63 D4
ngham Pl. Mang 51 F3

Buckingham Rd. Bris 64 B3
Buckingham Rd. W-S-M 105 D1
Buckingham St. Bris 63 E1
Buckingham Vale. Bris 63 D4
Buckland Green. W-S-M 89 D3
Bucklands Batch. Nail 75 F4
Bucklands Dr. Nail 76 A4
Bucklands End. Nail 75 F4
Bucklands Gr. Nail 75 F4
Bucklands La. Nail 75 F4
Bucklands View. Nail 76 A4
Bude Ave. Bris 65 D4
Bude Cl. Nail 60 A1
Bude Rd. Bris 36 A2
Bull La. Bris 64 C3
Bull La. E in G 47 E2
Bull's Hill. Well 118 C1
Bullens Cl. St Gif 24 B1
Buller Rd. Bris 64 B1
Bullocks La. K Sey 73 E2
Bully La. Yate 17 E1
Bumper's Batch. Sosto ... 119 D4
Bungay's Hill. Paul 115 F1
Bunting Cl. W-S-M 88 C1
Burbank Cl. Kingsw 66 A2
Burchells Ave. Bris 51 D1
Burchells Green Cl. Bris . 51 D1
Burchells Green Rd. Bris . 51 D1
Burcott Rd. Avon 33 E3
Burden Cl. St Gif 36 C3
Burfoot Gdns. Bris 80 C2
Burfoot Rd. Bris 80 C2
Burford Cl. Bath 101 D2
Burford Cl. Portis 45 F2
Burford St. Bris 47 F3
Burgage Cl. Ch Sod 40 A4
Burgess Green Cl. Bris ... 64 D4
Burghill Rd. Bris 35 D1
Burghley Rd. Bris 49 F1
Burgis Rd. Bris 80 B3
Burleigh Gdns. Bath 101 A1
Burleigh Way. Wickw 18 A3
Burley Ave. Mang 51 F4
Burley Crest. Mang 51 F3
Burley Gr. Mang 51 F2
Burlington Rd. Bris 49 D1
Burlington Rd. Mid No ... 132 B1
Burlington St. Bath 102 A4
Burlington St. W-S-M 104 C4
Burnbush Cl. Bris 80 C3
Burnell Dr. Bris 63 F4
Burneside Cl. Bris 35 E1
Burney Way. Kingsw 66 A2
Burnham Cl. Kingsw 51 F1
Burnham Cl. W-S-M 104 C1
Burnham Dr. Kingsw 51 F1
Burnham Cl. W-S-M 104 C1
Burnham Rd. Bath 101 E3
Burnham Rd. Bris 47 F3
Burrington Ave. W-S-M ... 104 C1
Burrington Cl. Nail 59 F1
Burrington Cl. W-S-M 104 C1
Burrington Wlk. Bris 79 D4
Burrough Way. Winsl 93 F3
Burrows La. Holl 138 A1
Burton Cl. Bris 63 F3
Burton Cl. Bris 64 C4
Burton Cl. Bris 63 D4
Burton Rd. A Tur 42 C3
Burton St. Bath 101 F3
Burwalls Rd. Lo Ash 62 C3
Bury Hill. Wint 37 F2
Bury La. Doyn 67 F4
Bury The. Lock 106 A2
Burycourt Cl. Bris 34 A1
Bush Ave. St Gif 36 B3
Bushes La. Hort 29 D3
Bushy Pk. Bris 63 F2
Bushy Thorn Rd. Ch St ... 112 C4
Butcombe La. Bul 111 D4
Butcombe Wlk. Bris 80 A3
Butcombe. W-S-M 105 D1
Butham La. Ch Mag 96 A2
Buttass Cl. Paul 115 E1
Butt's Batch. Wring 92 A2
Butt's La. Mon Far 103 F4
Butt's La. Tor 55 D2
Butterfield Cl. Bris 49 F4
Butterfield Park. Cleve .. 57 F1
Butterfield Rd. Bris 49 F4
Buttermead Rd. W-S-M 105 D3
Butterworth Ct. Bris 79 E4
Button Cl. Bris 80 A3
Butts Batch. Co Bi 124 A2
Buxton Wlk. Bris 50 A4
Byfields. Cleve 73 E4
Byron Cl. Bris 63 D4
Byron Pl. Bris 63 D4
Byron Pl. Kingsw 51 F2
Byron Rd. Bath 101 F2
Byron Rd. Lock 106 A2
Byron Rd. W-S-M 105 D2
Byron St. Bris 50 A1
Byron St. Bris 64 B4

Cabot Cl. Keyn 82 B1
Cabot Cl. Yate 27 F1
Cabot Green. Bris 64 A4

Cabot Rise. Portis 45 D3
Cabot Way. Bris 62 C3
Cabot Way. E in G 47 E2
Cabot Way. Bris 89 D2
Cabstand. Portis 45 E3
Cadbury Camp La W. Nail .. 58 B3
Cadbury Camp La. Nail 59 E3
Cadbury Farm Rd. Yatt 91 E4
Cadbury Halt. W in G 44 C1
Cadbury Heath Rd. Kingsw . 66 A3
Cadbury La. W in G 44 C1
Cadbury Rd. Keyn 82 A1
Cadbury Rd. Portis 45 F2
Cadbury Sq. Cong 91 E2
Caddick Cl. Kingsw 51 F1
Cade Cl. Kingsw 65 F3
Cade Cl. St Gif 36 C3
Cadogan Rd. Bris 80 A4
Caen Rd. Bris 63 E2
Caernarvon Rd. Keyn 81 E4
Caine Rd. Bris 49 F4
Cains Cl. Kingsw 65 F3
Cairn Cl. Nail 60 A1
Cairns Rd. Bris 49 E2
Cairns' Cres. Bris 49 F1
Cakenhill Rd. Bris 64 C1
Calcott Rd. Bris 64 A2
Caldbeck Cl. Bris 35 E1
Calder Cl. Keyn 82 A2
Caldicot Cl. Bris 34 B1
Caldicot Cl. Kingsw 66 A1
Caledonia Mews. Bris 62 C3
Caledonia Pl. Bris 62 C3
Caledonian Rd. Bath 101 E3
Callington Rd. Bris 64 B2
Callicroft Rd. Bris 36 A4
Callington Rd. Bris 64 B1
Callowhill Ct. Bris 63 F3
Calton Gdns. Bath 101 F3
Calton Rd. Bath 102 A3
Cam Brook Cl. Tims 132 C4
Camberley Dr. Fr Cot 37 F4
Camberley Rd. Bris 79 E4
Camborne Rd. Bris 50 A3
Cambrian Dr. Yate 27 F2
Cambridge Cres. Bris 49 D4
Cambridge Gr. Cleve 57 E3
Cambridge Park. Bris 49 D2
Cambridge Rd. Bris 49 D2
Cambridge Rd. Cleve 57 F3
Cambridge St. Bris 63 F2
Cambridge St. Bris 64 B4
Cambridge Terr. Bath 102 A3
Cambrook House. Clut 130 C4
Camden Cl. Bris 63 D4
Camden Rd. Bris 63 D4
Camden Row. Bath 101 F4
Camden Terr. Bris 63 D4
Camden Ter. W-S-M 104 C4
Cameley Cl. Clut 130 B4
Cameley Green. Bath 100 C3
Camerley Rd. Clut 130 B4
Cameron Wlk. Bris 50 B3
Camerons Cl. Keyn 51 F1
Camerton Cl. Keyn 82 C2
Camerton Hill. Tims 132 C4
Camerton Rd. Bris 50 B1
Camerton Rd. Tims 116 C1
Camp La. Tor 55 E2
Camp Rd N. W-S-M 104 B4
Camp Rd. Bris 62 C4
Camp Rd. O-on-S 7 D3
Camp Rd. W-S-M 87 E1
Camp View. Nail 59 E1
Campbell Farm Dr. Bris ... 33 F1
Campbell St. Bris 63 F4
Campion Cl. Thorn 8 B1
Campion Cl. W-S-M 105 E4
Campion Dr. St Gif 24 B1
Campion St. Bris 63 F4
Camplins. Cleve 57 E1
Camvale. P St J 133 D4
Camview. Paul 131 E3
Camwal Rd. Bris 64 A3
Canada Coombe. Blea 106 A1
Canada Coombe. Lock 106 A1
Canada Way. Bris 63 D3
Canberra Gr. Bris 36 A2
Canberra Rd. W-S-M 104 C2
Canford La. Bris 48 C4
Canford La. Bris 48 C4
Canford Rd. Bris 48 C4
Cann La. Bitt 66 C3
Cann La. Sist 66 C3
Cannans Cl. Wint 37 F4
Cannon St. Bris 63 E4
Cannon St. Bris 63 E4
Cannon St. Bris 64 B4
Cannons Gate. Cleve 73 E4
Canon's Rd. Bris 63 E3
Canon's Wlk. Kingsw 51 F1
Canons Wlk. W-S-M 88 C2
Canowie Rd. Bris 49 D2
Cantell Gr. Bris 80 C3
Canterbury Cl. W-S-M 89 D2
Canterbury Cl. Yate 27 F2
Canterbury Rd. Bath 101 E3

Canterbury St. Bris 64 A3
Canters Leaze. Wickw 18 A2
Cantock's Cl. Bris 63 E4
Canvey Cl. Bris 49 F4
Canynge Rd. Bris 62 C4
Canynge Sq. Bris 62 C4
Canynge St. Bris 63 F3
Capel Cl. Kingsw 66 A4
Capel Rd. Bris 34 A1
Capenor Cl. Portis 45 E2
Capgrave Cl. Bris 65 D2
Capgrave Cres. Bris 65 D2
Caple La. Ch St 112 A3
Caraway Gdns. Bris 50 B1
Cardigan Cres. W-S-M 105 E4
Cardigan Rd. Bris 49 D3
Cardill Ct. Bris 79 D4
Cardith Dro. Cong 108 A4
Carey's Cl. Cleve 57 F2
Carice Gdns. Cleve 73 E4
Carisbrooke Rd. Bris 79 E4
Carlingford Terr Rd. Rad 133 D1
Carlingford Terr. Rad ... 133 D1
Carlisle Rd. Bris 50 B1
Carlow Rd. Bris 79 F4
Carlton Cl. Clut 114 C2
Carlton Cl. Bris 66 B4
Carlton Mansions. W-S-M . 104 B4
Carlton Pk. Bris 64 B4
Carlton St. W-S-M 104 B4
Carmarthen Cl. Yate 27 F2
Carmarthen Gr. Kingsw 66 A1
Carmarthen Rd. Bris 49 D3
Carnarvon Rd. Bris 49 E1
Caroline Cl. Keyn 81 E2
Caroline Pl. Bath 101 F4
Carpenters La. Keyn 81 F3
Carre Gdns. W-S-M 88 C3
Carrington Rd. Bris 63 D2
Carroll Ct. Bris 36 C1
Carsons Rd. Sist 52 A1
Carter Rd. Paul 131 E3
Carter's Bldgs. Bris 62 C4
Carters Way. Chil 137 E2
Cartledge Rd. Bris 50 B1
Cashmore Ho. Bris 64 A4
Cassell Rd. Bris 51 D3
Cassey Bottom La. Bris ... 65 D4
Castle Cl. Back 76 C4
Castle Cl. Bris 34 C1
Castle St. Thorn 8 A1
Castle Farm La. Dun 78 A1
Castle Farm Rd. Kingsw ... 65 E1
Castle Gdns. Bath 101 F2
Castle Hill. Ban 107 E1
Castle La. Marsh 55 F1
Castle Rd. Cleve 57 F3
Castle Rd. Kingsw 51 E1
Castle Rd. Kingsw 66 B2
Castle Rd. Puck 53 E3
Castle Rd. W-S-M 88 C2
Castle St. Bris 63 F3
Castle St. Thorn 8 A1
Castle View Rd. Cleve 57 E3
Castlewood Cl. Cleve 57 E3
Caswell Hill. Portb 46 A1
Caswell La. Portb 46 B1
Catbrain Hill. Bris 35 D3
Catbrain La. Bris 35 D3
Catchpot La. Ch Sod 41 D3
Catemead. Cleve 73 E4
Cater Rd. Bris 79 D3
Catherine Hill. Olve 13 F1
Catherine Mead St. Bris .. 63 E2
Catherine Pl. Bath 101 F4
Catherine St. Avon 47 E4
Catherine Way. Bathe 86 A3
Catley Gr. Lo Ash 62 A1
Cato St. Bris 50 C1
Catsley Pl. Bath 85 E1
Cattistock Dr. Bris 65 D3
Cattle Market Rd. Bris ... 63 F3
Cattybrook Rd. Puck 52 B3
Cattybrook St. Bris 64 A4
Caulfield Rd. W-S-M 89 D2
Causeway The. Cong 91 E2
Causeway The. Fr Cot 38 B4
Causeway The. W in G 45 F1
Causeway The. Yatt 91 E4
Causeway View. Nail 59 E1
Causeway. Nail 59 D2
Causley Dr. Kingsw 66 A3
Cautletts Cl. Mid No 137 F4
Cavan Wlk. Bris 63 F1
Cave Ct. Bris 63 F4
Cave Dr. Bris 51 E3
Cave St. Bris 63 F4
Cavendish Ct. Cleve 57 E1
Cavendish Cl. Keyn 82 B1
Cavendish Cres. Bath 101 F4
Cavendish Gdns. Bris 48 B2
Cavendish Rd. Bath 101 F4
Cavendish Rd. Bris 35 F4
Cavendish Rd. Bris 49 D3
Cavendish Rd. Bris 48 B2
Caveners Ct. W-S-M 88 A1
Caversham Dr. Nail 60 A1
Cecil Ave. Bris 50 C1
Cecil Rd. Bris 62 C4

Cecil Rd. Kingsw 65 E4
Cecil Rd. W-S-M 87 F1
Cedar Ave. W-S-M 88 B1
Cedar Cl. Bris 35 F4
Cedar Cl. Kingsw 66 A2
Cedar Cl. Lo Ash 61 F1
Cedar Dr. Keyn 81 E2
Cedar Gr. Bath 101 E2
Cedar Gr. Bris 48 B3
Cedar Hall. Bris 51 E4
Cedar Park. Bris 48 B3
Cedar Row. Bris 47 F3
Cedar Terr. Rad 132 B1
Cedar Way. Bath 101 F3
Cedar Way. Nail 60 A1
Cedar Way. Portis 45 E2
Cedar Way. Puck 53 E3
Cedarhurst Rd. Portis 37 E3
Cedars The. Ch St 95 E1
Cedric Rd. Bath 101 E4
Celandine Cl. Thorn 8 B1
Celestine Rd. Yate 27 E2
Celtic Way. Blea 122 B4
Cemetery Rd. Bris 64 A2
Cennick Ave. Kingsw 51 F1
Centaurus Rd. Bris 35 E4
Central Ave. Avon 22 A2
Central Ave. Kingsw 65 E3
Central Way. Cleve 57 F1
Ceres Cl. Kingsw 65 F1
Cerimon Gate. St Gif 36 C3
Cerney Gdns. Nail 60 A1
Cerney La. Bris 47 F3
Cesson Cl. Ch Sod 40 B4
Chadleigh Gr. Bris 79 E4
Chaffinch Dr. Rod 138 A4
Chaffins The. Cleve 57 F1
Chaingate La. Ir Act 27 D3
Chakeshill Cl. Bris 35 E2
Chakeshill Dr. Bris 35 E2
Chalcombe Cl. St Gif 36 B4
Chalcroft Wlk. Bris 78 C2
Chalfont Rd. W-S-M 105 E4
Chalford Cl. Yate 39 D4
Chalks Rd. Bris 64 B4
Chalks The. Ch Mag 96 A2
Challender Ave. Bris 34 C1
Challoner Ct. Bris 63 E3
Challow Dr. W-S-M 88 A1
Champion Rd. Kingsw 52 A1
Champneys Ave. Bris 34 C2
Chancel Cl. Nail 59 E1
Chancellors Pound. Wring 93 E2
Chancery St. Bris 64 A4
Chandag Rd. Keyn 82 B2
Chandler Cl. Bath 84 A1
Chandos Rd. Bris 49 E1
Chandos Rd. Keyn 81 F4
Chandos Trading Est. Bris 64 A3
Channel Hts. W-S-M 104 C1
Channel Rd. Cleve 57 F3
Channel View Cres. Portis 45 D3
Channel View Rd. Portis .. 45 D3
Channi's Hill. Bris 49 D4
Channon's Hill. Bris 50 C3
Chantry Cl. Nail 59 E1
Chantry Dr. W-S-M 89 D2
Chantry Gr. Bris 34 C1
Chantry La. Mang 37 F1
Chantry Mead Rd. Bath ... 101 F2
Chantry Rd. Bris 49 D1
Chantry Rd. Thorn 8 A1
Chapel Barton. Bris 63 D1
Chapel Barton. Nail 59 E1
Chapel Cl. Ch St 112 C4
Chapel Cl. Kingsw 66 A4
Chapel La. Yate 59 F1
Chapel Cl. Paul 130 C3
Chapel Cl. Win 95 D3
Chapel Gdns. Bris 35 D3
Chapel Green La. Bris 49 D1
Chapel Hill. Back 76 B4
Chapel Hill. Clut 111 E3
Chapel Hill. Cleve 57 E2
Chapel Hill. Newp 4 A4
Chapel Hill. Wring 92 B2
Chapel La. A Tur 43 D3
Chapel La. Bris 34 B1
Chapel La. Bris 50 C1
Chapel La. Bris 51 D2
Chapel La. Brock 92 E4
Chapel La. Ch Sod 41 D4
Chapel La. Ch St 112 B4
Chapel La. Dyrh 58 E4
Chapel La. Hut 119 E4
Chapel La. Kingsw 66 A4
Chapel La. Thorn 9 D1
Chapel La. Win 95 D3
Chapel La. Yatt 91 A1
Chapel Pl. Bris 79 D3
Chapel Rd. Bris 50 C1
Chapel Rd. Bris 64 A4
Chapel Row. Bath 101 F3
Chapel Row. Bathf 86 B1

Chapel Row. E in G 47 E2
Chapel Row. Luck 31 F1
Chapel St. Bris 64 A3
Chapel St. Thorn 15 D4
Chaplin Rd. Bris 50 A1
Chapter St. Bris 63 F4
Charbon Gate. St Gil 36 C3
Charborough Rd. Bris 35 F1
Charbury Wlk. Bris 47 F3
Chard Cl. Nail 50 A1
Chard Rd. Cleve 57 E1
Chardstock Ave. Bris 48 B4
Chardyke Dr. Clut 114 C1
Charfield Rd. Bris 35 E1
Charfield. Kings 11 F3
Charfield. Kingsw 66 A4
Chargrove. Kingsw 66 B3
Chargrove. Yate 39 E4
Charis Ave. Bris 49 E4
Charity La. Hol 139 E1
Charity La. Kilm 139 E1
Charlcombe La. Bath 84 C2
Charlcombe La. Charl 84 C2
Charlcombe Rise. Bath 84 C1
Charlcombe View Rd. Bath 85 D1
Charlcombe Way. Bath 84 C1
Charlecombe Ct. Bris 48 C3
Charlecombe Rd. Bris 48 C3
Charles Ave. St Gil 36 C2
Charles Pl. Bris 63 D3
Charles Rd. Bris 36 A2
Charles St. Bath 101 D3
Charles St. Bris 63 E3
Charlotte St S. Bris 63 E3
Charlotte St. Bath 101 F3
Charlotte St. Bris 63 E4
Charlton Ave. Bris 35 F1
Charlton Ave. W-S-M 104 B2
Charlton Dr. Wrax 60 B4
Charlton Gdns. Bris 35 E2
Charlton La. Bris 35 D2
Charlton La. Kilm 81 D4
Charlton Mead Ct. Bris 35 E2
Charlton Mead Dr. Bris 35 E2
Charlton Park. Keyn 81 E3
Charlton Park. Rod 138 A4
Charlton Pl. Bris 35 E2
Charlton Rd. Bris 51 D1
Charlton Rd. Bris 51 D1
Charlton Rd. Co Dan 81 D2
Charlton Rd. Hol 138 B2
Charlton Rd. Keyn 81 D2
Charlton Rd. Kilm 138 B2
Charlton Rd. Rod 138 A4
Charlton Rd. W-S-M 104 B2
Charlton St. Bris 64 A4
Charlton View. Portis 45 E3
Charminster Rd. Bris 51 D2
Charmouth Rd. Bath 101 D4
Charnell Rd. Kingsw 51 F2
Charnhill Brow. Kingsw 52 A3
Charnhill Cres. Kingsw 51 F2
Charnhill Dr. Kingsw 51 F2
Charnhill Ridge. Kingsw 52 A2
Charnhill Vale. Kingsw 51 F2
Charnwood. Kingsw 52 A2
Charter Rd. W-S-M 105 D4
Charter Wlk. Bris 80 A3
Charterhouse Cl. Nail 59 F1
Charterhouse Rd. Bris 64 B4
Chase La. Kings 18 B3
Chase La. Wickw 18 B3
Chase Rd. Kingsw 51 E1
Chase The. Bris 51 E2
Chatcombe. Yate .....
Chatham Park. Bath 102 B3
Chatham Row. Bath 102 A4
Chatsworth Pk. Thorn 8 B1
Chatsworth Rd. Bris 51 D2
Chatsworth Rd. Bris 64 B2
Chatterton Green. Bris 79 F2
Chatterton Rd. Yate 27 E1
Chatterton Sq. Bris 63 F3
Chatterton St. Bris 63 F3
Chaucer Rd. Bath 101 F2
Chaucer Rd. Rod 138 A4
Chaucer Rd. W-S-M 105 D2
Chaucer Wlk. Bris 50 A4
Chaundey Gr. Bris 79 D3
Chavenage. Kingsw 66 A4
Cheap St. Bath 101 F3
Cheapside St. Bris 63 F2
Cheapside. Bris 63 F2
Cheddar Cl. Nail 75 F4
Cheddar Gr. Bris 79 D4
Cheddar Rd. Axb 125 E1
Chedworth Cl. Bath 102 C2
Chedworth Rd. Bris 50 A3
Chedworth. Kingsw 51 F2
Chedworth. Yate 39 D4
Cheese La. Bris 63 F4
Chelford Gr. St Gil 36 A4
Chelmer Gr. Keyn 81 F2
Chelmsford Wlk. Bris 64 C3
Chelscombe. Bath 84 B1
Chelsea Cl. Keyn 82 A3

Chelsea Rd. Bath 101 E4
Chelsea Rd. Bris 50 A1
Chelsea Rd. Bris 64 A4
Chelsfield. Back 76 A4
Chelston Rd. Bris 79 E4
Chelswood Ave. W-S-M 105 E4
Chelswood Gdns. W-S-M 105 E4
Cheltenham La. Bris 49 F1
Cheltenham Rd. Bris 49 F1
Cheltenham St. Bath 101 F3
Chelvey Batch. Brock 75 F2
Chelvey La. Brock 75 F3
Chelvey Rd. Nail 75 E3
Chelvey Rise. Nail 60 A1
Chelvy Cl. Bris 79 D1
Chelwood Dr. Bath 101 E1
Chelwood Rd. Bris 47 E4
Chelwood Rd. Nail 82 C2
Chepstow Park. Mang 37 F1
Chepstow Rd. Bris 79 E4
Chepstow Wlk. Keyn 81 E3
Chequers Cl. Kingsw 66 B2
Cherington Rd. Bris 49 E4
Cherington Rd. Nail 60 A1
Cherington. Kingsw 65 D3
Cherington. Yate 39 E3
Cheriton Pl. Bris 49 D4
Cheriton Pl. Kingsw 66 B3
Cherry Ave. Cleve 57 F1
Cherry Cl. Yatt 91 D4
Cherry Garden La. Kingsw 66 A1
Cherry Garden Rd. Kingsw 66 B1
Cherry Gdns. Kingsw 66 B1
Cherry Gr. Mang 52 A3
Cherry Gr. Yatt 91 D4
Cherry Hay. Cleve 57 E1
Cherry La. Bris 63 F4
Cherry Orchard La. Bris 64 C4
Cherry Orchard La. Luck 31 E3
Cherry Rd. Ch Sod 28 A1
Cherry Rd. Lo Ash 61 F1
Cherry Rd. Nail 59 E1
Cherry Tree Cl. Bris 51 F2
Cherry Tree Cl. Keyn 81 E2
Cherry Tree Ct. Rad 132 C1
Cherry Tree Cres. Bris 51 E1
Cherry Wood. Kingsw 66 A1
Cherrytree Rd. Bris 51 E1
Cherrywood Rd. W-S-M 88 C1
Cherrywood Rise. W-S-M 88 C1
Chertsey Rd. Bris 49 D1
Cherwell Cl. Thorn 15 E4
Cherwell Rd. Keyn 82 A2
Chescombe Rd. Yatt 91 D4
Chesham Road N. W-S-M 105 D4
Chesham Road S. W-S-M 105 D4
Chesham Way. Kingsw 51 E1
Cheshire Cl. Yate 27 F2
Chesle Cl. Portis 44 C2
Chesle Way. Portis 44 C2
Cheslefield. Portis 44 C2
Chesley Hill. Wick 66 C4
Chessel Cl. St Gil 24 B1
Chessel St. Bris 63 D2
Chessell Ave. Piln 22 B4
Chessington Ave. Bris 80 A3
Chester Park Rd. Bris 51 D1
Chester Rd. Bris 64 C4
Chester St. Bris 50 A1
Chesterfield Ave. Bris 49 F1
Chesterfield Cl. Ban 106 C2
Chesterfield Pl. Bris 49 F1
Chesterfield Rd. Mang 51 F3
Chestermaster Cl. Alm 24 A3
Chesters. Kingsw 66 A2
Chestnut Dr. Nail 60 A1
Chestnut Ave. Axb 125 E1
Chestnut Ave. W-S-M 89 D1
Chestnut Cl. Ban 107 D2
Chestnut Cl. Bris 80 C3
Chestnut Cl. Cong 91 E2
Chestnut Cl. Paul 131 F3
Chestnut Cl. Paul 132 C1
Chestnut Dr. Mang 52 A3
Chestnut Dr. Ch Sod 28 A1
Chestnut Dr. Thorn 8 B1
Chestnut Dr. Yatt 74 C1
Chestnut Gr. Bath 101 E2
Chestnut Gr. Cleve 57 F2
Chestnut Gr. Westw 120 C2
Chestnut La. Blea 122 A4
Chestnut Park Est. Kings 11 F2
Chestnut Rd. Kingsw 51 F3
Chestnut Rd. Lo Ash 62 A1
Chestnut Rd. Mang 51 E3
Chestnut Way. Kingsw 51 F2
Chestnut Wlk. Bris 79 D3
Chestnut Wlk. Keyn 81 F2
Chestnuts The. Wins 125 D4
Chetwode Cl. Bris 35 E2
Chevening Cl. St Gil 36 B2
Chever's La. N St P 135 F3
Cheviot Dr. Thorn 15 F4
Cheviot Way. Kingsw 66 B3
Chew Hill. Ch Mag 96 A2
Chew La. Ch Mag 95 F1
Chew La. Ch St 95 F1
Chew Rd. Ch Mag 95 E3

Chew Rd. Win 95 E3
Chew St. Ch Mag 96 A2
Chewton Cl. Bris 51 D2
Chewton Rd. Co Dan 81 F1
Chewton Rd. Keyn 81 F1
Cheyne Rd. Bris 48 B3
Che Ivey Rd. Brock 75 E3
Chichester Pl. Rad 133 D1
Chichester Way. Yate 27 E2
Chickwell La. Falk 135 D1
Chilcompton Rd. Chil 137 F4
Chilcompton Rd. Mid No 137 F4
Chillington Ct. Bris 23 F1
Chillyhill La. Ch Mag 95 F1
Chillyhill La. Ch St 95 F1
Chiltern Cl. Bris 80 A2
Chiltern Park. Thorn 15 F4
Chilton Cl. Bris 85 D1
Chilton Rd. Bath 85 D1
Chilton Rd. Bris 80 A4
Chilwood Cl Ir Act 26 C2
Chimes The. Nail 75 E4
Chine The. Bris 50 B3
Chine. Mang 51 F4
Chiphouse Rd. Kingsw 51 F2
Chippenham Rd. Marsh 70 A4
Chipperfield Dr. Kingsw 51 F1
Chipping Cross. Cleve 73 E4
Chipping The. Kings 11 F2
Chippings The. Bris 50 B3
Chisbury St. Bris 50 B2
Chittening Rd. Avon 33 F4
Chock La. Bris 49 D4
Christchurch Ave. Mang 51 E3
Christchurch Cl. Nail 59 F1
Christchurch La. Mang 51 E3
Christchurch Rd. Bris 63 D4
Christian Cl. W-S-M 89 D2
Christmas St. Bris 63 E4
Christmas Steps. Bris 63 E4
Christon Rd. Ban 107 D1
Christon Rd. Blea 123 E3
Christon Terr. W-S-M 104 C1
Chubb Cl. Kingsw 65 F3
Church Ave. Bris 48 C2
Church Ave. Bris 50 A1
Church Ave. Fall .....
Church Ave. Sist 66 B4
Church Cl. Bris 34 C1
Church Cl. Cleve 57 D1
Church Cl. Fr Cot 38 A4
Church Cl. Portis 45 E3
Church Cl. Salt 94 A2
Church Cl. Sist 66 B4
Church Cnr. Lymp 122 A1
Church Ct. Mid No 132 A1
Church Dr. Blea 122 A4
Church Dr. Cong 91 E2
Church Farm Cl. Marks 99 D1
Church Hayes Cl. Nail 75 F4
Church Hayes Dr. Nail 75 F4
Church Hill. Bris 64 A4
Church Hill. Hi Cha 120 A3
Church Hill. Klim 133 E2
Church La. O-on-S 7 D3
Church La. Cleve 14 A2
Church La. Tims 116 A1
Church La. Axb 125 E1
Church La. Back 76 B3
Church La. Back 76 C4
Church La. Bathe 85 F2
Church La. Bi Sut 113 E2
Church La. Bitt 82 C4
Church La. Blea 34 C1
Church La. Bris 63 D3
Church La. Bris 63 F3
Church La. Ch Sod 41 D4
Church La. Ch St 112 B4
Church La. Chil 137 E3
Church La. Chil 137 F1
Church La. Chur 108 B3
Church La. Clut 124 A2
Church La. Co Bi 124 A2
Church La. Co Dan 98 B3
Church La. Crom 10 A1
Church La. E Harp 128 C2
Church La. Farm 116 A3
Church La. Lim 38 B3
Church La. Lit St 120 A3
Church La. Lo Ash 62 B1
Church La. Lock 105 F1
Church La. Lymp 122 A1
Church La. Mang 51 F4
Church La. Marsh 70 A4
Church La. Mid No 132 A1
Church La. Nail 59 E2
Church La. Paul 131 F3
Church La. Paul 131 F3
Church La. Portb 46 C2
Church La. Tims 116 A1
Church La. Wickw 16 C1
Church La. Wins 124 C3
Church La. Wint 37 E3

Church La. Yatt 91 E4
Church Leaze. Bris 47 E3
Church Par. Bris 64 C1
Church Pl. E in G 47 E2
Church Rd N. Portis 45 E3
Church Rd S. Portis 45 E2
Church Rd. Ab Lei 62 A4
Church Rd. Alm 23 D1
Church Rd. Alm 24 A3
Church Rd. Alve 15 D1
Church Rd. Bath 84 B1
Church Rd. Bath 102 B1
Church Rd. Bris 48 B2
Church Rd. Bris 49 F3
Church Rd. Bris 51 D4
Church Rd. Bris 63 E2
Church Rd. Bris 64 B4
Church Rd. Bris 79 D3
Church Rd. Doyn 80 A2
Church Rd. Dun 78 B1
Church Rd. E in G 47 F2
Church Rd. Fr Cot 38 B4
Church Rd. Kingsw 51 F1
Church Rd. Lo Ash 62 B3
Church Rd. Luck 31 F2
Church Rd. Lymp 122 A1
Church Rd. O-on-S 7 D2
Church Rd. O-on-S 7 D3
Church Rd. P St J 133 D4
Church Rd. Plin 22 A3
Church Rd. St Gif 36 C2
Church Rd. Thorn 8 A1
Church Rd. W-S-M 88 C1
Church Rd. Whit 80 A2
Church Rd. Whit 97 D4
Church Rd. Wick 67 D3
Church Rd. Win 95 D4
Church Rd. Wins 124 C4
Church Rd. Wint 37 F2
Church Rise. Win 95 D4
Church Row. Chil 137 F1
Church Sq. Clut 114 C1
Church Sq. Mid No 132 A1
Church St. Ban 107 D2
Church St. Bath 84 A1
Church St. Bath 102 A2
Church St. Bath 102 A3
Church St. Bathf 85 F4
Church St. Blag 110 C1
Church St. Bris 50 A1
Church St. Bris 63 F3
Church St. Bris 63 A3
Church St. Charl 84 C3
Church St. N St P 135 F2
Church St. Paul 131 E3
Church St. Pens 97 E2
Church St. Rad 132 C1
Church St. Tom. Back 76 B3
Church View. Bris 36 A2
Church View. Mang 51 E3
Church View. Newp 45 D4
Church Wlk. Wring 92 B1
Churchdown Wlk. Bris 47 F3
Churchend La. Char 10 C2
Churchfarm Cl. Yate 27 F2
Churchill Ave. Bath 84 B2
Churchill Cl. Bris 64 B2
Churchill Ave. Cleve 57 E1
Churchill Cl. Cleve 57 E1
Churchill Cl. W-S-M 66 A3
Churchill Dr. Bris 48 B2
Churchill Green. Chur 108 A3
Churchill Rd. W-S-M 105 D4
Churchlands Rd. Bris 63 D1
Churchpath Rd. E in G 47 E2
Churchside. Bris 51 D4
Churchward Cl. Kingsw 65 D3
Churchward Rd. W-S-M 89 D2
Churchward Rd. Yate 27 D2
Churchway. Faulk 134 B1
Churchways Ave. Bris 49 F3
Churchways Cres. Bris 49 F3
Churchways. Whit 80 B2
Churston Cl. Bris 80 A1
Circle The. Bath 101 D1
Circular Rd. Bris 48 C1
Circus Mews. Bath 101 F4
Circus Pl. Bath 101 F4
Circus The. Bath 101 F4
City Bsns Pk. Bris 64 A4
City Rd. Bris 49 F1
Clamp The. Kingsw 66 A1
Clanage Rd. Bris 62 C2
Clanders Batch. Blag 110 B2
Clandown Rd. Paul 131 F2
Clapton Dro. W in G 45 E1
Clapton La. W in G 45 F1
Clapton Rd. Mid No 131 E1
Clapton Rd. Ston E 131 E1

Clare Ave. Bris .....49 E
Clare Gdns. Bath .....101 E
Clare Rd. Bris .....49 E
Clare Rd. Bris .....50 A
Clare Rd. Bris .....51 E
Clare St. Bris .....63 E
Clare St. Bris .....64 E
Clare Wlk. Thorn .....8 A
Claremont Ave. Bris .....49 F
Claremont Bldg. Bath .....85 D
Claremont Cres. W-S-M .....87 D
Claremont Gdns. Cleve .....57 F
Claremont Gdns. Nail .....59 E
Claremont Gdns. Paul .....131 E
Claremont Rd. Bath .....85 D
Claremont Rd. Bris .....49 E
Claremont St. Bris .....50 A
Claremont Terr. Bris .....64 B
Claremont Wlk. Bath .....85 E
Clarence Gdns. Mang .....51 F
Clarence Grove Rd. W-S-M .....104 C
Clarence Pl. Bath .....101 D
Clarence Pl. Bris .....63 E
Clarence Rd E. W-S-M .....104 C
Clarence Rd N. W-S-M .....104 C
Clarence Rd S. W-S-M .....104 C
Clarence Rd. Bris .....63 E
Clarence Rd. Bris .....64 A
Clarence Rd. Mang .....51 F
Clarence St. Bath .....102 A
Clarendon Rd. Bath .....102 B
Clarendon Rd. Bris .....49 E
Clarendon Rd. W-S-M .....104 C
Clark Dr. Bris .....51 E
Clark St. Bris .....64 A
Clarke St. Bris .....63 E
Clarken Cl. Nail .....59 F
Clarken Coombe. Lo Ash .....62 A
Clarkson Ave. W-S-M .....88 C
Claude Ave. Bath .....101 E
Clavell Rd. Bris 34
Claverham Cl. Yatt 91
Claverham Dro. Yatt 91
Claverham Park. Yatt 91
Claverham Rd. Bris 51
Claverham Rd. Nail 91
Claverton Cl. Bath 102
Claverton Down Rd. Bath 102
Claverton Rd W. Keyn 81
Claverton Rd. Keyn 81
Claverton St. Bath 102
Clay Bottom. Bris 50
Clay Hill. Bris 51
Clay La. Bitt 82
Clay La. St Gif 36
Clay La. Thorn 8
Clay Pit Rd. Bris 49
Claydon Green. Bris 79
Clayfield Rd. Bris 64
Clayfield. Yate 27
Claymore Cres. Bris 51
Claypiece Rd. Bris 79
Claypit Hill. Ch Sod 40
Claypool Rd. Kingsw 65
Clayton Cl. Avon 33
Clayton St. Avon 33
Clayton St. Bris 64
Cleave St. Bris 50
Cleeve Ave. Mang 51
Cleeve Dr. Brock .....
Cleeve Gdns. Mang 51
Cleeve Gr. Keyn 81
Cleeve Green. Bath 100
Cleeve Hill Extension. Mang 51
Cleeve Hill. Brock 92
Cleeve Hill. Co Mar 57
Cleeve Hill. Mang 51
Cleeve La. Wick 53
Cleeve Lawns. Mang 51
Cleeve Lodge Cl. Mang 51
Cleeve Lodge Rd. Mang 51
Cleeve Park Rd. Mang 51
Cleeve Pl. Nail 60
Cleeve Rd. Bris 51
Cleeve Rd. Bris 64
Cleeve Rd. Mang 51
Cleeve Rd. Yate 27
Cleeve Wood Rd. Mang 51
Cleevedale Rd. Bath 102
Clement St. Bris 64
Clevis Rd. Bris 36
Clevedale. Mang 51
Clevedon La. W in G 59
Clevedon Rd. Bris 51
Clevedon Rd. Lo Ash 61
Clevedon Rd. Nail 59
Clevedon Rd. Nail 59
Clevedon Rd. Portis 45
Clevedon Rd. W-S-M 104
Clevedon Rd. Wrax 60
Clevedon Terr. Bris 63
Cleveland Cl. Thorn 15
Cleveland Pl. Bath 102

...and Wlk. Bath 102 B3
...ourt Dr. Bris 51 D4
...d. Priddy 126 A1
...d. W-S-M 88 A1
...Dr. Li St 120 A3
...d Gdns. Bris 47 F3
...s Rd. Bris 51 E2
...ouse Rd. Bris 63 D2
...ouse Spur. Bris 62 C2
... Bris 63 E3
... Bris 63 D2
...Ave. W-S-M 104 C3
...Cl. Bris 62 C4
...Down Rd. Bris 63 D4
...Down. Bris 62 C4
...Hill. Bris 63 D3
...Park Rd. Bris 62 C4
...Park. Bris 63 D3
...Pl. Bris 64 A4
...Vale Cl. Bris 63 D3
...Rd. W-S-M 104 C3
...Rd. Bris 63 D3
...St. Bris 63 E3
...St. Bris 64 A4
...St. Portis 45 E1
...Vale Cl. Bris 63 D3
...Vale. Bris 63 D3
...View. Bris 63 F2
...Wood Rd. Bris 63 D3
...wood Cres. Bris 63 D3
...wood Terr. Bris 63 D3
...wood. Bris 63 E1
...er Rd. Bris 64 B4
...s Hill Ave. Bris 64 C4
...s Hill Rd. Bris 64 C4
...ly Cl. Bris 64 C4
...lly Rd. Bris 64 C4
...lly Rd. W-S-M 89 E1
...r Cl. Cleve 57 F2
...Ground. Bris 49 D4
...Leaze. St Gif 36 B3
...rdale Dr. Kingsw 66 A2
...rlea Rd. Kingsw 66 B3
...in Hill. Clut 115 D2
...Ave. Keyn 81 F2
...Gdns. Bath 101 D3
...Gdns. Bris 35 F1
...La. Bris 49 E1
...n Park. Bris 49 D1
...on Rd. Bris 64 D2
...on Rd. Bris 64 A2
...Rd. Fr Cot 38 A4
...Terr. Bris 63 E2
...n Terr. Bris 64 A2
...esdale Cl. Bris 80 A3
...ler Gr. Cleve 57 F3
...peration Rd. Bris 50 B1
...bridge Cl. W-S-M 88 C1
...ey Rd. Bris 47 E3
...oit La. Clut 137 D1
...nit Rd. Bathe 86 A2
...lack La. West 38 A2
...lle Rd. Fr Cot 38 B4
...e Bris. Bris 80 C3
...es Gr. Nail 75 A3
...es Wlk. Bris 79 E3
...estone Mews. Bris 51 F3
...orn Dr. Bris 78 C2
...y Croft. Cleve 73 F3
...urg Rd. Bris 49 F1
...oom Way. Cong 97 F3
...And Yew Tree Hill. Win 95 D1
...La. Dyrh 54 B3
...Rd. Kingsw 65 F3
...ers Hill. Co Dan 98 B3
...en St. Bris 64 A4
...ington Rd. Bris 49 E2
...Cl. Kingsw 65 D3
...n Rd. Bris 64 A2
...nll Rd. Kingsw 51 F2
...on Rd. Bris 80 C3

Coleridge Vale Rd S. Cleve 57 E1
Coleridge Vale Rd W. Cleve 57 E1
Coles Gdns. Kilm 139 D3
Colesborne Cl. Yate 39 E4
Coleshill Dr. Bris 79 D3
Coley Rd. E Harp 129 D2
Colin Rd. Thorn 8 B1
College Ave. Bris 51 D3
College Ct. Bris 51 D3
College Fields. Bris 62 C4
College Green. Bris 63 E3
College Park Dr. Bris 34 C1
College Rd. Bath 84 C1
College Rd. Bris 49 D4
College Rd. Bris 51 D3
College Rd. Bris 62 C4
College Sq. Bris 63 E3
College St. Bris 63 E3
Collet Cl Lock 89 E2
Collett Cl. Kingsw 65 D3
Collier Cl. Tims 132 B4
Colliers La. Charl 24 C2
Collin Rd. Bris 64 B2
Collingwood Ave. Kingsw 51 F1
Collingwood Cl. Keyn 82 C1
Collingwood Cl. W-S-M 88 C2
Collins Ave. St Gif 36 B3
Collins St. Avon 47 D4
Collinson Rd. Bris 79 D3
Colliter Cres. Bris 63 D1
Collum La W St L 88 C3
Collum La. W-S-M 88 B3
Coln Sq. Thorn 15 E4
Colne Green. Keyn 82 A2
Colombo Cres. W-S-M 104 C2
Colonnades The. Bath 101 F3
Colston Ave. Bris 63 E4
Colston Cl. Kingsw 51 F2
Colston Ct. Wint 37 F2
Colston Ct. Bris 49 E2
Colston Dale. Bris 50 C2
Colston Hill. Bris 50 B3
Colston Par. Bris 63 F3
Colston Rd. Bris 50 B1
Colston St. Bris 63 E4
Colston St. Kingsw 51 E2
Colthurst Dr. Kingsw 65 F3
Colts Green. Ch Sod 41 C2
Colwyn Rd. Bris 50 B1
Colyton. W-S-M 89 D1
Comb Paddock. Bris 49 D4
Combe Ave. Portis 45 E3
Combe End. Mid No 132 C2
Combe Fields. Portis 45 E3
Combe Hay La. Bath 118 A3
Combe Hay La. Sosto 118 A3
Combe La. Paul 131 D3
Combe Rd. Bath 101 F3
Combe Rd. Bath 102 A1
Combe Rd. Portis 45 E3
Combe Road Cl. Bath 102 A1
Combe Side. Back 76 A4
Combe The. Blag 109 F1
Combehaven. Thorn 15 E2
Combeside. Bath 102 A2
Combfactory La. Bris 64 A4
Commercial Rd. Bris 63 E3
Common (E). The. St Gif 24 B1
Common La. Chur 108 A3
Common La. E n G 47 E4
Common Mead La. Bris 37 D1
Common Rd. Kingsw 65 D2
Common Rd. Wint 37 F4
Common The. Bris 51 D4
Common The. St Gif 24 B1
Commonfield Rd. Bris 34 A1
Commonmead La. Ch Sod 29 D1
Compton Dr. Bris 48 B4
Compton Green. Keyn 81 F2
Comrade Ave. Ship 125 F4
Comyn Wlk. Bris 51 D3
Concorde Dr. Bris 35 D1
Concorde Rd. Bris 35 F4
Condor Cl. W-S-M 105 E4
Condover Rd. Bris 65 D2
Conduit Pl. Bris 50 A1
Conduit Rd. Bris 50 A1
Congleton Rd. Bris 64 B4
Conham Hill. Kingsw 65 D3
Conham Rd. Bris 64 C3
Conham Vale. Bris 65 D3
Conham Vale. Kingsw 65 D3
Conifer Cl. Bris 51 E3
Conifer Cl. Fr Cot 26 A1
Conifer Way. Lock 105 F3
Coniston Ave. Bris 48 C4
Coniston Cl. Kingsw 66 B3
Coniston Cres. W-S-M 104 C2
Coniston Rd. Bris 23 F1
Conkwell. Winsl 103 E1
Connaught Rd. Bris 79 F4
Connection Rd. Bath 101 D3
Constable Dr. W-S-M 88 C2
Constable Rd. Bris 50 A3
Constantine Ave. St Gif 36 C3
Constitution Hill. Bris 63 D3

Convent Cl. Bris 34 B2
Convocation Ave. Bath 102 C3
Conway Green. Keyn 82 A2
Conway Rd. Bris 64 B2
Conygar Cl. Cleve 57 F3
Conygre Gr. Bris 36 B2
Conygre Green. Tims 116 A1
Conygre Rd. Bris 36 A2
Conygre Rise. Farm 115 F3
Cook Cl. Kingsw 66 B2
Cook St. Avon 47 E4
Cook's Folly Rd. Bris 48 B2
Cook's La. Ban 107 D2
Cook's La. Cleve 58 A1
Cook's La. Cleve 58 B1
Cooke's Dr. Alm 23 D1
Cooks Bridle Path. Wring 93 E4
Cooks Cl. St Gif 24 B2
Cooks La. West 38 B2
Cooksley Rd. Bris 64 B4
Cookworthy Cl. Bris 64 A3
Coombe Ave. Thorn 8 A1
Coombe Bridge Ave. Bris 48 B3
Coombe Cl. Bris 34 B2
Coombe Dale. Bris 48 B3
Coombe Dale. Wring 94 A4
Coombe Gdns. Bris 48 C3
Coombe La. Bris 48 C3
Coombe La. Co Bi 124 A2
Coombe La. E Harp 128 C2
Coombe La. E n G 47 D1
Coombe Park. Bath 101 E4
Coombe Rd. Bris 50 B1
Coombe Rd. Nail 50 F1
Coombe Rd. W-S-M 104 C4
Coombe The. Blag 110 B2
Coombe The. Co Mar 128 A3
Coombe The. Cleve 57 E2
Coombes Way. Kingsw 66 B2
Cooper Rd. Thorn 15 D4
Cooper Rd. Bris 48 C3
Cooperage La. Bris 63 D3
Cooperage Rd. Bris 64 B4
Coots The. Bris 80 C3
Cope Park. Alm 24 B3
Copeland Dr. Bris 80 A3
Copford La. Lo Ash 62 A1
Copley Ct. Kingsw 65 F3
Copley Gdns. Bris 50 A2
Copley Gdns. W-S-M 88 C1
Copperfield Dr. W-S-M 88 C2
Coppice End Cnr. Lymp 122 B1
Coppice The. Bris 78 C2
Coppice The. St Gif 36 A4
Copse Cl. W-S-M 105 D1
Copse End. Winsc 107 F1
Copse Rd. Cleve 64 A2
Copse Rd. Keyn 82 B2
Copseland. Bath 102 B3
Copythorne Rd. Bris 50 A4
Coralberry Dr. W-S-M 88 C1
Corbet Cl. Bris 34 B1
Cordington Pl. Bris 63 D4
Cordwell Wlk. Bris 49 E4
Corey Cl. Bris 49 F1
Corfe Cl. Nail 59 E1
Corfe Cres. Keyn 81 F2
Corfe Pl. Kingsw 66 A1
Corfe Rd. Bris 79 E4
Coriander Wlk. Bris 50 A4
Corinthian Ct. Bris 63 F3
Cork St. Bath 101 E4
Corker's Hill. Bris 64 C3
Cormorant Cl. W-S-M 88 C1
Corn Meadow. Stone 3 F2
Corn St. Bris 63 E3
Corner Croft. Cleve 57 E1
Cornhill Dr. Bris 80 A4
Cornish Gr. Bris 80 C3
Cornish Rd. Bris 80 C3
Cornish's Grave. Kilm 139 F2
Cornleaze. Bris 79 D3
Cornwall Cres. Yate 27 F2
Cornwall Rd. Bris 49 D2
Cornwallis Ave. Bris 63 D3
Cornwallis Ave. W-S-M 88 C2
Cornwallis Cres. Bris 62 C3
Cornwallis Gr. Bris 63 D3
Coronation Ave. Bath 101 E2
Coronation Ave. Bris 51 D2
Coronation Ave. Keyn 81 F2
Coronation Cl. Kingsw 66 B3
Coronation Pl. Bris 63 E3
Coronation Rd. Ban 107 D2
Coronation Rd. Bath 101 E2
Coronation Rd. Bris 63 E2
Coronation Rd. Kingsw 66 A3
Coronation Rd. Mang 51 F3
Coronation Rd. W-S-M 104 C3
Corondale Rd. W-S-M 105 D4
Corridor The. Bath 102 A3
Corsley Wlk. Bris 79 F4
Corston View. Bath 101 E1
Corston Wlk. Bris 47 E4

Corston. W-S-M 105 D1
Cossham Cl. Thorn 8 B1
Cossham Rd. Bris 64 B4
Cossham Rd. Puck 53 E2
Cossham St. Mang 52 A3
Cossham Wlk. Bris 51 D1
Cossington Rd. Bris 79 F4
Cossins Rd. Bris 49 D2
Costers Cl. Alve 15 D3
Costiland Dr. Bris 78 C3
Cote Dr. Bris 49 D2
Cote House La. Bris 49 D2
Cote La. Bris 49 D3
Cote Lea Park. Bris 49 D4
Cote Paddock. Bris 48 C2
Cote Rd. Bris 49 D2
Cotham Brow. Bris 49 E1
Cotham Gdns. Bris 49 D1
Cotham Gr. Bris 49 E1
Cotham Hill. Bris 63 E4
Cotham Lawn Rd. Bris 49 E1
Cotham Park N. Bris 49 E1
Cotham Park. Bris 49 E1
Cotham Rd S. Bris 63 E4
Cotham Rd. Bris 63 E4
Cotham Side. Bris 49 E1
Cotham Vale. Bris 49 E1
Cotman Wlk. Bris 50 A3
Cotman. W-S-M 88 C1
Cotrith Gr. Bris 34 C2
Cotswold Cl. Portis 45 F2
Cotswold La. Ch Sod 41 D4
Cotswold Rd. Bath 101 E2
Cotswold Rd. Bris 63 F2
Cotswold Rd. Ch Sod 40 A4
Cotswold View. Bath 36 A2
Cotswold View. Char 11 D3
Cotswold View. Kingsw 51 E1
Cotswold View. Wickwar 18 A3
Cottage Pl. Bris 63 E4
Cottington Ct. Kingsw 65 F3
Cottisford Rd. Bris 50 A2
Cottle Gdns. Bris 80 C3
Cottle Rd. Bris 80 C3
Cottles La. Winsl 120 C3
Cotton Mead. Cor 100 A4
Cottonwood Dr. Kingsw 66 A2
Cottrell Ave. Bris 51 E1
Cottrell Rd. Bris 50 B2
Cotts The. Wring 92 B1
Coulson Dr. W-S-M 89 D2
Coulson Wlk. Bris 51 E1
Coulson's Cl. Bris 80 A2
Coulson's Rd. Bris 80 A2
Counterpool Rd. Kingsw 65 E4
Countership Gdns. Bris 80 B3
Countership. Bris 63 F3
Countess Wlk. Bris 50 C4
County St. Bris 64 A2
Court Ave. St Gif 36 C3
Court Ave. Yate 91 E4
Court Cl. Back 76 B3
Court Cl. Bris 49 E4
Court Cl. Portis 45 E2
Court Dr. Wins 108 A2
Court Farm Rd. Bris 79 F2
Court Farm Rd. Kingsw 65 F1
Court Gdns. Bathe 86 A2
Court Hay. E in G 47 D2
Court Hill. Co Dan 98 A4
Court La. Bath 86 A1
Court La. Cleve 58 A2
Court La. Wick 67 D3
Court La. Wins 125 F4
Court Mead. Stone 3 F2
Court Meadow. Stone 3 F2
Court Pl. W-S-M 88 A2
Court Rd. Bris 49 F3
Court Rd. Fr Cot 37 F4
Court Rd. Kingsw 65 F4
Court Rd. Kingsw 66 B2
Court Rd. W St L 88 A3
Court View Cl. Alm 24 A3
Court View. Wick 67 E3
Courtenay Rd. Keyn 82 A1
Courtenay Wlk. W-S-M 89 D2
Courteney Cres. Bris 79 E4
Courtfield Gr. Bris 50 A1
Courtlands La. Bris 62 C2
Courtlands. Keyn 81 F3
Courtlands. St Gif 24 B1
Courtmead. Sosto 118 C4
Courtney Rd. Kingsw 65 F4
Courtney Way. Kingsw 66 A4
Courtside Mews. Bris 49 E1
Courtville Cl. Alve 15 D2
Courtyard The. Nail 59 F1
Cousins Cl. Bris 34 A2
Cousins La. Bris 64 A4
Couzens Cl. Yate 28 A1
Couzens Pl. St Gif 36 C3
Coventry Wlk. Bris 64 C3
Cowdray Rd. Bris 79 E4
Cowleaze La. E Harp 128 B3
Cowler Wlk. Bris 78 C2
Cowling Dr. Bris 80 B3
Cowling Rd. Bris 80 B3
Cowper Rd. Bris 49 E1

Cowper St. Bris 64 B4
Cowship La. Crom 17 E3
Cowslip La. Wickw 17 E3
Cowslip La. Blea 123 E2
Cox Ct. Kingsw 65 F2
Cox's Green. Wring 92 C1
Coxley Dr. Bath 85 D1
Coxway. Cleve 57 F1
Crabtree Cl. Dun 78 B1
Crabtree La. Dun 78 B1
Crabtree Wlk. Bris 50 B1
Craddock Cl. Kingsw 66 A2
Cranberry Wlk. Bris 48 B4
Cranbourne Chase. W-S-M 88 A1
Cranbourne Rd. Bris 35 F4
Cranbrook Rd. Bris 49 E2
Crandale Rd. Bath 101 E3
Crandell Cl. Bris 34 C2
Crane Cl. Kingsw 66 A4
Cranford Cl. W-S-M 88 B1
Cranham Cl. Kingsw 51 F1
Cranham Dr. St Gif 24 B2
Cranham Rd. Bris 49 E4
Cranham. Yate 39 E4
Cranhill Rd. Bath 101 E4
Cranleigh Court Rd. Yate 27 E1
Cranleigh Gdns. Bris 48 C2
Cranleigh Rd. Bris 80 A3
Cranleigh. Sosto 118 C4
Cranmore Ave. Keyn 81 F3
Cranmore Cres. Bris 35 E1
Cranmore Pl. Bath 118 C4
Cranmore. W-S-M 105 D1
Cranside Ave. Bris 49 E2
Cransley Cres. Bris 49 E4
Crantock Ave. Bris 79 D4
Crantock Dr. Alm 24 B3
Crantock Rd. Yate 27 E1
Cranwell Gr. Bris 80 A3
Cranwells Park. Bath 101 E4
Crates Cl. Kingsw 65 F4
Craven Way. Kingsw 65 F3
Crawford Cl. Cleve 57 D1
Crawl La. Mid No 132 B2
Craydon Gr. Bris 80 B2
Craydon Rd. Bris 80 B3
Craydon Wlk. Bris 80 B3
Crediton Cres. Bris 63 F1
Crediton. W-S-M 89 D1
Crescent La. Bath 101 F4
Crescent Rd. Bris 51 E3
Crescent The. Back 76 A3
Crescent The. Bris 48 B3
Crescent The. Bris 48 B3
Crescent The. Kingsw 51 E3
Crescent The. Lymp 122 B2
Crescent The. Olve 14 B3
Crescent The. Paul 131 D2
Crescent The. Pens 96 C1
Crescent The. W-S-M 88 A1
Crescent The. Wick 66 C3
Cresswell Cl. W-S-M 89 D1
Crest The. Bris 64 B2
Cresswade Ave. Kingsw 65 E3
Creswicke Rd. Bris 79 F4
Crew's Hole Rd. Bris 64 C4
Crewkerne Cl. Nail 60 A1
Cribbs Causeway Centre.
  Bris 35 D3
Cribbs Causeway. Bris 35 D3
Crickback La. Ch Mag 96 A2
Cricket Field Green. Nail 59 E1
Cricklade Ct. Nail 60 A1
Cricklade Rd. Bris 49 E2
Cripps Rd. Bris 63 E2
Crispin La. Thorn 8 B1
Crispin Way. Kingsw 51 F1
Crockerne Dr. E in G 47 E2
Crocombe La. Tims 116 B2
Crocombe. Tims 116 B2
Croft Ave. Bris 50 B4
Croft Cl. Bitt 52 B4
Croft Rd. Bath 85 D1
Croft The. Back 76 A4
Croft The. Bath 102 C1
Croft The. Cleve 57 F2
Croft The. Kingsw 66 B2
Croft The. Lock 105 F2
Croft The. Mang 51 F3
Croft The. Westw 120 B3
Croft View. Bris 49 E3
Crofton Ave. Bris 49 F3
Crofts End Rd. Bris 50 C1
Crokeswood Wlk. Bris 34 A1
Crome Rd. Bris 50 A3
Cromer Rd. Bris 64 B1
Cromer Rd. W-S-M 104 C3
Cromhall La. Crom 9 F1
Cromwell Ct. Kingsw 66 B2
Cromwell Dr. W-S-M 89 D2
Cromwell Rd. Bris 49 F1
Cromwell Rd. Bris 50 A1
Cromwell St. Bris 63 F2
Cromwells Hide. Bris 50 C3
Crook's La. W-S-M 88 A3
Croomes Hill. Mang 51 E3
Cropthorne Rd. Bris 36 A1

Crosby Row. Bris 63 D3
Cross Combe Dr. Bris 79 E2
Cross Combez Wlk. Bris 79 D2
Cross Elms La. Bris 48 C3
Cross Hands Rd. Piln 22 B4
Cross La. Co Bi 125 D1
Cross Lanes. E in G 47 E2
Cross Manor Rd. Axb 125 D1
Cross Moor Dr. Axb 125 D1
Cross Moor Dro. Co Bi 124 C2
Cross St. Bris 51 E1
Cross St. Keyn 81 F4
Cross St. W-S-M 104 C4
Cross The. E Harp 128 C2
Cross Tree Gr. St Gif 36 B4
Cross Wlk. Bris 80 A3
Crossfield Rd. Kingsw 65 E2
Crossleaze Rd. Kingsw 65 E2
Crossley Cl. Wint 37 F4
Crossman Ave. Wint 37 F3
Crossman Wlk. Cleve 57 F1
Crosspot La. Co Dan 99 D2
Crossway La. Ston E 137 D4
Crossways Rd. Bris 64 A1
Crossways Rd. Thorn 8 A1
Crossways. Newp 4 C4
Crow La. Bris 34 C1
Crow La. Bris 63 E3
Crow Meadow. Kings 11 F2
Crowe Hill. Li St 120 A3
Crowe La. Hin Cha 120 A3
Crown Gdns. Kingsw 66 A4
Crown Glass Pl. Nail 59 F1
Crown Hill Wlk. Bris 50 C1
Crown Hill. Bath 84 B1
Crown Hill. Bris 64 C4
Crown Hill. Kingsw 66 B2
Crown Hill. Win 95 D2
Crown House. Nail 59 E1
Crown La. Kingsw 51 E2
Crown Rd. Bath 84 A1
Crown Rd. Bris 51 E1
Crown Rd. Kingsw 66 B3
Crowndale Rd. Bris 64 A2
Crownleaze. Kingsw 51 E2
Crows Gr. St Gif 24 B2
Crowther Park. Bris 50 A2
Crowther Rd. Bris 50 A2
Crowther St. Bris 63 D2
Crowthers Ave. Yate 27 F2
Croydon St. Bris 64 A4
Crunnis The. St Gif 36 C3
Cuck Hill. Ship 125 F4
Cuckoo La. Colst 115 D2
Cuckoo La. Wint 37 F2
Cuckoo La. Wrax 60 A3
Cuffington Ave. Bris 64 B2
Culleysgate La. Wick 67 F3
Culver La. E Harp 128 C2
Culver St. Bris 63 E3
Culverhay. Co Dan 98 B3
Culverhill Rd. Ch Sod 28 A1
Culverhill Rd. Keyn 81 F3
Culverwell Rd. Bris 79 D2
Cumberland Basin Rd. Bris .. 62 C3
Cumberland Cl. Bris 63 D3
Cumberland Pl. Bris 49 F1
Cumberland Pl. Bris 62 C3
Cumberland Rd. Bris 63 D3
Cumberland Row. Bath 101 F3
Cumberland St. Bris 63 F4
Cumbria Cl. Thom 8 C1
Cunningham Gdns. Bris 51 D3
Curland Gr. Bris 80 A3
Curlew Cl. Bris 50 C2
Curlew Gdns. W-S-M 88 C1
Currells La. Win 77 D1
Curtis La. St Gif 37 D2
Custom Cl. Bris 80 A4
Cutler Rd. Bris 79 D2
Cutsheath Rd. Tyth 16 B4
Cutsheath Rd. Thorn 16 B4
Cygnet Cres. W-S-M 88 C1
Cynthia Rd. Bath 101 E3
Cypress Cl. Bris 48 B2
Cypress Gdns. Lo Ash 62 C3
Cypress Gr. Bris 49 E3
Cypress Ter. Rad 132 B1
Cypress Wlk. Col 70 C3

Dafford St. Bath 85 E1
Dafford's Bldgs. Bath 85 E1
Daglands The. Tims 132 C4
Dairy Hill. Well 134 A3
Daisy Green La. N Nib 5 F1
Daisy Rd. Bris 50 B1
Dakota Dr. Bris 80 A2
Dalby Ave. Bris 63 E2
Daldry Gdns. Olve 14 A2
Dale St. Bris 63 F4
Dale St. Bris 64 A4
Daley Cl. W-S-M 89 D2
Dalkeith Ave. Bris 51 E1
Dalrymple Rd. Bris 49 F1
Dalston Rd. Bris 63 D2
Dalton Sq. Bris 63 F4
Dalwood. W-S-M 89 D1
Dame Court Cl. W-S-M 88 C2

Damery La. N Nib 4 A1
Damery La. Stone 4 A4
Dampier Rd. Bris 63 D2
Danbury Cres. Bris 35 E1
Danbury Wlk. Bris 35 E1
Dancey Mead. Bris 78 C4
Dane Cl. Winsl 120 C4
Dane Rise. Winsl 120 C4
Daneacre Rd. Mid No 133 D2
Dangerfield Ave. Bris 78 C3
Daniel Cl. Cleve 57 F2
Daniel Mews. Bath 102 A4
Daniel St. Bath 102 A4
Dapps Hill. Keyn 81 F3
Dapwell La. Co Dan 81 D1
Dark La. Back 76 A3
Dark La. Ban 107 E1
Dark La. Blag 110 C2
Dark La. Ch Mag 95 F2
Dark La. H Cha 120 A3
Dark La. Hol 138 B1
Dark La. Mang 53 D1
Dark La. Nol 139 D1
Darley Cl. Bris 34 B2
Darlington Mews. Bath 102 A4
Darlington Pl. Bath 102 A3
Darlington Rd. Bath 102 A4
Darlington St. Bath 102 A4
Darmead. W-S-M 89 D1
Darnley Ave. Bris 49 F3
Dart Cl. Thorn 8 C1
Dart Rd. Cleve 57 E1
Dartmoor St. Bris 63 D2
Dartmouth Ave. Bath 101 E3
Dartmouth Cl. W-S-M 89 D1
Dartmouth Wlk. Keyn 81 E2
Daubeny Cl. Bris 51 D2
Daventry Rd. Bris 63 F1
Davey St. Bris 49 F1
David St. Bris 63 F4
David's La. Alve 15 D2
David's Rd. Bris 80 B3
David's Rd. Thorn 8 B3
Davids Cl. Alve 15 D2
Davin Cres. E in G 47 E2
Davis Cl. Kingsw 65 F3
Davis Cl. Thom 8 A1
Davis La. Yatt 73 F4
Davis St. Avon 47 D4
Dawes Cl. Cleve 57 E1
Dawley Cl. Wint 37 F4
Dawlish Rd. Bris 64 A3
Dawn Rise. Kingsw 52 A1
Day Cres. Bath 100 C3
Day House La. Hill 19 E4
Day's Rd. Bris 64 A3
De Clifford Rd. Bris 34 B1
De Verose Ct. Kingsw 65 F3
Deacon Cl. Wint 37 F3
Deacons Cl. W-S-M 88 C1
Deadmill La. Bath 85 E2
Dean Ave. Thorn 8 B1
Dean Cl. Kingsw 65 D2
Dean Cl. W-S-M 89 D2
Dean Cres. Bris 63 E2
Dean Ct. Yate 27 E2
Dean La. Bris 63 E2
Dean Rd. Avon 33 E3
Dean Rd. Yate 27 E2
Dean St. Bris 63 E2
Dean St. Bris 63 F4
Dean's Dr. Bris 51 D1
Deanery Cl. Kingsw 66 A4
Deanery Rd. Bris 63 E3
Deanery Rd. Kingsw 66 A4
Deanhill La. Chalf 84 A1
Deans Mead. Bris 48 A4
Deans The. Portis 45 D2
Debecca's La. E in G 47 D2
Deep Coombe Rd. Bris 78 C3
Deep Pit Rd. Bris 50 C1
Deer Mead. Cleve 57 D1
Deerhurst. Kingsw 51 F2
Deerhurst. Yate 39 E4
Deerleap. Ship 125 F4
Deerswood. Kingsw 52 A1
Delabere Ave. Bris 51 D3
Delapre Rd. W-S-M 104 B2
Delius Gr. Bris 79 E4
Dell The. Bris 48 B2
Dell The. Kingsw 66 B3
Dell The. Nail 59 E1
Dell The. St Gif 36 C4
Dell The. W-S-M 88 C2
Delvin Rd. Bris 49 E4
Denbigh St. Bris 49 F1
Dene Cl. Keyn 81 F2
Dene Rd. Whit 80 B2
Denham House. Bris 79 E2
Denleigh Cl. Bris 80 A2
Denmark Ave. Bris 63 E3
Denmark Pl. Bris 49 F2
Denmark Rd. Bath 101 E3
Denmark St. Bris 63 E3
Denning Ct. W-S-M 89 D3
Dennisworth. Puck 53 D3
Dennor Park. Bris 80 A4
Denny Cl. Portis 45 D3

Denny Isle Dr. Piln 22 A3
Denny La. Ch Mag 96 A1
Denny View. Portis 45 D3
Dennyview Rd. Ab Lei 61 F4
Denston Dr. Portis 45 F2
Denston Wlk. Bris 79 D4
Dentwood Dr. Bris 48 A4
Denys Ct. Olve 14 A2
Derby Rd. Bris 64 B3
Derby St. Bris 64 B4
Derham Cl. Yatt 91 D4
Derham Park. Yatt 91 D4
Derham Rd. Bris 79 D3
Dermot St. Bris 50 B1
Derrick Rd. Kingsw 65 E4
Derricke Rd. Bris 80 C3
Derry Rd. Bris 63 D1
Derwent Cl. Bris 36 A4
Derwent Ct. Thom 15 E4
Derwent Gr. Keyn 82 A3
Derwent Rd. Bris 50 C1
Derwent Rd. W-S-M 105 D2
Desmond Rd. Lock 89 E2
Deveron Gr. Keyn 82 A2
Devil's La. Char 11 D1
Devon Gr. Bris 64 B4
Devon St. Bris 50 B1
Devonshire Bldgs. Bath 101 F2
Devonshire Ct. W-S-M 104 C2
Devonshire Dr. Portis 44 C3
Devonshire Pl. Bath 101 F2
Devonshire Rd. Bath 85 F1
Devonshire Rd. Bris 49 D2
Devonshire Rd. W-S-M 104 C2
Dial Hill Rd. Cleve 57 E2
Dial La. Ba Gu 77 E1
Dial La. Mang 51 E3
Dial La. Win 77 E1
Diamond St. Bris 63 E2
Dibden Cl. Mang 52 A4
Dibden La. Mang 52 A4
Dibden Rd. Mang 52 A4
Dickens Cl. Bris 50 A4
Dickenson Rd. W-S-M 104 C3
Dickenson's Gr. Cong 91 F2
Didsbury Cl. Bris 34 C1
Dighton Gate. St Gif 36 C3
Dighton St. Bris 63 E4
Dillon Ct. Bris 64 B4
Dimond Rd. Bris 64 C4
Dinder Cl. Nail 75 F4
Dinghurst Rd. Chur 108 C2
Dingle Cl. Bris 48 B3
Dingle Ct. Bris 48 B3
Dingle The. Mang 48 B4
Dingle The. Wint 37 F2
Dingle View. Bris 48 B3
Dinglewood Cl. Bris 48 B4
Dings Wlk. Bris 64 A3
Dipland Gr. Blag 110 C1
Dixon Gdns. Bath 84 C1
Dixon Rd. Bris 64 C1
Dock Gate La. Bris 63 D3
Dodington La. Dod 40 B3
Dodington Rd. Ch Sod 40 A4
Dodisham Wlk. Bris 51 D3
Dolberrow. Chur 108 C2
Dolemoor La. Cong 91 D2
Dolemoor La. Cong 91 E2
Dolman Cl. Bris 34 C2
Dolphin Sq. W-S-M 104 B4
Dominion Rd. Bath 101 D3
Dominion Rd. Bris 50 C2
Donald Rd. Bris 78 C4
Doncaster Rd. Bris 49 E4
Doncombe Hill. Col 70 C4
Doncombe La. Col 70 C4
Dongola Ave. Bris 49 F2
Dongola Rd. Bris 49 F2
Donnington Wlk. Keyn 81 E2
Doone Rd. Bris 49 F4
Dorcas Ave. St Gif 36 C3
Dorchester Cl. Nail 59 E1
Dorchester Rd. Bris 50 A4
Dorchester St. Bath 102 A3
Dorester Cl. Bris 35 E2
Dorian Cl. Bris 49 F4
Dorian Rd. Bris 49 F4
Dormer Cl. Fr Cot 38 B3
Dormer Rd. Bris 50 B2
Dorset Cl. Bath 101 E3
Dorset Gr. Bris 50 A1
Dorset Rd. Bris 48 C2
Dorset Rd. Kingsw 51 E1
Dorset St. Bath 101 E3
Dorset St. Bris 63 D2
Dorset Way. Yate 28 A2
Douglas Cl. W-S-M 104 C3
Douglas Rd. Bris 49 F4
Douglas Rd. Kingsw 65 E3
Douglas Rd. W-S-M 104 C3
Doulton Way. Bris 80 A3
Dove La. Bris 63 F4
Dove St S. Bris 63 E4
Dove St. Bris 63 E4
Dovecote. Yate 39 F4

Dovedale. Thom 15 E4
Dover Pl. Bath 85 D1
Dovercourt Rd. Bris 50 A3
Dovers La. Bathf 86 B1
Dovers Park. Bathf 86 B1
Dovey Ct. Kingsw 66 B3
Dowdeswell Cl. Bris 34 C2
Dowling Rd. Bath 85 D1
Dowland. W-S-M 89 D1
Dowling Rd. Bris 79 E2
Dowman Rd. Bris 102 A1
Down Cl. Portis 44 C3
Down Hill. Olve 14 B2
Down Leaze. Alve 15 D3
Down Rd. Alve 15 D3
Down Rd. Marsh 56 B1
Down Rd. Portis 45 D2
Down Rd. Wint 37 F2
Down The. Alve 14 C3
Down The. Olve 14 B2
Down View. Bris 49 F2
Downend Park Rd. Mang ... 51 E3
Downend Rd. Bris 49 F3
Downend Rd. Bris 51 E3
Downend Rd. Bris 51 E3
Downend Rd. Kingsw 51 E1
Downend Rd. Mang 51 E3
Downfield Cl. Alve 15 D3
Downfield Dr. Fr Cot 38 A4
Downfield Rd. Bris 49 D1
Downleaze Dr. Ch Sod 40 A4
Downleaze. Bris 48 C2
Downleaze. Mang 51 D3
Downman Rd. Bris 50 B3
Downs Cl. Alve 15 D3
Downs Cl. W-S-M 88 C1
Downs Cote Ave. Bris 48 C3
Downs Cote Gdns. Bris 49 D3
Downs Cote Park. Bris 49 D3
Downs Cote View. Bris 49 D3
Downs Park E. Bris 49 D2
Downs Park W. Bris 49 D2
Downs Rd. Bris 49 D3
Downs Rd. Dun 78 B1
Downs The. Portis 45 D2
Downs The. Wickw 17 F4
Downside Cl. Bath 85 F1
Downside Cl. Chil 137 E2
Downside Cl. Mang 65 F3
Downside Rd. Bris 49 D1
Downside Rd. W-S-M 104 C2
Downside Rd. Wring 63 F3
Downside. Portis 45 D3
Downsway. Paul 131 E3
Downton Rd. Bris 63 D3
Dowry Sq. Bris 63 D3
Doynton La. Doyn 54 A2
Dr White's Cl. Bris 63 D3
Dragon La. Dyrh 54 A2
Dragon Rd. Wint 37 E3
Dragon Wlk. Bris 50 C1
Dragons Hill Cl. Keyn 81 F3
Dragons Hill Ct. Keyn 81 F3
Dragons Hill Gdns. Keyn 81 F3
Dragonswell Rd. Bris 35 D1
Drake Ave. Bath 101 F1
Drake Cl. Keyn 82 B1
Drakes Cl. W-S-M 88 C2
Drakes Rd. Bris 63 E3
Drakes Way. Portis 45 D3
Draycot Pl. Bris 63 E3
Draycott Rd. Bris 50 B2
Drayton Cl. Bris 80 A4
Drayton Rd. Bris 48 B4
Dring. The. Rad 132 C1
Drive. The. W-S-M 105 D1
Druid Stoke Ave. Bris 48 B3
Druid Woods. Bris 48 B3
Drumhead Way The. Ship . 125 F4
Drummond Ct. Kingsw 65 F2
Drummond Rd. Bris 50 C2
Drummond Rd. Bris 64 A4
Dryleaze Rd. Bris 50 C3
Dryleaze. Keyn 81 F4
Drysdale Cl. W-S-M 88 C1
Dubbers La. Bris 50 C1
Dublin Cres. Bris 49 D3
Duchess Rd. Bris 49 D1
Duchess Way. Bris 50 B3

Duchy Cl. Mid No .... 1[
Duchy Rd. Mid No .... 1[
Ducie Rd. Mang 1
Ducie Rd. Bris
Duck Cl. Stur Court .... 1[
Duck St. Tyth
Duckmoor Rd. Bris
Dudley Cl. Keyn
Dudley Cl. Kingsw
Dudley Gr. Bris
Dugar Wlk. Bris
Duke St. Bath 1
Dulverton Rd. Bris
Dumaine Ave. St Gif
Dumfries Pl. W-S-M .... 1[
Dumpers La. Ch Mag .... 1[
Dunan Gdns. Bath
Duncombe La. Bris
Duncombe Rd. Bris
Dundas Cl. Bris
Dundonald Rd. Bris
Dundridge Gdns. Bris
Dundridge La. Bris
Dundry Cl. Kingsw
Dundry La. Dun
Dundry La. Win
Dundry View. Bris
Dunkeld Ave. Bris
Dunkerry Rd. Bris
Dunkerton Hill. P St J 1
Dunkerton Hill. Pris
Dunkery Cl. Nail
Dunkery Rd. W-S-M
Dunkirk Rd. Bris
Dunkite La. W-S-M
Dunmail Rd. Bris
Dunmore St. Bris
Dunsdown La. Tor
Dunster Cres. W-S-M 1
Dunster Ct. Wins
Dunster Gdns. Kingsw
Dunster Gdns. Nail
Dunster Rd. Bris
Dunster Rd. Keyn
Dunsters Rd. Yatt
Durban Rd. Bris
Durban Way. Yate
Durbin Park Rd. Cleve
Durbin Wlk. Bris
Durcott Rd. Tims
Durham Gr. Keyn
Durham Park. Bris
Durham Rd. Bris
Durham Rd. Char
Durleigh Cl. Bris
Durley Hill. Keyn
Durley Park. Bath
Durnford Ave. Bris
Durnford St. Bris
Durnford St. Bris
Durnhill. Co Mar
Dursley Cl. Yate
Dursley Rd. Bris
Durston. W-S-M
Durville Rd. Bris
Durweston Wlk. Bris
Dutton Cl. Bris
Dutton Rd. Bris
Dutton Wlk. Bris
Dyer's La. Yate
Dyers Cl. Bris
Dylan Thomas Ct. Kingsw
Dymboro Ave. Mid No ...
Dymboro Cl. Mid No
Dymboro Gdns. Mid No ...
Dymboro The. Mid No
Dyrham Cl. Bris
Dyrham Cl. Kingsw
Dyrham Par. St Gif
Dyrham Rd. Kingsw
Dyson Cl. Yatt

Eagle Cl. W-S-M
Eagle Cres. Puck
Eagle Dr. Bris
Eagle Park. Bathe
Eagle Rd. Bathe
Eagle Rd. Bris
Eagles The. Yatt
Eagles Wood Bsns Pk.
  St Gif
Earl Russell Way. Bris
Earlesfield. Nail
Earlham Gr. W-S-M
Earlsmead. Bris
Earlstone Cl. Kingsw
Earlstone Cres. Kingsw
Easedale Cl. Bris
East Cl. Bath
East Clevedon Triangle.
  Cleve
East Croft. Bris
East Dundry La. Dun

Dundry Rd. Bris 79 F1
Dundry Rd. Whit 79 F1
Gr. Bris 49 F1
Hill. Bris 49 D4
Lea Rd. Bath 101 D4
Mead. Mid No 132 A1
Par. Bris 48 B3
Park Dr. Bris 50 B1
Park. Bris 50 B1
Priory Cl. Bris 49 D4
Ridge Dr. Bris 78 C3
Shrubbery. Bris 49 E1
St. Avon 33 D1
St. Ban 107 E2
St. Bris 63 E2
St. Bris 63 F4
View. Mang 51 F3
Way. Bath 101 D3
Wlk. Yate 27 F1
Wood Pl. Portis 45 F4
bury Cl. Thorn 8 B1
bury Rd. Bris 51 D2
bury Rd. Thorn 8 B1
ombe Gdns. W-S-M 87 F1
ombe Rd. W-S-M 87 F1
ote Pk. Bris 80 A3
court Gdns. Bris 50 B3
court Rd. Clut 130 C4
croft Cl. Blag 110 C1
croft. Blag 110 C1
own Rd. Mid No 132 C3
ertown. Lymp 122 B1
field Ave. Bath 84 A1
field Gdns. W-S-M 87 F1
field Path. Bath 84 A1
field Rd. W-S-M 87 F1
field Rd. Bris 49 D4
field Rd. Bris 49 E1
field Rd. Lock 105 F1
field Terr. Bris 49 D3
field. Bris 49 D4
ake Office Centre. Bris 50 A2
ake Cl. Bris 50 A4
and Ave. Thorn 8 B1
und Rd. Thorn 8 B1
na. Cleve 57 D1
igh Rd. Kingsw 51 F2
igh Rd. Bris 35 E1
igh Rd. Kingsw 51 F2
y Cl. Falf 9 F4
or Rd. Bris 79 D4
ead La. Ban 107 D2
ead La. Bris 80 A2
or Rd. Bris 80 A2
h Hill Rd. Thorn 8 B1
s Rd. Bris 64 A4
s Rd. E in G 47 E2
Way. Bris 64 A4
er Gr. Bath 101 E1
er Rd. Paul 115 E1
le. Bath 85 D1
y Cl. Nail 59 E1
y Sq. Nail 59 F2
ay. Nail 59 F2
or Rd. Paul 115 E1
od Cres. Bris 64 C2
od Rd. Bris 64 C2
oods. Bathe 86 A2
s Cl. Bris 51 D2
Cl. Bris 80 C3
Cres. Bris 63 E2
St. Bris 63 E2
Rd. W ST L 89 D3
Rd. W-S-M 88 C2
La. Bris 48 C3
er St. Bris 64 B4
ombe Gdns. P St J 133 E4
La. P St J 133 F4
Rd. P St J 133 E4
Office Pk. Kingsw 51 E2
Bris 36 A1
ark Cl. Bathe 86 A2
ark Dr. Bathe 86 A2
ry Cl. Cleve 57 E3
ombe Gdns. W-S-M 88 B1
mbe Cl. Kingsw 51 F1
mer La. Burt 43 D2
mbe Rd. Bris 49 E1
d Cl. Bris 79 F2
d Rd. Bris 79 F2
d. Cleve 57 E3
are Rd. Kingsw 51 E2
od Cl. Bris 80 A4
d Cl. Kingsw 66 A2
orth Rd. Bath 101 E1
rth. Yate 39 D1
d. W-S-M 104 C4
n Gr. Bris 35 D1
Cl. Mang 51 F1
Cl. Puck 53 E3
are Cl. Bris 64 C2
Rd S. Cleve 57 F3
Rd W. Cleve 57 F3
Rd. Cleve 57 F3

Edward Rd. Kingsw 65 F4
Edward St. Bath 101 E4
Edward St. Bath 102 A4
Edward St. Bris 50 B1
Edward St. Bris 64 B4
Edwin Short Cl. Bitt 82 C4
Effingham Rd. Bris 49 F2
Egerton Brow. Bris 49 E2
Egerton Rd. Bris 49 E2
Egerton Rd. Bris 49 E2
Eggshill La. Yate 27 E1
Eighth Ave. Bris 36 A1
Eirene Terr. E in G 47 E2
Elberton Rd. Aust 14 A2
Elberton Rd. Bris 48 A4
Elberton Rd. Olive 46 A4
Elberton. Kingsw 66 A4
Elborough Ave. Yatt 91 D2
Elbury Ave. Bris 51 E1
Elderberry Wlk. W-S-M 89 D1
Elderbury Wlk. Bris 35 E2
Elderwood Dr. Kingsw 66 A2
Elderwood Rd. Bris 80 A4
Eldon Pl. Bath 85 D1
Eldon Terr. Bris 63 E2
Eldon Way. Bris 64 B3
Eleanor Cl. Bath 101 D3
Eleventh Ave. Bris 36 A1
Elfin Rd. Bris 51 D3
Elgar Cl. Bris 79 E3
Elgar Cl. Cleve 57 F2
Elgin Ave. Bris 35 F1
Elgin Croft. Bris 79 D2
Elgin Pk. Bris 49 D1
Elgin Rd. Bris 51 D1
Eliot Cl. W-S-M 105 D2
Elizabeth Cl. Lock 105 E2
Elizabeth Cl. Thorn 15 E4
Elizabeth Cres. St Gif 36 C2
Elizabeth House. E in G 47 E2
Elkstone Wlk. Kingsw 66 B1
Ellacombe Rd. Kingsw 65 F1
Ellan Hay Rd. St Gif 37 D3
Ellbridge Cl. Bris 48 B3
Ellenborough Park N. W-S-M 104 B3
Ellenborough Park Rd. W-S-M 104 C3
Ellenborough Park S. W-S-M 104 B3
Ellemcroft Rd. W-u-E 11 F4
Ellesmere Rd. Bris 64 B1
Ellesmere Rd. Kingsw 65 E1
Ellesmere Rd. W-S-M 104 B1
Ellesmere. Thorn 15 E4
Ellfield Cl. Bris 78 C3
Ellick Rd. Blag 126 B2
Ellicks Cl. St Gif 24 C1
Ellinghurst Cl. Bris 35 D1
Elliot Rd. Bris 49 F3
Elliott Ave. Bris 37 E1
Ellis Ave. Bris 79 D4
Elliston Dr. Bath 101 D2
Elliston La. Bris 49 E1
Elliston Rd. Bris 49 E1
Ellsbridge Cl. Keyn 82 A3
Ellsworth Rd. Bris 34 C2
Elm Cl. Ch Sod 28 A1
Elm Cl. Nail 59 D2
Elm Cl. Ship 108 B1
Elm Cl. St Gif 36 A4
Elm Cl. Yatt 91 D4
Elm Cl. Keyn 81 E2
Elm Gr. Bath 85 E1
Elm Gr. Bath 101 E2
Elm Gr. Lock 105 F2
Elm La. Bris 49 D1
Elm Park. Bris 36 A1
Elm Rd. Bris 49 F3
Elm Rd. Kingsw 65 F3
Elm Rd. Paul 131 F3
Elm Terr. Rad 132 B1
Elm Terr. Rod 138 B4
Elm Tree Ave. Mang 52 A4
Elm Tree Ave. Rad 132 B1
Elm Tree Cl. Cleve 57 E3
Elm Tree Rd. Lock 106 A2
Elm View. Mid No 132 B2
Elm Wlk. Yatt 91 D4
Elm Wood. Yate 39 F4
Elmcroft Cres. Bris 50 A2
Elmdale Cres. Thorn 8 B2
Elmdale Gdns. Bris 51 D2
Elmdale Rd. Bris 63 D4
Elmdale Rd. Bris 49 D4
Elmfield Cl. Kingsw 65 F3
Elmfield Rd. Bris 49 D4
Elmfield. Kingsw 65 F3
Elmgrove Ave. Bris 50 B1
Elmgrove Dr. Yate 27 F1
Elmgrove Park. Bris 49 E1
Elmgrove Rd. Bris 49 E1
Elmgrove Rd. Bris 50 C2
Elmhurst Ave. Bris 50 B2
Elmhurst Est. Bathe 86 A2
Elmhurst Gdns. Lo Ash 77 F4
Elmhurst Rd. Lock 105 F1

Elmhyrst Rd. W-S-M 104 C4
Elming Down Cl. St Gif 36 B3
Elmlea Ave. Bris 48 C3
Elmleigh Ave. Mang 52 A3
Elmleigh Cl. Mang 52 A3
Elmleigh Rd. Mang 52 A3
Elmore Rd. Bris 23 F1
Elmore Rd. Bris 50 A3
Elmore. Kingsw 51 F1
Elmore. Yate 39 E4
Elms Gr. St Gif 24 A1
Elms The. Bris 37 E1
Elmsleigh Rd. W-S-M 104 B2
Elmsley La. W St L 88 B3
Elmtree Cl. Kingsw 51 E1
Elmtree Dr. Bris 78 C3
Elmtree Way. Kingsw 51 E1
Elmvale Dr. Lock 105 F2
Elsbert Dr. Bris 78 C3
Elstree Rd. Bris 50 C1
Elton La. Bris 49 E1
Elton Rd. Bris 49 E1
Elton Rd. Bris 49 E1
Elton Rd. Bris 51 E1
Elton Rd. Bris 63 E4
Elton Rd. Cleve 57 E2
Elton Rd. W-S-M 89 D2
Elton St. Bris 63 F4
Elvard Cl. Bris 79 D2
Elvard Rd. Bris 79 D2
Elvaston Rd. Bris 63 F2
Elwell La. Dun 77 F1
Elwell La. Win 77 F1
Ely Gr. Bris 48 A4
Embassy Rd. Bris 50 C1
Embassy Wlk. Bris 50 C1
Embercourt Dr. Back 76 A3
Embleton Rd. Bris 35 E1
Emerson Sq. Bris 36 A4
Emery Gate. Ban 107 D2
Emery Rd. Bris 64 C1
Emlyn Cl. W-S-M 89 D2
Emlyn Rd. Bris 50 B1
Emmett Wood. Bris 80 A2
Emra Cl. Bris 50 C1
Enderleigh Gdns. Chur 108 C2
Enfield Rd. Bris 51 D2
Engine Common La. Yate 27 E3
Engine La. Nail 75 D4
England's Cres. Wint 37 F4
Englishcombe La. Bath 101 E2
Englishcombe Rd. Bris 101 E2
Englishcombe Way. Bath 101 E2
Enmore. W-S-M 88 C2
Ennerdale Cl. W-S-M 105 D3
Ennerdale Rd. Bris 35 E3
Entry Hill Dr. Bath 101 F2
Entry Hill Gdns. Bath 101 F2
Entry Hill Park. Bath 101 F1
Entry Hill. Bath 101 F1
Entry Rise. Bath 101 F1
Epney Cl. Bris 23 F1
Epsom Cl. Mang 37 F1
Epworth Rd. Bris 35 D2
Equinox. St Gif 36 A3
Erin Wlk. Bris 79 E4
Ermine Way. Bris 47 E4
Ermleet Rd. Bris 49 E1
Ernestville Rd. Bris 50 C2
Ernst Barker Cl. Bris 64 A4
Ervine Terr. Bris 63 F4
Esgar Rise. W-S-M 88 C2
Eskdale Cl. W-S-M 105 E4
Eskdale. Thorn 15 E4
Esmond Gr. Cleve 57 E3
Esplanade Rd. Portis 45 D4
Essery Rd. Bris 50 B1
Essex St. Bris 63 E2
Esson Rd. Bris 51 D1
Estoril. Yate 27 F1
Estune Wlk. Lo Ash 62 A1
Etloe Rd. Bris 49 D2
Eton La. Ban 106 C4
Eton Rd. Bris 64 B2
Ettlingen Way. Cleve 57 F1
Ettricke Dr. Bris 51 D3
Eugene St. Bris 63 E4
Eugene St. Bris 63 F4
Evans Rd. Bris 49 D1
Eve Rd. Bris 50 A1
Evelyn Rd. Bath 101 B4
Evelyn Rd. Bris 49 E4
Evelyn Terr. Bath 85 D1
Evenlode Gdns. Bris 47 F3
Evenlode Way. Keyn 82 A2
Evercreech Rd. Bris 80 A2
Everest Ave. Bris 50 C2
Everest Rd. Bris 50 C2
Evergreen Cl. Winsc 107 F1
Ewart Rd. W-S-M 105 D2
Excelsior La. Bath 102 A3
Excelsior St. Bath 102 A3
Excelsior Terr. Mid No 132 A1
Exchange Ave. Bris 63 E3
Exeter Bldgs. Bris 49 D1
Exeter Rd. Bris 63 E2
Exeter Rd. Portis 45 F2
Exeter Rd. W-S-M 104 C3
Exford Cl. W-S-M 104 C1

Exley Cl. Kingsw 66 B3
Exmoor Rd. Bath 101 F1
Exmoor St. Bris 63 D2
Exmouth Rd. Bris 63 F1
Exton Cl. Bris 80 A3
Exton. W-S-M 105 D1
Eyer's La. Bris 63 F4
Faber Gr. Bris 79 E2
Fabian Dr. St Gif 36 C3
Factory Rd. Wint 37 F4
Failand Cres. Bris 48 B3
Failand La. Portb 46 C1
Failand La. Wrax 61 D4
Failand Wlk. Bris 48 B3
Fair Cl. N St P 135 F2
Fair Furlong. Bris 79 D2
Fair Hill. Ship 125 F4
Fair Lawn. Kingsw 66 A2
Fair View Dr. Bris 49 E1
Fairacre Cl. Bris 50 A3
Fairacre. Lock 106 A2
Fairacres Cl. Keyn 81 F3
Fairfax St. Bris 63 E4
Fairfield Ave. Bath 85 D1
Fairfield Cl. Back 76 B4
Fairfield Cl. Marsh 46 A4
Fairfield Cl. W-S-M 88 A1
Fairfield Mead. Back 76 B4
Fairfield Park Rd. Bath 85 D1
Fairfield Pl. Bris 63 D2
Fairfield Rd. Bath 85 D1
Fairfield Rd. Bris 49 F1
Fairfield Rd. Bris 63 E2
Fairfield St. Bris 64 A4
Fairfield Terr. P St J 133 E4
Fairfield Way. Back 76 B3
Fairfield. Rode 138 C1
Fairfoot Rd. Bris 64 A2
Fairford Cl. Kingsw 51 F1
Fairford Cres. St Gif 36 B4
Fairford Rd. Bris 47 E4
Fairhaven Rd. Bris 49 E2
Fairhaven. Yate 27 F1
Fairlawn Ave. Bris 36 A2
Fairlawn Rd. Bris 49 F1
Fairlyn Dr. Kingsw 51 F2
Fairoaks. Kingsw 66 A2
Fairseat Workshops. Ch St 112 C4
Fairview Rd. Kingsw 66 A2
Fairview. W-S-M 88 C2
Fairway Cl. Kingsw 66 A2
Fairway Ind Centre. Bris 35 F2
Fairway. Bris 64 B1
Fairways. Keyn 82 C1
Fairy Hill. Co Dan 98 B3
Falcon Cl. Bris 35 F4
Falcon Cl. Bris 48 C2
Falcon Cl. Portis 45 E2
Falcon Cres. W-S-M 105 E4
Falcon Way. Thorn 8 B1
Falcon Wlk. Bris 23 F1
Falcondale Rd. Bris 48 C4
Falcondale Wlk. Bris 49 D4
Falconer Rd. Bath 84 A2
Falfield Rd. Bris 64 B2
Falfield Wlk. Bris 49 E4
Falkland Rd. Bris 49 F1
Falloden Ct. Bris 49 D3
Fallodon Way. Bris 49 D3
Fallowfield. Kingsw 66 B3
Fallowfield. W-S-M 88 C2
Falmouth Cl. Nail 60 A1
Falmouth Rd. Bris 49 F3
Fane Cl. Bris 35 D2
Fanshawe Rd. Bris 80 A4
Far Handstones. Kingsw 66 A2
Faraday Rd. Bris 62 C3
Farington Rd. Bris 49 E4
Farleigh Hospital Cotts. Back 77 D2
Farleigh La. Crom 10 B3
Farleigh Rd. Back 76 B4
Farleigh Rd. Cleve 57 D1
Farleigh Rd. Keyn 81 E2
Farleigh Rd. N St P 136 A3
Farleigh Rise. Mon Far 86 C1
Farleigh View. Westw 120 C2
Farleigh Wick. Mon Far 103 F3
Farleigh Wlk. Bris 79 D4
Farler's End. Nail 75 F4
Farley Cl. St Gif 36 B4
Farm Cl. Mang 51 F4
Farm Cl. Alm 22 C1
Farm La. Plm 22 C2
Farm La. Well 118 C1
Farm Lees. Char 11 D1
Farm Rd. Lock 105 F1
Farm Rd. Mang 51 F4
Farmer Rd. Bris 78 C2
Farmhouse Cl. Nail 59 F1
Farmhouse Ct. Nail 59 F1
Farmwell Cl. Bris 79 D3
Farndale Rd. W-S-M 105 E4
Farndale. Bris 65 D3
Farne Cl. Bris 49 D3

Farr St. Avon 47 D4
Farr's La. Bris 63 E3
Farrant Cl. Bris 79 E3
Farrington Fields. Paul 131 E2
Farrington Rd. Paul 131 E3
Farrington Way. Paul 131 D2
Farrs La. Bath 102 A1
Farthing Row. Rode 136 C1
Faulkland View. P St J 133 F4
Faulkland La. Well 134 B2
Faulkland Rd. Bath 101 E3
Faversham Dr. W-S-M 105 D1
Fawkes Cl. Kingsw 66 A4
Fearnville Est. Cleve 57 E1
Featherbed La. Clut 114 B3
Featherbed La. Pens 114 B3
Featherbed La. Win 95 C2
Fedden Village. Portis 44 C3
Feeder Rd. Bris 64 A3
Felix Rd. Bris 64 A4
Felstead Rd. Bris 35 F1
Feltham Rd. Puck 53 E3
Felton Dr. Win 94 B4
Felton La. Win 94 B4
Felton St. Win 94 B4
Fenbrook Cl. Bris 37 D1
Feniton. W-S-M 105 D1
Fennel La. Axb 125 D1
Fennel Gr. Bris 35 D1
Fenners. W-S-M 89 D2
Fenshurst Gdns. Lo Ash 77 F4
Fenswood Mead. Lo Ash 61 F1
Fenswood Rd. Lo Ash 61 F1
Fenton Cl. Keyn 82 B2
Fenton Rd. Bris 49 E2
Ferenberge Cl. Farm 116 A3
Fermaine Ave. Bris 64 C2
Fern Cl. Bris 35 D2
Fern Gr. Nail *75 E4
Fern Gr. Nail 75 E4
Fern Lea. Blea 122 A3
Fern Rd. Mang 51 E3
Fernbank Rd. Bris 49 E1
Ferndale Ave. Bris 65 D1
Ferndale Ave. Kingsw 66 A2
Ferndale Rd. Bath 85 E2
Ferndale Rd. Bris 36 A1
Ferndale Rd. Portis 45 E3
Ferndean. St Gif 24 B1
Ferndown Cl. Bris 48 A4
Ferndown. Yate 27 F1
Fernhill La. Bris 34 A1
Fernhill. Alve 24 B4
Fernhurst Rd. Bris 50 C1
Fernhurst Rd. Bris 50 C1
Fernlea Gdns. E in G 47 D2
Fernlea Rd. W-S-M 105 E4
Fernleaze. Fr Cot 38 B3
Fernside. Back 76 C3
Fernsteed Rd. Bris 78 C3
Ferry La. Bath 102 A3
Ferry Rd. Kingsw 65 F3
Ferry St. Bris 63 F3
Ferry Steps Ind Est. Bris 64 A2
Fiddes Rd. Bris 49 E1
Field La. Aust 14 A4
Field La. Dyrh 54 C3
Field La. Kingsw 65 F2
Field La. Ston E 130 A1
Field La. Tyth 15 F2
Field Rd. Bris 51 E3
Field View Dr. Bris 51 E3
Fielders The. W-S-M 89 D2
Fieldgardens Rd. Clut 114 C1
Fielding Rd. Bath 101 B3
Fieldings. Winsl 120 C4
Fieldway. Wins 108 A2
Fiennes Cl. Kingsw 51 F2
Fifth Ave. Bris 36 A1
Fifth Way. Avon 33 F1
Filby Dr. St Gif 36 C4
Filer Cl. P St J 133 E4
Filton Ave. Bris 36 A1
Filton Ave. Bris 36 A2
Filton Gr. Bris 49 F3
Filton La. Bris 36 B1
Filton Rd. Bris 36 B1
Filton Rd. Bris 37 D1
Filwood Broadway. Bris 79 F4
Filwood Dr. Kingsw 65 F4
Filwood Rd. Bris 50 C1
Finch Cl. Thorn 8 B1
Finch Cl. W-S-M 105 F4
Finch Rd. Ch Sod 40 A4
Finmere Gdns. W-S-M 89 D2
Fir La. Priddy 126 B4
Fir Leaze. Nail 59 D1
Fir Rd. Col 70 C3
Fir Tree Ave. Lock 105 F2
Fir Tree Ave. Paul 131 F2
Fir Tree Cl. Bris 35 F4
Fir Tree La. Bris 65 D4
Fircliff Park. Portis 45 D4
Fire Engine La. Fr Cot 38 B4
Fireclay Rd. Bris 64 B3
Firework Cl. Mang 52 A4
Firgrove Cres. Yate 28 A1

150

Firgrove La. P St J	117	D1
Firs Ct. Keyn	81	E2
Firs The. Bath	102	A1
Firs The. U St	120	A3
Firs The. Mang	51	F3
First Ave. Bath	101	E2
First Ave. Bris	64	C3
First Ave. Portb	46	C3
First Ave. Rod	138	B4
First Way. Avon	33	E1
Fisher Ave. Kingsw	52	A1
Fisher Rd. Kingsw	52	A1
Fishponds Rd. Bris	50	C2
Fishpool Hill. Bris	35	D2
Fitchett Wlk. Bris	34	C2
Fitzgerald Rd. Bris	63	F2
Fitzroy Pl. Bris	51	D1
Fitzroy St. Bris	64	A2
Fitzroy Terr. Bris	49	D1
Five Acre Dr. Bris	50	C4
Five Arches Cl. Mid No	132	B1
Flagstaff Rd. Blea	123	E4
Flamingo Cres. W-S-M	105	F4
Flat The. Clut	114	B3
Flatwoods Cres. Bath	102	C2
Flatwoods Rd. Bath	102	C2
Flax Bourton Rd. Wrax	61	D2
Flaxman Cl. Bris	50	A3
Flaxpits La. Wint	37	F3
Florence Gr. W-S-M	105	D4
Florence Park. Alm	24	B3
Florence Park. Bris	49	D2
Florence Rd. Kingsw	51	F2
Florida Terr. Mid No	132	B1
Flowers Hill Cl. Bris	64	C1
Flowers Hill. Bris	64	C1
Flowerwell Rd. Bris	79	D3
Folleigh Cl. Lo Ash	62	A1
Folleigh Dr. Lo Ash	62	A1
Folleigh La. Lo Ash	62	A1
Folliot Cl. Bris	51	D4
Folly Bridge Cl. Yate	27	E1
Folly La. Bris	64	A3
Folly La. Ship	125	F4
Folly La. W-S-M	104	C1
Folly Rd. Ir Act	25	F2
Folly The. Keyn	82	C1
Folly The. Mang	51	F4
Fontana Cl. Kingsw	66	A2
Fonthill Rd. Bath	84	C1
Fonthill Rd. Bris	35	E1
Fonthill Way. Kingsw	66	B3
Fontmell Ct. Bris	80	B4
Fontwell Dr. Mang	37	F1
Footes La. Fr Cot	38	A4
Footshill Cl. Kingsw	65	E3
Footshill Dr. Kingsw	65	E3
Footshill Rd. Kingsw	65	E3
Ford Rd. P St J	133	E4
Ford La. Litt	129	E1
Ford Rd. Well	137	E4
Ford St. Bris	64	B3
Forde Cl. Kingsw	65	F3
Fordell Pl. Bris	64	A2
Fordfield Pl. Bath	102	A3
Fordfield Rise. Bath	102	A3
Forest Ave. Bris	51	D2
Forest Dr. Bris	35	E2
Forest Edge. Kingsw	65	E4
Forest Hills. Alm	24	A3
Forest Rd. Bris	51	D2
Forest Rd. Kingsw	65	E4
Forest Wlk. Bris	51	D1
Forest Wlk. Kingsw	65	E4
Forester Ave. Bath	102	A4
Forester La. Bath	102	A4
Forester Rd. Bath	102	A4
Forester Rd. Portis	45	E2
Forge End. Portb	46	C2
Fortescue Rd. Rad	132	C1
Fortfield Rd. Bris	80	A3
Forty Acre La. Alve	15	D2
Foss La. O-o-S	7	F3
Fosse Barton. Nail	59	E1
Fosse Cl. Nail	59	E1
Fosse Gdns. Bath	118	B4
Fosse Green Rd. Mid No	132	C2
Fosse La. Bathe	86	A2
Fosse La. Mid No	132	B2
Fosse La. Nail	59	E1
Fosse Way Cotts. Rad	132	B1
Fosse Way. Nail	59	E1
Fossedale Ave. Bris	80	B3
Fossefield Rd. Kilm	138	A4
Fosseway Gdns. Rad	132	B1
Fosseway S. Kilm	138	A4
Fosseway The. Bris	50	C3
Fosseway. Chil	137	F1
Fosseway. Chil	138	A2
Fosseway. Cleve	57	E1
Fosseway. Mid No	132	C2
Fosseway. Rod	138	B4
Foster St. Bris	50	C1
Foundry La. Bris	50	C1
Fountain Cl. St Gif	24	B2
Fountain La. Wins	125	D4
Fountaine Ct. Bris	50	B1
Fountains Dr. Kingsw	65	F3
Four Acre Ave. Mang	51	F4
Four Acre Cres. Mang	37	F1
Four Acre Rd. Mang	51	F4
Four Acres Cl. Bris	78	C2
Four Acres Cl. Nail	75	F4
Four Acres Cl. Bris	78	C2
Fourth Ave. Bris	36	A1
Fourth Ave. Rod	138	B4
Fourth Way. Avon	33	F1
Fowey Cl. Nail	76	A4
Fowey Rd. W-S-M	89	D2
Fox And Hounds La. Keyn	81	F3
Fox Ave. Yate	27	E1
Fox Ct. Kingsw	65	F2
Fox Den Rd. St Gif	36	B2
Fox Hill. Bath	102	A1
Fox House. Bris	64	C2
Fox Rd. Bris	50	A1
Foxe Rd. Fr Cot	38	A4
Foxfield Ave. St Gif	24	B2
Foxglove Cl. Bris	50	C2
Foxglove Cl. Thorn	8	B1
Foxhole La. Clve	14	B2
Foye House. Lo Ash	62	B3
Fraley Rd. Bris	49	D4
Frampton Cres. Bris	51	E2
Frampton Ct. Kingsw	65	F2
Frampton End Rd. Fr Cot	38	B4
Frampton End Rd. Ir Act	26	B2
France La. H Up	20	A1
Francis Fox Rd. W-S-M	104	C4
Francis Pl. Kingsw	65	F2
Francis Rd. Bris	49	E4
Francis Rd. Bris	63	E1
Francombe Gr. Bris	49	F3
Frankland Cl. Bath	84	A1
Frankley Bldgs. Bath	85	D1
Franklin Cl. Bris	63	F3
Franklin's Way. Yate	74	C1
Franklyn La. Bris	49	F1
Franklyn St. Bris	49	F1
Fraser Cl. W-S-M	88	C2
Fraser St. Bris	63	E2
Frayne Rd. Bris	62	C3
Frederick Ave. P St J	133	E4
Frederick Pl. Bris	63	D3
Fredrick St. Bris	64	A2
Free Tank. Bris	63	F3
Freeland Bldgs. Bris	50	B1
Freeland Pl. Bris	62	C3
Freelands. Cleve	73	D4
Freemans La. Ba Gu	77	D1
Freemantle Gdns. Bris	50	B2
Freemantle La. Bris	49	E1
Freemantle Rd. Bris	50	B2
Freemantle Sq. Bris	49	E1
Freestone Rd. Bris	64	A3
Freeview Rd. Bath	101	D3
Freezinghill La. Co Ash	68	A2
French Cl. Nail	59	F2
French Cl. P St J	133	E4
Frenchay Cl. Bris	51	E4
Frenchay Hill. Bris	51	E4
Frenchay Park Rd. Bris	50	C3
Frenchay Rd. W-S-M	104	C3
Frenchfield Rd. P St J	133	E4
Freshford La. Hi Cha	120	A3
Freshland Way. Bris	64	A2
Freshmoor. Cleve	57	F2
Friar Ave. W-S-M	88	C2
Friary Cl. Cleve	57	E3
Friary Cl. Westw	120	C2
Friary Grange Park. Wint	37	F3
Friary Rd. Bris	49	D2
Friary Rd. Portis	45	D3
Friendly Row. E in G	47	E3
Friendship Gr. Nail	59	F1
Friendship Rd. Bris	64	A1
Friendship Rd. Nail	59	F2
Friezewood Rd. Bris	63	D2
Fripp Cl. Bris	64	A3
Frith La. Yate	17	F2
Frobisher Ave. Portb	45	D3
Frobisher Cl. W-S-M	88	C2
Frobisher Rd. Bris	63	D2
Frog La. Bris	63	D3
Frog La. Co Mar	111	E1
Frog La. Nib	5	E3
Frog La. Win	94	B4
Frog La. Wint	37	D4
Frog La. Yate	38	C4
Frogmore St. Bris	63	E3
Frome Ct. Thorn	15	E4
Frome Glen. Wint	37	F2
Frome Old Rd. Rad	133	D1
Frome Pl. Bris	50	C3
Frome Rd. Ch Sod	28	A1
Frome Rd. Kilm	139	E4
Frome Rd. N St P	135	F2
Frome Rd. Rad	133	D1
Frome St. Bris	63	F4
Frome Terr. Bris	50	C3
Frome Valley Rd. Bris	50	C3
Frome View. Fr Cot	38	A4
Frome Way. Wint	37	F3
Fromeside Park. Bris	51	D4
Fromside Cl. Chur	108	C2
Froomshaw Rd. Bris	51	D4
Frost Hill. Yatt	91	E4
Fry's Cl. Bris	50	B2
Fry's La. Blag	109	F2
Fry's Well. Chil	137	E2
Fry's Hill. Kingsw	51	F1
Fryth House. Wrax	60	B2
Fryth Way. Nail	59	E1
Gibson Rd. Bris	49	E1
Fulford Rd. Bris	79	D3
Fulford Wlk. Bris	79	D3
Fullens Cl. W-S-M	105	E4
Fuller Rd. Bath	85	E1
Fullers La. Wins	125	D3
Fullers Way. Bath	101	E4
Fulmar Cl. Thorn	8	B1
Fulmar Rd. W-S-M	88	C1
Fulwell Cl. Faulk	134	B1
Fulwell La. Faulk	134	B1
Furber Cl. Bris	65	D3
Furber Rd. Bris	65	D3
Furber Ridge. Bris	65	D3
Furber Vale. Bris	65	D3
Furland Rd. W-S-M	88	B1
Furlong Cl. Mid No	137	F4
Furnleaze. Clut	114	B2
Furnwood. Bris	65	D3
Furze Cl. W-S-M	88	A1
Furze Rd. Bris	51	E2
Furze Rd. W-S-M	88	A2
Furzewood Rd. Kingsw	65	F4
Fussell Ct. Kingsw	65	F4
Fylton Croft. Bris	80	A2
Gable Cl. Alm	23	D1
Gable Rd. Bris	50	A1
Gables Cl. Ban	107	D2
Gadshill Dr. St Gif	36	C3
Gadshill Rd. Bris	50	B1
Gages Cl. Kingsw	66	C3
Gages Rd. Kingsw	65	F3
Gainsborough Dr. W-S-M	88	C2
Gainsborough Gdns. Bath	101	E4
Gainsborough Rd. Keyn	81	F3
Gainsborough Sq. Bris	50	A4
Gallivan Cl. St Gif	36	A4
Galway Rd. Bris	63	E4
Gambril La. Crom	9	F3
Gander Cl. Bris	79	D3
Garden Cl. Bris	48	A3
Gardeners Wlk. Lo Ash	62	A1
Gardens Rd. Cleve	57	E2
Gardens The. Kingsw	51	E2
Gardner Ave. Bris	78	C4
Gardner Rd. Portis	45	E3
Garfield Rd. Bris	65	D4
Garner Cl. W-S-M	89	D2
Garnet St. Bris	63	D2
Garnett Pl. Mang	51	F4
Garonor Way. E in G	46	C3
Garrett Dr. St Gif	36	B4
Garrick Rd. Bath	100	C3
Garsdale Rd. W-S-M	105	E4
Garston La. Blag	110	C2
Garstons Cl. Wring	92	C1
Garstons Orch. Wring	92	B1
Garstons The. Portis	45	E2
Garstons. Bathf	86	B1
Garstons. Cleve	73	D4
Garstons. Wring	92	C1
Garth Rd. Bris	79	D4
Gas La. Bris	64	A3
Gasferry Rd. Bris	63	D3
Gaskins The. Bris	50	A4
Gaston Ave. Keyn	81	F3
Gastons The. Bris	48	A4
Gatcombe Dr. St Gif	36	C2
Gatcombe Rd. Bris	79	D3
Gatehouse Ave. Bris	79	D3
Gatehouse Cl. Bris	79	D3
Gatesby Mead. St Gif	36	C3
Gathorne Rd. Bris	63	D3
Gatton Rd. Bris	50	A1
Gaunt's Earthcott La. Alve	25	D3
Gaunts Cl. Bris	23	D1
Gaunts Ct. Portis	44	C2
Gaunts Rd. Ch Sod	44	A3
Gay Elms Rd. Bris	79	D2
Gay St. Bath	101	F4
Gays Hill. Bath	102	A4
Gayner Rd. Bris	36	A1
Gays Rd. Kingsw	65	D2
Gaythorne Cres. Yate	27	E1
Gazelle Rd. W-S-M	105	D2
Gazzard Cl. Wint	37	F4
Gazzard Rd. Wint	37	F4
Gee Moors. Kingsw	66	A3
Geldof Dr. Mid No	132	A1
Gefle Cl. Bris	63	D3
Geoffrey Cl. Bris	78	C3
George & Dragon La. Bris	64	B4
George La. Marsh	55	F1
George St. Bath	101	F4
George St. Bris	64	B4
George St. Portis	45	E1
George St. W-S-M	104	C4
George's Bldgs. Bath	102	A4
George Whitefield Ct. Bris	63	F4
George's Bldgs. Bath	102	A4
George's Rd. Bath	85	D1
Georgian View. Bath	101	E1
Gerald Rd. Bris	63	D2
Gerard Rd. W-S-M	104	C4
Gerrish Ave. Bris	64	B4
Gerrish Ave. Mang	51	F3
Gibbet La. Whit	80	B1
Gibbets Brow. Priddy	128	A2
Gibbsfold Rd. Bris	79	E2
Gibson Rd. Bris	49	E1
Gifford Cl. Bris	34	C3
Gifford Cl. Wickw	27	D4
Gifford Cres. St Gif	36	B3
Gifford Rd. Bris	34	C2
Gilbeck Rd. Nail	59	E1
Gilbert Rd. Bris	64	B4
Gilbert Rd. Kingsw	51	E1
Gilberyn Dr. W-S-M	89	D2
Gilda Cl. Bris	80	B3
Gilda Cres. Bris	80	A3
Gilda Par. Bris	80	B3
Gilda Sq W. Bris	80	A3
Gill Ave. Bris	51	D3
Gill Mews. W-S-M	89	D2
Gillard Cl. Bris	65	D4
Gillard Rd. Bris	65	D4
Gillebank Cl. Bris	80	B2
Gillingham Hill. Bris	65	D3
Gillingham Terr. Bath	85	D1
Gillingstool. Thorn	15	E4
Gillmore Cl. W-S-M	88	B1
Gillmore Rd. W-S-M	88	B1
Gillray Cl. Bris	50	A3
Gilpin Cl. Lock	105	E1
Gilpin Cl. Kingsw	51	F1
Gilroy Cl. Kingsw	66	A2
Gilslake Ave. Bris	35	D2
Gimblet Rd. W-S-M	89	D2
Gingell's Green. Bris	65	D4
Gipsy Patch La. St Gif	36	B3
Glades The. Bris	50	C1
Gladstone Dr. Kingsw	51	F2
Gladstone La. Fr Cot	38	B4
Gladstone Rd. Bath	102	B1
Gladstone Rd. Bris	80	A3
Gladstone Rd. Kingsw	51	E1
Gladstone St. Bris	63	D2
Gladstone St. Bris	64	B4
Gladstone St. Kingsw	51	F2
Gladstone St. Mid No	132	A2
Glaisdale Rd. Bris	51	D3
Glanville Dr. Hn Ble	129	F3
Glanville Gdns. Kingsw	65	F4
Glass House La. Bris	64	A3
Glastonbury Cl. Kingsw	65	F3
Glastonbury Cl. Nail	60	A1
Glebe Ave. Portis	45	F2
Glebe Field. Alm	34	A4
Glebe Rd. Bath	101	D2
Glebe Rd. Bris	64	C4
Glebe Rd. Cleve	57	E1
Glebe Rd. Lo Ash	62	B1
Glebe Rd. Portis	45	F2
Glebe Rd. W-S-M	104	C3
Glebe The. Ch Cha	120	A2
Glebe The. Hin Cha	119	E1
Glebe The. Piln	22	B4
Glebe The. Tims	116	A2
Glebe The. Wring	92	C1
Glebe Wlk. Keyn	81	E2
Glebelands Rd. Bris	36	A2
Glebelands. Rad	132	B1
Gledemoor Dr. Fr Cot	38	B4
Glen Ave. Ab Lei	61	F4
Glen Dr. Bris	48	B3
Glen Park Gdns. Bris	65	D4
Glen Park. Bris	50	B1
Glen Park. Bris	65	D4
Glen The. Bris	49	F2
Glen The. Keyn	82	C1
Glen The. Kingsw	65	D2
Glen The. W-S-M	88	A1
Glen The. Wring	92	C3
Glena Ave. Bris	79	F4
Glenarm Rd. Bris	64	C1
Glenarm Wlk. Bris	64	C1
Glenavon Park. Bris	48	B2
Glencairn Cl. Bris	64	A2
Glencoyne Sq. Bris	35	E1
Glendale. Bris	51	E2
Glendale. Bris	65	D4
Glendare St. Bris	64	B3
Glendevon Rd. Bris	79	E2
Gleneagles Cl. Nail	60	A1
Gleneagles Cl. W-S-M	88	C2
Gleneagles Dr. Bris	34	B2
Gleneagles Rd. Kingsw	66	A3
Gleneagles. Yate		27
Glenfall. Yate		39
Glenfrome Rd. Bris		50
Glenroy Ave. Bris		51
Glenside Cl. Bris		51
Glenside Park. Bris		50
Glentworth Rd. Bris		49
Glentworth Rd. Bris		63
Glenview Rd. Bris		64
Glenwood Dr. Kingsw		66
Glenwood Rise. Portis		44
Glenwood. Bris		51
Gloster Ave. Bris		51
Gloucester Cl. St Gif		36
Gloucester La. Bris		63
Gloucester Rd N. Bris		36
Gloucester Rd. Alm		24
Gloucester Rd. Avon		33
Gloucester Rd. Bath		85
Gloucester Rd. Bathe		85
Gloucester Rd. Bris		49
Gloucester Rd. Kingsw		51
Gloucester Rd. Thorn		8
Gloucester Row. W-u-E		11
Gloucester St. Bath		101
Gloucester St. Bris		51
Gloucester St. Bris		62
Gloucester St. Bris		63
Gloucester St. W-S-M		104
Glovers Field. Ship		125
Glyn Vale. Bris		63
Goddard Dr. W-S-M		89
Godfrey Ct. Kingsw		65
Goffenton Dr. Bris		51
Goldcrest Rd. Ch Sod		39
Golden La. Kingsw		65
Golden Lion Ct. Bris		11
Golden Valley La. Bitt		66
Goldfinch Way. Puck		53
Goldney Ave. Bris		63
Goldney Ave. Sist		66
Goldney Cl. Clut		114
Goldney Rd. Bris		63
Goldney Way. Clut		114
Goldsbury Wlk. Bris		34
Golf Club La. Keyn		99
Golf Course La. Bris		35
Golf Course Rd. Bath		103
Golledge Cl. Chil		137
Gooch Way. W-S-M		89
Good Shepherd Cl. Bris		49
Goodeve Park. Bris		48
Goodeve Rd. Bris		48
Goodhind St. Bris		64
Goodneston Rd. Bris		51
Gooding Hill. Bris		54
Goodwin Dr. Bris		79
Goodwin Dr. Nail		59
Goodwood Gdns. Mang		37
Goold Ct Cor		100
Goolden St. Bris		64
Goosard La. Paul		131
Goose Acre. St Gif		36
Goose Green. Yate		27
Goose Green. Frcot		38
Goose Green. Frcot		38
Gooseland Cl. Bris		79
Goosy La. Lock		89
Gordano Gaine. E in G		47
Gordano Rd. E in G		46
Gordano View. Portis		45
Gordano Way. E in G		46
Gordon Ave. Bris		51
Gordon Cl. Bris		50
Gordon Rd. Bath		102
Gordon Rd. Bris		63
Gordon Rd. Bris		64
Gordon Rd. P St J		133
Gordon Rd. W-S-M		104
Gore Rd. Bris		63
Gore's Marsh Rd. Bris		63
Gorham Cl. Bris		34
Gorlands Rd. Ch Sod		28
Gorlangton Cl. Bris		80
Gorse Cover Rd. Piln		22
Gorse Hill. Bris		51
Gorse La. Bris		63
Gorse La. Co Ash		68
Gorse La. Marsh		54
Gosforth Rd. Bris		35
Goslet Rd. Bris		80
Goss Barton. Nail		59
Goss Cl. Nail		59
Goss La. Nail		59
Goss View. Nail		59
Gotley Rd. Bris		64
Gott Dr. Bris		64
Goulston Rd. Bris		79
Goulston Wlk. Bris		79
Goulter St. Bris		64
Gournay Cl. Paul		131
Gourney Ct. Bris		34
Grace Cl. Ch Sod		28
Grace Cl. Yatt		91

ace Ct. Mang ... 51 E3
ace Dr. Kingsw ... 66 A4
ace Dr. Mid No ... 132 A1
ace Park Rd. Bris ... 64 B1
ace Rd. Mang ... 51 E3
ace Rd. W-S-M ... 89 D2
adwell Cl. W-S-M ... 89 D2
aeme Cl. Bris ... 51 D2
aham Rd. Bris ... 50 A1
aham Rd. Bris ... 63 E2
aham Rd. Mang ... 51 F3
aham Rd. W-S-M ... 104 C4
ainger Ct. Bris ... 47 F4
aitney Cl. Brock ... 92 A4
ampian Ct. Kingsw ... 66 B2
anby Hill. Bris ... 62 C3
and Par. Bath ... 102 A3
andmother's Rock La.
  Bitt ... 67 E1
ange Ave. Kingsw ... 65 E3
ange Ave. St Gif ... 36 B3
ange Cl N. Bris ... 49 D3
ange Cl. St Gif ... 24 B1
ange Cl. W-S-M ... 104 C1
ange Court Rd. Bris ... 49 D3
ange Ct. Kingsw ... 65 E3
ange Dr. Bris ... 51 E3
ange End. Rod ... 138 A4
ange Park. Bris ... 49 D3
ange Park. Bris ... 51 E4
ange Rd. Bris ... 63 D4
ange Rd. Bris ... 79 D3
ange Rd. Keyn ... 82 B2
ange Rd. W-S-M ... 104 C1
ange The. Bris ... 48 B4
angeville Ct. Kingsw ... 66 A2
angewood Cl. Bris ... 51 E3
inny's La. Kingsw ... 65 F3
intham La. Bris ... 65 E4
intham Rd. Bris ... 51 E1
intson Cl. Bris ... 64 C1
inville Ct. Kingsw ... 65 D2
inville Rd. Bath ... 84 C2
inville St. Bris ... 64 B3
inville Cl. Bris ... 49 D4
ismere Dr. W-S-M ... 104 C2
ss Meers Dr. Bris ... 80 A2
ssington Dr. Ch Sod ... 40 A4
ssmere Gdns. Kingsw ... 66 B3
ssmere Rd. Yatt ... 91 D4
ltitude Rd. Bris ... 50 B1
vel Hill Rd. Yate ... 28 A3
vel Hill. Ch S ... 112 A4
vel Hill. Win ... 112 A4
eney Cl. Bris ... 64 B1
y's Cl. Bris ... 34 C1
ile Rd. Bris ... 35 D1
es Hill. Well ... 134 C4
t Ann St. Bris ... 63 F4
st Bedford St. Bath ... 101 F4
t Brockeridge. Bris ... 48 C3
t Dowles. Kingsw ... 66 A2
t George St. Bris ... 63 D3
t George St. Bris ... 63 F4
t Hayles Rd. Bris ... 80 A4
t Leaze. Kingsw ... 66 A2
t Meadow Rd. St Gif ... 36 C3
t Meadow. St Gif ... 37 D3
t Park Rd. St Gif ... 24 B2
t Pulteney St. Bath ... 102 A4
t Stanhope St. Bath ... 101 F3
t Stoke Way. St Gif ... 36 B2
t Stoke. St Gif ... 37 D3
Western Bridge.
  S-M ... 104 C4
t Western La. Bris ... 64 A3
t Western Rd. Cleve ... 57 E3
t Western Way. Bris ... 63 F3
stone La. Win ... 94 C3
n Cl. Bris ... 50 A4
t Croft. Bris ... 51 D1
t Dell Cl. Bris ... 34 B2
t Ditch La. Chil ... 137 D3
t Ditch La. Ston E ... 137 D3
t Dragon Rd. Wint ... 37 E3
t Hayes. Ch Sod ... 40 B4
t La. Avon ... 33 D1
t La. But ... 94 B2
t La. But ... 111 D4
t La. But ... 137 F1
t La. Hin Cha ... 119 F1
t La. Marsh ... 69 F4
t La. Paul ... 130 C3
t La. Thorn ... 16 A3
t La. Win ... 94 B2
t La. Wrax ... 61 E2
Park Rd. Bath ... 101 F3
t Park. Bath ... 101 F3
t Parlour Rd. Kilm ... 133 E1
Side. Mang ... 52 A3
t St. Bath ... 102 A2
t St. Bris ... 63 F2
t Well ... 133 F3
The. Back ... 75 F3
The. Bath ... 101 E1
The. Crom ... 17 D4
The. E in G ... 47 E2
The. Hin Cha ... 119 F1

Green The. Kingsw ... 51 F1
Green The. Lock ... 106 A2
Green The. Olve ... 14 A1
Green The. St Gif ... 36 C2
Green The. Wins ... 125 D4
Green Tree Rd. Mid No ... 132 A2
Green Wlk. Bris ... 64 A1
Greenacre Rd. Bris ... 80 A2
Greenacre. W-S-M ... 88 A1
Greenacres. Bath ... 84 A2
Greenacres. Bris ... 48 C4
Greenacres. Mid No ... 131 F1
Greenbank Ave W. Bris ... 50 B1
Greenbank Ave. Bris ... 50 B1
Greenbank Gdns. Bath ... 84 A1
Greenbank Rd. Bris ... 50 B1
Greenbank Rd. Bris ... 63 D2
Greenbank Rd. Kingsw ... 50 B1
Greenbank View. Bris ... 50 B1
Greendale Rd. Bris ... 49 D2
Greendale Rd. Bris ... 63 F1
Greenditch Ave. Bris ... 79 E3
Greenditch Cl. Chil ... 137 E2
Greenditch St. Pltn ... 13 E1
Greendown Pl. Bath ... 102 A1
Greendown. Bris ... 65 D4
Greenfield Ave. Bris ... 48 C4
Greenfield Cres. Nail ... 59 F2
Greenfield Park. Portis ... 45 E2
Greenfield Pl. W-S-M ... 104 B4
Greenfield. Bris ... 35 E1
Greenfields Ave. Ban ... 107 D2
Greenfinch Lodge. Bris ... 50 C3
Greenhaven. Bris ... 50 B1
Greenhill Cl. Nail ... 59 E1
Greenhill Down. Alve ... 15 D2
Greenhill Gdns. Alve ... 15 D2
Greenhill La. Alve ... 15 D2
Greenhill La. Bris ... 34 B1
Greenhill La. Wins ... 108 A2
Greenhill Par. Alve ... 15 D3
Greenhill Pl. Mid No ... 132 A2
Greenhill Rd. Alve ... 15 D3
Greenhill. Alve ... 15 D2
Greenland Rd. W-S-M ... 88 B1
Greenlands Rd. P St J ... 133 E4
Greenlands Way. Bris ... 34 C2
Greenleaze Way. Mang ... 37 F1
Greenleaze. Bris ... 64 A1
Greenmore Rd. Bris ... 64 A1
Greenore. Kingsw ... 65 E4
Greenpark Rd. Bris ... 35 F1
Greenridge Cl. Bris ... 78 C2
Greenridge. Clut ... 114 C2
Greenside Cl. Bris ... 34 A2
Greenslade Gdns. Nail ... 59 E2
Greensplott Rd. Avon ... 33 F4
Greenvale Cl. Tims ... 116 A1
Greenvale Dr. Tims ... 116 A1
Greenvale Rd. Paul ... 131 E3
Greenvale. Tims ... 116 A1
Greenview. Kingsw ... 66 A1
Greenway Bush La. Bris ... 63 D2
Greenway Ct. Bath ... 101 F2
Greenway Dr. Bris ... 49 E4
Greenway La. Bath ... 102 A1
Greenway La. Co Ash ... 68 C3
Greenway Park. Bris ... 49 E4
Greenway Park. Cleve ... 57 F2
Greenway Rd. Bris ... 49 D1
Greenway The. Bris ... 51 E2
Greenways Rd. Yate ... 27 F2
Greenways. Chil ... 137 E1
Greenways. Kingsw ... 52 A1
Greenwich La. Chur ... 109 E4
Greenwood Cl. Bris ... 51 D1
Greenwood Dr. Alve ... 14 C2
Greenwood Rd. Bris ... 64 A1
Greenwood Rd. W-S-M ... 88 C1
Gregory Ct. Bris ... 66 A3
Gregorys Tyning. Paul ... 131 F3
Greinton. W-S-M ... 105 D1
Grenville Ave. Lock ... 106 A4
Grenville Cl. Bris ... 64 C4
Grenville Pl. Bris ... 62 C3
Grenville Rd. Bris ... 49 F2
Greve Cl. Kingsw ... 65 F3
Greville Rd. Bris ... 63 D2
Greville St. Bris ... 63 D2
Grey Hollow. E Harp ... 128 C2
Greyfield Comm. Paul ... 115 E1
Greyfield Rd. Paul ... 115 E1
Greyfield View. Clut ... 114 C1
Greylands Rd. Bris ... 78 C4
Greystoke Ave. Bris ... 35 E1
Greystoke Gdns. Bris ... 49 D4
Greystones. Mang ... 37 F1
Grib La. Blag ... 110 C1
Griffin Cl. W-S-M ... 89 D1
Griffin Rd. Cleve ... 57 F2
Griggfield Wlk. Bris ... 80 A4
Grimsbury Rd. Kingsw ... 66 A4
Grindell Rd. Bris ... 64 B4

Grinfield Ave. Bris ... 79 E2
Grinfield Cl. Bris ... 79 E2
Grinfield Ct. Bris ... 79 E2
Gritleton Rd. Bris ... 49 F4
Grosvenor Bridge Rd. Bath ... 85 E1
Grosvenor Park. Bath ... 85 E1
Grosvenor Pl. Bath ... 85 E1
Grosvenor Rd. Bris ... 63 F3
Grove Ave. Bris ... 48 B4
Grove Ave. Bris ... 50 C2
Grove Ave. Bris ... 63 E3
Grove Bank. Bris ... 37 E1
Grove Ind Est The. Bris ... 36 A4
Grove La. Dyrh ... 54 B3
Grove La. Faulk ... 134 B1
Grove La. W-S-M ... 104 B4
Grove Leaze. Bris ... 47 E3
Grove Park Ave. Bris ... 64 B1
Grove Park Rd. Bris ... 64 B1
Grove Park Rd. W-S-M ... 87 E1
Grove Park Terr. Bris ... 50 C2
Grove Park. Bris ... 49 E1
Grove Pk. Bris ... 64 B1
Grove Rd. Bris ... 48 B4
Grove Rd. Bris ... 49 D1
Grove Rd. Bris ... 50 C2
Grove Rd. W-S-M ... 88 B1
Grove Rd. W-S-M ... 104 B4
Grove St. Bath ... 102 A4
Grove The. Bris ... 62 B2
Grove The. Kingsw ... 66 A2
Grove The. Wickw ... 27 D4
Grove The. Winsc ... 107 F1
Grove The. Wrax ... 60 B2
Grove View. Bris ... 50 C3
Grove Wood Rd. Rod ... 138 C4
Grovesend Rd. Thorn ... 15 E4
Guernsey Ave. Bris ... 64 C2
Gug The. Paul ... 115 E1
Guildford Rd. Bris ... 64 C3
Guinea La. Bath ... 101 F4
Guinea La. Bris ... 51 D2
Guinea St. Bris ... 63 E3
Gullen. Wall ... 134 A3
Guilliford's Bank. Cleve ... 57 F1
Gullimores Gdns. Bris ... 79 D2
Gullivers Pl. Ch Sod ... 40 A4
Gullon Wlk. Bris ... 78 C3
Gullons Cl. Bris ... 79 D3
Gully La. Rock ... 8 C4
Gully The. Wint ... 37 F4
Gullybrook La. Bris ... 64 A3
Gunter's Hill. Bris ... 65 D3
Guthrie Rd. Bris ... 63 D4
Gwilliam St. Bris ... 63 E3
Gwyn St. Bris ... 49 F1
Gypsy La. Keyn ... 99 D4

Haberfield Hill. Ab Lei ... 47 F1
Habield Cl. Bris ... 48 B2
Hacket La. Thorn ... 15 F4
Hadley Cl. Kingsw ... 66 A3
Hadley Rd. Bath ... 102 A1
Hagg Hill. Tims ... 116 A1
Hague Cl. Bris ... 50 C1
Haig Cl. Bris ... 48 A4
Halbrow Cres. Bris ... 51 E3
Haldon Cl. Bris ... 63 E4
Hales Horn Cl. St Gif ... 36 B3
Half Yd. Wring ... 109 E4
Halfacre Cl. Bris ... 80 A2
Halfacre La. Bris ... 80 A2
Halfpenny Row. Rode ... 136 C1
Halifax Rd. Yate ... 27 E2
Hall End La. Yate ... 17 E1
Hall La. Co Ash ... 68 A2
Hall La. Co Ash ... 68 C2
Hall La. Hort ... 29 F3
Hall St. Bris ... 63 D1
Hallam Rd. Cleve ... 57 E2
Hallards Ct. Bris ... 47 E3
Hallatrow Rd. Paul ... 131 E3
Hallen Cl. Bris ... 34 B2
Hallen Dr. Bris ... 48 B4
Hallen Rd. Bris ... 34 B2
Halletts Way. Portis ... 45 E3
Halliwell Rd. Portis ... 45 E4
Halls Rd. Kingsw ... 65 E4
Halsbury Rd. Bris ... 49 D2
Halstock Ave. Bris ... 50 C2
Halston Dr. Bris ... 63 F4
Halswell Gdns. Bris ... 79 D2
Halswell Rd. Cleve ... 57 E1
Halt End. Whit ... 80 B2
Ham Cl. Clut ... 114 C1
Ham Gr. Paul ... 131 F4
Ham Green. E in G ... 47 F2
Ham La. Bi Sut ... 113 E3
Ham La. Bris ... 50 C3
Ham La. Dun ... 78 B2
Ham La. K Sey ... 72 C1
Ham La. O-on-S ... 7 E3
Ham La. Paul ... 130 C3
Ham La. Paul ... 131 F3
Ham La. Wick ... 53 F1
Ham La. Wrax ... 60 A2
Ham La. Yatt ... 74 A2

Ham Link. Blag ... 109 F2
Ham Rd. Berr ... 121 D2
Ham Wood Cl. W-S-M ... 105 D1
Hamble Cl. Thorn ... 15 E4
Hambledon Rd. Lock ... 89 E2
Hambrook La. Bris ... 37 D2
Hambrook La. St Gif ... 37 D2
Hamersmith Rd. Bris ... 64 B4
Hamilton Rd. Bath ... 84 C4
Hamilton Rd. Bris ... 63 D2
Hamilton Rd. Bris ... 64 A4
Hamilton Rd. W-S-M ... 87 E1
Hamlet The. Nail ... 60 A2
Hammer La. Faulk ... 135 E1
Hammond Cl. Bris ... 64 C4
Hammond Gdns. Bris ... 48 C4
Hampden Cl. Yate ... 27 E2
Hampden Rd. Bris ... 64 A2
Hampden Rd. W-S-M ... 88 C1
Hampshire Way. Yate ... 27 F2
Hampstead Rd. Bris ... 64 B2
Hampton Cl. Kingsw ... 66 A3
Hampton Cnr. Bris ... 47 F3
Hampton La. Bris ... 49 D1
Hampton Park. Bris ... 49 D1
Hampton Rd. Bris ... 49 D1
Hampton Row. Bath ... 102 A4
Hampton St. Kingsw ... 51 E1
Hampton View. Bath ... 85 D1
Hams La. Badg ... 123 E1
Hams Rd. Keyn ... 81 F4
Hanbury Cl. Kingsw ... 65 E3
Hanbury Rd. Bris ... 63 D4
Handel Ave. Bris ... 64 B4
Handel Rd. Keyn ... 81 F3
Handford Way. Kingsw ... 66 A2
Hanford Ct. Bris ... 65 D4
Hang Hill. Well ... 134 A3
Hanham Bsns Pk. Kingsw ... 65 D3
Hanham La. Paul ... 131 F4
Hanham Rd. Kingsw ... 65 E4
Hanham Way. Nail ... 59 E1
Hannah More Cl. Wring ... 92 C1
Hannah More Rd. Nail ... 75 E4
Hanny's La. Ch Mag ... 96 A2
Hanover Cl. W-S-M ... 89 D2
Hanover Ct. Bris ... 63 F4
Hanover Ct. Rad ... 133 E1
Hanover Pl. Bris ... 63 D3
Hanover St. Bath ... 85 D1
Hanover St. Bris ... 63 E3
Hanover St. Bris ... 64 B4
Hansford Cl. Bath ... 101 F1
Hansford Sq. Bath ... 101 F1
Hanson's Way. Cleve ... 57 E1
Hapenny La. E in G ... 47 E1
Hapstog Cl. W-S-M ... 89 D2
Harbour Rd. Portis ... 45 E3
Harbour Wall. Bris ... 48 B2
Harbour Way. Bris ... 63 E3
Harbury Rd. Bris ... 49 E4
Harbutts. Bath ... 85 F1
Harcombe Hill. Wint ... 37 F3
Harcombe Rd. Wint ... 37 E3
Harcourt Ave. Bris ... 65 D3
Harcourt Cl. Keyn ... 82 C1
Harcourt Gdns. Bath ... 84 A1
Harcourt Hill. Bris ... 49 D2
Harcourt Rd. Bris ... 49 D2
Harden Rd. Bris ... 80 C3
Hardenhuish Rd. Bris ... 64 B3
Harding Pl. Keyn ... 82 A3
Hardington Dr. Keyn ... 82 A2
Hardwick Cl. Bath ... 102 C2
Hardwick Cl. Bris ... 66 B3
Hardwick Rd. E in G ... 47 E3
Hardwicke. Yate ... 39 E4
Hardy Ave. Bris ... 63 D2
Hardy Ct. Kingsw ... 65 F4
Hardy La. Olive ... 14 A1
Hardy Rd. Bris ... 63 D1
Haredive Rd. Bris ... 79 E2
Harefield Cl. Kingsw ... 65 E1
Harescombe. Yate ... 39 F3
Harewood Rd. Bris ... 51 D1
Harford Cl. Bris ... 48 B4
Harford Dr. Bris ... 37 E1
Harford La. Bath ... 96 A3
Harford Sq. Ch Mag ... 96 A2
Harington Pl. Bath ... 101 F3
Harlech Way. Kingsw ... 65 E3
Harleston La. Bris ... 64 A4
Harley La. Cleve ... 58 B3
Harley St. Bath ... 101 F4
Harmer Cl. Bris ... 34 A4
Harmony Dr. Portis ... 44 C2
Harnhill Cl. Bris ... 79 D2
Harolds Way. Kingsw ... 65 E3
Harptree Cl. Kingsw ... 65 E3
Harptree Gr. Bris ... 63 D1
Harptree Hill. E Harp ... 128 A3
Harptree. W-S-M ... 105 D1
Harrier Path. W-S-M ... 105 F4
Harrington Ave. Bris ... 80 C3
Harrington Gr. Bris ... 80 C3
Harrington Rd. Bris ... 80 C3
Harrington Wlk. Bris ... 80 C3
Harris Barton. Fr Cot ... 38 A4

Harris Ct. Kingsw ... 65 F2
Harris La. Ab Lei ... 61 F4
Harrow Rd. Bris ... 64 B2
Harrowdene Rd. Bris ... 64 A2
Harry Stoke Rd. St Gif ... 36 C1
Hart's La. Paul ... 131 D4
Hartcliffe Rd. Bris ... 79 F4
Hartcliffe Way. Bris ... 79 E4
Hartcliffe Wlk. Bris ... 79 F4
Hartcombe Rd. E in G ... 47 D1
Hartfield Ave. Bris ... 49 E1
Hartgill Cl. Bris ... 79 D2
Hartington Park. Bris ... 49 E1
Hartland. W-S-M ... 89 D1
Hartley Cl. Ch Sod ... 28 A1
Harts Paddock. Mid No ... 131 F2
Harvey Cl. W-S-M ... 88 D2
Harveys La. Bris ... 64 C4
Harwood Gdns. W-S-M ... 88 C2
Haselbury Gr. Keyn ... 82 C1
Haskins Cl. Kingsw ... 66 A3
Haslands. Nail ... 75 E4
Haslemere Ind Est. Avon ... 33 E1
Hassage Hill. Well ... 134 C4
Hassell Dr. Bris ... 64 A4
Hastings Cl. Bris ... 63 E1
Hastings Rd. Bris ... 63 E1
Hatchet Hill. Kilm ... 139 F2
Hatchet La. St Gif ... 36 C2
Hatchet Rd. St Gif ... 36 C3
Hatchmere. Thorn ... 15 E4
Hatfield Bldgs. Bath ... 102 A3
Hatfield Rd. Bath ... 101 F2
Hatfield Rd. W-S-M ... 105 D4
Hatherley Rd. Bris ... 49 F2
Hatherley. Yate ... 39 F4
Hathway Wlk. Bris ... 64 A4
Hatters' La. Ch Sod ... 28 A1
Havage Dro. Ban ... 107 E4
Haven The. Kingsw ... 51 F1
Haversham Cl. W-S-M ... 88 B1
Haverstock Rd. Bris ... 64 A2
Haviland Gr. Bath ... 84 A2
Haviland Park. Bath ... 84 A1
Havory. Bath ... 85 E1
Hevyat Rd. Wring ... 109 F4
Haw La. Olve ... 14 A2
Hawarden Terr. Bath ... 85 D1
Hawburn Ct. Bris ... 64 B1
Haweswater Cl. Kingsw ... 66 B3
Hawke Rd. W-S-M ... 88 C2
Hawkesbury Rd. Bris ... 50 C2
Hawkesbury Rd. Hill ... 19 F4
Hawkesley Dr. St Gif ... 36 B3
Hawkfield Cl. Bris ... 79 E3
Hawkfield Rd. Bris ... 79 E3
Hawkfield Way. Bris ... 79 E3
Hawkins Cl. Kingsw ... 66 B3
Hawkins St. Bris ... 63 F4
Hawkley Dr. St Gif ... 24 B2
Hawkridge Dr. Puck ... 53 E3
Hawksmoor Cl. Bris ... 80 A3
Hawksworth Dr. Kingsw ... 65 D3
Hawksworth Dr. W-S-M ... 89 D2
Hawlyn Cl. Bris ... 48 B3
Hawthorn Ave. Kingsw ... 65 D3
Hawthorn Cl. Bris ... 35 F4
Hawthorn Cl. Chur ... 11 D2
Hawthorn Coombe. W-S-M ... 88 C2
Hawthorn Cres. Thorn ... 8 B1
Hawthorn Cres. Yatt ... 74 A1
Hawthorn Gdns. W-S-M ... 88 B1
Hawthorn Gr. Bath ... 101 F1
Hawthorn Hill. W-S-M ... 88 C1
Hawthorn Hts. W-S-M ... 88 B1
Hawthorn Park. W-S-M ... 88 C2
Hawthorn Rd. Rad ... 133 D1
Hawthorn Way. Nail ... 60 A1
Hawthorn Way. St Gif ... 36 C2
Hawthorne Cl. Puck ... 53 E3
Hawthorne Gdns. Kingsw ... 51 F2
Hawthorne Ms. Keyn ... 81 F3
Hawthorns The. Kingsw ... 51 F1
Hawthorns La. Keyn ... 81 F3
Hay Hill. Bath ... 101 F4
Hay La. Win ... 94 B3
Hay Leaze. Yate ... 27 E2
Hay St. Marsh ... 70 A4
Hay St. Ston E ... 137 D4
Haycombe Dr. Bath ... 101 D2
Haycombe La. Engl ... 100 C2
Haycombe. Bris ... 79 F3
Haycroft La. Newp ... 4 B3
Haycroft Rd. Bris ... 36 A2
Hayden Cl. Bath ... 101 F3
Haydock Cl. Mang ... 37 F1
Haydon Gate. Rod ... 138 C4
Haydon Gdns. Bris ... 50 A3
Hayeley Dr. St Gif ... 36 C3
Hayes Cl. Bris ... 64 A4
Hayes La. Gr Bad ... 30 C1
Hayes Park Rd. Mid No ... 131 F3
Hayes Rd. Mid No ... 131 F3
Hayesfield Park. Bath ... 101 F3
Hayeswood Rd. Farm ... 115 F2

Hayeswood Rd. Tims 116 A1
Hayfield. Marsh 70 A4
Hayleigh House. Bris 79 E2
Haymarket The. Bris 63 E4
Haymarket Wlk. Bris 63 E4
Haynes La. Mang 51 E3
Haythorn Cl. Mang 51 F3
Haytor Park. Bris 48 B3
Hayward Cl. Cleve 57 E1
Hayward Rd. Bris 64 B4
Hayward Rd. Kingsw 51 E2
Haywood Cl. W-S-M 105 D1
Haywood Gdns. W-S-M 105 D1
Hazel Ave. Bris 49 D1
Hazel Cres. Thorn 8 B1
Hazel Gdns. Alve 14 C2
Hazel Gr. Bath 101 E2
Hazel Gr. Bris 50 A4
Hazel La. Clve 14 C2
Hazel Terr. Rod 138 B4
Hazelbury Dr. Kingsw 66 A3
Hazelbury Rd. Nail 59 E1
Hazelcote Rd. Bris 80 A2
Hazeldene Rd. Bris 36 A4
Hazeldene Rd. W-S-M 105 D4
Hazell Cl. Cleve 57 F1
Hazelton Rd. Bris 49 E2
Hazelwood Ct. Bris 48 B2
Hazelwood Rd. Bris 48 B2
Hazleton Gdns. Bath 102 C2
Headford Ave. Bris 65 D4
Headford Rd. Bris 63 E1
Headley La. Bris 79 D3
Headley Park Ave. Bris 79 D4
Headley Park Rd. Bris 79 D4
Headley Rd. Bris 79 D4
Headley Wlk. Bris 79 D4
Healey Dr. Dyrh 54 B3
Heart Meers. Bris 80 A3
Heath Cl. Wint 37 F3
Heath Cl. Mang 51 E4
Heath Cl. W-S-M 105 F4
Heath Gdns. Fr Cot 38 B3
Heath Gdns. Mang 51 E4
Heath Rd. Bris 50 A2
Heath Rd. Kingsw 65 F4
Heath Rd. Mang 51 E4
Heath Rd. Nail 59 F2
Heath Ridge. Lo Ash 62 A1
Heath Rise. Kingsw 66 A3
Heath St. Bris 50 B2
Heath Wlk. Mang 51 E4
Heathcote Dr. Fr Cot 38 B4
Heathcote La. Fr Cot 38 B4
Heathcote Rd. Bris 51 D1
Heathcote Rd. Mang 51 F3
Heathcote Wlk. Bris 51 D1
Heather Ave. Fr Cot 38 A3
Heather Cl. Bris 65 D4
Heatherdene. Bris 79 F4
Heathfield Cl. Bath 84 A2
Heathfield Cl. Keyn 81 E3
Heathfield Cres. Bris 80 A2
Heathfield Rd. Nail 59 F2
Heathfield Way. Nail 59 F1
Heathgate. Yatt 91 D4
Hebden Rd. Westw 120 C2
Hebor St. Bris 64 B4
Hebron Rd. Bris 63 E2
Hedgemead Cl. Bris 50 B3
Hedgemead View. Bris 50 C3
Hedges Cl. Cleve 57 D1
Hedges The. Lock 89 E1
Hedwick Ave. Bris 64 C4
Hedwick St. Bris 64 C4
Heggard Cl. Bris 79 D3
Helens Rd. Wins 108 A2
Hellier Wlk. Bris 79 E2
Helston Rd. Nail 60 A1
Hemming Way. Lock 105 F2
Hemmings Par. Bris 64 A4
Hemplow Cl. Bris 80 B4
Hempton La. St Gif 24 A1
Hen La. Win 54 C2
Henacre Rd. Bris 47 F4
Henbury Gdns. Bris 34 C1
Henbury Hill. Bris 34 C1
Henbury Rd. Bris 34 C1
Henbury Rd. Kingsw 65 E2
Hencliffe Rd. Bris 80 B4
Hencliffe Way. Kingsw 65 D2
Henderson Rd. Kingsw 65 D3
Hendre Rd. Bris 63 D1
Henfield Cres. Bris 8 F4
Henfield Cres. Kingsw 66 A2
Henfield Rd. Fr Cot 38 B2
Henfield Rd. West 38 B2
Hengaston St. Bris 63 D1
Hengrove Ave. Bris 80 A4
Hengrove La. Bris 80 A4
Hengrove Rd. Bris 64 A1
Hengrove Way. Bris 79 E3
Henleaze Ave. Bris 49 D3
Henleaze Gdns. Bris 49 D3
Henleaze Park Dr. Bris 49 E3
Henleaze Park. Bris 49 E3
Henleaze Rd. Bris 49 D3
Henleaze Terr. Bris 49 D3
Henley Gr. Bris 49 D3

Henley La. Yatt 91 E4
Henley Lodge. Yatt 91 E4
Henley Park. Yatt 91 E4
Henley View. Yatt 118 B1
Hennessy Cl. Bris 79 F2
Henrietta Gdns. Bath 102 A4
Henrietta Mews. Bath 102 A4
Henrietta Pl. Bath 102 A4
Henrietta Rd. Bath 102 A4
Henrietta St. Bath 102 A4
Henrietta St. Bris 63 E4
Henrietta St. Bris 50 A1
Henry St. Bath 102 A3
Henry St. Bris 63 F2
Henry Williamson Ct.
    Kingsw 66 A3
Henshaw Cl. Bris 51 E1
Henshaw Rd. Bris 51 E1
Henshaw Wlk. Bris 51 E1
Hensley Gdns. Bath 101 F2
Hensley Rd. Bath 101 F2
Hensman's Hill. Bris 63 D3
Hepburn Rd. Bris 49 F1
Herald Cl. Bris 48 B3
Heraspath St. Bris 64 B3
Herbert Cres. Bris 50 B2
Herbert Rd. Bath 101 E3
Herbert Rd. Cleve 57 E2
Herbert Rd. Bris 63 E2
Herbert St. Bris 64 B4
Hercules Cl. St Gif 36 B3
Hereford Rd. Bris 50 A1
Hereford St. Bris 63 F2
Heritage Cl. P St J 133 E4
Herkomer Cl. Bris 36 A4
Herluin Way. W-S-M 105 D3
Hermes Cl. Keyn 82 B1
Hermitage Cl. Bris 47 F4
Hermitage Rd. Bath 84 C1
Hermitage Rd. Mang 51 F3
Hern La. Ba Gu 77 F4
Heron Cl. W-S-M 105 F4
Heron Rd. Bris 50 A1
Heron Way. Ch Sod 41 A4
Heron Gdns. P. Bris 79 D2
Hersey Gdns. Bris 78 C2
Hesding Cl. Kingsw 65 E2
Hestercombe Rd. Bris 79 D3
Heyford Ave. Bris 50 A2
Heyron Wlk. Bris 79 D2
Heywood Rd. E in G 47 E2
Heywood Terr. E in G 47 E2
Hibbs Cl. Marsh 69 F4
Hicks Common Rd. Wint ... 37 F3
Hicks Cl. Kingsw 65 F2
High Acre. Paul 131 F2
High Bannerdown. Bathe ... 86 B4
High Elm. Kingsw 65 F3
High Gr. Bris 48 A4
High Mead Gdns. Bi Suf .. 113 E2
High Meadows. Mid No ... 131 F1
High Park. Bris 64 A1
High Park. Paul 131 A3
High St. Axb 125 D1
High St. Ban 107 D1
High St. Bath 84 A1
High St. Bath 101 D3
High St. Bath 102 A3
High St. Bathe 85 F2
High St. Bathf 86 B1
High St. Bitt 82 C4
High St. Blag 110 B2
High St. Bris 47 E4
High St. Bris 89 D4
High St. Bris 50 A1
High St. Bris 63 E3
High St. Ch Mag 96 A2
High St. Ch Sod 28 A1
High St. Cong 91 E2
High St. Doyn 53 F1
High St. Dyrh 54 B2
High St E Harp 128 C3
High St. Gr Bad 30 C1
High St. H Up 19 F1
High St. Hi Cha 120 A3
High St. Hill 19 E4
High St. Hin Cha 119 F1
High St. H U 51 D1
High St. Keyn 81 F3
High St. Keyn 82 C2
High St. Kings 11 F2
High St. Kingsw 51 E2
High St. Kingsw 65 F4
High St. Kingsw 66 A4
High St. Kingsw 51 E2
High St. Mang 51 E2
High St. Marsh 69 F4
High St. Mid No 132 A1
High St. N St P 135 F2
High St. Nail 59 F1
High St. Paul 115 E1
High St. Paul 131 F2
High St. Pens 97 F2

High St. Portb 46 B2
High St. Portis 45 E3
High St. Rode 136 C1
High St. Ston E 130 C1
High St. Thorn 15 D4
High St. Tims 116 A1
High St. W-S-M 104 B4
High St. Well 118 B1
High St. Wick 67 E3
High St. Wickw 18 A3
High St. Win 95 D4
High St. Wint 37 E3
High St. Wring 92 B2
High St. Yatt 74 C1
High St. Yatt 91 D4
High View. Portis 45 D2
Higham St. Bris 64 C4
Highbury Pl. Bath 85 D1
Highbury Rd. Bris 49 F4
Highbury Rd. Bris 63 E1
Highbury Rd. Paul 131 D4
Highbury St N. Bris 87 E1
Highbury Terr. Bath 85 D1
Highbury Villas. Bris 63 E3
Highcroft. Kingsw 66 B3
Highdale Ave. Cleve 57 F2
Highdale Cl. Bris 80 A2
Highdale Pl. Cleve 57 E2
Highdale Rd. Cleve 57 F2
Highett Dr. Bris 50 A1
Highfield Ave. Kingsw 65 E3
Highfield Cl. Bath 101 D3
Highfield Cl. St Gif 36 C2
Highfield Cres. Chil 137 E2
Highfield Dr. Portis 44 C2
Highfield Gdns. Kingsw 66 B1
Highfield Gr. Bris 49 E3
Highfield La. Co Mar 128 A3
Highfield La. E Harp 129 D2
Highfield La. H Up 29 F4
Highfield La. Hort 29 F4
Highfield Rd. Ch Sod 28 A1
Highfield Rd. Keyn 81 F3
Highfield Rd. P St J 133 E4
Highfield Rd. W-S-M 105 D1
Highfields. H Up 19 F1
Highfields. Pens 96 C1
Highfields. Rad 132 B1
Highgrove St. Bris 64 A2
Highland Cl. W-S-M 88 A1
Highland Cres. Bris 49 D1
Highland Rd. Bath 101 D3
Highland Sq. Bris 49 D1
Highland Terr. Bath 101 D3
Highlands Dr. N Nib 5 F2
Highlands Rd. Lo Ash 62 A1
Highlands Rd. Portis 45 D3
Highleaze Rd. Kingsw 66 B2
Highleaze Gdns. Bris 78 C2
Highmore Cl. Bris 50 A4
Highmore Gdns. Bris 50 B4
Highnam Cl. St Gif 24 A1
Highridge Cres. Bris 78 C3
Highridge Green. Bris 78 C3
Highridge Rd. Bris 78 C3
Highridge Rd. Bris 63 D1
Highridge Rd. Dun 78 C2
Highridge Rd. Dun 78 C2
Highridge Wlk. Bris 78 C4
Highview Rd. Kingsw 51 F1
Highwall La. Co Dan 80 C1
Highway. Yate 27 F1
Highwood La. Bris 35 E4
Highwood Rd. Bris 35 F4
Highworth Cres. Yate 26 B4
Highworth Rd. Bris 64 B3
Hill Ave. Bath 101 F1
Hill Ave. Bris 63 F2
Hill Burn. Bris 49 E3
Hill Crest. Bris 64 E1
Hill Dr. Wrax 61 E2
Hill End Dr. Bris 34 B2
Hill Gay Cl. Portis 44 C2
Hill Gr. Bris 49 E3
Hill House Rd. Mang 51 F3
Hill La. Sod 41 D4
Hill La. Nail 58 B2
Hill La. O-On-S 1 C1
Hill La. Rock 2 A2
Hill La. Ship 109 D1
Hill Lawn. Bris 64 B2
Hill Moor. Cleve 57 F1
Hill Park. Cong 91 F3
Hill Rd E W-S-M 88 C1
Hill Rd. Cleve 57 E1
Hill Rd. Dun 78 C2
Hill Rd. W-S-M 88 C1
Hill Rd. W-S-M 104 C4
Hill Rd. Wins 108 A2
Hill St. Bris 63 E3
Hill St. Bris 63 E3
Hill St. Bris 64 C4
Hill St. Kingsw 65 F4
Hill The. Alm 24 B2
Hill The. Hi Cha 120 B3
Hill Top. Portis 45 D2
Hill View Cl. Kingsw 66 B2

Hill View Ct. W-S-M 105 E4
Hill View Rd. Bath 85 D1
Hill View Rd. Bris 79 D4
Hill View Rd. Puck 53 E3
Hill View Rd. W-S-M 105 D4
Hill View. Bris 36 A2
Hill View. Bris 49 E3
Hill View. Bris 80 A4
Hill View. Kingsw 51 E1
Hill View. Marks 99 D1
Hill View. Paul 131 D2
Hill View. Pens 117 D3
Hillbrook Rd. Thorn 15 E4
Hillburn Rd. Bris 65 D4
Hillcrest Cl. Nail 59 F1
Hillcrest Dr. Bath 101 E2
Hillcrest Rd. Nail 59 F1
Hillcrest Rd. Portis 44 C3
Hillcrest. P St J 133 E4
Hillcrest. Pens 97 F2
Hillcrest. Thorn 8 A1
Hillcroft Cl. W-S-M 88 A1
Hilldale Rd. Back 76 A3
Hillesley Rd. Kings 11 F2
Hillfields Ave. Bris 51 E2
Hillgrove St N. Bris 63 E4
Hillgrove Terr. W-S-M 104 B1
Hilliers La. Chur 108 B2
Hillmead La. Chur 109 D3
Hillmer Rise. Ban 106 C2
Hillpath. Ban 107 D1
Hills Cl. Keyn 82 A3
Hillsborough Rd. Bris 64 B2
Hillsborough. Bris 63 D3
Hillsdon Rd. Bris 48 C4
Hillside Ave. Bris 65 E4
Hillside Ave. Mid No 137 F4
Hillside Cl. Fr Cot 38 B4
Hillside Cres. Mid No 137 F4
Hillside Gdns. Bi Suf 113 E2
Hillside Gdns. W-S-M 88 A1
Hillside La. Fr Cot 38 B4
Hillside Rd. Back 76 A2
Hillside Rd. Bath 85 E1
Hillside Rd. Blea 122 A4
Hillside Rd. Bris 65 D4
Hillside Rd. Cleve 57 E2
Hillside Rd. Lo Ash 62 A1
Hillside Rd. Mid No 137 F4
Hillside Rd. Portis 44 B2
Hillside Rd. Bris 64 A2
Hillside. P St J 133 E4
Hillside. W. Lock 105 F1
Hillside. Bris 64 A2
Hillside. Mang 52 A3
Hillside. Portb 46 C2
Hilltop Gdns. Bris 65 D4
Hilltop Gdns. Kingsw 51 E1
Hilltop View. Bris 65 D4
Hillview Ave. Cleve 57 E1
Hillview Gdns. Win 94 B4
Hillview Rd. Blea 123 E2
Hillview. Time 116 A1
Hillyfield Rd. Bris 79 D3
Hillyfields Way. Wins 125 D4
Hillyfields. Wins 125 D4
Hilverton Gdns. Bris 49 F1
Hind Pitts. Wins 125 F4
Hinton Cl. Bath 100 C3
Hinton Cl. Keyn 82 C2
Hinton Dr. Kingsw 66 B3
Hinton Hill. Hin Cha 119 D1
Hinton La. Bris 62 C3
Hinton Rd. Bris 50 B1
Hinton Rd. Bris 64 C4
Hinton Villas. Hin Cha 119 F1
Hinton. W-S-M 104 C1
Hippisley Dr. Axb 125 E1
Hiscocks Dr. Bath 101 F2
Hitchen Cl. Marsh 69 F4
Hither Green. Cleve 57 F1
Hoare's La. Kilm 139 D2
Hobart Rd. W-S-M 104 C2
Hobb's La. Bris 63 E3
Hobbiton Rd. W-S-M 88 B2
Hobbs Cl. Nail 59 F1
Hobbs La. Ba Gu 77 F2
Hobbs La. Sist 52 A1
Hobhouse Cl. Bris 49 E4
Hobwell La. Lo Ash 62 B1
Hockey's La. Bris 51 D2
Hoddon La. Puck 53 E3
Hodshill. Sosto 118 C3
Hoecroft Gdns. Chil 137 E2
Hogarth Mews. W-S-M 89 D2
Hogarth Wlk. Bris 50 B4
Hogarth Wlk. W-S-M 89 D2
Hogues Wlk. Bris 79 D2
Holbeach Way. Bris 80 A2
Holbrook Cres. Bris 79 E2
Holbrook La. Wick 67 D4
Holcombe Cl. Bath 85 F1
Holcombe Gn. Bath 84 A1
Holcombe Gr. Keyn 81 E3
Holcombe La. Bath 85 F1
Holcombe Vale. Bath 85 F1

Holcombe. Bris 80
Holdenhurst Rd. Bris 51
Holders Wlk. Lo Ash 61
Holford Cl. Nail 59
Holford Ct. Bris 80
Holland Rd. Bath 85
Holland Rd. Cleve 57
Holland St. Bris 63
Holland St. W-S-M 105
Hollidge Gdns. Bris 63
Hollies La. Bathe 86
Hollies Ave. Portis 45
Hollis Cl. Lo Ash 78
Hollis Cres. Portis 45
Hollis Gdns. Luck 31
Hollister's Dr. Bris 79
Hollow La. W-S-M 88
Hollow Marsh La. Hin Ble . 130
Hollow Rd. Alm 24
Hollow Rd. Kingsw 65
Hollow Rd. Wins 125
Hollow The. Bath 101
Hollow The. Bath 101
Holloway. Bath 101
Hollowbrook La. Ch Mag . 113
Hollowmead Cl. Yatt 91
Hollows The. West 38
Holly Cl. Bris 80
Holway Rd. Bris 80
Holly Cl. Alve 14
Holly Cl. Bris 51
Holly Cl. Nail 60
Holly Cl. Puck 53
Holly Cl. W-S-M 89
Holly Cres. Kingsw 51
Holly Dr. Col 70
Holly Gr. Bris 51
Holly Green. Kingsw 52
Holly Hill Rd. Kingsw 51
Holly Hill. Ir Act 26
Holly La. Cleve 57
Holly Lodge Rd. Bris 50
Holly Ridge. Portis 45
Holly Wlk. Keyn 132
Holly Wlk. Rad 82
Hollybush Cl. A Tur 43
Hollybush Cl. Winsl 120
Hollybush La. Bris 48
Hollybush Rd. Kingsw 65
Hollyguest Rd. Kingsw 66
Hollyleigh Ave. Bris 35
Hollyman Wlk. Cleve 57
Hollymead La. Bris 48
Hollyridge. Bris 80
Hollywood La. Alm 35
Hollywood Rd. Bris 64
Holm La. Piln 13
Holm Rd. Lock 105
Holmdale Rd. Bris 36
Holmes Gr. Bris 49
Holmes Hill Rd. Bris 64
Holmes St. Bris 64
Holmesdale Rd. Bris 63
Holmoak Rd. Keyn 81
Holms Rd. W-S-M 105
Holmwood Cl. Wint 37
Holmwood. Kingsw 65
Holsom Cl. Bris 80
Holsom Rd. Bris 80
Holst Gdns. Bris 79
Holtsdown Cl. Bris 89
Holwell. Yate 27
Homeground. Cleve 57
Homelea Park E. Bath 101
Homelea Park W. Bath 101
Homeleaze Rd. Bris 35
Homemead Dr. Bris 80
Homemead Gdns. Bris 51
Homestead Rd. Bris 35
Homestead The. Cleve 57
Homestead The. Keyn 81
Homestead Way. Wins ... 125
Homestead. Portis 44
Honey Garston Cl. Bris 79
Honey Garston Rd. Bris 79
Honey Hill Rd. Kingsw 66
Honey Mead. Kingsw 65
Honey Way. Kingsw 66
Honeyborne Way. Wickw .. 18

...hall La. Cong 108 B4
...lands. Portis 45 E2
...mead. Bris 80 B3
...suckle Cl. St Gif 24 C1
...rysuckle La. Bris 50 C2
...on Rd. Bris 51 D2
...on Rd. Cleve 57 F1
...on. W-S-M 89 D1
...La. Hin Ble 129 F2
...Batch. Blag 110 B2
...st Rd. Bris 80 B3
...Cl. Bris 63 D3
...Rd. Bris 63 E2
...Rd. Ir Act 27 F2
...Sg. Bris 62 C3
...Ter. Mid No 132 A1
...hapel Hill. Bris 62 C3
...oun Rd. Bris 49 F2
...well Gdns. Bris 47 F4
...s Ct. Bris 49 D1
...s. W-S-M 104 C4
...nd Cl. Kingsw 66 A2
...t Rd. Kingsw 65 E4
...ham Gr. Bris 79 E3
...ld Rd. Bris 63 E4
...r Rd. Bris 50 A1
...e Rd. Bath 125 D1
...ream Wlk. Keyn 81 E2
...eams The. Bris 37 D1
...La. Thom 8 B3
...leaze La. Ship 108 B1
...pool La. Doyn 47 F4
...pool Rd. Bris 78 C2
...shoe La. Bris 48 B2
...shoe La. Ch Sod 28 A1
...shoe La. Thorn 24 C3
...La. Ave 24 C3
...Hill. Horr 29 E3
...rd. Ch Sod 28 B2
...shoe Wlk. Bath 102 A3
...La. Ave 24 C3
...Hill. Horr 29 E3
...ood Ct. Kingsw 66 A2
...ood La. Wickw 18 A2
...ood Rd. Nail 59 F1
...y Wlk. Bris 79 D3
...Cl. Bris 63 E4
...ath St. Bath 101 F3
...n Gdns. Bris 50 A4
...all Rd. Bris 62 C3
...gate Way. Axb 125 D1
...d Cl. Bris 63 F4
...ds Cl. Ch Sod 28 A1
...ds Rd. Ch Sod 28 A1
...'s La. Fr Cot 26 A2
...Hill. Bath 101 D3
...rd Ave. Bris 64 C4
...rd Cl. Keyn 82 B2
...rd Rd. Bris 49 D2
...rd Rd. Bris 63 D2
...rd Rd. Kingsw 51 E2
...rd Rd. Thom 8 B1
...st Rd. Bris 50 C1
...rcroft Gdns. Bris 48 C2
...a Cl. Kingsw 66 A3
...nd Rd. Bris 54 B4
...moor La. Mang 52 B4
...oke Dr. Kingsw 66 A3
...oke. Yate 39 F4
...iord La. West 38 A2
...ord Rd. Wint 37 F3
...ey Way. St Gif 36 C3
...'s Hill Gdns. Bris 64 C4
...'s Hill Rd. Bris 64 C4
...Ison Hill Rd. Bris 34 B2
...on Cl. Ch Sod 39 F4
...s Vale Rd. Bris 49 D1
...enden Rd. Bris 49 F3
...enden Rd. W-S-M 105 D4
...Ct. Rad 133 D1
...rt Cl. Bris 65 D1
...Rd. Bris 64 B1
...eer Way. Avon 33 E3
...erstan Wlk. Bris 47 F4
...shy Davy Way. Bris 62 C3
...Rd. Bris 47 F3
...arford Cl. Bris 80 C4
...arford Cres. Bris 80 C4
...arford Gdns. Bris 80 C4
...arford Rd. Bath 101 E4
...arford Rd. Bris 80 C4
...arford Terr. Well 118 B1
...arford Wlk. Bris 64 C1
...rete Rd. Farm 115 F3
...s La. Tur 91 F4
...r's La. A Tur 42 C3
...r's Way. Bris 80 C4
...rs Cl. Kingsw 65 E3

Hunters Dr. Kingsw 51 F1
Hunters Mead. H Up 20 A1
Hunters Rd. Kingsw 65 E3
Huntingham Rd. Bris 78 C2
Huntley Gr. Nail 46 A3
Hunts La. Bris 49 F3
Hurle Cres. Bris 49 D1
Hurle Rd. Bris 49 D1
Hurlingham Rd. Bris 49 F1
Hurn La. Keyn 82 A2
Hurn Rd. Cleve 57 F1
Hursley Hill. Pens 97 E4
Hursley La. Pens 80 C1
Hurst Rd. Bris 79 F4
Hurst Rd. W-S-M 105 D3
Hurst Wlk. Bris 79 F4
Hurston Rd. Bris 79 E4
Hurstwood Rd. Mang 51 E3
Hutton Cl. Bris 48 C4
Hutton Cl. Keyn 82 A1
Hutton Hill. Lock 105 F1
Hutton Moor Rd. W-S-M 105 E4
Huyton Rd. Bris 50 C2
Hyde Ave. Thorn 8 A2
Hyde The. Cleve 73 E4
Hyde's La. Co Ash 69 D3
Hyland Gr. Bris 48 C4

I.S.F Rd. Avon 33 E2
Ida Rd. Bris 64 B4
Iddesleigh Rd. Bris 49 D1
Idstone Rd. Bris 51 D2
Idwal Cl. P St J 133 E4
Iford Cl. Keyn 82 C2
Iford Hill. Westw 120 C1
Iford Rd. Hi Cha 120 B2
Ilchester Cres. Bris 78 C1
Ilchester Rd. Bris 79 D4
Ilex Ave. Cleve 57 F1
Ilex Cl. Bris 78 C3
Ilex La. Winsc 107 F1
Ilminster Ave. Bris 64 A1
Ilminster Cl. Cleve 57 F1
Ilminster Cl. Nail 75 E4
Ilminster. W-S-M 105 D1
Ilsyn Gr. Bris 80 B4
Imber Court Cl. Bris 80 A4
Imperial Rd. Bris 49 D1
Imperial Rd. Bris 80 B4
Imperial Wlk. Bris 64 A1
Ingleside Rd. Bris 51 E1
Inglestone Rd. Wickw 18 A3
Ingleton Dr. W-S-M 89 D2
Ingmire Rd. Bris 50 A2
Ingst Hill. Aust 13 E2
Ingst Rd. Aust 13 F2
Inkerman Cl. Bris 49 F4
Inner Down The. Olve 14 B2
Inner Elm Terr. Rad 132 B1
Innicks Cl. Co Mar 111 E1
Innocks Est. N Nib 5 E2
Innox Dr. Bris 79 D3
Innox Gr. Engl 78 C2
Innox La. Bathe 85 D3
Innox Rd. Bath 101 D3
Inns Court Ave. Bris 79 E4
Inns Court Dr. Bris 79 E3
Instow Rd. Bris 79 F4
Instow Wlk. Bris 79 D1
Inverness Rd. Bath 101 E3
Ipswich Dr. Bris 64 C3
Irby Rd. Bris 63 D2
Irena Rd. Bris 50 C1
Ireton Rd. Bris 63 D2
Iron Hogg La. Fail 9 E2
Ironchurch Rd. Avon 33 E3
Ironmould La. Bris 65 D1
Irving Cl. Cleve 57 F2
Irving Cl. Kingsw 51 F2
Island Gdns. Bris 50 B2
Island The. Mid No 132 A1
Isleys Ct. Kingsw 65 F2
Islington Rd. Bris 63 D2
Ison Hill Rd. Bris 34 B2
Itchington Rd. Alve 15 F2
Itchington Rd. Tyth 15 F2
Itchington Rd. Tyth 16 A2
Ivo Peters Rd. Bath 101 F3
Ivor Rd. Bris 64 B4
Ivy Ave. Bath 101 E2
Ivy Bank Park. Bath 101 F1
Ivy Ct. Portis 44 C3
Ivy Gr. Bath 101 E2
Ivy La. Bris 51 E3
Ivy Pl. Bath 101 E2
Ivybridge. W-S-M 89 D1
Ivywell Rd. Bris 48 C2
Iwood La. Cong 92 A1

Jackson Cl. Piln 22 B4
Jacob St. Bris 63 F4
Jacob's Wells Rd. Bris 63 E4
Jamaica St. Bris 63 F4
James Cl. Kingsw 51 F2
James Pl. Bris 62 C4
James Rd. Kingsw 51 F2
James St W. Bath 101 F3

James St. Bris 50 A1
James St. Bris 63 F4
Jane St. Bris 64 A4
Jarvis St. Bris 64 A3
Jasmine Cl. W-S-M 89 D1
Jasmine Gr. Bris 35 D4
Jasmine La. Yatt 74 C1
Jasper St. Bris 63 D2
Jays The. Tyth 16 A3
Jean Rd. Bris 64 C1
Jefferies Hill Bottom. Bris 65 D3
Jeffery Ct. Kingsw 51 F3
Jellicoe Ct. W-S-M 88 C2
Jena Ct. Keyn 82 B2
Jenner Cl. Ch Sod 40 B4
Jersey Ave. Bris 64 C2
Jesmond Rd. Cleve 57 E2
Jesse Hughes Ct. Bath 85 E1
Jessop Underpass. Bris 62 C2
Jews La. Bath 101 E3
Jews La. Chur 108 C2
Jocelin Dr. W-S-M 88 C2
Jocelyn Rd. Bris 49 F4
Jockey La. Bris 65 D4
John Cabot Ct. Bris 63 D3
John Carr's Terr. Bris 63 D3
John Cozens Rd. Bris 64 A4
John St. Bath 101 F4
John St. Bris 50 A1
John St. Bris 63 E4
John St. Bris 65 E4
John Wesley Rd. Bris 64 C2
Johnson Dr. Kingsw 65 F3
Johnsons La. Bris 50 B1
Johnsons Rd. Bris 50 B1
Johnstone St. Bath 102 A3
Jones Cl. Yatt 73 F1
Joy Hill. Bris 62 C3
Jubilee Cres. Mang 52 A3
Jubilee Dr. Thorn 8 B1
Jubilee Dr. Wrax 61 D2
Jubilee La. Chur 109 D3
Jubilee La. Croom 17 D4
Jubilee Pl. Bris 63 E3
Jubilee Pl. Cleve 57 E1
Jubilee Rd. Axb 125 E1
Jubilee Rd. Bris 50 A1
Jubilee Rd. Bris 64 C4
Jubilee Rd. Kingsw 51 F2
Jubilee Rd. Rad 132 B1
Jubilee Rd. W-S-M 104 C4
Jubilee Terr. Paul 131 F3
Jubilee Way. Avon 33 D1
Julian Cl. Bris 48 C2
Julian Rd. Bath 101 F4
Julian Rd. Bris 48 C2
Julius Rd. Bris 49 E2
Junction Ave. Bath 101 F3
Junction Rd. Bath 101 F3
Junction Rd. Bris 64 B2
Juniper Ct. Bris 50 B1
Jupiter Rd. Bris 35 F4
Justice Ave. Keyn 82 C2
Justice Rd. Bris 51 D2
Jutland Rd. Avon 33 D1

Karen Dr. Back 76 A3
Kathdene Gdns. Bris 49 F2
Kathrine Dr. Char 11 D3
Keats Rd. Rod 138 D4
Keble Ave. Bris 78 C3
Keeds La. Lo Ash 61 F1
Keedwell Hill. Lo Ash 61 F1
Keedwell House. Bris 79 E2
Keel's Hill. P St J 133 E4
Keen's Gr. Piln 22 B4
Keene's Way. Cleve 57 E1
Keep The. Kingsw 66 A4
Keep The. W-S-M 89 D2
Keinton Wlk. Bris 35 D1
Kellaway Ave. Bris 49 E3
Kellaway Cres. Bris 49 E3
Kellways. Back 76 C2
Kelston Cl. Keyn 82 B2
Kelston Cl. Yate 39 E4
Kelston Gdns. Bris 49 E4
Kelston Gdns. W-S-M 89 D3
Kelston Rd. Bath 100 A4
Kelston Rd. Bris 49 E4
Kelston Rd. Keyn 81 E3
Kelston Rd. W-S-M 89 D3
Kelston View. Bath 101 D3
Kelston Wlk. Bris 51 E3
Kelting Gr. Cleve 57 F1
Kemble Cl. Kingsw 66 A3
Kemble Cl. Nail 60 A1
Kemble Gdns. Bris 47 F3
Kempe's Cl. Lo Ash 62 A2
Kempenfeay Way. St Gif 36 B4
Kempton Cl. Mang 37 F1
Kempton Cl. Thorn 8 A2
Kencot Wlk. Bris 79 D2
Kendall Gdns. Kingsw 51 E2
Kendall Rd. Kingsw 51 E2

Kendon Dr. Bris 49 E4
Kenilworth Cl. Keyn 81 E2
Kenilworth Dr. Kingsw 66 A1
Kenilworth Rd. Bris 49 E1
Kenilworth. Yate 27 F1
Kenmare Rd. Bris 63 F1
Kenmeade Cl. Ship 125 F4
Kenmore Cres. Bris 35 F1
Kenmore Dr. Bris 35 F1
Kenmore Gr. Bris 35 F1
Kenn Cl. W-S-M 105 D3
Kenn Est. Yatt 73 F3
Kenn Moor Dr. Cleve 57 F1
Kenn Rd. Bris 65 D4
Kenn Rd. Yatt 73 F4
Kennard Cl. Bris 65 E4
Kennard Rd. Bris 65 E4
Kennard Rise. Bris 65 E4
Kennaway Rd. Cleve 57 E1
Kennedy Way. Ch Sod 40 A4
Kennedy Way. Yate 27 E3
Kennel Dr. Gr Bad 30 C1
Kennel La. Co Bi 123 F2
Kennel Lodge Rd. Bris 62 C2
Kennet Park. Bath 85 F1
Kennet Rd. Keyn 82 A2
Kennet Way. Thorn 15 E4
Kenneth Rd. Bris 64 B1
Kennford. W-S-M 89 D1
Kennington Ave. Bris 49 E1
Kennington Ave. Kingsw 51 E1
Kennington Rd. Bath 101 D4
Kenmoor Cl. Kingsw 66 A3
Kenmoor Rd. Yatt 74 A3
Kensal Ave. Bris 63 F2
Kensal Rd. Bris 63 F2
Kensington Cl. Thorn 8 A1
Kensington Cl. Bath 85 D1
Kensington Gdns. Bath 85 D1
Kensington Park Rd. Bris 64 B1
Kensington Park. Bris 50 A1
Kensington Pl. Bris 63 D4
Kensington Rd. Bris 49 E1
Kensington Rd. Kingsw 51 E2
Kensington Rd. W-S-M 104 C3
Kent Ave. Yate 27 F2
Kent Cl. St Gif 36 B2
Kent Rd. Bris 49 E2
Kent Rd. Cong 91 E3
Kent St. Bris 63 E3
Kent Way. W-S-M 89 D2
Kenton Mews. Bris 49 D3
Kents Green. Kingsw 51 F1
Kentshare La. Win 95 D3
Keppel Cl. Keyn 82 B1
Kerry Rd. Bris 63 F1
Kersteman Rd. Bris 49 E2
Kestrel Cl. Bris 35 D4
Kestrel Cl. Ch Sod 39 F4
Kestrel Cl. Thorn 8 B1
Kestrel Dr. Puck 53 E2
Kestrel Dr. W-S-M 88 C1
Kestrel Pl. Rod 138 A4
Keswick Wlk. Bris 35 E1
Ketch Rd. Bris 63 F2
Ketley Hill. Mid No 132 B2
Kew Rd. W-S-M 89 D4
Kew Wlk. Bris 80 A3
Kewside. W-S-M 88 A2
Kewstoke Rd. Bath 102 A1
Kewstoke Rd. Bris 48 C2
Kewstoke Rd. W-S-M 88 B2
Keyes Path. W-S-M 88 C1
Keynsham By-pass. Keyn 81 F4
Keynsham Rd. Bitt 82 A2
Keys Ave. Bris 49 F4
Kielder Dr. W-S-M 88 C2
Kilbirnie Rd. Bris 80 A1
Kilburn St. Bris 64 A4
Kildare Rd. Bris 63 F1
Kilkenny La. Engl 118 A4
Kilkenny St. Bris 63 F3
Killcott Rd. Hill 1 E1
Kilmersdon Hill. Kilm 139 D3
Kilmersdon Rd. Bris 79 D2
Kilmersdon Rd. Rod 138 C4
Kilmington Cl. Bris 47 E4
Kiln Cl. Bris 51 F1
Kiln Park. W-S-M 105 D3
Kilnhurst Cl. Kingsw 65 F1
Kilve. W-S-M 104 C1
Kilvert Cl. Bris 64 B3
Kimberley Ave. Bris 51 E3
Kimberley Cl. Mang 51 F3
Kimberley Cres. Bris 51 E3
Kimberley Rd. Bris 51 E3
Kimberley Rd. Cleve 57 E1
Kimberley Rd. Kingsw 51 E1
Kinber Cl. Bath 84 C2
King Alfred Way. Winsl 120 B4
King Dick's La. Bris 64 B4
King Edward Cl. Bris 80 A3
King Edward Rd. Bath 101 E3
King George V Pl. Bris 63 E4
King George's Rd. Bris 79 D2

King George's Rd. Bris 78 C3
King John's Rd. Bris 51 D1
King La. Clut 114 C2
King La. Hort 29 D4
King Rd. Bris 64 C1
King Rd. Chur 108 C3
King Road Ave. Avon 33 D1
King Sq. Bris 63 E4
King Square Ave. Bris 63 E4
King St. Avon 33 D1
King St. Bris 50 B1
King St. Bris 63 E3
King St. Bris 63 D4
King William Ave. Bris 63 D3
King William St. Bris 63 D2
Kings Ave. Bris 49 E2
King's Ave. Bris 49 F2
King's Dr. Bris 49 E2
King's Head La. Bris 78 C4
King's La. W-S-M 104 C4
Kings Parade Ave. Bris 49 D1
King's Parade Mews. Bris 49 D1
Kings Rd. Bris 63 D4
King's Rd. Cleve 57 E3
King's Rd. Portis 44 C2
Kingfisher Cl. Thorn 8 B1
Kingfisher Dr. Bris 50 C3
Kingfisher Dr. Rod 138 A4
Kingfisher Rd. Ch Sod 40 A4
Kingfisher Rd. W-S-M 105 F4
Kingrove Cres. Ch Sod 40 B4
Kingrove La. Ch Sod 40 B4
Kings Ave. Kingsw 65 D2
Kings Chase. Kingsw 65 E3
Kings Dr. Kingsw 65 D2
Kings Oak Meadow. Clut 114 C1
Kings Park Ave. Bris 64 B3
Kings Weston Ave. Bris 47 E4
Kings Weston La. Avon 33 F2
Kings Weston La. Bris 48 A4
Kings Weston Rd. Bris 34 B1
Kingscote Wlk. Bris 80 A3
Kingscote. Yate 39 E3
Kingscourt Cl. Bris 80 A2
Kingsdown Par. Bris 63 E4
Kingsdown View. Bath 85 D1
Kingsfield La. Kingsw 65 F2
Kingsfield La. Kingsw 65 F3
Kingsfield. Bath 101 E2
Kingshill Gdns. Nail 59 E1
Kingshill House. Bris 64 A1
Kingshill La. Ch St 112 B3
Kingshill. Nail 59 E1
Kingsholm Rd. Bris 50 A4
Kingsholme Rd. Kingsw 51 E1
Kingsland Cl. Bris 64 A3
Kingsland Rd Br. Bris 64 A3
Kingsland Trading Est. Bris 64 A4
Kingsleigh Cl. Kingsw 65 F4
Kingsleigh Gdns. Kingsw 65 F4
Kingsleigh Park. Kingsw 65 F4
Kingsley Rd. Bris 49 E1
Kingsley Rd. Bris 50 B1
Kingsley Rd. Cleve 57 E1
Kingsley Rd. Rad 132 B1
Kingsley Rd. W-S-M 104 C2
Kingsmead Cl. Bath 101 F3
Kingsmead Rd. Bris 51 D3
Kingsmead Sq. Bath 101 F3
Kingsmead St. Bath 101 F3
Kingsmead Wlk. Bris 51 D1
Kingsmead. Bath 101 F3
Kingsmead. Nail 59 E1
Kingsmill. Bris 48 B3
Kingston Ave. Cleve 57 E1
Kingston Ave. Keyn 82 B2
Kingston Cl. Mang 52 A4
Kingston Dr. Mang 52 A4
Kingston Dr. Thorn 8 B2
Kingston La. Win 94 C4
Kingston Mead. Win 94 C4
Kingston Par. Bath 102 A3
Kingston Rd. Bath 102 A3
Kingston Rd. Bris 63 D3
Kingston Rd. Nail 75 E4
Kingston Way. Nail 75 E4
Kingstree St. Bris 64 A2
Kingsway Ave. Bris 65 D4
Kingsway Cres. Bris 65 D4
Kingsway. Bris 65 D4
Kingsway. Bris 50 B1
Kingsway. St Gif 36 B3
Kingswear. Bris 65 D4
Kingswear. W-S-M 89 D1
Kingswood Trading Est. Kingsw 51 E1
Kington La. Thorn 7 F1
Kington Rd. O-on-S 7 F2
Kington. Rd. Thorn 7 F2
Kingwell View. Paul 115 E1
Kinsale Rd. Bris 80 B4
Kinsale Wlk. Bris 63 F1

Kinvara Rd. Bris 79 F4
Kipling Rd. Bris 36 A1
Kipling Rd. Rad 132 B1
Kipling Rd. W-S-M 105 D2
Kiplingave. Bath 101 F2
Kirkby Rd. Bris 34 A1
Kirkstone Gdns. Bris 35 E1
Kirttington Rd. Bris 50 A2
Kite Hay Cl. Bris 50 C3
Kite Wlk. W-S-M 105 F4
Kites Cl. St Gif 24 B1
Kitland La. Chur 109 E4
Knapp La. Crom 10 A2
Knapp Rd. Thorn 8 C1
Knapps Cl. Wins 124 C4
Knapps Dr. Wins 124 C4
Knapps La. Bris 50 C1
Knightcott Gdns. Ban 106 C2
Knightcott Ind Est Ban ... 106 C2
Knightcott Park. Ban 107 D2
Knightcott Rd. Ab Lei 61 F4
Knightcott Rd. Ban 107 D2
Knighton Rd. Bris 35 F1
Knights Cl. W-S-M 89 D3
Knightstone Cl. Axb 125 E1
Knightstone Cl. P St J 133 D4
Knightstone Cswy. W-S-M 104 B4
Knightstone Ct. Bris 50 B1
Knightstone Pl. Bath 84 A1
Knightstone Pl. Kingsw 65 D2
Knightstone Rd. W-S-M ... 104 B4
Knightstone Sq. Bris 80 B3
Knightwood Rd. St Gif 36 C3
Knobsbury Hill. Kilm 139 E3
Knobsbury La. Rad 139 E4
Knobsbury La. Rad 133 E1
Knole Cl. Alm 23 F2
Knole La. Bris 35 D2
Knole Park. Alm 23 F2
Knoll Hill. Bris 48 B2
Knoll The. Portis 45 D4
Knovill Cl. Bris 34 A1
Knowle Rd. Bris 63 F2
Knowles Rd. Cleve 57 E1
Knowsley Rd. Bris 50 C2
Kyilross Ave. Bris 80 A3
Kynges Mill Cl. Bris 51 D4
Kyrle Gdns. Bath 85 F2

Labbott The. Keyn 81 F3
Laburnham Wlk. Keyn 81 E2
Laburnum Ct. Mid No 137 F4
Laburnum Ct. W-S-M 105 D4
Laburnum Ct. Mid No 137 F4
Laburnum Rd. Kingsw 65 E1
Laburnum Rd. W-S-M 105 D4
Lacey Rd. Bris 80 C3
Lacock Dr. Kingsw 65 F4
Ladd Cl. Kingsw 65 F4
Ladden Ct. Thom 15 E4
Ladies Mile. Bris 48 C4
Ladman Dr. Bris 80 C3
Ladman Rd. Bris 80 C3
Ladycroft. Cleve 57 D1
Ladye Bay. Cleve 57 D1
Ladye Wake. W-S-M 88 C2
Ladymead La. Chur 108 C3
Ladymeade. Back 76 A4
Ladysmith Rd. Bris 49 D2
Ladywell. Wring 92 B1
Laggan Gdns. Bath 84 C1
Lake Rd. Bris 49 E4
Lake Rd. Portis 45 D4
Lake View Rd. Bris 64 B4
Lakemead Gdns. Bris 78 C2
Lakemead Gr. Bris 78 C3
Lakeside. Bris 50 C2
Lakewood Cres. Bris 49 D4
Lakewood Rd. Bris 49 D4
Lamb St. Bris 63 F4
Lambert Pl. Bris 79 E3
Lambley Rd. Bris 64 C2
Lambourn Cl. Bris 63 E2
Lambourn Rd. Keyn 82 A2
Lambridge Mews. Bath 85 E1
Lambridge Pl. Bath 85 E1
Lambridge St. Bath 85 E1
Lambrook Rd. Bris 51 D2
Lamford Gate. St Gif 36 C3
Lampard's Bldgs. Bath ... 101 F4
Lampeter Rd. Bris 49 D4
Lampley Rd. K Sey 73 E1
Lampley Rd. Yatt 73 F1
Lampton Ave. Bris 79 F2
Lampton Gr. Bris 79 F2
Lampton Rd. Lo Ash 61 F1
Lanaway Rd. Bris 51 D3
Lancashire Rd. Bris 49 F2
Lancaster Cl. St Gif 36 B2
Lancaster Rd. Bris 50 A1
Lancaster Rd. Yate 27 F2
Lancaster St. Bris 64 B4
Land The. Fr Cot 38 B4
Landemann Cir. W-S-M 87 F1
Landsdown View. Kingsw .. 65 F4
Landseer Ave. Bris 50 A4
Landseer Cl. W-S-M 88 C2

Landseer Rd. Bath 101 D3
Lane The. Alm 22 C1
Lanercost Rd. Bris 35 E1
Lanesborough Rise. Bris ... 80 B4
Laneys Dro. Lock 105 F3
Langdale Rd. Bris 50 C2
Langdon Rd. Bath 101 D2
Langdon Ct. Bris 80 C3
Langfield Cl. Bris 34 C3
Langford La. Blag 109 F3
Langford Rd. Bris 78 C4
Langford Rd. Chur 109 D3
Langfords La. Paul .... 13! E4
Langham Pl. Rode 136 C1
Langham Rd. Bris 64 A1
Langhill Ave. Bris 79 E4
Langley Cres. Bris 62 C1
Langley's La. Ston E 131 E1
Langport Gdns. Nail 75 F4
Langport Rd. W-S-M 104 C3
Langridge La. Charl 84 A4
Langthorn Cl. Fr Cot 38 B4
Langton Court Rd. Bris 64 B3
Langton Park. Bris 63 E2
Langton Rd. Bris 64 B3
Langton Way. Bris 64 C3
Lansdown Cl. Kingsw 51 E1
Lansdown Cres. Bath 101 F4
Lansdown Cres. Tims 116 B1
Lansdown Gdns. W-S-M ... 89 D3
Lansdown Gr. Bath 101 F4
Lansdown La. Bath 84 B1
Lansdown Pl. Bath 67 E1
Lansdown La. Charl 84 A4
Lansdown Park. Bath 84 C2
Lansdown Pl. Bris 63 D4
Lansdown Pl. Paul 115 E1
Lansdown Pl E. Bath 84 C1
Lansdown Rd. Bath 84 C2
Lansdown Rd. Bris 85 E1
Lansdown Rd. Bris 64 A4
Lansdown Rd. Keyn 82 A2
Lansdown Rd. Kingsw 51 E1
Lansdown Rd. Puck 53 E3
Lansdown Terr. Bath 84 D2
Lansdown Terr. Bris 49 E3
Lansdown View. Bath 84 A1
Lansdown View. Bath 101 E3
Lansdown View. Fauk 34 C3
Lansdown View. Tims 116 B1
Lantern La. Bris 51 E4
Laphams La. Tor 41 E1
Laphams Ct. Kingsw 65 F2
Lapwing Cl. St Gif 24 B1
Lapwing Gdns. Bris 50 C3
Lapwing Gdns. W-S-M 88 C1
Larch Cl. Chur 109 D3
Larch Cl. Nail 60 A1
Larch Ct. Rad 138 B4
Larch Rd. Col 70 C2
Larch Rd. Kingsw 51 F2
Larch Way. Bris 35 F4
Larches The. W-S-M 89 D2
Larchgrove Cres. W-S-M ... 88 C1
Larchgrove Wlk. W-S-M 89 D1
Lark's Field. Bris 50 C3
Lark's La. Fr Cot 44 A4
Larkfield. Fr Cot 38 B4
Larkhall Pl. Bath 85 E1
Larksleaze Rd. Kingsw 65 F1
Larkspur Cl. Thorn 8 B1
Lasbury Gr. Bris 79 E3
Latchmoor House. Bris 79 D4
Late Broads. Winsl 120 B4
Latimer Cl. Bris 64 C2
Latteridge La. Ir Act 26 A4
Latteridge La. Tyth 26 A4
Latteridge Rd. Ir Act 26 B2
Latton Rd. Bris 49 F4
Launceston Ave. Kingsw ... 65 D3
Launceston Rd. Bris 51 D1
Laura Pl. Bath 102 A4
Laurel Dr. Col 70 C3
Laurel Dr. Paul 131 F3
Laurel Dr. Yate 10 C4
Laurel Gdns. Yatt 74 A1
Laurel St. Kingsw 65 E4
Laurel Terr. Yatt 74 A1
Laurels The. Mang 52 A3
Laurie Cres. Bris 49 E3
Laurie Lee Ct. Kingsw 66 A3
Lavender Cl. Thorn 8 B1
Lavington Cl. Cleve 57 D1
Lavington Dr. Bris 65 D3
Lawford Ave. St Gif 36 B3
Lawford St. Bris 64 A4
Lawfords Gate. Bris 64 A4
Lawfords Gate. Bris 63 F4
Lawn Ave. Bris 51 D3
Lawn Rd. Bris 51 D3

Lawns Rd. Yate 27 F1
Lawns The. Bris 47 F4
Lawns The. W-S-M 89 D2
Lawns The. Yatt 74 A4
Lawnside. Back 76 A3
Lawnwood Rd. Bris 64 A4
Lawrence Ave. Bris 50 A1
Lawrence Cl. W-S-M 88 C1
Lawrence Cl. Yate 27 D1
Lawrence Gr. Bris 49 D3
Lawrence Hill Ind Pk. Bris . 64 A4
Lawrence Hill Roundabout.
Bris 64 A4
Lawrence Mews. W-S-M 88 C1
Lawrence Rd. W-S-M 88 C1
Lawrence Rd. Wring 92 C1
Lawrence Weston Rd. Avon 33 F3
Lawrence Weston Rd. Bris . 34 A1
Lawrence Weston Rd. Bris . 34 B1
Lawson Cl. Keyn 82 B1
Laxey Rd. Bris 49 F4
Laxton Cl. Olve 14 A2
Laxton Dr. Kings 11 F2
Laxton Way. P St J 133 E4
Lays Dr. Keyn 81 E3
Lays La. Blag 110 B2
Lea Croft. Bris 79 D2
Lea Grove Rd. Cleve 57 E2
Leach Cl. Cleve 57 E1
Leafy Way. Lock 106 A2
Leaholme Gdns. Bris 80 A2
Leaman Cl. Ch Sod 28 A1
Leap Vale. Mang 52 A4
Leap Valley Cres. Mang 52 A4
Leaze La Priddy 126 C4
Leaze The. Rod 138 B4
Leaze The. Yate 27 E1
Leda Ave. Bris 80 A4
Ledbury Rd. Bris 51 E2
Lee Cl. Bris 35 F4
Leechpool Way. Yate 27 F3
Leeming Way. Avon 47 E4
Lees Hill. Kingsw 51 F1
Lees La. Kingsw 66 A3
Lees The. Cong 91 E2
Leeside. Portis 45 E3
Leewood Rd. W-S-M 87 F1
Leg La. Blag 110 A2
Leicester Sq. Kingsw 51 E2
Leicester St. Bris 63 E2
Leicester Wlk. Bris 64 C3
Leigh Cl. Bath 85 D1
Leigh La. Co Ash 69 D2
Leigh La. West 39 E1
Leigh Rd. Bris 63 D3
Leigh St. Bris 63 D2
Leigh View Rd. Portis 45 F3
Leighton Cres. W-S-M 122 A4
Leighton Rd. Bath 84 A2
Leighton Rd. Bris 63 D2
Leighton Rd. Bris 64 A1
Leighwood Dr. Nail 59 D1
Leighwood House. Lo Ash . 62 B3
Leinster Ave. Bris 79 E4
Lemon La. Bris 63 F4
Lena Ave. Bris 50 B1
Lena St. Bris 50 B1
Lenover Gdns. Bris 79 D2
Leonard La. Bris 63 E4
Leonard Rd. Bris 64 B4
Leopold Rd. Bris 49 F1
Lescren Way. Avon 33 E1
Leslie Rise. Westw 120 C2
Lester Dr. W-S-M 89 D2
Lewin St. Bris 64 B4
Lewington Rd. Bris 51 E2
Lewis Mead. Bris 63 E4
Lewis Cl. Kingsw 66 B3
Lewis Rd. Bris 79 D4
Lewis St. Bris 64 A4
Lewisham Gr. W-S-M 105 D4
Lewton La. Wint 37 F4
Leyes La. Olve 13 F2
Leyland Wlk. Bris 78 C2
Leys The. Cleve 57 D1
Leyton Vilas. Bris 49 D1
Liberty Ind Park. Bris 63 D1
Liberty La. Blag 110 C1
Lichfield Rd. Bris 64 C3
Lilac Cl. Bris 35 F4
Lilac Ct. Keyn 81 E2
Lilac Terr. Mid No 132 B1
Lilian Terr. Paul 131 F3
Lilian St. Bris 64 B4
Lillington Cl. Rad 133 D1
Lillington Rd. Rad 133 D1
Lilliput Ave. Ch Sod 28 C4
Lilliput Ct. Ch Sod 40 A4
Lilstock Ave. Bris 49 F2
Lilton Wlk. Bris 63 D1
Lilymead Ave. Bris 64 B2
Lime Cl. Bris 35 F4
Lime Cl. Col 70 C3
Lime Cl. Lock 106 A2
Lime Cl. W-S-M 89 D1
Lime Croft. Yate 27 F2

Lime Ct. Keyn 81 E2
Lime Gr. Alve 14 C3
Lime Gr. Bath 102 A3
Lime Grove Gdns. Bath ... 102 A3
Lime Kiln Gdns. St Gif 24 B2
Lime Kiln Rd. Bris 63 D2
Lime Rd. Kingsw 65 D3
Lime Terr. Rad 132 B1
Lime Tree Gr. E in G 47 E2
Limeburn Hill. Ch Mag 95 F3
Limekiln La. Bath 102 C2
Limekiln Rd. Yate 27 E4
Limerick Rd. Bris 49 E1
Limes The. Bris 37 D1
Limes The. Gr Bad 30 C1
Limpley Stoke Rd. Winsl .. 120 B3
Lincoln Cl. Keyn 81 E2
Lincoln St. Bris 64 A4
Lincombe Ave. Mang 51 E3
Lincombe Rd. Mang 51 E3
Lincombe Rd. Rod 138 B4
Lincott View. P St J 133 E4
Linden Ave. W-S-M 105 D4
Linden Cl. Bris 51 F3
Linden Cl. Bris 80 C3
Linden Cl. Col 70 C3
Linden Cl. Rod 138 C4
Linden Cl. Wint 37 F3
Linden Dr. St Gif 36 C4
Linden Gdns. Bath 101 F4
Linden Rd. Bris 49 D2
Linden Rd. Cleve 57 E2
Lindens The. W-S-M 88 C2
Lindrea St. Bris 63 D2
Lindsay Rd. Bris 50 A2
Lindsey Cl. Portis 44 C2
Linemere Cl. Back 76 B3
Lines Way. Whit 80 B2
Lingfield Park. Mang 37 F1
Link La. Blag 109 F2
Link Rd. Bris 35 F2
Link Rd. Nail 59 F1
Link Rd. Portis 45 E3
Link Rd. Yate 27 F1
Links Rd. W-S-M 104 B1
Linkside. Cleve 57 F3
Linley Cl. Bath 101 D3
Linleys The. Bath 101 E4
Linnell Cl. Bris 50 A3
Linnet Cl. Bris 35 F4
Linnet Cl. W-S-M 88 C1
Linnet Way. Rad 138 A4
Lintern Cres. Kingsw 66 A3
Lintham Dr. Kingsw 65 F3
Linton Rd. Bris 63 F2
Lion Cl. Nail 59 E1
Lippiat Hill. Faulk 134 B2
Lippiatt La. Ship 125 F4
Lippiatt La. Tims 116 A2
Lisburn Rd. Bris 63 F1
Lisle Rd. W-S-M 89 D2
Lister Gr. Westw 120 C2
Litfield Rd. Bris 62 C4
Litt Hill. Litt 129 F1
Little Ann St. Bris 63 F4
Little Birch Croft. Bris 80 A2
Little Bishop St. Bris 63 F4
Little Bristol La. Char 11 D2
Little Caroline Pl. Bris 62 C3
Little Dowles. Kingsw 66 A2
Little Green La. Bris 63 F4
Little George St. W-S-M ... 104 C4
Little Green La. Pln 22 A4
Little Halt. Portis 44 C2
Little Ham. Cleve 73 E4
Little Headley Cl. Bris 79 E4
Little King St. Bris 63 E3
Little La. Farm 116 A3
Little Mead Cl. Lock 105 F2
Little Mead. Bris 34 A1
Little Mead. Bris 34 A1
Little Meadow End. Nail 75 F4
Little Meadow. St Gif 37 D3
Little Orch. W-S-M 104 B1
Little Paradise. Bris 63 E2
Little Stanhope St. Bath ... 101 F3
Little Stoke La. St Gif 36 B4
Little Stoke Rd. Bris 48 C2
Little Withey Mead. Bris 48 C3
Littlebrook. Paul 131 F3
Littledean. Yate 39 F4
Littlefields Ave. Ban 107 D2
Littlefields Rd. Ban 107 D2
Littleton Ct. Bris 23 F1
Littleton La. Ch Mag 95 E2
Littleton La. Win 93 F4
Littleton La. Well 134 B4
Littleton Rd. Bris 63 E2
Littleton St. Bris 50 B1
Littlewell. Lo Ash 61 E1
Littlewood La. Brock 75 E1
Litton. W-S-M 105 D1
Livingstone Rd. Bath 101 E3
Llewellyn Ct. Bris 49 D4

Llewellyn Way. W-S-M 89
Lock Gdns. Bris 78
Lockemor Rd. Bris 79
Locking Head Dro. Lock ... 106
Locking Moor Rd. W-S-M . 105
Locking Rd. W-S-M 105
Lockingwell Rd. Keyn 81
Lockleaze Rd. Bris 50
Locksbrook Rd. Bath 101
Locksbrook Rd. W-S-M 89
Lodge Causeway. Bris 51
Lodge Cl. Yatt 91
Lodge Dr. Kingsw 66
Lodge Dr. Lo Ash 62
Lodge Dr. W-S-M 88
Lodge Gdns. Bath 101
Lodge Hill. Bris 51
Lodge La. Wrax 60
Lodge Pl. Bris 63
Lodge Rd. Wick 53
Lodge Rd. Yate 27
Lodge St. Bris 63
Lodge Wlk. Mang 51
Lodgeside Ave. Bris 51
Lodgeside Gdns. Bris 51
Lodore Rd. Bris 50
Lodway Cl. E in G 47
Lodway Gdns. E in G 47
Lodway Rd. Bris 64
Lodway. E in G 47
Logan Rd. Bris 49
Logus Ct. Kingsw 65
Lombard St. Bris 63
Lomond Rd. Bris 35
London Rd E. Bathe 86
London Rd. Bath 85
London Rd. Bath 102
London Rd. Bris 49
London Rd. Bris 66
London Rd. Wick 67
London St. Bath 102
London St. Kingsw 65
Long Acres Cl. Bris 48
Long Ashton Rd. Lo Ash ... 62
Long Ave. Cleve 57
Long Barnaby. Mid No 132
Long Beach Rd. Kingsw 66
Long Cl. Bris 51
Long Cl. St Gif 36
Long Croft. Yate 27
Long Cross. Bris 34
Long Cross. Win 94
Long Eaton Dr. Bris 80
Long Handstones. Kingsw . 66
Long Hay. Kingsw 66
Long La. Kingsw 101
Long La. Back 6
Long La. Wring 93
Long Leaze. Burt 43
Long Mead. Yate 27
Long Meadow. Bris 50
Long Rd. Mang 52
Long Row. Bris 63
Long Thorn La. Win 111
Longacre Rd. Bris 80
Longbrook Trad Est. Bris ... 63
Longbottom. Ched 125
Longcross. Crom 10
Longden Rd. Mang 51
Longdown Dr. W-S-M 89
Longfellow Ave. Bath 101
Longfellow Rd. Rad 132
Longfellow Rd. Rod 138
Longfield Rd. Bris 49
Longford Ave. Bris 49
Longford. Yate 39
Longleat Cl. Bris 49
Longleaze Gdns. Lock 105
Longmead Ave. Bris 79
Longmead Croft. Bris 78
Longmeadow Rd. Keyn 81
Longmoor Rd. Bris 63
Longney Pl. Bris 23
Longreach Gr. Bris 80
Longs Dr. Yate 27
Longs View. Char 11
Longton Grove Rd. W-S-M 104
Longton Ind Est. W-S-M .. 104
Longway Ave. Bris 79
Longwell House. Kingsw ... 66
Longwood La. Lo Ash 61
Longwood. Bris 66
Lonsdale Ave. W-S-M 105
Lorain Wlk. Bris 34
Lorne Rd. Bath 101
Lorton Rd. Bris 35
Louise Ave. Bris 52
Louise Ave. Kingsw 52
Love La. Yate 28
Love's La. Farm 115
Lovelinch Gdns. Lo Ash 61
Lovell Ave. Kingsw 66
Lovell Mill. Bi But 113
Loveringe Cl. Bris 34
Lovers La. Paul 132

ers' Wlk. W-S-M 104 B4
ies Hill. Tims 116 A1
...bourne. Bris 79 F3
...er Ashley Rd. Bris 50 A1
...er Ashley Rd. Bris 50 A1
...er Batch. Ch Mag 96 A2
...er Borough Walls. Bath .. 101 F3
...er Bristol Rd. Bath 101 E3
...er Bristol Rd. Clut 114 C2
...er Castle St. Bris 63 F4
...er Chapel La. Fr Cot 38 B4
...er Chapel Rd. Kingsw 65 E3
...er Cheltenham Pl. Bris ... 49 F1
...er Church La. Bris 63 E4
...er Church Rd. W-S-M 104 B4
...er Claverham. Yatt 74 C2
...er Clifton Hill. Bris 63 D3
...er Cock Rd. Kingsw 65 F4
...er College St. Bris 63 E3
...er Court Rd. Alm 24 A3
...er Down Rd. Portis 45 D3
...er Fallow Cl. Bris 79 F2
...er Gay St. Bris 63 E4
...er Grove Rd. Bris 50 C2
...er Maudlin Rd. Kingsw 65 E3
...er High St. Bris 63 E4
...er House Cres. Bris 36 A2
...er Kingsdown Rd. Box 86 C2
...er Knole La. Bris 35 D2
...er Knowles Rd. Cleve 57 E1
...er Lamb St. Bris 63 E3
...er Linden Rd. Cleve 57 E2
...er Maudlin St. Bris 63 E4
...er Moor Rd. Yate 27 F2
...er Northend Est. Bathe ... 85 F3
...er Norton La. W St L 88 B2
...er Norton La. W-S-M 88 C2
...er Oldfield Park. Bath .. 101 F3
...er Park Row. Bris 63 E4
...er Queen's Rd. Cleve 57 E2
...er Rd. Hin Ble 129 F3
...er Redland Rd. Bris 49 D3
...er Sidney St. Bris 63 D2
...er St. Rode 136 C1
...er Station Rd. Bris 51 E2
...er Station Rd. Kingsw 51 E2
...er Stoke. Bath 103 D1
...er Stoke. Li St 120 A4
...er Stone Cl. Fr Cot 38 B4
...er Strode Rd. Cleve 73 D4
...er Strode. Win 112 A4
...er Thirtmere Rd. Bris 36 A4
...er Tockington Rd. Olv 14 A1
...er Whitelands. Mid No .. 133 D2
...owlis Cl. Bris 34 C2
...owther Rd. Bris 35 E1
...oxalm Bath. Bath 101 E2
...oxton Dr. Bath 101 D3
...oxton Rd. W-S-M 104 C1
...oxton Sq. Bris 80 A3
...cas Cl. Bris 64 B1
...ccombe Hill. Bris 79 D4
...uckington Cross. Hol ... 139 D1
...uckington Rd. Bris 79 D2
...ucklands Rd. Bath 84 B1
...uckley Ave. Bris 79 E3
...uckwell Rd. Bris 63 D2
...ucky La. Bris 63 E1
...udlow Cl. Bris 49 F1
...udlow Cl. Keyn 81 E3
...udlow Cl. Kingsw 66 A1
...udlow Rd. Bris 50 A4
...udwell Cl. Wint 37 F4
...udwells Orch. Paul 131 F3
...dlington Rd. Bris 64 A1
...ilsgate Rd. Bris 79 D4
...ulworth Cres. Mang 51 F4
...ulworth Rd. Keyn 81 E3
...urgan Wlk. Bris 63 E1
...uvers La. Blag 110 B1
...ucky La. Bris 48 A4
...uxton St. Bris 64 A4

Lynchmead. Wins 124 C4
Lyncombe Hill. Bath 102 A3
Lyncombe Vale Rd. Bath . 102 A2
Lyncombe Vale. Bath 102 A2
Lyncombe Wlk. Bris 51 D1
Lyndale Ave. Bris 48 B3
Lyndale Rd. Bris 64 B4
Lyndale. Yate 27 E1
Lynde Cl. Bris 79 D2
Lyndhurst Rd. Bath 101 E3
Lyndhurst Rd. Bris 48 C4
Lyndhurst Rd. Keyn 81 F2
Lyndhurst Rd. Rod 138 A4
Lyndhurst Rd. W-S-M 104 C2
Lynfield Park. Bath 84 B1
Lynmouth Cl. W-S-M 89 D1
Lynmouth Rd. Bris 50 A1
Lynn Rd. Bris 50 B3
Lynton Cl. Portis 45 F4
Lynton Pl. Bris 63 F3
Lynton Rd. Bris 138 A4
Lynton Way. Bris 37 D1
Lynton. Kingsw 66 A4
Lynwood Cl. Rod 138 A4
Lynx Cres. W-S-M 105 D2
Lyons Court Rd. Bris 80 B4
Lyons Cl. W-S-M 104 C4
Lyppiatt Rd. Bris 64 B4
Lyppincourt Rd. Bris 35 D2
Lysander Rd. Bris 35 E3
Lysander Wlk. St Gif 36 C3
Lytchet Dr. Mang 51 F4
Lytes Cary Rd. Keyn 82 A2
Lytton Gdns. Bath 101 D2
Lytton Gr. Bris 50 A4
Lytton Gr. Keyn 82 A2
Lyveden Gdns. Bris 79 D3
Lyvedon Way. Lo Ash 62 A1

Macaulay Bldgs. Bath ... 102 B2
Macaulay Rd. Bris 50 A4
Macey's Rd. Bris 79 E2
Machin Cl. Bris 34 C2
Machin Rd. Bris 34 C2
Machley La. N St P 135 F2
Macies The. Bath 84 A2
Mackie Ave. Bris 36 A1
Mackie Gr. Bris 36 A1
Mackie Rd. Bris 36 A1
Macleod Cl. Cleve 57 D1
Madam La. W-S-M 89 C1
Madam's Paddock. Ch Mag 96 A2
Maddocke House. Bris ... 79 E2
Madeira Rd. Bris 51 E4
Madeira Rd. W-S-M 87 E1
Madeline Rd. Bris 50 C1
Madison Cl. Yate 27 E1
Maesbury Rd. Keyn 82 A1
Maesbury. Bris 65 F3
Maesknoll La. Whit 97 D4
Maesknoll Rd. Bris 64 A1
Magdalen Ave. Bath 101 F3
Magdalen Rd. Bath 101 F3
Magdalene Way. W-S-M ... 89 D2
Magdalene Pl. Bris 49 F1
Magdalene Rd. Rad 133 E1
Magellan Cl. W-S-M 88 C1
Maggs Folly. Paul 115 E1
Maggs La. Whit 80 C4
Maggs La. Bris 65 E1
Magnolia Ave. W-S-M 89 D1
Magnolia Rd. Rad 132 C1
Magpie Bottom La. Bris . 65 E3
Magpie Bottom La. Kingsw 65 E3
Magpie Cl. W-S-M 105 F4
Maiden Way. Avon 47 E4
Maidenhead Rd. Bris 79 F2
Maidstone Gr. W-S-M ... 105 D1
Maidstone St. Bris 64 A4
Main Rd. Back 76 C4
Main Rd. Brock 75 F1
Main Rd. Lock 105 F1
Main Rd. Puck 52 B3
Main St. Paul 131 D2
Main View. Fr Cot 38 B4
Maisemore Ave. St Gif .. 24 A1
Maisemore. Yate 39 F3
Makin Cl. Kingsw 66 B3
Malago Rd. Bris 64 A3
Malago Vale Est. Bris ... 78 C2
Malago Wlk. Bris 78 C2
Maldowers La. Bris 65 F2
Mall The. Bath 102 A3
Mall The. Bris 52 C4
Mallard Cl. Ch Sod 40 A4
Mallard Cl. St Gif 36 C3
Mallard Wlk. W-S-M 105 F4
Mallow Cl. Clev 57 F1
Mallow Cl. Thorn 8 B3
Malmains Dr. Bris 37 D1
Malmesbury Cl. Bris 49 E2
Malmesbury Cl. Kingsw .. 66 A3
Maltings Ind Est The. Bath 101 D4
Maltings The. W-S-M 105 E4
Maltlands. W-S-M 105 D1
Maltravers Cl. St Gif ... 36 B4
Malvern Bldgs. Bath 85 D1

Malvern Ct. Bris 64 C4
Malvern Dr. Kingsw 66 B3
Malvern Dr. Thorn 15 E4
Malvern Rd. Bris 64 B2
Malvern Rd. Bris 64 C4
Malvern Rd. W-S-M 104 C3
Mancroft Ave. Bris 47 F4
Mandy Meadows. Mid No 131 F1
Mangotsfield Rd. Mang .. 52 A3
Manilla Pl. W-S-M 87 E1
Manilla Rd. Bris 63 D4
Manmoor La. Cleve 58 A1
Manor Cl The. Ab Le 62 A4
Manor Cl. E in G 47 D2
Manor Cl. Fr Cot 38 B3
Manor Cl. Olve 14 B1
Manor Cl. Paul 131 D2
Manor Cl. Well 118 B1
Manor Copse Rd. Rad ... 133 E1
Manor Court Dr. Bris 49 F4
Manor Ct. Back 76 C3
Manor Ct. Bris 50 C3
Manor Ct. E in G 47 D2
Manor Farm Cl. W-S-M .. 105 D1
Manor Farm Cres. W-S-M 105 D1
Manor Farm. St Gif 36 B2
Manor Gdns. Farm 115 F3
Manor Gdns. Lock 106 A2
Manor Gdns. Paul 131 D2
Manor Gdns. W-S-M 88 A2
Manor Pk. Kingsw 52 A2
Manor Pk. St Gif 24 A1
Manor Grange. Blea 122 A4
Manor La. Ab Lei 61 F4
Manor La. Char 11 D2
Manor La. Wint 37 F4
Manor Park. Bath 101 D4
Manor Park. Bris 49 D2
Manor Park. Olve 14 A1
Manor Pk. Rad 133 E1
Manor Pl. Bris 37 E1
Manor Rd. Ab Lei 61 F4
Manor Rd. Bris 49 F2
Manor Rd. Bris 50 C3
Manor Rd. Bris 79 D3
Manor Rd. Fr Cot 27 D4
Manor Rd. Ir Act 52 A2
Manor Rd. Kingsw 52 A2
Manor Rd. Rad 133 E1
Manor Rd. W-S-M 105 D4
Manor Rd. Wick 67 E3
Manor Terr. Rad 133 E1
Manor Villas. Bath 84 B1
Manor Way. Ch Sod 28 A1
Manor Way. Wrax 61 E2
Mansel Cl. Keyn 82 B2
Mansfield Ave. W-S-M .. 105 D2
Mansfield St. Bris 63 D1
Manston Cl. Bris 80 A3
Manvers St. Bath 102 A3
Manworthy Rd. Bris 64 C2
Manx Rd. Bris 49 E3
Maple Ave. Bris 51 E2
Maple Ave. Thorn 8 B1
Maple Cl. Bris 80 B2
Maple Cl. St Gif 36 B4
Maple Cl. W-S-M 105 D4
Maple Cl. Rad 132 C1
Maple Gdns. Bath 101 F2
Maple Leaf Ct. Bris 49 D3
Maple Rd. Bris 64 B3
Maple Rd. Bris 64 C2
Maple Wlk. Keyn 81 E2
Maple Wlk. Puck 53 E3
Maplemeade. Bris 49 D2
Maplemeade. Bris 49 D2
Mapleridge La. Hort 28 B4
Mapleridge La. Yate 28 B4
Maples The. Nail 59 E1
Maplestone Rd. Bris 80 A2
Marbeck Rd. Bris 35 D1
Marchfields Way. W-S-M 105 E1
Marconi Rd. Portis 44 C3
Mardale Cl. Bris 35 E1
Marden Rd. Keyn 82 A1
Mardon Rd. Bris 64 B3
Mardyke Ferry Rd. Bris . 63 D3
Margaret Rd. Bris 78 C4
Margaret's Bldgs. Bath . 101 F4
Margaret's Hill. Bath .. 102 A4
Margate St. Bris 63 F2
Marguerite Rd. Bris 78 C4
Marigold Wlk. Bris 63 D1
Marina Gdns. Bris 50 C2
Marindrin Dr. W-S-M ... 89 D3
Marine Hill. Cleve 57 E2
Marine Par. Cleve 57 D2
Marine Par. E in G 47 E2
Marine Par. W-S-M 104 B3
Mariner's Cl. W-S-M 88 B1
Mariner's Way. E in G .. 47 E3

Mariners Cl. Back 76 A3
Mariners Dr. Back 76 A3
Mariners Dr. Bris 48 B2
Marion Way. Kingsw 65 D2
Marion Wlk. Bris 65 D4
Marissal Cl. Bris 34 C2
Marissal Rd. Bris 34 C2
Mariston Way. Kingsw .. 66 B3
Mark La. Bris 63 E3
Market Ind Est. Yatt 74 A1
Market La. W-S-M 104 B4
Market Pl. Marsh 70 A4
Market Pl. Win 94 C4
Market Sq. Bris 51 E2
Markham Cl. Bris 47 E4
Marksbury Rd. Bris 63 E1
Marksbury. Marks 99 D1
Marlborough Ave. Bris .. 50 C2
Marlborough Bldgs. Bath 101 F4
Marlborough Dr. Bris ... 37 D1
Marlborough Dr. W-S-M . 89 D1
Marlborough Hill Pl. Bris 63 E4
Marlborough Hill. Bris .. 63 E4
Marlborough La. Bath .. 101 F4
Marlborough St. Bath .. 101 F4
Marlborough St. Bris 63 E4
Marlborough St. Bris 63 E4
Marlepit Gr. Bris 78 C4
Marling Rd. Bris 64 C4
Marlwood Dr. Bris 35 D2
Marmaduke St. Bris 64 A4
Marmion Cres. Bris 34 C2
Marne Cl. Bris 80 B2
Marsden Rd. Bath 101 E2
Marsh Cl. Wint 37 F3
Marsh Comm. Piln 22 B3
Marsh La. Bris 63 D1
Marsh La. Bris 64 B3
Marsh La. Clut 115 D1
Marsh La. E in G 46 C3
Marsh La. Paul 131 D2
Marsh Rd. Bris 63 D2
Marsh Rd. Rode 136 C1
Marsh St. Avon 47 E4
Marsh St. Bris 63 E3
Marshacre La. Aust 13 F3
Marsham Way. Kingsw .. 66 B3
Marshfield La. Bitt 67 E1
Marshfield Pk. Bris 51 E2
Marshfield Rd. Mang 51 E4
Marshfield Rd. Tor 41 F1
Marshfield Way. Bath ... 85 D1
Marshwall La. Alm 23 E1
Marson Rd. Cleve 57 E2
Marston Rd. Bris 64 A2
Martin Cl. Bris 35 F4
Martin St. Bris 63 D2
Martindale Cl. W-S-M .. 105 E4
Martindale Rd. W-S-M . 105 E4
Martingale Rd. Bris 64 C2
Martins Cl. Kingsw 65 E3
Martins Gr. W-S-M 88 C1
Martock Cres. Bris 63 E1
Martock Rd. Bris 63 E1
Martock Rd. Keyn 82 A2
Martock. W-S-M 104 C1
Martor Ind Est. Marsh .. 56 A1
Marwood Rd. Bris 79 F4
Mary Carpenter Pl. Bris 49 F1
Mary St. Bris 64 A4
Marybush La. Bris 63 F4
Marygold Leaze. Kingsw 66 A2
Mascot Rd. Bris 63 E2
Masefield Way. Bris 50 A4
Maskelyne Ave. Bris 36 A3
Masons View. Wint 37 F4
Matchells Cl. Bris 64 C3
Materman Rd. Bris 80 C3
Matford Cl. Bris 35 E2
Matford Cl. Wint 37 F3
Matford La. Stone 3 F2
Matthew's Rd. Bris 64 A3
Matthews Cl. Bris 80 C3
Maules La. St Gif 36 C1
Maunsell Rd. Bris 34 B4
Maurice Rd. Bris 49 F1
Max Mill La. Wins 124 B4
Maxse Rd. Bris 64 A2
May St. Bris 51 E1
May Tree Cl. Nail 59 F3
May Tree Cl. Rad 132 C1
May Tree Wlk. Keyn 81 E2
May's La. Pux 90 B2
Maybank Rd. Yate 27 E1
Maybec Gdns. Bris 65 D3
Maybourne. Bris 65 D1
Maybrick Rd. Bath 101 E3
Maycliffe Park. Bris 49 F1
Maylair Ave. Nail 59 F1
Mayfield Ave. Bris 51 D1
Mayfield Ave. W-S-M ... 88 C2
Mayfield Pk N. Bris 51 D1
Mayfield Pk S. Bris 51 D1
Mayfield Pk. Bris 51 D1
Mayfield Rd. Bath 101 E3
Mayfields. Keyn 81 F3

Mayflower Gdns. Nail ... 60 C3
Maynard Cl. Bris 79 E3
Maynard Cl. Cleve 57 F2
Maynard Rd. Bris 79 E3
Maynard Terr. Clut 115 D2
Maypole Cl. Clut 114 C2
Maysfield Cl. Portis 44 C3
Maysgreen Rd. Pux 90 A2
Maysmead La. Chur 109 E3
Maytree Ave. Bris 79 D4
Maytree Cl. Bris 79 D4
Mayville Ave. Bris 36 A2
Maywood Ave. Bris 51 D2
Maywood Cres. Bris 51 D2
Maywood Rd. Bris 51 E2
Maze St. Bris 64 C3
McAdam Way. Bris 62 C3
Mead Cl. Bath 101 F2
Mead Cl. Bris 47 F3
Mead La. Keyn 82 C2
Mead La. Keyn 83 D2
Mead La. Winsc 107 F2
Mead Rd. Lamb. Cor ... 100 A4
Mead Rd. Ch Sod 28 A1
Mead Rd. Portis 45 E1
Mead Rise. Bris 63 F2
Mead The. Alve 15 D3
Mead The. Bris 36 A2
Mead The. Chil 137 F1
Mead The. Chil 114 C2
Mead The. Tim 72 B1
Mead The. Farm 116 A3
Mead The. Ship 125 F4
Mead The. Tims 116 B2
Mead The. Win 95 D3
Mead The. Winsc 120 C4
Mead Way. W-S-M 15 D4
Meadow Cl. Back 76 A3
Meadow Cl. Mang 51 F4
Meadow Cl. Nail 59 E1
Meadow Cl. Portis 44 C3
Meadow Court Dr. Kingsw 66 B2
Meadow Croft. W-S-M .. 105 D1
Meadow Dr. Lock 106 A2
Meadow Dr. W in G 44 C1
Meadow Gdns. Bath 84 A1
Meadow Vale. Bris 51 D1
Meadow View. Fr Cot ... 38 B4
Meadow View. Rad 133 D1
Meadow Way. St Gif 36 C4
Meadowbank. W-S-M ... 88 C2
Meadowland Rd. Bris .. 34 C2
Meadowland. Yatt 74 A1
Meadowlands. Lock 89 F1
Meadows The. Kingsw .. 65 E2
Meadowside Dr. Bris ... 80 A2
Meadowside. Thorn 15 E4
Meadowsweet Ave. Bris 36 A2
Meads The. Burt 92 D2
Meads The. Mang 51 F4
Meadway Ave. Nail 59 E1
Meadway. Bris 48 B3
Meadway. Clut 114 C3
Meadway. Farm 116 A3
Mearcombe La. Blea ... 122 C3
Meardon Rd. Bris 80 C3
Meare Rd. Bath 102 A1
Meare. W-S-M 104 C1
Meers Bank. Bris 34 B4
Meetinghouse La. Brock 75 D1
Meg Thatchers Cl. Bris 65 D3
Meg Thatchers Gdns. Bris 65 D3
Melbourne Dr. Bris 66 A2
Melbourne Rd. Bris 49 E2
Melbourne Terr. Cleve . 57 E1
Melbury Rd. Bris 64 A1
Melcombe Rd. Bath ... 101 E3
Melita Rd. Bris 49 F2
Mellent Ave. Bris 79 E2
Mells Cl. Keyn 82 A1
Mells La. Kilm 133 D1
Mells La. Rad 133 D1
Melrose Ave. Bris 63 D4
Melrose Ave. Yate 28 A1

Melrose Cl. Yate 28 A1
Melrose Gr. Bath 101 D2
Melrose Pl. Bris 63 D4
Melton Cres. Bris 50 A4
Melville Rd. Bris 49 D1
Melville Terr. Bris 63 E2
Memorial Cl. Kingsw 65 D2
Memorial Cotts. Bath 84 B1
Memorial Rd. Kingsw 65 D2
Memorial Rd. Wring 92 C1
Mendip Ave. W-S-M 88 C1
Mendip Cl. Axb 125 E1
Mendip Cl. Keyn 81 E3
Mendip Cl. Nail 59 F1
Mendip Cl. Paul 131 F2
Mendip Cl. Yatt 91 D4
Mendip Cres. Mang 52 A4
Mendip Edge. W-S-M 121 F4
Mendip Gdns. Bath 118 B4
Mendip Gdns. Yatt 91 D4
Mendip Rd. Bris 63 E2
Mendip Rd. Portis 45 D3
Mendip Rd. W-S-M 105 D4
Mendip Rd. Yatt 91 D4
Mendip Rise. Lock 106 A2
Mendip View Ave. Bris 51 D2
Mendip View. Wick 67 E4
Mendip Villas. Co Mar 127 F4
Mendip Way. 132 C2
Menlea. Blag 110 B2
Merchant St. Bris 63 F4
Merchants Ct. Bris 63 D3
Merchants Quay. Bris 63 E3
Merchants Rd. Bris 63 D3
Merchants Rd. Bris 63 D4
Mercia Dr. Bris 50 A1
Mercier Cl. Yate 27 F1
Meredith Ct. Bris 63 D3
Merfield Rd. Bris 64 A1
Meridian Pl. Bris 63 D4
Meridian Rd. Bris 49 E1
Meridian Vale. Bris 63 D4
Meriet Ave. Bris 79 D2
Merioneth St. Bris 63 F2
Meriton St. Bris 64 A3
Merlin Cl. Bris 48 C4
Merlin Cl. W-S-M 105 F4
Merlin Park. Portis 45 D2
Merlin Rd. Bris 35 E3
Merlin Ridge. Puck 53 E2
Merlin Way. Ch Sod 39 F4
Merrimans Rd. Bris 47 E4
Merryweathers. Bris 64 C1
Merrywood Cl. Bris 63 E2
Merrywood Rd. Bris 63 E2
Merstham Rd. Bris 50 A1
Merton Rd. Bris 49 F3
Mervyn Rd. Bris 49 F2
Metford Gr. Bris 49 D2
Metford Pl. Bris 49 E2
Metford Rd. Bris 49 E2
Methwyn Cl. W-S-M 105 E4
Mews The. Bath 101 D4
Michaels Mead. Bath 84 A1
Middle Ave. Bris 63 E3
Middle La. Bath 85 D1
Middle La. K Sey 73 D2
Middle Rd. Kingsw 51 F2
Middle St. E Harp 128 C2
Middle Stoke. Li St 120 A3
Middle Yeo Green. Nail 59 E2
Middledown Rd. Marsh 55 E1
Middleford House. Bris 79 E2
Middlemead. Chil 137 F2
Middlepiece La. Keyn 99 D4
Middleton Rd. Bris 47 F4
Midford Hill. Hin Cha 119 E2
Midford La. Hi Cha 120 A3
Midford La. Li St 119 F4
Midford Rd. Bath 101 F1
Midford Rd. Sosto 119 D4
Midford. W-S-M 104 C1
Midhaven Rise. W-S-M 88 C2
Midland Bridge Rd. Bath 101 F3
Midland Rd. Bath 101 E4
Midland Rd. Bris 63 F4
Midland Rd. Kingsw 51 E2
Midland Terr. Bris 50 C2
Midland Way. Thorn 15 D4
Midsomer Enterprise Park. Mid No 132 B1
Midsummer Bldgs. Bath 85 D1
Milbourn Cl. Winsl 120 B4
Milburn Rd. W-S-M 104 C4
Mildred St. Bris 64 B4
Mile Wlk. Bris 80 A3
Miles Ct. Kingsw 65 F2
Miles Rd. Bris 49 D1
Miles St. Bath 102 A3
Miles's Bldgs. Bath 101 F4
Milestone Ct. Lock 89 E1
Milford Ave. Wick 67 D4
Milford St. Bris 63 E2
Milk St. Bath 101 F3
Mill Ave. Bris 63 E3
Mill Cl. Fr Cot 38 B4
Mill Cl. Portb 46 B1
Mill Cres. West 39 D2
Mill Hill. Well 118 C1
Mill La. Bath 85 F1
Mill La. Bath 101 D3
Mill La. Bath 119 F4
Mill La. Bitt 66 C1
Mill La. Bitt 82 C4
Mill La. Bris 63 E2
Mill La. But 111 D4
Mill La. Ch Sod 28 A1
Mill La. Ch Sod 40 C3
Mill La. Ch St 112 B4
Mill La. Co Mar 128 A4
Mill La. Cong 91 E2
Mill La. Doyn 53 F1
Mill La. Falf 9 F4
Mill La. Fr Cot 26 A1
Mill La. Kingsw 66 B3
Mill La. Olve 14 A1
Mill La. Portb 46 C1
Mill La. Pris 117 D4
Mill La. Tims 116 A1
Mill La. Wring 109 F4
Mill Leg. Cong 91 F2
Mill Pool Ct. Bris 35 D1
Mill rd. Mid No 133 D1
Mill Rd. Wint 37 E2
Mill Stream Cl. Axb 125 D1
Millard Cl. Bris 35 E1
Millard's Hill. Mid No 132 A2
Millbank Cl. Bris 64 C2
Millbrook Ave. Bris 64 C2
Millbrook Pl. Bath 102 A3
Millbrook Rd. Yate 27 D1
Millcross. Cleve 73 E4
Millers Cl. E in G 47 E2
Millers Dr. Kingsw 66 B3
Millers Rise. W-S-M 89 D2
Millfield Dr. Kingsw 66 B3
Millfield. Mid No 137 F4
Millfield. Thorn 8 B1
Millground Rd. Bris 78 C3
Millier Rd. Brock 92 A4
Milliman Cl. Bris 79 E3
Millmead House. Bris 79 E2
Millmead Rd. Bath 101 E3
Millpond St. Bris 50 A1
Millward Gr. Bris 51 E2
Milner Green. Kingsw 66 A3
Milner Rd. Bris 49 F3
Milsom St. Bath 101 F4
Milsom St. Bris 64 A4
Milton Ave. Bath 101 F2
Milton Ave. W-S-M 105 D4
Milton Brow. W-S-M 88 A1
Milton Cl. Nail 59 F2
Milton Cl. Yate 27 E1
Milton Green. W-S-M 88 B1
Milton Hill. W-S-M 88 A1
Milton Park Rd. W-S-M 88 B1
Milton Pk. Bris 64 B4
Milton Rd. Bris 49 F3
Milton Rd. Rad 132 B1
Milton Rd. Yate 27 E1
Milton Rise. W-S-M 88 B1
Miltons Cl. Bris 79 E2
Milverton. W-S-M 104 C1
Milward Rd. Keyn 81 F3
Mina Rd. Bris 50 A1
Minehead Rd. Bris 64 A1
Minerva Gdns. Bath 101 E2
Minor's La. Avon 34 A4
Minsmere Rd. Keyn 82 A2
Minster Way. Bath 102 B4
Minto Rd. Bris 50 A1
Minto Road Ind Centre. Bris 49 F1
Mission Rd. Ir Act 27 D2
Mitchell Ct. Bris 63 F3
Mitchell La. Bris 63 F3
Mitford-Slade Ct. Yatt 91 E4
Mivart St. Bris 50 A1
Mizzymead Cl. Nail 59 E1
Mizzymead Rd. Nail 59 F1
Mizzymead Rise. Nail 59 E1
Modecombe Gr. Bris 34 C2
Mogg St. Bris 50 A1
Molesworth Cl. Bris 79 D2
Molesworth Dr. Bris 79 D2
Molesworth Dr. Bris 79 D2
Molly Cl. Clut 130 C4
Monger La. Mid No 132 A2
Monk Rd. Bris 49 E2
Monk's Park Ave. Bris 49 F4
Monks Ave. Bris 65 D4
Monks Hill. W-S-M 88 A2
Monksdale Rd. Bath 101 E2
Monkton Ave. W-S-M 105 D1
Monkton Farleigh. Mon Far 103 F4
Monkton Rd. Kingsw 65 D3
Monmouth Cl. Portis 44 C2
Monmouth Hill. Alm 23 F2
Monmouth Paddock. N St P 135 F2
Monmouth Pl. Bath 101 F3
Monmouth Rd. Bris 49 E2
Monmouth Rd. E in G 47 E3
Monmouth Rd. Keyn 81 E3
Monmouth St. Bath 101 F3
Monmouth St. Bris 63 F2
Monsdale Cl. Bris 35 D2
Monsdale Dr. Bris 35 D1
Montague Cl. St Gif 36 C3
Montague Hill S. Bris 63 E4
Montague Hill. Bris 63 E4
Montague Pl. Bris 63 E4
Montague Rd. Keyn 82 B1
Montague Rd. Well 133 F3
Montague St. Bris 63 E4
Montgomery St. Bris 63 F2
Montpelier E. W-S-M 87 F1
Montpelier. W-S-M 104 C4
Montreal Ave. Bris 50 A4
Montrose Ave. Bris 49 E1
Montrose Dr. Kingsw 66 A3
Montrose Pk. Bris 64 B1
Montroy Cl. Bris 49 E3
Moon St. Bris 63 F4
Moor Croft Dr. Kingsw 65 F2
Moor Croft Rd. Lock 105 F2
Moor End Spout. Nail 59 E1
Moor Gr. Bris 48 A4
Moor Green. Axb 125 E1
Moor La. Back 75 F3
Moor La. Cleve 58 A1
Moor La. Lock 105 E2
Moor La. Nail 58 C2
Moor La. Olve 24 A4
Moor La. Piln 23 F4
Moor La. W in G 45 F1
Moor La. W-S-M 105 F4
Moor Park. Cleve 57 F1
Moor Rd. Ban 107 D3
Moor Rd. Yatt 74 A1
Moordell Cl. Yate 27 E1
Moorend Gdns. Bris 47 F4
Moorend Rd. Wint 37 E2
Moorfield Rd. Back 76 A3
Moorfields Cl. Bath 101 E2
Moorfields Ct. Nail 59 E1
Moorfields Rd. Bath 101 E2
Moorfields Rd. Nail 59 E1
Moorham Rd. Wins 108 A1
Moorhill St. Bris 50 A1
Moorhouse La. Avon 34 A2
Moorings The. E in G 47 E2
Moorland Rd. Bath 101 E3
Moorland Rd. W-S-M 104 C2
Moorland Rd. Yate 27 E1
Moorland St. Axb 125 E1
Moorlands Cl. Nail 59 E1
Moorlands Rd. Bris 50 C2
Moorlands Rd. Bris 51 D1
Moorledge La. Ch Mag 96 B1
Moorledge La. Pens 113 F4
Moorledge Rd. Ch Mag 96 A1
Moorpark Ave. Yate 27 E1
Moorsfield. Clut 114 C2
Moorside Ct. Cleve 57 F1
Moorside Villas. Cleve 57 E1
Moorslade La. Falf 3 E1
Moorslade La. Stone 3 E1
Moravian Ct. Kingsw 65 E4
Moravian Rd. Kingsw 65 E4
Morden Wlk. Bris 80 B4
Moreton Cl. Bris 80 A2
Moreton St. Bris 63 F4
Morford St. Bath 101 F4
Morgan Cl. Keyn 82 B1
Morgan St. Bris 49 F1
Morgan's La. E Harp 128 C2
Morgans Hill Cl. Nail 75 E4
Morley Ave. Kingsw 52 A2
Morley Cl. Kingsw 51 E2
Morley Cl. St Gif 36 B4
Morley Rd. Bris 63 E2
Morley Rd. Kingsw 51 E2
Morley Sq. Bris 49 F2
Morley St. Bris 49 F1
Morley St. Bris 64 A4
Morley Terr. Kingsw 51 E1
Morley Terr. Mid No 133 D2
Mornington Rd. Bris 49 D1
Morpeth Rd. Bris 79 E4
Morris La. Bathe 86 A2
Morris Rd. Bris 50 A3
Morse Rd. Bris 64 B4
Mortimer Cl. Bath 84 A1
Mortimer Rd. Bris 36 A1
Mortimer Rd. Bris 63 D4
Morton St. Bris 64 A4
Morton St. Thorn 8 B2
Morton Way. Thorn 8 B1
Moseley Gr. W-S-M 104 C1
Mount Beacon Row. Bath 84 C1
Mount Beacon. Bath 85 D1
Mount Cl. Fr Cot 37 F4
Mount Cres. Wint 37 F3
Mount Gdns. Kingsw 65 E3
Mount Gr. Bath 101 D2
Mount Hill Rd. Kingsw 65 E3
Mount Pleasant Terr. Bris 63 E2
Mount Pleasant. Bath 102 B1
Mount Pleasant. E in G 47 E2
Mount Pleasant. Rad 133 D1
Mount Rd. Bath 101 D2
Mount Rd. Bath 101 F4
Mount View. Bath 101 D2
Mountain Ash. Bath 84 B1
Mountain Wood. Bathf 86 B1
Mountbatten Cl. W-S-M 88 C2
Mountbatten Cl. Yate 27 E2
Mounteney's La. Kings 18 B4
Mow Barton. Bris 78 C3
Mow Barton. Yate 27 E1
Mowbray Rd. Bris 80 B4
Mowcroft Rd. Bris 79 E2
Moxham Dr. Bris 79 E2
Mud La. Yatt 74 C1
Muddy La. W ST L 89 D4
Muirfield. Kingsw 66 A3
Muirfield. Yate 39 F4
Mulberry Cl. Back 76 A3
Mulberry Cl. Kingsw 65 F4
Mulberry Dr. Kingsw 51 F1
Mulberry La. Blea 122 B3
Mulberry Rd. Cong 91 F2
Mulberry Wlk. Bris 48 B4
Mule St. N Nib 4 A2
Mullberry Cl. W-S-M 89 D1
Muller Ave. Bris 49 F2
Muller Rd. Bris 50 A2
Mulready Cl. Bris 50 B3
Mumbleys Hill. Thorn 14 C4
Mumbleys La. Thorn 14 C4
Murford Ave. Bris 79 D2
Murford Wlk. Bris 79 D2
Murray St. Bris 63 E2
Musgrove Cl. Bris 34 B1
Myrtle Dr. Bris 47 F3
Myrtle Hill. E in G 47 E2
Myrtle Rd. Bris 63 E4
Myrtle St. Bris 63 D2
Myrtles The. Lock 105 E1

Nags Head Hill. Bris 65 D4
Nailsea Cl. Bris 79 D4
Nailsea Park Cl. Nail 59 F1
Nailsea Park. Nail 59 F1
Nailsea Wall. Nail 74 B4
Nailsea Wall. Yatt 74 B4
Nailsworth Dr. Yate 27 F1
Naish Hill. Wrax 59 F4
Naish La. Ba Gu 77 E2
Naish's Cross. Chil 137 E2
Naishcombe Hill. Wick 67 E4
Naishes Ave. P St J 133 E4
Naite The. O-on-S 7 E3
Nanny Hurn's La. Bi Sut 114 A1
Nanny Hurn's La. Clut 130 A4
Napier Ct. Bris 63 D3
Napier Miles Rd. Bris 48 A4
Napier Rd. Avon 33 D1
Napier Rd. Bath 84 A2
Napier Rd. Bris 49 D1
Napier Rd. Bris 50 A1
Napier Sq. Avon 33 D1
Napier St. Bris 64 A3
Narrow La. Kingsw 51 F2
Narrow Plain. Bris 63 F3
Narrow Quay. Bris 63 E3
Narroways Rd. Bris 50 A2
Naseby Wlk. Bris 50 C1
Nash Cl. Keyn 82 A3
Nash Dr. Bris 50 B4
Nates La. Wring 92 C1
Naunton Way. W-S-M 88 A1
Neath Rd. Bris 64 B4
Nelson Ct. W-S-M 88 C2
Nelson Pl W. Bath 101 F3
Nelson Pl. Bath 102 A4
Nelson Rd. Mang 51 E2
Nelson St. Bris 63 D1
Nelson St. Bris 63 E4
Nelson Terr. Bath 102 A4
Nelson Villas. Bath 101 F3
Nempnett St. But 111 E3
Neston Wlk. Bris 79 F4
Netham Park Ind Est. Bris 64 B3
Netham Rd. Bris 64 B4
Netham View Ind Park. Bris 64 B4
Netherways. Cleve 57 D1
Nettlestone Cl. Bris 34 C2
Nettleton Rd. Burt 43 D2
Neva Rd. W-S-M 104 C3
Nevalan Dr. Bris 65 D3
Nevil Rd. Bris 49 F2
Neville Rd. Kingsw 51 F1
New Bldgs. Bris 50 C2
New Bldgs. P St J 133 D4
New Bond St. Bath 102 A3
New Bond Street Pl. Bath 102 A3
New Bristol Rd. W-S-M 88 C1
New Brunswick Ave. Bris 65 D4
New Charlotte St. Bris 63 E2
New Cheltenham Rd. Kingsw 51 F1
New Cut Bow. K Sey 73 D3
New Fosseway Rd. Bris 80 A3
New John St. Bris 63 E2
New King St. Bath 101 F3
New Kingsley Rd. Bris 63 F3
New La. Alve 15 E3
New Leaze. St Gif 24 B2
New Orchard St. Bath 102 A3
New Queen St. Bris 63 F2
New Queen St. Bris 65 D4
New Rd. Bathf 86
New Rd. Bris 36
New Rd. Bris 36
New Rd. Chur 108
New Rd. E in G 47
New Rd. Farm 115
New Rd. Hi Cha 120
New Rd. Kilm 139
New Rd. N Nib 5
New Rd. Olve 14
New Rd. Paul 115
New Rd. Pens 97
New Rd. Ship 108
New Rd. Tyth 16
New Rd. W-u-E 11
New Rd. Wickw 27
New Rd. Wring 93
New Rd. Yate 17
New Rock Ind Est. Chil 137
New St. Bath 101
New St. Bris 63
New St. Char 11
New Station Rd. Bris 51
New Thomas St. Bris 63
New Tyning La. Hort 29
New Walls. Bris 63
New Wlk. Kingsw 65
Newark St. Bath 102
Newbolt Cl. W-S-M 105
Newbourne Rd. W-S-M 105
Newbridge Cl. Bris 64
Newbridge Ct. Bath 101
Newbridge Gdns. Bath 101
Newbridge Hill. Bath 101
Newbridge Rd. Bath 101
Newbridge Rd. Bris 64
Newbury Rd. Bris 50
Newchurch Rd. W-S-M 104
Newclose La. Co Mar 128
Newcombe Dr. Bris 48
Newcombe Rd. Bris 48
Newditch La. Ba Gu 77
Newent Ave. Bris 65
Newfields. Blag 126
Newfoundland Rd. Bris 63
Newfoundland St. Bris 63
Newfoundland Way. Bris 49
Newgate. Bris 63
Newhaven Pl. Portis 44
Newhaven Rd. Portis 44
Newland Dr. Bris 79
Newland Rd. Bris 79
Newland Rd. W-S-M 104
Newland Wlk. Bris 79
Newlands Ave. Fr Cot 38
Newlands Green. Cleve 57
Newlands Hill. Portis 45
Newlands Rd. Keyn 81
Newlands The. Bris 51
Newlyn Ave. Bris 48
Newlyn Way. Yate 27
Newlyn Wlk. Bris 64
Newman Cl. West 39
Newmans La. Tims 116
Newmarket Ave. Bris 63
Newnham Cl. Bris 80
Newnham Pl. Bris 23
Newpit La. Bitt 66
Newport Cl. Cleve 57
Newport Cl. Portis 44
Newport Rd. E in G 47
Newport St. Bris 63
Newquay Rd. Bris 63
Newry Wlk. Bris 63
Newsome Ave. E in G 47
Newton Cl. E Harp 128
Newton Cl. Kingsw 52
Newton Dr. Kingsw 66
Newton Green. Nail 75
Newton Rd. Bath 100
Newton Rd. Kingsw 66
Newton Rd. W-S-M 104
Newton St. Bris 64
Newton's Rd. W-S-M 88
Newtown. Char 11
Niblett Cl. Kingsw 65
Niblett's Hill. Bris 65
Nibley La. Ir Act 26
Nibley Rd. Bris 47
Nichol's Rd. Portis 44
Nicholas La. Bris 65
Nicholas Rd. Bris 50
Nicholas St. Bris 63
Nicholettes. Kingsw 66
Nicholls La. Wint 37
Nigel Park. Bris 47
Nightingale Cl. Fr Cot 38
Nightingale Cl. Thorn 8
Nightingale Cl. W-S-M 88
Nightingale Gdns. Nail 59
Nightingale La. Wint 38
Nightingale Rise. Portis 44
Nightingale Way. Rod 138
Nine Tree Hill. Bris 49
Ninth Ave. Bris 36
Nippors Way. Wins 124
Nithsdale Rd. W-S-M 104
Noble Ave. Kingsw 66

Nomis Park. Cong 91 F1
lore Gdns. Portis 45 E3
lore Park Dr. Portis 44 C3
lore Rd. Portis 45 D3
orfolk Ave. Bris 49 F1
orfolk Ave. Bris 63 F4
orfolk Bldg. Bath 101 F3
orfolk Cres. Bath 101 F3
orfolk Gr. Keyn 81 E2
orfolk Pl. Bris 63 E2
orfolk Rd. Portis 45 F2
orland Rd. Bris 62 C4
orley Rd. Bris 49 F4
orman Gr. Bris 51 E1
orman Rd. Bris 50 A1
orman Rd. Keyn 82 C2
orman Rd. Sist 66 A4
ormanby Rd. Bris 50 A1
ormans The. Bath 85 F1
orman's The. Bris 49 D1
orrisville Rd. Bris 49 D1
orth Croft. Kingsw 66 B2
orth Devon Rd. Bris 51 D3
orth Down Cl. Ship 125 F4
orth Down La. Ship 125 F4
orth East Rd. Thorn 8 B1
orth End Rd. Yatt 133 F2
orth End. Yatt 74 A1
orth Gr. E in G 47 E2
orth Green St. Bris 62 C3
orth Hills Cl. W-S-M 105 D1
orth La. Bath 102 B3
orth La. Nail 59 D1
orth La. W-S-M 104 C4
orth Leaze. Lo Ash 62 A1
orth Meadows. P St J 133 F4
orth Par. Bath 102 A2
orth Par. Yate 27 F1
orth Parade Bldgs. Bath 102 A2
orth Parade Pas. Bath 102 A3
orth Parade Rd. Bath 102 A2
orth Pk. Kingsw 51 F1
orth Rd. Ban 107 D2
orth Rd. Bath 102 B1
orth Rd. Bris 49 F1
orth Rd. Bris 63 D2
orth Rd. Nr I Act 27 D2
orth Rd. Lymp 122 B1
orth Rd. Mid No 132 A1
orth Rd. St Gif 36 C2
orth Rd. Thorn 8 B1
orth Rd. Tims 116 A1
orth Rd. Wint 37 F4
orth Rd. Qur 27 D2
orth Side Rd. Yate 94 A4
orth St. Bris 63 D2
orth St. Bris 63 E4
orth St. Kingsw 66 B2
orth St. Mang 51 F3
orth St. N St P 135 F2
orth St. Nail 59 D1
orth St. Nail 104 C4
orth St. Wickw 18 A3
orth Stoke La. Bitt 83 E1
orth View Cl. Bath 101 D3
orth View Dr. Ban 107 D1
orth View. Bris 49 D2
orth View. Kingsw 51 E2
orth View. Mang 51 F3
orth View. Rad 133 D1
orth View. Yatt 133 F3
orth Way. Mid No 132 A1
orth Wlk. Yate 27 F2
orthampton Bldgs. Bath 101 F4
orthampton House. Wrax 60 B2
orthampton St. Bath 101 F4
orthaven Bsns Centre.
  Yate 27 E2
orthcote Rd. Bris 48 C1
orthcote Rd. Bris 64 C4
orthcote Rd. Mang 51 F3
orthcote St. Bris 50 A1
orthcot Rd. Paul 132 C3
orthend Ave. Kingsw 51 E1
orthend Gdns. Kingsw 51 E1
orthend Rd. Kingsw 51 F1
orthend Way. Cleve 57 F2
orthfield Ave. Kingsw 65 E3
orthfield Rd. Portis 44 C3
orthfield. Mid No 133 D2
orthfield. Tims 116 B2
orthfield. Winsl 120 C4
orthfield. Yate 39 E4
orthfields Cl. Bath 84 C1
orthfields. Bath 84 C1
orthgate St. Bath 102 A3
orthleach Wlk. Bris 47 F3
orthleigh Ave. W-S-M 88 B1
orthmead Ave. Mid No 131 F1
orthmead Cl. Mid No 131 F1
orthmead La. Ir Act 26 B3
orthmead Rd. Mid No 131 F1
orthover Rd. Bris 35 D1
orthridge Bsns Centre.
  Yate 27 E1

Northumberland Pl. Bath 102 A3
Northumberland Rd. Bris 49 E1
Northumbria Dr. Bris 49 D3
Northville Rd. Bris 36 A2
Northway. Bris 36 A2
Northwick Gdns. Bi Sut 113 E2
Northwick Rd. Ch Mag 96 B4
Northwick Rd. Piln 22 B4
Northwick Rd. Wint 96 B4
Northwoods Wlk. Bris 35 E2
Norton Cl. Ch Mag 96 A2
Norton Cl. Kingsw 65 F4
Norton La. Ch Mag 96 B3
Norton La. Hin Cha 135 E4
Norton La. W St L 88 B2
Norton La. Whit 135 E4
Norton La. Whit 80 B1
Norton La. Whit 96 B3
Norton Rd. Bris 64 C2
Nortons Wood La. Cleve 58 A3
Norwich Dr. Bris 64 C3
Norwood Ave. Bath 102 C3
Norwood Gr. Portis 44 C3
Notgrove Cl. W-S-M 88 A1
Nottingham Rd. Bris 49 F2
Nottingham St. Bris 63 F2
Nova Scotia Pl. Bris 63 D3
Novers Cres. Bris 79 E4
Novers Hill Trading Est. Bris 63 E1
Novers Hill. Bris 79 E4
Novers La. Bris 79 E4
Novers Park Dr. Bris 79 E4
Novers Park Rd. Bris 79 E4
Novers Rd. Bris 79 E4
Nugent Hill. Bris 49 F1
Nunney Cl. Keyn 82 A1
Nupdown Rd. O-On-S 1 C3
Nupdown Rd. Rock 2 A2
Nursery Gdns. Bris 35 D2
Nursery The. Bris 63 D2
Nutfield Gr. Bris 36 A1
Nutgrove Ave. Bris 63 F2
Nuthatch Dr. Ch Mag 96 A2
Nuthatch Dr. Bris 50 C3
Nutwell Rd. W-S-M 88 C1
Nutwell Sq. W-S-M 88 C1
Nye Rd. Winsc 107 F3
Nympsfield. Kingsw 51 F1

Oak Ave. Bath 101 E2
Oak Cl. St Gif 36 B4
Oak Cl. Yate 26 C2
Oak Dr. Portis 45 D2
Oak Gr. E in G 47 E3
Oak La. Bris 50 C1
Oak Rd. Bris 49 F3
Oak Rd. Cor 70 C3
Oak Rd. Wins 125 D4
Oak St. Bath 101 F3
Oak Terr. Rad 132 B2
Oak Tree Ave. Puck 53 D2
Oak Tree Cl. Kingsw 65 F1
Oak Tree Wlk. Keyn 81 E2
Oakdale Ave. Mang 51 E4
Oakdale Cl. Mang 51 F4
Oakdale Ct. Mang 51 F4
Oakdale Gdns. W-S-M 88 C1
Oakdale Rd. Bris 80 D4
Oakdale Rd. Mang 51 F4
Oakenhill Wlk. Bris 64 C1
Oakes La. Tor 42 C1
Oakes Cl. Tor 42 C1
Oakfield Gr. Bris 63 D4
Oakfield Pl. Bris 63 D4
Oakfield Rd. Bath 101 E4
Oakfield Rd. Bris 63 D4
Oakfield Rd. Keyn 81 F1
Oakfield Rd. Kingsw 65 E4
Oakford Ave. W-S-M 104 C4
Oaklord La. Marsh 70 A1
Oakhanger Dr. Bris 34 A1
Oakhill Ave. Kingsw 65 F1
Oakhill Cl. Nail 60 A1
Oakhill Rd. Bath 101 F1
Oakhill. Bris 34 B2
Oakhill. W-S-M 105 D1
Oakhurst Rd. Bris 48 C3
Oakland Dr. Dock 105 F2
Oakland Rd. Bris 49 D1
Oakland Rd. Bris 64 C4
Oaklands Cl. Mang 52 A3
Oaklands Dr. Aust 24 A2
Oaklands Dr. Bris 51 D4
Oaklands Dr. Kingsw 66 B1
Oaklands Rd. Mang 52 A3
Oaklands. Clav 114 C1
Oaklands. Paul 131 F2
Oakleaze Rd. Thorn 8 B1
Oakleaze. Fr Col 38 B4
Oakleigh Ave. Bris 64 B4
Oakleigh Cl. Back 76 A3
Oakleigh Gdns. Kingsw 66 B1
Oakley Rd. Bris 49 F4
Oakley. Bath 102 C3
Oakley. Cleve 73 D4
Oakmead Pk. Bris 64 A1
Oakridge Cl. Kingsw 66 A4

Oakridge Cl. Wins 125 D4
Oaks La. Wins 125 D4
Oaks The. Win 94 C4
Oaksey Gr. Nail 60 A1
Oaktree Cres. St Gif 24 B1
Oaktree Ct. Bris 47 F4
Oaktree Gdns. Bris 78 C3
Oakwood Ave. Bris 49 D3
Oakwood Rd. Bris 49 D3
Oatlands Ave. Bris 80 A3
Oberon Ave. Bris 50 C1
Oclite Rd. Bath 101 E1
Odins Rd. Bath 101 E1
Okebourne Cl. Bris 35 D2
Okebourne Rd. Bris 35 D2
Old Ashley Hill. Bris 49 F1
Old Aust Rd. Alm 24 B3
Old Banwell Rd. Lock 106 A2
Old Barn La. But 94 A3
Old Barrow Hill. Bris 47 E4
Old Bond St. Bath 101 F3
Old Bread St. Bris 63 F3
Old Bristol Rd. Priddy 128 A2
Old Bristol Rd. W-S-M 89 D1
Old Chelsea La. Wrax 61 E2
Old Church Rd. Axb 125 E1
Old Church Rd. Cleve 57 E2
Old Church Rd. Nail 75 E4
Old Church Rd. W-S-M 104 B4
Old Coach Rd. Co Bi 124 C2
Old Coach Rd. Ch Sod 42 B4
Old Down Rd. Gr Bad 30 C1
Old England Way. P St J 133 F4
Old Farm La. Bris 65 D3
Old Ferry Rd. Bath 101 E3
Old Fosse Rd. Bath 101 E1
Old Fosse Way. Mid No 132 C3
Old Frome Rd. Bath 118 C4
Old Gloucester Rd. Alve 15 D3
Old Gloucester Rd. Bris 25 E2
Old Gloucester Rd. Bris 37 D1
Old Gloucester Rd. Fr Cot 25 E2
Old Gloucester Rd. St Gif 37 D2
Old Gloucester Rd. Ston 37 D4
Old Gloucester Rd. Thorn 9 D1
Old Gloucester Rd. Wint 37 D4
Old Hill. Winn 92 C2
Old King St. Bath 101 F4
Old King St. Bris 63 E3
Old La. Farm 101 F4
Old La. Nail 59 E3
Old Manor Cl. Char 11 D3
Old Market St. Bris 63 F3
Old Midford Rd. Sosto 119 D4
Old Mill Rd. Portis 45 E3
Old Millard's Hill. Mid No 132 A2
Old Mills End. Paul 131 F1
Old Mills La. Paul 131 E2
Old Newbridge Hill. Bath 100 C3
Old Orchard St. Bath 102 A3
Old Orchard. Bath 102 A4
Old Park Hill. Bris 63 E4
Old Park Rd. Bris 47 E4
Old Park Rd. Cleve 57 E4
Old Pit Terr. Mid No 132 C2
Old Post Office La. W-S-M 104 B4
Old Priory Rd. E in G 47 D2
Old Quarry Rd. Bris 47 F4
Old Quarry Rise. Bris 47 F4
Old Quarry. Bath 101 E1
Old Rd. Rad 133 E1
Old Rectory Rd. Kings 11 F2
Old School La. Blea 122 B3
Old Sneed Ave. Bris 48 B2
Old Sneed Park. Bris 48 B2
Old Sneed Rd. Bris 48 B2
Old St. Cleve 57 F3
Old Station Cl. Wring 92 B1
Old Tarnwell. Pens 97 D1
Old Track. Li St 119 F4
Old Vicarage Green. Keyn 81 F3
Old Wall. Blea 121 E1
Old Water Gdns The. Blea 110 C1
Old Wells Rd. Bath 101 F2
Old Weston Rd. Back 77 D4
Old Weston Rd. Cong 91 D3
Oldacre Rd. Bris 80 A2
Oldbury Chase. Kingsw 66 A1
Oldbury Court Dr. Bris 51 D3
Oldbury Court Rd. Bris 51 D3
Oldbury La. Thorn 8 A2
Oldbury La. Wick 67 E3
Oldfield La. Bath 101 E2
Oldfield Pl. Bris 62 C3
Oldfield Rd. Bath 101 E2
Oldfield Rd. Bris 62 C3
Oldfield. Cleve 57 F3
Oldfields La. Alve 25 E4
Oldlands Ave. Fr Col 38 B3
Oldmead Wlk. Bris 78 C4
Oldmixon Cres. W-S-M 105 D2
Oldmixon Rd. W-S-M 105 D1
Oldmixon Rd. W-S-M 105 D1
Oldown Hill. Olve 14 B1

Oldville Ave. Cleve 57 E1
Olive Gdns. Alve 14 C2
Olveston Rd. Bris 49 F3
Olympus Cl. St Gif 36 B3
Olympus Rd. Bris 35 E4
Ooite Gr. Bath 118 B4
Oram Ct. Keyn 65 F2
Orange Gr. Bath 102 A3
Orange St. Bris 63 F4
Orchard Ave. Mid No 131 F1
Orchard Ave. Nail 58 C2
Orchard Ave. Thorn 8 B1
Orchard Bvd. Kingsw 66 A2
Orchard Cl. Back 77 D4
Orchard Cl. Ban 107 D2
Orchard Cl. Bi Sut 113 E2
Orchard Cl. Bris 48 C3
Orchard Cl. Char 11 D3
Orchard Cl. Keyn 81 E3
Orchard Cl. Kingsw 65 F4
Orchard Cl. Portis 45 E3
Orchard Cl. W-S-M 88 A2
Orchard Cl. Westw 120 C2
Orchard Cl. Win 94 B4
Orchard Cl. Wring 92 C1
Orchard Cl. Yate 27 F1
Orchard Cres. Bris 47 E4
Orchard Dr. Aust 13 D4
Orchard Dr. Bris 79 D3
Orchard Dr. Wink 108 A2
Orchard End. E Harp 128 C2
Orchard Gdns. Kingsw 65 F4
Orchard Grange. Thorn 8 A1
Orchard La. Bris 63 E3
Orchard Lea. Alve 15 D3
Orchard Lea. E in G 47 E2
Orchard Pl. W-S-M 104 C4
Orchard Rd. Axb 125 E1
Orchard Rd. Back 76 A3
Orchard Rd. Back 76 A3
Orchard Rd. Bris 64 C4
Orchard Rd. Cleve 57 E1
Orchard Rd. Fr Cot 38 B4
Orchard Rd. Kingsw 65 F4
Orchard Rd. Lo Ash 61 F3
Orchard Rd. Nail 59 E1
Orchard Rd. Paul 131 F3
Orchard Rd. Puck 53 D3
Orchard Rise. Olve 14 A2
Orchard St. Bris 63 D3
Orchard St. W-S-M 104 C4
Orchard Terr. Bath 101 D3
Orchard The. Ban 107 D2
Orchard The. E in G 47 E2
Orchard The. Fr Col 38 A4
Orchard The. Hi Cha 120 B3
Orchard The. Lock 106 A3
Orchard The. Pens 97 D1
Orchard The. Pens 97 F2
Orchard Vale. Kingsw 65 F4
Orchard Vale. Mid No 131 F1
Orchard Wlk. Chur 108 C2
Orchards The. Kingsw 65 E1
Oriel Gdns. Bath 85 E1
Oriel Gr. Bath 101 D2
Orion Dr. St Gif 36 B3
Orland Way. Kingsw 66 A2
Orlebar Gdns. Bris 34 A1
Orme Dr. Cleve 57 F3
Ormerod Rd. Bris 48 C3
Ormonds Cl. St Gif 24 C1
Ormsley Cl. St Gif 36 B4
Orpen Gdns. Bris 50 B3
Orpen Park. St Gif 24 B2
Orpheus Ave. St Gif 36 B3
Orwell Dr. Keyn 81 F4
Orwell St. Bris 63 F2
Osborne Ave. W-S-M 104 C4
Osborne Ave. W-S-M 104 C4
Osborne Cl. St Gif 36 B2
Osborne Rd. Bath 101 D4
Osborne Rd. Bris 63 E2
Osborne Rd. Bris 63 E4
Osborne Rd. Bris 64 A1
Osborne Rd. W-S-M 104 C4
Osborne Terr. Bris 63 D1
Osborne Villas. Bris 63 E4
Oslings La. Bathf 86 A1
Osprey Dr. W-S-M 105 F2
Osprey Gdns. W-S-M 88 C1
Osprey Pk. Thorn 8 C2
Osprey Rd. Bris 64 B4
Ottawa Rd. W-S-M 104 C4
Otter Rd. Cleve 57 F1
Otterford Cl. Bris 80 A3
Ottery Cl. Bris 34 A1
Otrells Mead. St Gif 24 B2
Oval The. Bath 101 D2
Over La. Alm 23 F1
Overdale. Mid No 132 C2
Overdale. Tims 116 B2
Overhill. E in G 47 E2

Overndale Rd. Mang 51 E3
Overhill Ct. Mang 51 E3
Overhill Rd. Mang 51 E3
Overhurst Ct. Mang 51 E3
Overton Rd. Bris 49 F1
Owen Dr. Wrax 91 D2
Owen Gr. Bris 49 D3
Owen St. Bris 64 A4
Owls Head Rd. Kingsw 65 F3
Oxbarton. St Gif 36 C3
Oxen Leaze. St Gif 24 C1
Oxford Pl. 102 B1
Oxford Pl. Bris 50 A1
Oxford Pl. Bris 62 C3
Oxford Pl. W-S-M 104 B4
Oxford St. Bris 63 E4
Oxford St. Bris 63 F2
Oxford St. Bris 64 A3
Oxford St. Bris 64 B4
Oxford St. W-S-M 104 B4
Oxhouse La. Win 94 B4
Oxhouse La. Wrax 61 D3
Oxlease. Bris 79 E2
Oxleaze La. Bris 78 C2
Ozleworth. Kingsw 66 A4

Pack Horse La. Sosto 119 D4
Paddock Cl. St Gif 24 B1
Paddock Gdns. Alve 15 D3
Paddock Gdns. Bris 79 F2
Paddock The. Ban 107 D2
Paddock The. Cor 107 D2
Paddock The. Portis 45 E2
Paddock Woods. Bath 102 B1
Paddocks The. Bath 102 A1
Paddocks The. Chur 108 B2
Paddocks The. Thorn 8 A1
Paddocks The. W-S-M 104 B1
Padfield Cl. Bath 101 D3
Padleigh Hill. Bath 101 D1
Padmore Ct. Bris 64 B4
Padstow Rd. Bris 79 F4
Pagans Hill. Ch Mag 95 E1
Pagans Hill. Ch St 95 E1
Page Rd. Kingsw 51 F2
Page's Ct. Yatt 91 E4
Pages Mead. Avon 47 E4
Painswick Ave. St Gif 36 A4
Painswick Dr. Yate 27 F1
Palace Yd Mews. Bath 101 F3
Palmdale Cl. Kingsw 66 A2
Palmer Row. W-S-M 104 C4
Palmer St. W-S-M 104 C4
Palmers Cl. Kingsw 66 B3
Palmers Leaze. St Gif 37 D4
Palmers Way. Lock 105 E1
Palmerston Rd. Bris 49 E2
Palmerston St. Bris 63 D2
Palmyra Rd. Bris 63 D1
Par The. Bath 101 D3
Parade The. Bris 23 F1
Parade The. Bris 47 F3
Parade The. Ch Sod 28 A1
Paradise Row. Pens 98 A3
Paragon Rd. W-S-M 87 E1
Paragon The. Bris 62 C3
Park Ave. Bath 101 F3
Park Ave. Bris 50 B2
Park Ave. Bris 64 C3
Park Ave. Bris 63 F4
Park Ave. Fr Cot 38 A4
Park Ave. St Gif 24 A1
Park Ave. Win 37 F4
Park Ave. Yatt 91 E4
Park Batch. Blag 110 C2
Park Cl. Keyn 81 E3
Park Cl. Kingsw 65 F4
Park Cl. Kingsw 66 A3
Park Cres. Bris 51 E1
Park Cres. Bris 64 B4
Park Cres. Kingsw 66 A3
Park Farm Ct. Kingsw 65 F2
Park Gdns. Bath 101 E4
Park Gr. Bris 49 E3
Park Hill. Bris 47 F3
Park La. Bath 101 E4
Park La. Blag 110 C2
Park La. Bris 63 E4
Park La. Faulk 134 A1
Park La. Fr Cot 38 A4
Park La. N Nib 5 F4
Park Pl. Bath 101 F4
Park Pl. Bris 50 C2
Park Pl. Bris 63 D4
Park Rd. Bath 101 D4
Park Rd. Bris 36 A1
Park Rd. Bris 50 B3
Park Rd. Bris 63 D3
Park Rd. Cleve 57 E2
Park Rd. Cong 91 F2
Park Rd. Keyn 81 E3
Park Rd. Kingsw 65 F4
Park Rd. Mang 51 F3

158

Park Rd. Paul Puxton Rd. Pu

Park Rd. Paul 131 E3
Park Rd. Thorn 8 A1
Park Row. Bris 63 E4
Park Row. Fr Cot 38 A4
Park St Ave. Bris 63 E4
Park St Mews. Bath 101 F4
Park St. Bath 101 F4
Park St. Bris 63 E4
Park St. Bris 64 A2
Park St. Bris 64 C4
Park St. H Up 20 A1
Park St. Ir Act 26 B2
Park The. Bitt 66 A1
Park The. Bris 37 D1
Park The. Keyn 81 F3
Park The. Kingsw 65 F4
Park The. St Gif 24 B2
Park The. Yatt 74 A1
Park View Ave. Thorn 8 B1
Park View Terr. Bris 64 C4
Park View. Kingsw 65 F4
Park View. Paul 131 E3
Park Way. Kingsw 66 A3
Park Way. Mid No 138 A4
Park Wood Cl. Bris 79 F2
Parker St. Bris 63 D2
Parkers Ave. Wick 67 E4
Parkers Barton. Bris 64 A3
Parkers Cl. Bris 35 E2
Parkfield Ave. Bris 64 B4
Parkfield Gdns. Bi Sut 113 E2
Parkfield Rd. Axb 125 E1
Parkfield Rd. Puck 53 D3
Parkhouse La. Keyn 81 E1
Parkhurst Ave. Bris 51 D2
Parkhurst Rd. W-S-M 105 D4
Parkland Way. Thorn 8 B2
Parklands Ave. W-S-M 88 C2
Parklands Rd. Bris 62 C2
Parklands. Kingsw 65 F4
Parklands. Paul 115 E1
Parkside Ave. Wint 37 F3
Parkside Gdns. Bris 50 A2
Parkstone Ave. Bris 49 F3
Parkwall Cres. Kingsw 66 A2
Parkwall Rd. Kingsw 66 A3
Parkway La. Tims 116 B2
Parkway. Tims 116 C1
Parliament St. Bris 64 A2
Parnall Cres. Yate 27 E2
Parnall Rd. Bris 51 D2
Parry Cl. Bath 101 D2
Parry's Cl. Bris 48 C3
Parry's La. Bris 48 C3
Parslow Barton. Bris 65 D4
Parson St. Bris 63 E1
Parsonage Cl. Win 94 C3
Parsonage La. Bath 101 F3
Parsonage La. Ched 125 F1
Parsonage La. Chil 137 E2
Parsonage La. Pens 97 E3
Parsonage La. Win 94 C3
Parsonage Rd. Lo Ash 62 B1
Parsons Ave. St Gif 36 C3
Parsons Gn. Cleve 73 E4
Parsons Green. W-S-M 89 D2
Parsons Mead. Back 76 C4
Parsons Paddock. Bris 80 A4
Parsons Way. Wins 124 B3
Partis College. Bath 101 D4
Partis Way. Bath 101 D4
Partition St. Bris 63 E3
Partridge Cl. W-S-M 88 C1
Partridge Cl. Yate 27 F2
Partridge Rd. Puck 53 E2
Passage Leaze. Bris 47 E3
Passage Rd. Bris 35 D1
Passage Rd. Bris 35 D2
Passage Rd. Bris 35 D3
Passage St. Bris 63 F3
Pastures The. Westw 120 C2
Patch Croft. Cleve 73 E4
Patch Elm La. Wickw 26 C4
Patch La. Wickw 27 D4
Patchway Trading Est. Bris 35 F4
Paul St. Bris 63 E4
Paul's Cswy. Cong 91 E2
Paulman Gdns. Lo Ash 77 F4
Paulmont Rise. Clut 114 C1
Paulto' Hill. Paul 132 A3
Paulton Dr. Bris 49 E2
Paulton La. Tims 132 B4
Paulton Rd. Mid No 131 F1
Paulton Rd. Paul 131 D4
Paulton Rd. Paul 131 E3
Paultow Ave. Bris 63 F2
Paultow Rd. Bris 63 F2
Paulwood Rd. Clut 114 C1
Pavey Cl. Bris 79 E2
Pavey Rd. Bris 79 E2
Pawlett Rd. Bris 79 E2
Pawlett Wlk. Bris 79 E2
Pawlett. W-S-M 105 D1
Paybridge Rd. Bris 78 C2
Payne Dr. Bris 64 A4
Payne Rd. Lock 105 E1
Peach Rd. Mang 51 F3
Peacock La. Kingsw 65 E4
Pear Tree Hey. Yate 27 F3
Pear Tree Rd. St Gif 24 B2
Pearces Hill. Bris 51 D4
Pearl St. Bris 63 D2
Pearsall Rd. Kingsw 65 F1
Pearse Cl. W-S-M 89 D3
Peart Cl. Bris 78 C3
Peart Dr. Bris 78 C2
Peartree La. Bris 65 D3
Peartree La. Kingsw 51 F1
Pedder Rd. Cleve 57 E1
Peel St. Bris 63 F4
Pegasus Rd. Bris 35 E4
Pelican Cl. W-S-M 105 F4
Pemberton Ct. Bris 51 E3
Pembery Rd. Bris 63 D2
Pembroke Ave. Bris 47 F3
Pembroke Gr. Bris 63 D4
Pembroke Pl. Bris 63 D3
Pembroke Rd. Bris 47 F3
Pembroke Rd. Bris 63 D4
Pembroke Rd. Bris 63 E2
Pembroke Rd. Kingsw 51 F1
Pembroke Rd. Portis 44 C2
Pembroke Rd. W-S-M 104 C2
Pembroke St. Bris 63 F4
Pembroke Vale. Bris 63 D4
Pen Park Rd. Bris 35 E1
Penard Way. Kingsw 65 F4
Penarth Dr. W-S-M 105 D1
Pendennis Ave. Mang 51 E2
Pendennis Pk. Bris 64 B1
Pendennis Rd. Mang 51 E3
Pendlesham Gdns. W-S-M 88 A1
Pendock Cl. Kingsw 66 B1
Pendock Rd. Bris 51 E3
Pendock Rd. Wint 37 F3
Penfield Rd. Bris 50 A1
Penlea Ct. Bris 47 E4
Penn Gdns. Bath 101 D4
Penn Hill Rd. Bath 84 A1
Penn Lea Rd. Bath 84 A1
Penn Lea Rd. Bath 101 D4
Penn St. Bris 63 F4
Penn Way. Axb 125 E1
Pennard Ct. Bris 80 A3
Pennard Green. Bath 101 D3
Pennard. W-S-M 105 D1
Penngrove. Kingsw 66 A2
Pennine Gdns. W-S-M 88 A1
Pennine Rd. Kingsw 66 B2
Pennlea. Bris 79 E4
Penns The. Cleve 57 F1
Pennycress. W-S-M 105 E4
Pennyquick View. Bath 100 C3
Pennyquick. Cor 100 B3
Pennyroyal Gr. Bris 50 C2
Pennywell Rd. Bris 64 A4
Penpole Ave. Bris 47 F3
Penpole Cl. Bris 47 E4
Penpole La. Bris 47 F4
Penpole Pl. Bris 47 F3
Penrice Cl. W-S-M 88 B1
Penrith Gdns. Bris 49 E4
Penrose. Bris 79 F4
Pensfield Park. Bris 35 E2
Pensford Ct. Bris 80 B3
Pensford Hill. Pens 97 E3
Pensford La. Pens 97 D1
Pensford Old Rd. Pens 97 F2
Pentagon The. Bris 48 A3
Pentire Ave. Bris 79 D4
Pentland Ave. Thorn 15 F4
Peppershells La. Co Dan 98 B3
Pepys Cl. Keyn 82 B1
Pera Pl. Bath 102 A4
Pera Rd. Bath 102 A4
Percival Rd. Bris 62 C4
Percy St. Bris 63 E2
Peregrine Cl. W-S-M 88 C1
Perrin Cl. Clut 130 C4
Perrings The. Nail 75 F4
Perrinpit Rd. Fr Cot 25 F1
Perrott Rd. Kingsw 52 A1
Perry Cl. Wint 37 E3
Perry Rd. Bris 63 E4
Perry St. Bris 64 A4
Perrycroft Ave. Bris 79 D3
Perrycroft Rd. Bris 79 D3
Perrymans Cl. Bris 51 D3
Perrymead. Bath 102 A2
Perrymead. W-S-M 89 D3
Perrys Lea. St Gif 24 B1
Pesley Cl. Bris 79 D2
Peter's Terr. Bris 64 A4
Petercole Dr. Bris 79 D3
Peterside. Clut 130 C4
Peterson Sq. Bris 79 E2
Petersway Gdns. Bris 65 D3
Petherton Cl. Kingsw 65 F4
Petherton Gdns. Bris 80 A4
Petherton Rd. Bris 80 A4
Peto Gr. Westw 120 C2
Pettigrove Gdns. Kingsw 65 F4
Pettigrove Rd. Kingsw 65 F3
Pevensey Wlk. Bris 79 E4
Peverell Cl. Bris 34 C2
Peverell Dr. Bris 34 C2
Philadelphia Ct. Bris 63 F4
Philip St. Bris 63 E2
Philip St. Bris 64 A3
Philippa Cl. Bris 80 A4
Phillips Rd. W-S-M 105 D3
Phillis Hill. Paul 131 F2
Phippen St. Bris 63 F3
Phipps St. Bris 63 D2
Phoenix Gr. Bris 49 E3
Piccadilly Pl. Bath 102 A4
Pickedmoor La. O-on-S 7 E3
Pickwick Rd. Bath 85 D1
Picton La. Bris 49 F1
Picton St. Bris 49 F1
Pier Rd. Portis 45 F4
Pierrepont Pl. Bath 102 A3
Pierrepont St. Bath 102 A3
Pigeon La. Wring 93 F1
Pigott Ave. Bris 79 D2
Pilgrims Way. Avon 47 E4
Pilgrims Way. Ch St 112 B4
Pilgrims Way. Mang 51 E4
Pilgrims Way. W-S-M 88 C2
Pilgrims Wharf. Bris 64 C4
Pilkington Cl. Bris 36 B1
Pill Rd. Ab Lei 47 F1
Pill St. E in G 47 E2
Pill Way. Cleve 57 D1
Pillingers Rd. Kingsw 65 E4
Pilning St. Piln 23 E4
Pimm's La. W-S-M 88 A1
Pinchay La. Win 95 D2
Pinckney Green. Mon Far 103 F3
Pincots La. Wickw 18 A2
Pine Cl. Thorn 8 B1
Pine Cl. W-S-M 88 B1
Pine Ct. Ch Mag 96 A2
Pine Ct. Keyn 81 E2
Pine Ct. Rad 133 D1
Pine Gr. Bris 36 A1
Pine Grove Pl. Bris 49 E2
Pine Hill. W-S-M 88 B1
Pine Lea. Blea 122 A4
Pine Rd. Bris 35 D2
Pine Ridge Cl. Bris 48 B2
Pine Wlk. Rad 132 C1
Pinecroft. Bris 79 F4
Pinecroft. Portis 44 C3
Pines Cl. Chil 137 E2
Pines La. Olve 14 B2
Pines Rd. Kingsw 66 B1
Pines Way. Bath 101 F3
Pines Way. Rad 133 D1
Pinewood Ave. Mid No 131 F1
Pinewood Cl. Bris 49 D4
Pinewood Gr. Mid No 131 F1
Pinewood Rd. Mid No 131 F1
Pinewood Way. Col 70 C4
Pinewood. Kingsw 51 F1
Pinhay Rd. Bris 79 D3
Pinkhams Twist. Bris 80 A3
Pioneer Ave. Bath 101 F1
Pipe La. Bris 63 E3
Pipe La. Bris 63 F3
Pipehouse La. Hi Cha 120 A2
Pipehouse La. Hin Cha 119 F2
Piper Rd. Yate 27 F2
Pippin Cl. P St J 133 E4
Pippin Ct. Kingsw 65 F2
Pit La. Back 76 A2
Pit La. Win 111 F3
Pit Rd. Mid No 132 A1
Pitch And Pay La. Bris 48 C2
Pitch And Pay Park. Bris 48 C2
Pitch La. Bris 49 E1
Pitchcombe Gdns. Bris 48 B4
Pitchcombe. Yate 39 E4
Pitcot La. Hol 138 A1
Pithay Ct. Bris 63 E4
Pithay The. Bris 63 E4
Pithay The. Paul 131 F3
Pitman Ct. Bath 85 E1
Pitman Rd. W-S-M 104 C3
Pitt Rd. Bris 49 F3
Pittville Cl. Thorn 8 B2
Pitville Pl. Bris 49 D1
Pitway Cl. Paul 130 C2
Pitway La. Paul 130 B2
Pixash Bsns Centre. Keyn 82 A3
Pixash La. Keyn 82 A3
Pizey Ave. Cleve 57 D1
Pizey Cl. Cleve 57 D1
Plain The. N St P 135 F2
Plain The. Thorn 8 A1
Players Cl. St Gif 37 D2
Playford Gdns. Bris 47 F4
Pleasant Pl. Bathf 86 B1
Pleasant Rd. Mang 51 E3
Pleshey Cl. W-S-M 88 B1
Ploughed Paddock. Nail 59 E1
Plover Cl. W-S-M 88 C1
Plover Cl. Yate 27 E1
Plovers Rise. Mid No 133 D2
Plumbers Hill. Bris 64 C4
Plumers Cl. Cleve 57 F1
Plumpton Ct. Mang 37 F1
Plumptre Cl. Paul 131 F3
Plumptre Rd. Paul 131 F3
Plumtree Cl. Wins 108 A1
Plunder St. Brock 92 A4
Podium The. Bath 102 A3
Poets Cnr. Rad 132 B1
Poets' Cl. Bris 64 B4
Polden Cl. Nail 59 F1
Polden Rd. Portis 45 D3
Polden Rd. W-S-M 104 C4
Police Station Hill. Puck 53 D2
Polly Barnes Cl. Kingsw 65 D3
Polly Barnes Hill. Kingsw 65 D3
Polygon Rd. Bris 63 D3
Polygon The. Bris 62 C3
Pomfret House. Bris 79 E2
Pomfrett Gdns. Bris 80 C3
Pomphrey Hill. Mang 52 A2
Ponsford Rd. Bris 80 A4
Ponting Cl. Bris 51 D1
Pool La. Win 95 D1
Pool Rd. Kingsw 51 F2
Poole Court Dr. Yate 27 F1
Poole St. Avon 47 D4
Poolemead Rd. Bath 100 C3
Poor Hill. Farm 115 F3
Pope's Wlk. Bath 102 A2
Poplar Ave. Bris 48 B3
Poplar Cl. Bath 101 E2
Poplar Cl. Kingsw 66 B3
Poplar Dr. Puck 53 D3
Poplar La. Wickw 18 A2
Poplar Pl. Bris 51 D2
Poplar Pl. W-S-M 104 C4
Poplar Rd. Bris 50 C1
Poplar Rd. Bris 65 D3
Poplar Rd. Bris 78 C4
Poplar Rd. Kingsw 66 B3
Poplar Way. Col 70 C3
Poplar Wlk. Lock 105 F3
Poplars The. E in G 47 D2
Poplars The. W-S-M 89 D1
Pople's La. Kilm 139 F1
Popular Terr. Kingsw 65 F4
Porlock Cl. Cleve 57 F1
Porlock Cl. W-S-M 104 C1
Porlock Gdns. Nail 59 F1
Porlock Rd. Bath 102 A1
Porlock Rd. Bris 63 E2
Port Elizabeth House. Bris 35 D1
Port View. E in G 47 E3
Portbury Comm. Portis 45 F2
Portbury Gr. Bris 47 E3
Portbury Hundred The. Portb 46 B2
Portbury La. Wrax 60 C3
Portbury Way. Portb 46 C3
Portbury Wlk. Bris 47 E3
Portishead Rd. W-S-M 89 D2
Portishead Way. Bris 62 C2
Portland Cl. Nail 59 E1
Portland Ct. Bris 63 D3
Portland Dr. Portis 45 F2
Portland Pl. Bath 101 F4
Portland Pl. Kingsw 51 E2
Portland Sq. Bris 63 F4
Portland St. Bris 62 C4
Portland St. Bris 63 E4
Portland St. Kingsw 51 E2
Portmeade Dro. Axb 125 E1
Portmeirion Cl. Bris 80 A3
Portview Rd. Avon 47 D4
Portwall La E. Bris 63 F3
Portwall La. Bris 63 F3
Portway La. Ch Sod 29 D1
Portway. Bris 48 B2
Post Office La. Back 76 C4
Post Office La. Blag 110 B2
Poston Way. Winsl 120 C4
Pottery Cl. W-S-M 105 D3
Potts Cl. Bathe 85 F2
Pound Dr. Bris 50 C3
Pound La. Bris 50 C2
Pound La. Nail 59 E2
Pound Mead. Win 94 B4
Pound Rd. Kingsw 51 F1
Pound The. Alm 24 A3
Pound The. O-on-S 7 D3
Pound The. Wring 93 E2
Pountney Dr. Bris 64 A4
Pow's Hill. Paul 132 B3
Pow's Orch. Mid No 132 A1
Pow's Rd. Kingsw 65 E4
Powis Cl. W-S-M 88 B1
Powlett Rd. Bath 102 A4
Poyntz Ct. Kingsw 65 F2
Poyntz Rd. Bris 79 F4
Pratten's La. Mang 51 E2
Preanes Green. W-S-M 89 D1
Preddy's La. Bris 65 D3
Prescot Cl. W-S-M 88 A1
Prescott. Yate 39 E4
Press Moor Dr. Kingsw 65 F2
Prestbury. Yate 39 E4
Preston Wlk. Bris 64 A1
Prestwick Cl. Bris 64 B1
Pretoria Rd. Bris 35 F4
Prewett St. Bris 63 F3
Priddy Cl. Bath 101 D3
Priddy Ct. Bris 80 A3
Priddy Dr Bris 80
Priests Way. W-S-M 88
Priestwood Cl. Bris 35
Primrose Cl. Bris 65
Primrose Cl. St Gif 24
Primrose Dr. Thorn 8
Primrose Hill. Bath 84
Primrose La. Bris 51
Primrose La. Mid No 132
Primrose Terr. Bris 51
Prince St. Bris 63
Prince's Pl. Bris 49
Prince's Rd. Cleve 57
Prince's St. Bris 63
Prince's St. Mid No 132
Princes Ct. Kingsw 65
Princes St. Bath 101
Princes' La. Bris 62
Princess Cl. Keyn 81
Princess Gdns. Bris 50
Princess Row. Bris 63
Princess St. Bris 63
Princess St. Bris 64
Princess Victoria St. Bris 62
Priors Hill. Tims 116
Priors Lea. Yate 27
Priory Ave. Bris 49
Priory Cl. Bath 102
Priory Cl. Mid No 132
Priory Court Rd. Bris 49
Priory Ct. Kingsw 65
Priory Dene. Bris 49
Priory Gdns. Bris 47
Priory Gdns. Bris 49
Priory Gdns. E in G 47
Priory Park Rd. Bath 102
Priory Rd. Bris 47
Priory Rd. Bris 63
Priory Rd. Bris 64
Priory Rd. E in G 47
Priory Rd. Keyn 81
Priory Rd. Portb 46
Priory Rd. W-S-M 105
Priory Wlk. Portb 46
Priston Cl. W-S-M 89
Priston La. Pris 117
Priston Rd. Engl 117
Priston Rd. Pris 117
Pritchard St. Bris 63
Probyn Cl. Bris 51
Proctor Cl. Bris 64
Prospect Ave. Bris 51
Prospect Cl. Alm 22
Prospect Cl. Alm 23
Prospect Cl. Fr Cot 37
Prospect Cl. Wint 37
Prospect Cres. Kingsw 51
Prospect Gdns. Bathe 85
Prospect La. Fr Cot 37
Prospect Pl. Bath 84
Prospect Pl. Bathf 86
Prospect Pl. Bris 63
Prospect Pl. Bris 64
Prospect Pl. W-S-M 104
Prospect Rd. Bath 102
Prospect Rd. Piln 22
Providence La. Lo Ash 61
Providence Pl. Bris 63
Providence St. Bris 63
Prowse's La. Axb 125
Prudham St. Bris 50
Publow La. Pens 97
Pucklechurch Trading Est. Puck 53
Pudding Pie Cl. Chur 109
Pudding Pie La. Chur 109
Puffin Cl. W-S-M 105
Pullen's Green. Thorn 8
Pullin Ct. Kingsw 66
Pulteney Ave. Bath 102
Pulteney Bridge. Bath 102
Pulteney Gdns. Bath 102
Pulteney Gr. Bath 102
Pulteney Mews. Bath 102
Pulteney Rd. Bath 102
Pump La. Bathf 86
Pump La. Bris 63
Pump La. Olve 14
Pump La. Wring 93
Pump Sq. E in G 47
Purcell Wlk. Bris 79
Purdey Rd. Bris 50
Purdue Cl. W-S-M 89
Purn La. W-S-M 122
Purn Rd. W-S-M 121
Purn Way. Blea 122
Purplewent Dr. Bath 84
Pursey Dr. St Gif 36
Purton Cl. Kingsw 65
Purton Rd. Bris 49
Purving Row La. Lymp 122
Purving Row. Lymp 122
Puttingthorpe Dr. W-S-M 105
Puxley Cl. Bris 80
Puxton La. Ban 90
Puxton La. Pux 90
Puxton Rd. Ban 90
Puxton Rd. Pux 90

159

Pye Cnr. Chur

Rows The. W-S-M

ye Cnr. Chur 108 B2
ye Croft. St Gif 24 C2
yecroft Ave. Bris 49 E4
ylewell La. Ship 108 B1
yle Hill Cres. Bris 63 F2
yne Point. Cleve 57 E2
ynne Cl. Bris 80 C3
ynne Rd. Bris 80 C3
yracantha Wlk. Bris 80 A3

uadrangle The. West 39 E2
uadrant E. Bris 51 E2
uadrant The. Bris 49 D2
uadrant The. St Gif 24 A2
uadrant W. Bris 51 E2
uadrant. St Gif 24 A2
uaker La. Thorn 8 A1
uaker's Cl. Mang 51 E4
uaker's Rd. Mang 51 F4
uakers' Friars. Bris 63 F4
uantock Cl. Kingsw 66 B3
uantock Rd. Bris 63 E2
uantock Rd. Portis 45 D3
uantock Rd. W-S-M 104 C3
uantocks. Bath 102 A1
uarries The. Alm 24 B3
uarrington Rd. Bris 49 F3
uarry Barton. Wint 37 E2
uarry Cl. Bath 101 F1
uarry Hay. Ch St 112 B4
uarry Head. Alve 14 C3
uarry La. Wint 37 F2
uarry Rd. Alve 14 C3
uarry Rd. Bath 102 B3
uarry Rd. Bris 51 E4
uarry Rd. Ch Sod 28 A1
uarry Rd. Kingsw 65 E3
uarry Rd. Wins 108 A1
uarry Stps. Bris 49 D1
uarry Way. Bris 50 C3
uarry Way. Nail 59 E1
uay St. Bris 63 E4
uayside. Bris 64 C3
uedgeley. Yate 39 E4
ueen Ann Rd. Bris 64 A3
ueen Charlotte St. Bris 63 E3
ueen Charlton La. Co Dan 80 C1
ueen Charlton La. Whit 80 C1
ueen Sq Ave. Bris 63 E3
ueen Sq Pl. Bath 101 F4
ueen Sq. Bath 101 F4
ueen Sq. Bris 63 E3
ueen Sq. Keyn 82 C2
ueen St. Avon 33 D1
ueen St. Bath 101 F3
ueen St. Bris 50 B2
ueen St. Bris 63 F4
ueen St. Bris 65 D4
ueen Victoria Rd. Bris 49 D2
ueen Victoria St. Bris 64 A3
ueen's Ave. Bris 63 D4
ueen's Ave. Portis 45 E3
ueen's Dr. Bath 102 A1
ueen's Dr. Bris 49 E3
ueen's Par Pl. Bath 101 F4
ueen's Par. Bris 63 E3
ueen's Rd. Bris 49 F3
ueen's Rd. Bris 63 D4
ueen's Rd. Bris 64 C4
ueen's Rd. Bris 78 C2
ueen's Rd. Cleve 57 E2
ueen's Rd. Kingsw 66 A2
ueen's Rd. Nail 59 E1
ueen's Rd. Portis 44 C2
ueen's Rd. Puck 53 D3
ueen's Rd. Rad 133 D1
ueen's Rd. W-S-M 87 E1
ueen's Way. Portis 44 C2
ueen's Way. W-S-M 89 D2
ueens Down Gdns. Bris 64 B2
ueens Dr. Kingsw 65 D2
ueens Par. Bath 101 F4
ueens Rd. Ban 107 D2
ueens Rd. Bris 64 B1
ueens Rd. Keyn 81 E2
ueens Wlk. Thorn 8 A2
ueensdale Cres. Bris 64 A1
ueenshill Rd. Bris 64 A1
ueensholm Ave. Mang 37 F1
ueensholm Cl. Mang 37 F1
ueensholm Dr. Mang 37 F1
ueensway. St Gif 36 B3
ueenwood Ave. Bath 85 D1
uickthorn Cl. Bris 80 A3
uiet St. Bath 101 F3
uilter Gr. Bris 79 E4

aby Mews. Bath 102 A4
ackfield Pl. Bath 101 D3
ackham Cl. Bris 50 A3
ackhay. Bris 63 E3
ackley La. Co Bi 124 A1
ackvernal Rd. Mid No 132 A1
adford Hill. Paul 132 B4
adford Hill. Tims 116 B1
adley Rd. Bris 51 D2
adnor Rd. Bris 49 D3
adnor Rd. Bris 49 F3
Radstock Rd. Mid No 132 B1
Raeburn Rd. Bris 65 D3
Rag Hill. P St J 133 E3
Rag La. Wickw 17 E3
Raglan Cl. Chil 137 E2
Raglan La. Bris 65 D4
Raglan La. Win 94 C4
Raglan Pl. Bris 49 E2
Raglan Pl. Thorn 15 D4
Raglan Pl. W-S-M 87 E1
Raglan Rd. Bris 49 E2
Raglan Wlk. Keyn 81 E2
Ragland La. Bath 85 D1
Ragland St. Bath 85 D1
Railton Jones Cl. St Gif 36 C2
Railway Pl. Bath 102 A3
Railway St. Bath 102 A3
Railway Terr. Bris 51 E2
Railway View Pl. Mid No 132 A1
Rainham Ct. W-S-M 87 E1
Rains Batch. Priddy 126 C3
Raleigh Cl. Keyn 82 B1
Raleigh Rd. Bris 63 D2
Raleigh Rise. Portis 45 D3
Ralph Allen Dr. Bath 102 B2
Ralph Rd. Bris 49 F2
Ram Hill. West 38 B2
Ramscombe La. Bathe 85 F3
Ramsey Cl. W-S-M 88 C2
Ramsey Rd. Bris 49 F4
Ranchways. Portis 44 C2
Randall Cl. Kingsw 51 F1
Randall Rd. Bris 63 D3
Randolph Ave. Bris 79 D3
Randolph Ave. Yate 27 E3
Randolph Cl. Bris 79 D3
Rangers Wlk. Kingsw 65 E2
Rankers La. Co Dan 98 B3
Rannoch Rd. Bris 35 F1
Ranscombe Ave. W-S-M 88 B1
Ransford. Cleve 57 D1
Raphael Ct. Bris 63 F3
Ratcliffe Dr. St Gif 36 C3
Rathbone Cl. Fr Cot 38 B3
Raven Cl. W-S-M 88 C1
Ravendale Dr. Kingsw 66 A1
Ravenglass Cres. Bris 35 E1
Ravenhead Dr. Bris 80 A4
Ravenhill Ave. Bris 63 F1
Ravenhill Rd. Bris 63 F2
Ravens Wood. Kingsw 66 A2
Ravenscourt Rd. Bris 36 A4
Ravenswood Rd. Bris 49 E1
Rawlins Ave. W-S-M 89 D3
Rayens Cl. Lo Ash 61 F1
Rayens Cross Rd. Lo Ash 61 F1
Rayleigh Rd. Bris 48 C4
Raymend Rd. Bris 63 F2
Raymend Wlk. Bris 63 F1
Raymill. Bris 65 D1
Raymore Rise. Lo Ash 61 F1
Raynes Rd. Bris 63 D2
Reach Hill La. Ch St 112 B3
Rector's Way. W-S-M 104 C3
Rectory Cl. Farm 116 A3
Rectory Cl. Yate 27 F2
Rectory Dr. Yatt 91 E4
Rectory La. Bris 36 A2
Rectory La. Co Mar 128 A3
Rectory La. Crom 17 D4
Rectory La. Tims 116 B1
Rectory Rd. E in G 47 D2
Rectory Rd. Fr Cot 38 A4
Rectory Way. Lymp 121 F1
Rectory Way. Yatt 91 E4
Red Hill. Tims 116 C1
Red Hill. Wring 93 E1
Red House La. Alm 24 A2
Red House La. Bris 48 C3
Red Rd. Berr 121 D1
Redacre. Wring 93 E2
Redcatch Rd. Bris 63 F1
Redcliff Backs. Bris 63 F3
Redcliff Hill. Bris 63 F3
Redcliff Mead La. Bris 63 F3
Redcliff St. Bris 63 F3
Redcliffe Cl. Portis 44 C2
Redcliffe Par E. Bris 63 F3
Redcliffe Par W. Bris 63 E3
Redcliffe Way. Bris 63 F3
Redcroft. Wring 93 E2
Redcross La. Bris 63 F4
Redcross St. Bris 63 F4
Redding Pit La. Win 94 C2
Reddings The. Co Mar 128 A4
Reddings The. Kingsw 51 F1
Redfield Gr. Mid No 138 A4
Redfield Hill. Bitt 66 C2
Redfield Rd. Bris 36 A4
Redfield Rd. Mid No 132 A1
Redford Cres. Bris 78 C2
Redford La. Puck 53 E2
Redford Wlk. Bris 78 C2
Redham La. Piln 23 D4
Redhill Cl. Bris 50 C2
Redhill Dr. Bris 50 C2
Redhill La. Aust 13 F3
Redland Ave. E in G 46 C3
Redland Court Rd. Bris 49 E1
Redland Gr. Bris 49 E1
Redland Green Rd. Bris 49 E2
Redland Hill. Bris 49 D1
Redland Park. Bath 100 C3
Redland Park. Bris 49 D1
Redland Rd. Bris 49 D1
Redland Terr. Bris 49 D1
Redlands Terr. Mid No 137 F4
Redlynch La. Co Dan 81 E1
Redshard La. Chur 109 D4
Redshelf Wlk. Bris 35 E2
Redwick Cl. Bris 34 B1
Redwick Gdns. Piln 22 B4
Redwick Rd. Piln 22 B4
Redwing Dr. W-S-M 88 C1
Redwood Cl. Kingsw 66 A2
Redwood Cl. Nail 60 A1
Redwood Cl. Rod 138 C4
Redwood La. Lo Ash 77 E4
Redwoods The. Keyn 81 E3
Reed Ct. Kingsw 65 F2
Reed's Row. Hill 19 E4
Reedley Rd. Bris 48 C3
Reedling Cl. Bris 50 C3
Regency Dr. Bris 65 D1
Regent Rd. Bris 63 E2
Regent St. Kingsw 65 E4
Regent St. W-S-M 104 B4
Regents Cl. Thorn 8 A1
Regents St. Bris 63 D4
Regil La. Win 94 C2
Regil La. Win 95 D3
Remenham Dr. Bris 49 D3
Remenham Park. Bris 49 D3
Rendcomb Cl. W-S-M 88 A1
Rene Rd. Bris 50 A1
Repton Rd. Bris 64 B2
Retort Rd. Avon 33 E2
Retreat The. Faulk 133 F2
Reubens Ct. W-S-M 88 C2
Reynold's Wlk. Bris 50 A4
Reynolds Cl. Keyn 82 A3
Rhode Cl. Keyn 82 A2
Rhodyate Hill. Brock 92 A4
Rhodyate Hill. Cong 91 F3
Rhodyate La. Brock 92 A4
Rhodyate The. Ban 107 E1
Rhodyate. Blag 110 B1
Rhyne Terr. W-S-M 104 B1
Ribblesdale. Thorn 15 E4
Richards Cl. W-S-M 89 D2
Richeson Cl. Bris 34 C1
Richeson Wlk. Bris 34 C1
Richmond Ave. Bris 49 F1
Richmond Ave. St Gif 36 C3
Richmond Cl. Bath 84 C1
Richmond Cl. Keyn 81 E2
Richmond Cl. Portis 45 F3
Richmond Dale. Bris 49 D1
Richmond Green. Nail 59 F1
Richmond Hill Ave. Bris 63 D4
Richmond Hill. Bath 84 C1
Richmond Hill. Bris 63 D4
Richmond Hts. Bath 84 C1
Richmond La. Bath 84 C1
Richmond La. Bris 63 D4
Richmond Park Rd. Bris 63 D4
Richmond Pl. Bath 84 C1
Richmond Rd. Bath 84 C1
Richmond Rd. Bris 49 F1
Richmond Rd. Bris 64 C4
Richmond Rd. Mang 52 A3
Richmond St. Bris 63 F2
Richmond St. W-S-M 104 B4
Richmond Terr. Avon 33 D1
Richmond Terr. Bris 63 D4
Ricketts La. W-S-M 89 D1
Rickford La. Blag 110 A2
Rickford Rd. Nail 59 F1
Rickford Rise. Blag 110 A2
Rickyard Rd. Wring 92 C1
Ride The. Kingsw 52 A1
Ridge Cl. Portis 45 D2
Ridge Cres. E Harp 128 C3
Ridge La. E Harp 128 B3
Ridge The. Bris 47 F4
Ridge The. Fr Cot 38 B4
Ridge The. Yatt 91 D4
Ridge View. Lo Ash 62 A1
Ridgehill. Bris 49 E3
Ridgemeade. Bris 80 A2
Ridgeway Ave. W-S-M 104 C3
Ridgeway Cl. E Harp 128 C3
Ridgeway Ct. Bris 35 D1
Ridgeway Gdns. Bris 80 B3
Ridgeway La. Bris 80 B3
Ridgeway Par. Bris 50 C2
Ridgeway Rd. Bris 50 C2
Ridgeway Rd. Lo Ash 62 A1
Ridgeway The. Bris 35 D1
Ridgeway The. W-S-M 88 A1
Ridgeway. Fr Cot 38 B4
Ridgeway. Nail 59 E1
Ridgeway. Yate 27 F1
Riding Barn Hill. Wick 67 D3
Ridingleaze. Bris 34 A1
Ridings Cl. Ch Sod 28 A1
Ridings Rd. Fr Cot 38 B3
Ridings The. Bris 78 C2
Ridings The. Fr Cot 38 B3
Ringspit La. Pens 97 F4
Ringswell Gdns. Bath 85 E1
Ringwell La. N St P 135 F2
Ringwell. N St P 135 F2
Ringwood Cres. Bris 35 E1
Ringwood Gr. W-S-M 88 A1
Ringwood Rd. Bath 101 E3
Ripley Rd. Bris 51 D1
Ripon Ct. Mang 37 F1
Ripon Rd. Bris 64 C3
Ripple The. Nail 59 E2
Rippleside Rd. Cleve 57 F3
Rippleside. Portis 45 E3
Risdale Rd. Bris 62 C1
Risedale Rd. Wins 125 D4
Rivendell. W-S-M 89 D2
River Rd. Ch Sod 28 A1
River Rd. E in G 46 C4
River St. Bris 63 F4
River Terr. Keyn 81 F3
River View. Bris 50 C3
Riverland Dr. Bris 78 C3
Riverleaze. Bris 48 A3
Riverleaze. Portis 44 C3
Rivers Rd. Bath 85 D1
Rivers St Mews. Bath 101 F4
Rivers St. Bath 101 F4
Riverside Bsns Park. Bris 64 B3
Riverside Cl. Bris 47 F3
Riverside Cl. Cleve 57 D1
Riverside Cl. Mid No 137 F4
Riverside Cotts. Kingsw 65 D1
Riverside Cotts. Rad 133 D1
Riverside Ct. Bath 101 F3
Riverside Ct. Bris 64 C3
Riverside Gdns. Mid No 137 F4
Riverside Mews. Bris 64 C3
Riverside Rd. Bath 101 F3
Riverside Rd. Mid No 137 F4
Riverside Way. Kingsw 65 E2
Riverside Wlk. Mid No 137 F4
Riverside. Ban 107 D3
Riverway. Nail 59 F2
Riverwood Rd. Bris 37 E1
Riviera Cres. Kingsw 51 F2
Roach's La. Gr Bad 30 B1
Road Hill. Col 70 B1
Road Two. Avon 22 A2
Roath Rd. Portis 45 E3
Robbins Cl. Marsh 69 F4
Robbins Cl. St Gif 36 C3
Robel Ave. Fr Cot 37 F4
Robert St. Bris 50 A1
Robert St. Bris 64 A4
Robertson Rd. Bris 50 B1
Robin Cl. Rod 138 A4
Robin Cl. W-S-M 105 F4
Robin Dr. Lock 105 F1
Robin La. Cleve 57 E3
Robin Way. Ch Sod 40 A4
Robinia Wlk. Bris 80 A4
Robinson Cl. Back 76 A3
Robinson Way. Back 76 A3
Rochester Cl. W-S-M 105 D1
Rochester Rd. Bris 64 C3
Rock Ave. Nail 59 E1
Rock Cl. Bris 64 C1
Rock Hall La. Bath 102 A1
Rock La. Bath 102 A1
Rock La. St Gif 36 C3
Rock Rd. Chil 137 E1
Rock Rd. Mid No 132 A1
Rock Rd. Wick 67 E4
Rock Rd. Yatt 91 E4
Rock St. Thorn 15 D4
Rock The. Bris 64 C2
Rockhill Est. Keyn 81 F2
Rockingham Gr. W-S-M 88 A1
Rockland Gr. Bris 50 B3
Rockland Rd. Mang 51 E4
Rockleaze Ave. Bris 48 C2
Rockleaze Rd. Bris 48 C2
Rockliffe Ave. Bath 102 A4
Rockliffe Rd. Bath 102 A4
Rocks La. Ba Gu 77 F1
Rocks La. Win 77 F1
Rockside Ave. Mang 51 F4
Rockside Dr. Bris 49 E3
Rockside Gdns. Fr Cot 38 B4
Rockside Gdns. Mang 51 F4
Rockstowes Way. Bris 35 E2
Rockwell Ave. Bris 34 A1
Rodborough Way. Kingsw 66 A4
Rodborough. Yate 39 E4
Rodbourne Rd. Bris 49 F3
Rode Hill. Rode 136 C1
Rodford Way. Yate 39 E4
Rodfords Mead. Bris 80 A4
Rodmead Wlk. Bris 79 D2
Rodmoor Rd. Portis 45 E3
Rodney Ave. Bris 65 D4
Rodney Cres. Bris 36 A2
Rodney Pl. Bris 63 D4
Rodney Rd. Back 76 A3
Rodney Rd. Bris 65 D4
Rodney Rd. Keyn 82 C1
Rodney Wlk. Bris 51 D1
Rodney. W-S-M 105 D1
Rodway Hill Rd. Kingsw 52 A2
Rodway Hill. Sist 52 A2
Rodway Rd. Bris 36 A4
Rodway Rd. Mang 52 A3
Rodway View. Kingsw 51 F2
Roebuck Cl. W-S-M 89 D2
Roegate Dr. Bris 64 C3
Rogers Cl. Clut 114 C2
Rogers Cl. Kingsw 66 A3
Rokeby Ave. Bris 49 E1
Roman Rd. Bris 50 A1
Roman Rd. Winsc 107 F2
Roman Way. Bris 48 B2
Roman Way. Paul 131 E3
Roman Wlk. Bris 64 B2
Roman Wlk. St Gif 36 C3
Romney Ave. Bris 50 A3
Ronald Rd. Bris 50 C3
Ronayne Wlk. Bris 51 E3
Rook Rd. Keyn 81 F3
Rookery Cl. W-S-M 88 C2
Rookery La. Doyn 53 F2
Rookery La. Piln 23 D3
Rookery Rd. Bris 64 A2
Rookery Way. Bris 79 F2
Rooksbridge Wlk. Bath 101 D3
Roper's La. Wring 92 C2
Rose Acre. Bris 35 D2
Rose Cl. Wint 37 F2
Rose Gdns. W-S-M 89 D2
Rose Green Cl. Bris 50 C1
Rose Green Rd. Bris 50 C1
Rose Hill. Bath 85 E2
Rose La. Fr Cot 38 B3
Rose Mead. Bris 50 A4
Rose Meare Gdns. Bris 78 C4
Rose Oak La. Fr Cot 38 B4
Rose Rd. Bris 64 C4
Rose St. Bris 63 F3
Rose Wlk. Bris 51 E2
Rosebay Mead. Bris 50 C2
Roseberry Pk. Bris 64 B4
Roseberry Rd. Bath 101 E3
Roseberry Rd. Bris 64 B4
Rosebery Ave. Bris 50 A1
Rosedale Ave. W-S-M 105 D4
Rosedale Rd. Bris 51 E2
Roselarge Gdns. Bris 35 D1
Rosemary La. Bris 50 B1
Rosemary La. Hi Cha 120 A2
Rosemont Terr. Bris 63 D3
Rosemount La. Bath 102 A2
Rosery Cl. Bris 49 D4
Rosery The. Bris 51 E2
Rosevear. Bris 64 A4
Roseville Ave. Kingsw 66 A1
Rosewarn Cl. Bath 101 D2
Rosewell Ct. Bath 101 F3
Rosewood Gdns. Alve 14 C3
Rosling Rd. Bris 49 F3
Roslyn Ave. W-S-M 88 B1
Roslyn Rd. Bris 49 E1
Rossall Ave. St Gif 36 B3
Rossall Rd. Bris 64 B2
Rossendale Cl. W-S-M 88 C2
Rossiter Rd. Bath 102 A3
Rossiter's La. Bris 65 D3
Rosslyn Rd. Bath 101 D4
Rosslyn Way. Thorn 8 B2
Rotcombe La. Paul 115 E1
Rotcombe Vale. Paul 115 E1
Rounceval St. Ch Sod 28 A1
Roundhill Gr. Bath 101 D2
Roundhill Park. Bath 101 D2
Roundmoor Cl. Keyn 82 B2
Roundmoor Gdns. Bris 80 B4
Roundways. Fr Cot 38 B3
Rousham Rd. Bris 50 A2
Row La. Faulk 135 E1
Row Of Ashes La. But 94 A2
Row Of Ashes La. Wring 93 F2
Row The. Aust 13 D4
Rowacres. Bath 101 D2
Rowacres. Bris 79 F3
Rowan Cl. Bris 51 D1
Rowan Cl. Nail 60 A1
Rowan Ct. Rad 132 C1
Rowan Way. Chur 109 D3
Rowan Way. Kingsw 65 D2
Rowan Wlk. Keyn 81 E2
Rowans The. Bris 37 D1
Rowans The. Portis 45 E2
Rowberrow La. Ship 108 C1
Rowberrow La. Ship 125 F4
Rowberrow Way. Nail 59 F1
Rowberrow. Bris 79 F4
Rowland Ave. Bris 50 B2
Rowlands Cl. Bathf 86 A1
Rowlandson Gdns. Bris 50 A3
Rowley St. Bris 63 E2
Rownham Cl. Bris 62 C2
Rownham Ct. Bris 63 D3
Rownham Hill. Lo Ash 62 C3
Rownham Mead. Bris 63 D3
Rows The. W-S-M 88 C1

160

Roy King Gdns. Kingsw

Seymour Rd. Ba

Roy King Gdns. Kingsw 66 B3
Royal Albert Rd. Bris 49 D2
Royal Ave. Bath 101 F4
Royal Cl. Bris 34 B2
Royal Cres. Bath 101 F4
Royal Cres. W-S-M 104 B4
Royal Fort Rd. Bris 63 E4
Royal Park. Bris 63 D4
Royal Portbury Dock Rd. E in G 46 C3
Royal Prom. Bris 63 D4
Royal York Cres. Bris 62 C3
Royal York Cres. Bris 63 D3
Royate Hill. Bris 50 B1
Roycroft Rd. Bris 36 A1
Royston Wlk. Bris 35 E1
Rozel Rd. Bris 49 F3
Rubens Cl. Keyn 82 A3
Ruby St. Bris 63 D2
Ruddymead. Cleve 57 E1
Rudford Cl. St Gif 24 A1
Rudgeway Park. Alve 14 C1
Rudgeway Rd. Paul 131 F2
Rudgewood Cl. Bris 79 E2
Rudgleigh Ave. E in G 47 E2
Rudgleigh Rd. E in G 47 E2
Rudhall Gr. Bris 49 F4
Rudhall Green. W-S-M 89 D2
Rudmore Park. Bath 101 D4
Rudthorpe Rd. Bris 49 F3
Ruffet Rd. West 38 B2
Rugby Rd. Bris 64 B2
Runnymead Ave. Bris 64 B1
Runnymede. Kingsw 51 F1
Runswick Rd. Bris 64 B2
Rupert St. Bris 63 E4
Rupert St. Bris 64 B4
Rurdown Rd. Bris 49 F3
Rush Cl. St Gif 24 B1
Rush Hill. Bath 101 D1
Rush Hill. Paul 130 C2
Rush Hill. Ston E 130 C2
Rushgrove Gdns. Bi Sut 113 E2
Rushmead La. Marsh 55 F1
Rushmoor Gr. Back 76 A3
Rushmoor La. Back 76 A3
Rushmoor. Cleve 57 D1
Rushton Dr. Fr Cot 38 B4
Rushway. Blag 110 A2
Rushy. Kingsw 66 A2
Ruskin Gr. Bris 50 A4
Ruskin Rd. Rad 132 B1
Russ St. Bris 63 F3
Russell Ave. Kingsw 65 F4
Russell Cl. Win 95 D3
Russell Gr. Bris 49 E3
Russell Rd. Bris 49 D2
Russell Rd. Bris 51 D1
Russell Rd. Cleve 57 E2
Russell St. Bath 101 F4
Russell Town Ave. Bris 64 A4
Russet Cl. Olve 14 A2
Russet Ct. Kings 11 F2
Russet Way. P St J 133 E4
Russett Cl. Back 76 A3
Russett Gr. Nail 75 E4
Rutherford Cl. Kingsw 66 A2
Ruthven Rd. Bris 79 F4
Rutland Ave. Kingsw 66 A1
Rutland Cl. W-S-M 105 E4
Rutland Rd. Bris 49 F2
Rydal Ave. Lock 106 A2
Rydal Rd. W-S-M 104 C2
Ryde Rd. Bris 64 A1
Rye Cl. Bris 78 C3
Ryecroft Ave. W-S-M 88 C1
Ryecroft Rd. Fr Cot 38 B4
Ryecroft Rise. Lo Ash 62 A1
Ryedown La. Bitt 66 B1
Ryland Pl. Bris 50 A1
Rylestone Cl. Fr Cot 37 F4
Rylestone Gr. Bris 48 C3
Rysdale Rd. Bris 48 C3

Sabrina Way. Bris 48 B2
Sadbury Cl. W-S-M 89 D2
Sadlier Cl. Bris 48 A4
Saffron Ct. Bath 102 A4
Saffrons The. W-S-M 89 D2
Sage Cl. Portis 44 C2
Sailsburt St. Bris 64 C4
Sailsbury Rd. Bris 64 B3
St John's Rd. Back 76 A3
St Agnes Ave. Bris 63 F1
St Agnes Cl. Nail 60 A1
St Agnes Wlk. Bris 63 F1
St Aidan's Cl. Bris 65 D3
St Aidan's Rd. Bris 65 D3
St Alban's Rd. Bris 49 D2
St Aldams Dr. Puck 53 D3
St Aldwyn's Cl. Bris 49 F4
St Andrew's Cl. Cong 91 E2
St Andrew's Dr. Cleve 57 D1
St Andrew's Par. W-S-M 104 C2
St Andrew's Rd. Avon 33 D2
St Andrew's Rd. Bris 49 F1
St Andrew's Terr. Bath 101 F4
St Andrews Cl. Nail 60 A1
St Andrews Cl. W-S-M 88 C2
St Andrews Rd. Back 76 A3
St Andrews Trading Est. Avon 33 E1
St Andrews. Kingsw 66 A3
St Andrews. Yate 27 F1
St Ann's Way. Bath 102 A3
St Anne's Ave. Keyn 81 E3
St Anne's Cl. Kingsw 66 A2
St Anne's Ct. Keyn 81 E3
St Anne's Dr. Fr Cot 38 B3
St Anne's Dr. Wick 67 D4
St Anne's Park Rd. Bris 64 C3
St Anne's Rd. Bris 64 B3
St Anne's Rd. Bris 65 D3
St Anne's Terr. Bris 64 C3
St Annes Dr. Kingsw 66 B2
St Anthony's Dr. Wick 67 D4
St Anthonys Cl. Mid No 132 A1
St Anway. Kingsw 66 B1
St Aubin's Ave. Bris 64 C2
St Aubyn's Ave. W-S-M 104 B1
St Augustine's Cl. Portis 44 C2
St Augustine's Par. Bris 63 E3
St Augustine's Pl. Bris 63 E3
St Austell Cl. Nail 76 A4
St Austell Rd. W-S-M 105 D4
St Barnabas Cl. Bris 63 F1
St Barnabas Cl. Mid No 132 A2
St Barnabas Cl. Sist 66 B4
St Bartholomew's Rd. Bris 49 F2
St Bede's Rd. Bris 51 E1
St Bernard's Rd. Bris 47 F3
St Brelades Gr. Bris 64 C3
St Brendan's Way. Avon 33 D1
St Briavels Dr. Yate 39 E4
St Bridges Cl. W St L 88 A3
St Catherine's Cl. Bath 102 B3
St Catherine's Ind Est. Bris 63 E2
St Catherine's Mead. E in G 47 E2
St Catherine's Pl. Bris 63 E2
St Chad's Ave. Mid No 132 A1
St Chad's Green. Mid No 132 A1
St Charles Cl. Mid No 132 A1
St Christophers Cl. Bath 102 B4
St Clements Ct. Keyn 81 F2
St Clements Rd. Keyn 81 F2
St David's Ave. Kingsw 66 A3
St David's Cl. W-S-M 88 A1
St David's Cres. Bris 64 C3
St Dunstan's Rd. Bris 63 E1
St Edward's Rd. Bris 63 D3
St Edyth's Rd. Bris 48 B3
St Fagans Ct. Kingsw 66 A1
St Francis Dr. Wick 67 D4
St Francis Dr. Wint 37 F3
St Francis Rd. Bris 63 D2
St Francis Rd. Keyn 81 E3
St Gabriel's Rd. Bris 64 A4
St George's Hill. Bath 102 B4
St George's Hill. E in G 47 D2
St George's Rd. Bris 63 E3
St George's Rd. E in G 46 C4
St George's Rd. Keyn 81 E3
St Giles Barton. Hill 19 E4
St Gregory's Rd. Bris 49 F4
St Gregory's Wlk. Bris 49 F4
St Helen's Wlk. Bris 51 D1
St Helena Rd. Bris 49 D2
St Helens Dr. Kingsw 66 B1
St Helens Dr. Wick 67 E4
St Helier Ave. Bris 64 C2
St Hilary Cl. Bris 48 B3
St Ivel Way. Kingsw 66 B3
St Ives Cl. Nail 60 A1
St Ives Rd. W-S-M 105 D3
St James Cl. Thorn 8 B2
St James Ct. St Gif 24 B2
St James St. W-S-M 104 B4
St James' Barton. Bris 63 F4
St James's Par. Bath 101 F3
St James's Park. Bath 101 F4
St James's Pl. Mang 52 A3
St James's Sq. Bath 101 F4
St James's St. Bath 101 F4
St James's St. Mang 52 A3
St John St. H Up 20 A2
St John St. Thorn 8 A1
St John's Ave. Cleve 57 E2
St John's Bridge. Bris 63 E4
St John's Cl. P St J 133 D4
St John's Cl. W-S-M 87 E1
St John's Cres. Bris 63 F1
St John's Cres. Mid No 132 A1
St John's La. Bris 63 F1
St John's Pl. Bath 101 F3
St John's Rd. Bath 101 E4
St John's Rd. Bath 102 A4
St John's Rd. Bris 63 E2
St John's Rd. Cleve 57 E2
St John's St. Bris 63 E2
St John's Steep. Bris 63 E4
St Johns Ct. Keyn 81 F3
St Johns Way. Ch Sod 28 A1
St Johns' Rd. Bris 49 D1
St Jonhs Rd. Tims 116 A1
St Joseph's Rd. Bris 35 D2
St Joseph's Rd. W-S-M 87 F1
St Jude's Terr. W-S-M 88 B1
St Julian's Rd. Well 133 F3
St Kenya Ct. Keyn 81 F3
St Keyna Rd. Keyn 81 F3
St Kilda's Rd. Bath 101 E3
St Ladoc Rd. Keyn 81 E3
St Laud Cl. Bris 48 B3
St Leonard's Rd. Bris 49 F3
St Leonard's Rd. Bris 50 B1
St Lucia Cl. Bris 49 F4
St Lucia Cres. Bris 49 F4
St Luke St. Bris 64 A4
St Luke's Cres. Bris 63 F2
St Luke's Gdns. Bris 64 C1
St Luke's Rd. Bath 101 F2
St Luke's Rd. Bris 63 F2
St Luke's Rd. Mid No 131 F1
St Margaret's Cl. Back 76 A3
St Margaret's Cl. Keyn 81 E3
St Margaret's Dr. Bris 49 E3
St Margaret's La. Back 76 A3
St Margaret's Terr. W-S-M 104 B4
St Mark's Gr. Bris 50 A1
St Mark's Rd. Bath 102 A3
St Mark's Rd. Bris 50 A1
St Mark's Rd. Mid No 132 A1
St Mark's Terr. Bris 50 A1
St Marks Cl. Keyn 81 F3
St Marks Rd. W-S-M 89 D2
St Martin's Cl. Bris 64 A1
St Martin's Ct. Bath 101 F1
St Martin's Gdns. Bris 64 A1
St Martin's La. Marsh 69 F4
St Martin's Park. Marsh 69 F4
St Martin's Rd. Bris 64 A1
St Martin's Wlk. Bris 64 A1
St Martins Cl. W-S-M 88 C2
St Mary St. Thorn 15 D4
St Mary's Bldgs. Bath 101 F3
St Mary's Cl. Bath 102 A3
St Mary's Cl. Tims 116 A1
St Mary's Ct. W-S-M 105 D1
St Mary's Gdns. Chur 109 D3
St Mary's Gr. Nail 75 E4
St Mary's Park Rd. Portis 45 E2
St Mary's Park. Nail 75 E4
St Mary's Rd. Bris 47 E4
St Mary's Rd. Lo Ash 62 B3
St Mary's Rd. Lock 105 E1
St Mary's Rd. Portis 45 E2
St Mary's Rise. Rad 133 E1
St Mary's St. Axb 125 E1
St Mary's Way. Yate 27 F1
St Mary's Wlk. Bris 47 E3
St Marys Cl. Lock 105 E1
St Marys Way. Thorn 8 A1
St Matthew's Cl. W-S-M 87 E1
St Matthew's Rd. Bris 63 E4
St Matthias Park. Bris 63 F4
St Michael's Ave. Cleve 57 E1
St Michael's Cl. Wint 37 F4
St Michael's Hill. Bris 63 E4
St Michael's Park. Bris 63 E4
St Michael's Rd. Bath 101 E4
St Michaels Ct. Bris 65 D4
St Michaels Rd. Bath 101 D3
St Micheal's Ave. W-S-M 89 D2
St Nicholas Cl. Winsl 120 B4
St Nicholas Ct. Bath 85 F1
St Nicholas Park. Bris 50 A1
St Nicholas Rd. W-S-M 104 B1
St Nicholas Rd. Whit 80 B2
St Nicholas St. Bris 63 E3
St Nicholas' Rd. Bris 49 F1
St Oswald's Ct. Bris 49 D2
St Oswald's Rd. Bris 49 D2
St Patrick's Ct. Bath 102 A3
St Patricks Ct. Keyn 81 F3
St Paul St. Bris 63 F4
St Paul's Rd. Bris 63 D4
St Paul's Rd. Bris 63 E2
St Paul's Rd. W-S-M 104 C3
St Pauls Pl. Bath 101 F3
St Pauls Pl. Mid No 132 A1
St Peter's Ave. W-S-M 87 E1
St Peter's Cres. Fr Cot 38 A4
St Peter's Rd. Rod 138 B4
St Peter's Rise. Bris 79 D4
St Peter's Wlk. Bris 49 D3
St Peters Rd. Portis 45 E2
St Phillips Causeway. Bris 64 A3
St Phillips Rd. Bris 64 A4
St Pierre Dr. Kingsw 66 A3
St Ronan's Ave. Bris 49 E1
St Saviour's Rd. Bath 85 E1
St Saviours Way. Bath 85 E1
St Silas St. Bris 64 A3
St Stephen's Ave. Bris 63 E3
St Stephen's Cl. Bath 101 F4
St Stephen's Ct. Bath 101 F4
St Stephen's Rd. Kingsw 51 E1
St Stephen's St. Bris 63 E3
St Stephens Bsns Centre. Kingsw 66 B3
St Stephens Cl. Kingsw 51 F2
St Stephens Rd. Bath 101 F4
St Swithin's Pl. Bath 102 A4
St Thomas Rd. Mid No 132 A1
St Thomas St E. Bris 63 F3
St Thomas St. Bris 63 F3
St Vincent's Hill. Bris 49 D1
St Vincent's Rd. Bris 63 D3
St Werburgh's Park. Bris 50 A1
St Werburgh's Rd. Bris 49 F1
St Whytes Rd. Bris 79 E4
St Winifreds Dr. Bath 102 B1
Salcombe Gdns. W-S-M 89 D1
Salcombe Rd. Bris 64 A1
Salem Rd. Wint 37 F4
Salisbury Ave. Bris 65 D4
Salisbury Gdns. Mang 51 F3
Salisbury Rd. Bath 85 D1
Salisbury Rd. Bris 49 E1
Salisbury Rd. Mang 51 F3
Salisbury Rd. Paul 131 F2
Salisbury Rd. W-S-M 105 E4
Salisbury St. Bris 64 A3
Salisbury Terr. W-S-M 104 B4
Sally In The Wood Rd. Bathf 103 E3
Sallybarn Cl. Kingsw 65 F1
Sallys Way. Wint 37 F4
Sallysmead Cl. Bris 79 D2
Saltford Ct. Keyn 82 C2
Salthouse Ct. Cleve 57 D1
Salthouse Rd. Cleve 57 D1
Salthrop Rd. Bris 49 F2
Saltings Cl. Cleve 57 D1
Saltmarsh Dr. Bris 34 A1
Saltwell Ave. Whit 80 B3
Sambourne La. E in G 47 E2
Samian Way. St Gif 36 C3
Sampsons Rd. Bris 79 E2
Samuel St. Bris 64 B4
Samuel White Rd. Kingsw 65 E2
Samuel Wright Cl. Kingsw 66 B3
Sanctuary Gdns. Bris 48 B2
Sand Farm La. W St L 88 A3
Sand Hill. Bris 64 B2
Sand Rd. W St L 88 A3
Sandbach Rd. Bris 64 B2
Sandbed Rd. Bris 50 A1
Sandburrows Rd. Bris 78 C3
Sandburrows Wlk. Bris 78 C3
Sandcroft Ave. W-S-M 104 B1
Sandcroft. Bris 79 F3
Sandford Cl. Cleve 57 D1
Sandford Rd. Bris 63 D3
Sandford Rd. W-S-M 105 D4
Sandford Rd. Winsc 107 F1
Sandgate Rd. Bris 64 B2
Sandholm Rd. Bris 64 B2
Sandholme Cl. Mang 51 F4
Sandhurst Cl. St Gif 24 A1
Sandhurst Rd. Bris 64 B2
Sandhurst. Yate 39 E4
Sandling Ave. Bris 50 A4
Sandmead Rd. Wins 108 A2
Sandown Cl. Mang 37 F1
Sandown Rd. Bris 36 B2
Sandown Rd. Bris 64 B2
Sandpiper Dr. W-S-M 88 C1
Sandpits La. H Up 19 F1
Sandringham Ave. Mang 51 F4
Sandringham Park. Mang 51 F4
Sandringham Rd. Bris 64 B2
Sandringham Rd. Kingsw 65 F1
Sandringham Rd. St Gif 36 B2
Sandringham Rd. W-S-M 104 C3
Sands Hill. Dyrh 54 C2
Sands La. Fr Cot 25 F1
Sandwich Rd. Bris 64 B2
Sandy Cl. St Gif 36 C3
Sandy La. Ab Lei 61 E4
Sandy La. Aust 13 D4
Sandy La. Bris 50 B2
Sandy La. Pens 96 C2
Sandy La. Wrax 47 D1
Sandy La. Wrax 61 E4
Sandy Lodge. Yate 39 F4
Sandy Park Rd. Bris 64 B2
Sandyleaze. Bris 48 C4
Sarabeth Dr. Pris 117 D2
Saracen St. Bath 102 A4
Sarah St. Bris 64 A4
Sargent St. Bris 63 F2
Sarum Cres. Bris 35 E1
Sassoon Ct. Kingsw 65 F3
Satchfield Cl. Bris 34 C1
Satchfield Cres. Bris 34 C1
Sates Way. Bris 49 E3
Saunders Rd. Kingsw 51 F2
Saunton Wlk. Bris 79 F4
Savages Wood Rd. St Gif 36 B4
Savages Wood Rd. St Gif 36 C4
Savernake Rd. W-S-M 88 C2
Saville Cres. W-S-M 105 E4
Saville Gate Cl. Bris 48 C2
Saville Pl. Bris 63 D3
Saville Rd. Bris 48 C2
Saville Rd. W-S-M 105 E4
Saville Row. Bath 101 F4
Savoy Rd. Bris 64 B2
Saw Cl. Bath 101 F3
Saw Mill La. Thorn 8 A1
Sawyers Ct. Cleve 57
Saxby Cl. Cleve 57
Saxby Cl. W-S-M 89
Saxon Rd. Bris 50
Saxon Rd. W-S-M 105
Saxon Way. St Gif 24
Saxon Way. Winsl 120
Says La. Chur 109
Sbi Centre. Kingsw 65
Scandrett Cl. Bris 34
Scaurs The. W-S-M 88
School Cl. Bris 79
School Cl. Hill 19
School Cl. St Gif 36
School La. Ba Gu 77
School La. Bathe 85
School La. Bris 50
School La. Ch St 112
School La. Paul 131
School La. Ship 109
School La. Wring 94
School Rd. Bris 64
School Rd. Bris 64
School Rd. Fr Cot 38
School Rd. Kingsw 65
School Rd. Kingsw 66
School Rd. Wring 92
School Way. Piln 22
School Wlk. Bris 50
School Wlk. Yate 27
Scobell Rise. Paul 115
Scop The. Alm 24
Score La. Blag 110
Score The. Blag 110
Scot La. Ch St 95
Scotch Horn Cl. Nail 59
Scotch Horn Way. Nail 59
Scots Pine Ave. Nail 60
Scott Ct. Kingsw 65
Scott Lawrence Cl. Bris 51
Scott Rd. W-S-M 105
Scott Way. Ch Sod 39
Scumbrum La. Farm 115
Scumbrum La. Paul 115
Sea Bank Rd. E in G 32
Sea Mills La. Bris 48
Seabrook Rd. W-S-M 88
Seagry Cl. Bris 35
Searl Court Ave. Bris 64
Searle Cres. W-S-M 105
Seaton Rd. Bris 50
Seavale Rd. Cleve 57
Seaview Rd. Portis 44
Seaview Rd. Portis 44
Seawalls Rd. Bris 48
Seawalls. Bris 48
Second Ave. Bath 101
Second Ave. Rod 138
Second Way. Avon 33
Seddon Rd. Bris 50
Sedgefield Gdns. Mang 37
Sedgemoor Cl. Nail 75
Sedgemoor Rd. Bath 101
Sedgemoor Rd. W-S-M 87
Sefton Park Rd. Bris 49
Selbourne Cl. Bath 101
Selbourne Rd. Bris 49
Selbourne Rd. W-S-M 104
Selbrooke Cres. Bris 51
Selby Rd. Bris 50
Selden Rd. Bris 80
Selkirk Rd. Bris 51
Selley Wlk. Bris 79
Selwood Cl. W-S-M 105
Selworthy Cl. Keyn 81
Selworthy Gdns. Nail 59
Selworthy Rd. Bris 64
Selworthy Rd. W-S-M 105
Selworthy. Kingsw 65
Seneca Pl. Bris 64
Seneca St. Bris 64
Sercombe Park. Cleve 57
Serlo Ct. W-S-M 88
Seven Acres La. Bathe 85
Seventh Ave. Bris 36
Severn Ave. W-S-M 104
Severn Cl. Char 11
Severn Dr. Thorn 8
Severn Grange. Bris 34
Severn Rd. Avon 33
Severn Rd. Avon 33
Severn Rd. Bris 47
Severn Rd. E in G 47
Severn Rd. Piln 22
Severn Rd. Portis 45
Severn View Rd. Thorn 8
Severn Way. Bris 23
Severn Way. Keyn 81
Severnmeade. Portis 44
Severnwood Gdns. Piln 22
Sevier Rd. Blea 123
Sevier St. Bris 50
Seville Rd. Portis 45
Seward Terr. Rad 133
Seymour Ave. Bris 49
Seymour Cl. Cleve 57
Seymour Cl. W-S-M 88
Seymour Rd. Bath 102 A4

Seymour Rd. Bris 49 F2
Seymour Rd. Bris 50 A1
Seymour Rd. Kingsw 51 E1
Seymour Rd. Kingsw 51 F2
Seyton Wlk. St Gif 36 C3
Shackleton Ave. W-S-M 39 F4
Shadwell Rd. Bris 49 E2
Shaft Rd. Bath 102 B1
Shaft Rd. Plin 22 A4
Shaftesbury Ave. Bris 49 F1
Shaftesbury Rd. Bath 101 E3
Shaftesbury Rd. W-S-M 105 D4
Shaftesbury Terr. Bris 64 B4
Shaftesbury Terr. Mid No 133 D2
Shakespeare Ave. Bath 101 F2
Shakespeare Ave. Bris 50 A4
Shakespeare Rd. Rad 132 B1
Shaldon Rd. Bris 50 A2
Shallows The. Keyn 82 C2
Sham Castle La. Bath 102 B4
Shamrock Rd. Bris 50 B2
Shanklin Dr. Bris 36 A2
Shannon Ct. Thorn 15 E4
Shapcott Cl. Bris 64 A1
Shaplands. Bris 48 C3
Sharland Cl. Bris 48 C2
Shaw Cl. Bris 64 B4
Shaws Way. Bath 101 D3
Shaymoor La. Alm 23 D2
Sheene La. Bris 63 E2
Sheep Fair La. Marsh 69 F4
Sheeps Croft. Bris 79 D3
Sheepway. Portb 46 B3
Sheepwood Cl. Bris 35 D1
Sheepwood Rd. Bris 35 D1
Sheldare Barton. Bris 65 D4
Sheldon Cl. Cleve 57 F1
Sheldrake Dr. Bris 50 C3
Shellard Rd. Bris 36 A1
Shellards La. Alve 15 E2
Shellards Rd. Kingsw 65 E3
Shelley Ave. Cleve 57 E1
Shelley Cl. Bris 64 C4
Shelley Rd. Bath 101 F2
Shelley Rd. W-S-M 132 B1
Shelley Way. W-S-M 105 D2
Shellmor Ave. St Gif 24 A4
Shellmor Cl. St Gif 24 B1
Shelly Way. Bris 50 A4
Shepherds Cl. Mang 51 F3
Sheppard Rd. Bris 51 E3
Sheppards Gdns. Bath 84 A1
Sheppardine Rd. O-On-S 1 B1
Sheppy's Mill. Cong 91 E3
Shepton Wlk. Bris 63 F1
Shepton. W-S-M 105 D1
Sherbourne Ave. St Gif 36 C4
Sherbourne Cl. Kingsw 51 F1
Sherbourne St. Bris 64 C4
Sherbourne's Brake. St Gif 36 C3
Sheridan Rd. Bath 100 C3
Sheridan Rd. Bris 50 A4
Sheridan Way. Kingsw 66 A1
Sherrin Way. Bris 78 C2
Sherrings The. St Gif 36 B4
Sherston Cl. Bris 51 D3
Sherston Cl. Nail 60 A1
Sherston Rd. Bris 49 F4
Sherston Rd. Luck 31 F3
Sherwell Rd. Bris 64 B2
Sherwood Cl. Keyn 81 F3
Sherwood Cres. W-S-M 88 C2
Sherwood Rd. Bris 51 D1
Sherwood Rd. Keyn 81 F3
Shetland Rd. Bris 35 E1
Shetland Way. Nail 60 A1
Shickle Gr. Bath 101 E1
Shields Ave. Bris 36 A1
Shilde Dr. St Gif 36 B4
Shilton Cl. Kingsw 65 F4
Shimsey Cl. Bris 51 E3
Shiners Elms. Yatt 91 D4
Ship La. Bris 63 F3
Shipham Cl. Bris 20 A3
Shipham Cl. Nail 75 F4
Shipham La. Ship 108 A1
Shipham La. Wins 108 A1
Shipham Rd. Ched 125 F3
Shiplate Rd. Blea 123 D4
Shipley Rd. Bris 49 D4
Shire Gdns. Bris 47 E4
Shire La. Tor 56 A3
Shire Way. Yate 39 E3
Shirehampton Rd. Bris 48 B3
Shockerwick La. Bathf 86 B2
Shop La. Gr Bad 30 C1
Shophouse Rd. Bath 101 D3
Shoreditch. Ch St 112 B4
Short La. Litt 129 F1
Short La. Lo Ash 62 A1
Short St. Bris 64 A3
Short Way. Thorn 15 D4
Short Way. Wrax 61 D2
Shorthill Rd. West 39 D2
Shortlands Rd. Bris 34 A1
Shortwood Hill. Puck 52 C2

Shortwood Rd. Bris 79 F2
Shortwood Rd. Puck 53 D3
Shortwood View. Kingsw 65 F4
Shortwood Wlk. Bris 79 F2
Showering Rd. Bris 80 B3
Shrubbery Ave. W-S-M 87 E1
Shrubbery Cotts. Bris 49 D1
Shrubbery Rd. Mang 51 E3
Shrubbery Rd. W-S-M 87 E1
Shrubbery Terr. W-S-M 87 E1
Shrubbery Wlk W. W-S-M 87 E1
Shrubbery Wlk. W-S-M 87 E1
Shuter Rd. Bris 78 C3
Sibland Cl. Thorn 15 E4
Sibland Rd. Thorn 15 E4
Sibland Way. Thorn 15 E4
Sibland. Thorn 15 E4
Sidcot La. Wins 125 D4
Sidcot. Bris 65 D1
Sidcot La. Bris 65 D1
Sideland Cl. Bris 80 C3
Sidelands Rd. Bris 51 D3
Sidings The. Char 11 D3
Sidlings The. Co Mar 127 E4
Sidmouth Gdns. Bris 63 E1
Sidmouth Rd. Bris 63 F1
Sidney Hill Cottage Homes.
  Chur 108 C2
Signal Rd. Kingsw 51 F2
Silbury Rd. Bris 62 C1
Silbury Rise. Keyn 82 A1
Silcox Rd. Bris 79 E2
Silklands Gr. Bris 48 B4
Silver Birch Cl. St Gif 36 B4
Silver Ct. Nail 59 E1
Silver Mead. Cong 91 E1
Silver Moor La. Ban 106 C4
Silver St. Bris 63 E4
Silver St. Ch Mag 96 A2
Silver St. Cong 91 E1
Silver St. Hol 138 B1
Silver St. Kilm 139 D3
Silver St. Mid No 138 A4
Silver St. Nail 59 E1
Silver St. Rad 138 A4
Silver St. W in G 44 C1
Silver St. Wring 92 C1
Silverhill Rd. Bris 34 C2
Silverlow Rd. Nail 59 E1
Silverstone Way. Cong 91 E2
Silverthorne La. Bris 64 A3
Silverthorne Wharf. Bris 64 A3
Silverton Ct. Bris 63 F1
Simon's Cl. Haut 51 A3
Simons Cl. W-S-M 89 D1
Simplex Ind Est The.
  Kingsw 66 B2
Singapore Rd. W-S-M 104 C4
Single Hill. Well 134 A3
Sion Hill Pl. Bath 84 C1
Sion Hill. Bath 84 C1
Sion Hill. Bath 101 E4
Sion La. Bris 62 C4
Sion Pl. Bris 62 C4
Sion Rd. Bath 84 C1
Sion Rd. Bris 63 E2
Sir John's La. Bris 50 A3
Siskin Wlk. W-S-M 105 F4
Siston Centre The. Kingsw 52 A1
Siston Cl. St Gif 52 A1
Siston Comm. Sist 52 A1
Siston La. Puck 52 C1
Six Ways. Cleve 57 E2
Sixpence. Paul 115 E1
Sixth Ave. Bris 36 A2
Sixty Acres Cl. Wrax 61 D2
Skinner's Hill. Times 132 C4
Skinners La. Char 108 C2
Skippon Ct. Kingsw 65 F3
Sladacre La. Blag 110 C1
Slade La. Ba Gu 77 E2
Slade La. Lymp 122 A1
Slade Rd. Portis 45 E3
Sladebrook Ave. Bath 101 E2
Sladebrook Rd. Bath 101 D2
Slate La. Co Dan 98 A4
Sleep La. Whit 80 B2
Slimbridge Cl. Ch Sod 39 F4
Sloan St. Bris 64 B2
Slough La. Co Ash 68 C3
Slymbridge Ave. Bris 35 D2
Small Down End. Winsc 107 F1
Small La. Bris 64 C3
Small St. Bris 63 E4
Small St. Bris 63 E4
Smallbrook La. Co Dan 98 A3
Smallcombe Rd. Mid No 132 C2
Smallcombe Rd. Bath 102 C2
Smallway. Cong 91 F2
Smarts Green. Ch Sod 40 B4
Smeaton Rd. Bris 62 C3
Smithcourt Dr. St Gif 36 B4
Smithmead. Bris 79 D3
Smoke La. Avon 33 E4
Smyth Rd. Bris 63 D2
Smythe Croft. Bris 80 A2

Smyths Cl. Avon 33 D1
Snow Hill. Bath 85 D1
Snowberry Cl. W-S-M 89 D1
Snowberry Wlk. Bris 50 C1
Snowdon Cl. Bris 50 C2
Snowdon Rd. Bris 50 C2
Snowdon Vale. W-S-M 88 A1
Sodbury Rd. Wickw 18 A2
Solent Way. Thorn 15 E4
Soldale Cl. Bath 85 F2
Solsbury Way. Bath 85 D1
Somer Ave. Mid No 131 F1
Somer Lea. Chil 137 E3
Somer Rd. Mid No 131 F1
Somerby Cl. St Gif 36 B4
Somerdale Ave. Bath 101 E1
Somerdale Ave. Bris 64 A1
Somerdale Cl. W-S-M 105 E4
Somerdale Cl. W-S-M 105 E4
Somerdale Rd N. Keyn 81 F4
Somerdale Rd. Keyn 81 F4
Somerdale View. Bath 101 E1
Somermead. Bris 63 E1
Somerset Ave. Yate 27 F2
Somerset Cl. Kings 17 F2
Somerset Cres. St Gif 36 C3
Somerset Folly. Tims 116 A1
Somerset La. Bath 84 C1
Somerset Mews. W-S-M 104 C3
Somerset Pl. Bath 84 C1
Somerset Pl. Bris 64 A2
Somerset Rd. Cleve 57 F2
Somerset Rd. Portis 44 C3
Somerset Sq. Bris 63 F3
Somerset Sq. Nail 59 F1
Somerset St. Bris 63 E4
Somerset St. Bris 63 F4
Somerset Terr. Bris 63 E2
Somerset Way. Paul 131 F3
Somerton Cl. Kingsw 65 F4
Somerton Rd. Bris 49 F3
Somerton Rd. Cleve 57 F4
Somerton. W-S-M 105 D1
Somervale Rd. Rad 132 C1
Somerville Cl. Keyn 82 C1
Somerville Rd. Wins 108 A3
Somerville Rd S. Bris 49 F1
Somerville Rd. Bris 49 F1
Sophia Gdns. W-S-M 89 D2
Sorrel Cl. Thorn 8 A1
Soundwell Rd. Bris 65 E4
Soundwell Rd. Kingsw 51 E4
South Ave. Bath 101 E3
South Ave. Portis 45 E3
South Ave. Yate 27 F4
South Combe. Blea 122 A3
South Croft. Bris 48 C4
South Croft. Winsc 107 F1
South Dene. Bris 48 B4
South Gr. Bris 49 E3
South Gr. E in G 47 E2
South Green St. Bris 62 C3
South Hayes. Bris 50 A2
South Hill. Winsc 107 F1
South Lawn Cl. Lock 105 F2
South Lawn. Lock 105 F2
South Lea Rd. Bath 101 D4
South Liberty La. Bris 63 D1
South Meadows. Wring 92 C1
South Par. Bath 102 A3
South Par. Ch Mag 96 A2
South Par. W-S-M 104 B4
South Par. Yate 27 F1
South Rd. Alve 24 C3
South Rd. Bris 49 E1
South Rd. Bris 63 E2
South Rd. Kingsw 65 E4
South Rd. Lymp 122 A1
South Rd. Mid No 132 A1
South Rd. Portis 116 A1
South Rd. W-S-M 87 E1
South Rock Ind Est. Chil 137 E1
South Side. Cong 91 F3
South St. Chil 137 F1
South Terr. Bris 49 E4
South Terr. W-S-M 104 B4
South View Cres. Fr Cot 38 B3
South View Pl. Mid No 132 A1
South View Rd. Bath 101 E3
South View Rise. Fr Cot 38 B3
South View Terr. Yatt 74 B1
South View. Fr Cot 38 A4
South View. Kilm 139 D2
South View. Mid No 132 C3
South View. Portis 45 D4
South View. Tims 116 A1
South Wlk. Yate 27 F1
Southbournes Gdns. Bath 85 D1
Southcot Pl. Bath 102 A2
Southdown Ave. Bath 101 D2
Southdown Rd. Bath 101 D2
Southdown Rd. Bris 35 E1
Southdown. W-S-M 88 C4
Southend Rd. W-S-M 104 C2
Southern Way. Cleve 57 D1

Southernhay Ave. Bris 63 D3
Southernhay. Bris 63 D3
Southernhay. Kingsw 51 E2
Southey Ave. Kingsw 51 F1
Southey Cl. Kingsw 51 F1
Southey Rd. Cleve 57 E1
Southey St. Bris 49 F1
Southfield Ave. Kingsw 51 F1
Southfield Cl. Nail 59 F2
Southfield Cl. W-S-M 104 B1
Southfield Rd. Bris 49 D4
Southfield Rd. Bris 63 E2
Southfield Rd. Bris 49 D4
Southfield Rd. Nail 59 F2
Southfield Road Trading Est.
  Nail 59 F2
Southfield. W St P 135 F2
Southfield. Rad 133 D1
Southgate. Bath 102 A3
Southlands Way. Cong 91 F3
Southlands. Bath 84 A1
Southlands. Tyth 16 A2
Southleaze. Wins 125 D3
Southleigh Rd. Bris 63 D4
Southmead Rd. Bris 35 F1
Southmead Rd. W-S-M 105 D4
Southmead. Wins 125 D4
Southover Cl. Bris 49 D4
Southover Rd. Paul 115 E1
Southridge Hts. W-S-M 122 A4
Southsea Rd. Bris 36 A4
Southside Cl. Bris 48 A4
Southside Cres. W St L 88 C2
Southstoke La. Sosto 118 C4
Southstoke Rd. Bath 101 F1
Southview Cl. Lock 105 F1
Southville Rd. Bris 63 E2
Southville Rd. W-S-M 104 C2
Southway Dr. Kingsw 66 B3
Southwell St. Bris 63 E4
Southwood Ave. Bris 48 B4
Southwood Dr E. Bris 48 B4
Southwood Dr. Bris 48 A4
Sovereign Gdns. Bris 48 C2
Spa La. Bath 85 D1
Spalding Cl. Bris 50 A2
Spaniorum View. Alm 22 C1
Spar Rd. Avon 33 E2
Spar Rd. Yate 27 E1
Spartley Dr. Bris 78 C3
Spartley Wlk. Bris 78 C3
Specklemead. Paul 131 E3
Speedwell Ave. Bris 64 B4
Speedwell Cl. Thorn 8 B1
Speedwell Rd. Bris 51 D1
Spencer Dr. W-S-M 89 D2
Spey Cl. Thorn 15 E4
Spider La. W-S-M 104 B4
Spindleberry Gr. Nail 60 A1
Spinners End. W-S-M 89 D2
Spinney Croft. Bris 78 C3
Spinney The. Fr Cot 38 A4
Spinney The. W-S-M 104 C1
Spires View. Bris 50 C3
Spratts Bridge. Ch Mag 96 A2
Spring Cres. Bath 102 A3
Spring Gardens Rd. Bath 102 A4
Spring Gardens Rd. Bath 102 A4
Spring Gdns. Bris 64 A1
Spring Ground Rd. Paul 131 F3
Spring Hill Dr. W-S-M 88 C1
Spring Hill. Bris 63 E4
Spring Hill. Kingsw 51 F1
Spring Hill. W-S-M 88 B1
Spring La. Bath 85 D1
Spring Rise. Portis 45 E2
Spring St Pl. Bris 63 F2
Spring St. Bris 63 F2
Spring Terr. W-S-M 88 B1
Spring Valley. W-S-M 88 B1
Springfield Ave. Bris 47 E3
Springfield Ave. Bris 49 F3
Springfield Ave. Mang 52 A4
Springfield Ave. W-S-M 88 B1
Springfield Bldgs. Mid No 133 D2
Springfield Bldgs. Paul 131 E1
Springfield Cl. Bath 101 D3
Springfield Cl. Mang 52 A4
Springfield Gr. Bris 49 E3
Springfield Hts. Mid No 132 C2
Springfield Lawns. Bris 47 E3
Springfield Pl. Mid No 132 C2
Springfield Rd. Bris 49 E1
Springfield Rd. E in G 47 E2
Springfield Rd. Mang 52 A4
Springfield Rd. Portis 45 D3
Springfield. P St J 133 E3
Springfield. Thorn 15 E4
Springfields. Bris 36 A1
Springhill Cl. Paul 131 E3
Springleaze. Bris 64 A1
Springleaze. Mang 52 A4
Springville Cl. Kingsw 66 A2

Springwater Park Ind Est.
  Bris 64 C4
Springwell. N St P 135 F2
Springwood Dr. Bris 34 B2
Spruce Way. Bris 35 F4
Square The. Ave 125 E1
Square The. Axb 125 E1
Square The. Ban 107 D2
Square The. Blag 109 F2
Square The. Bris 64 A1
Square The. Clut 114 C1
Square The. Mang 51 F2
Square The. Ship 125 F4
Square The. Tims 116 A1
Square The. Well 118 B1
Square The. Wins 124 C3
Squire La. Co Mar 111 E1
Squire's Cl. Kingsw 65 F2
Squires Leaze. Thorn 8 B1
Stabbins Cl. W-S-M 89 D3
Stable Yd. Bath 101 E3
Stackpool Rd. Bris 63 E2
Staddlestones. Mid No 137 F4
Stadium Rd. Bris 49 E3
Stafford Cres. Thorn 8 A1
Stafford Pl. W-S-M 104 C4
Stafford Rd. Bris 50 A1
Stafford Rd. Portis 45 F2
Stafford Rd. W-S-M 104 C4
Stafford St. Bris 63 E2
Staffords Cl. Kingsw 66 A3
Stall St. Bath 102 A3
Stambrook Park. Bathe 65 F3
Stanbridge Cl. Mang 51 F3
Stanbridge Rd. Mang 51 F3
Stanbury Ave. Bris 51 E3
Stanbury Rd. Bris 63 F2
Stancombe La. Back 76 C4
Standfast Rd. Bris 34 C2
Standish Ave. St Gif 24 B1
Standish Cl. Bris 34 C1
Standon Way. Bris 35 E1
Stane Way. Avon 47 E4
Stanfield Cl. Bris 50 B3
Stanford Cl. Fr Cot 37 F4
Stanhope Pl. Bath 101 F3
Stanhope Rd. Bath 101 F3
Stanhope Rd. W-S-M 104 C2
Stanhope St. Bris 64 A3
Stanier Rd. Bath 101 F3
Stanley Hill. Bris 64 A2
Stanley Ave. Bris 36 A1
Stanley Ave. Bris 49 F2
Stanley Chase. Bris 50 C1
Stanley Cres. Bris 36 A1
Stanley Gdns. Kingsw 66 A1
Stanley Gr. W-S-M 104 C4
Stanley Park Rd. Kingsw 51 F2
Stanley Park. Bris 50 B1
Stanley Rd. Bris 101 E3
Stanley Rd. Bris 49 E1
Stanley Rd. Kingsw 66 A1
Stanley Rd. W-S-M 63 E2
Stanley St N. Bris 63 E2
Stanley St S. Bris 63 E2
Stanley St. Bris 63 E2
Stanley Terr. Bris 63 E2
Stanley Terr. Mid No 133 D2
Stanshalls Cl. Win 94 B4
Stanshalls Dr. Win 94 B4
Stanshalls La. Win 94 B4
Stanshawe Cres. Yate 27 E1
Stanshawes Dr. Yate 27 E1
Stanshawes Dr. St Gif 27 D1
Stanton Cl. Kingsw 52 A1
Stanton La. Pens 97 D1
Stanton Rd. Bris 35 F1
Stanton Wick La. Pens 97 D1
Stanway Cl. Bath 101 E1
Stanway. Bris 80 C1
Staple Grove Cres. Bris 65 D4
Staplehill Rd. Bris 51 E2
Staples Cl. Cleve 57 F2
Staples Green. W-S-M 89 D2
Stapleton Cl. Bris 50 B3
Stapleton Rd. Bris 50 B3
Stapleton Rd. Bris 50 A1
Star Barn Rd. Wint 37 F4
Star La. Bris 50 C2
Starcross Rd. W-S-M 105 D4
Starling Cl. W-S-M 105 F4
Starrs Cl. Axb 125 D1
Station App. Pens 97 E1
Station Rd. W-S-M 104 C4
Station Rd. Axb 125 E1

Station Rd. Back

Station Rd. Back ... 76 A3
Station Rd. Back ... 77 D4
Station Rd. Bath ... 101 E4
Station Rd. Bag ... 110 C2
Station Rd. Bris ... 34 C2
Station Rd. Bris ... 36 A1
Station Rd. Bris ... 36 A2
Station Rd. Bris ... 47 E3
Station Rd. Bris ... 49 F1
Station Rd. Bris ... 49 F2
Station Rd. Bris ... 51 D2
Station Rd. Bris ... 64 B1
Station Rd. Char ... 11 D3
Station Rd. Cleve ... 57 E2
Station Rd. Clut ... 114 C2
Station Rd. Cong ... 91 E2
Station Rd. E in G ... 47 E2
Station Rd. Fr Cot ... 38 B3
Station Rd. Gr Bad ... 30 C1
Station Rd. Hi Cha ... 120 B3
Station Rd. In Act ... 26 B2
Station Rd. Keyn ... 81 F3
Station Rd. Kingsw ... 51 F2
Station Rd. Kingsw ... 66 B4
Station Rd. Lock ... 89 E1
Station Rd. Mid No ... 132 A1
Station Rd. Nail ... 59 F1
Station Rd. Piln ... 22 C2
Station Rd. Portb ... 46 B2
Station Rd. Portis ... 45 E3
Station Rd. St Gif ... 36 B4
Station Rd. W-S-M ... 88 C1
Station Rd. W-S-M ... 104 C4
Station Rd. Winsc ... 107 F3
Station Rd. Wint ... 37 F2
Station Rd. Wring ... 92 B1
Station Rd. Yate ... 27 E1
Station Rd. Yatt ... 74 A1
Station R d. Wickw ... 18 A4
Staunton Fields. Whit ... 80 B2
Staunton La. Whit ... 80 B2
Staunton Rd. Ch Mag ... 96 A2
Staunton Way. Whit ... 80 B2
Staveley Cres. Bris ... 35 E1
Staverton Cl. St Gif ... 24 B1
Staverton Way. Kingsw ... 66 A3
Stavordale Gr. Bris ... 80 A3
Steam Mills. Mid No ... 137 F4
Stean Bridge Rd. St Gif ... 36 C3
Steel Cl. Kingsw ... 65 F2
Steel Mills. Keyn ... 81 F2
Stella Gr. Bris ... 63 D1
Stephen St. Bris ... 64 A4
Stephens Dr. Kingsw ... 65 F3
Stepney Rd. Bris ... 50 B1
Stepney Wlk. Bris ... 50 B1
Stepping Stones The. Bris ... 64 C3
Sterncourt Rd. Bris ... 51 D4
Stevens Cres. Bris ... 63 F2
Stevens La. Lymp ... 122 B2
Steway La. Bathe ... 86 A3
Stibbs Cl. Kingsw ... 65 F2
Stibbs Hill. Bris ... 65 D2
Stickland. Cleve ... 57 E1
Stidcot La. Tyth ... 16 B3
Stidcote La. Wickw ... 16 C3
Stile Acres. Bris ... 34 A1
Stilemead La. Co Mar ... 111 E1
Stillhouse La. Bris ... 63 E2
Stillingfleet Rd. Bris ... 79 E3
Stillman Cl. Bris ... 78 C2
Stinchcombe. Yate ... 27 F1
Stirling Cl. Yate ... 27 E2
Stirling Rd. Bris ... 64 B2
Stirling Way. Keyn ... 81 F2
Stirtingale Ave. Bath ... 101 E2
Stirtingale Rd. Bath ... 101 E2
Stitchings La. Engl ... 117 E4
Stitchings Shord La. Bi Sut ... 113 E2
Stock Hill. Thorn ... 7 E1
Stock La. Chur ... 109 D4
Stock La. Cong ... 91 F1
Stock Way N. Nail ... 59 F1
Stock Way S. Nail ... 59 F1
Stockhill Cl. Chil ... 137 E2
Stockhill Rd. Chil ... 137 E2
Stockmead. Chur ... 109 D3
Stockton Cl. Bris ... 79 F2
Stockton Cl. Kingsw ... 66 A2
Stockwell Ave. Mang ... 52 A3
Stockwell Cl. Mang ... 51 F4
Stockwell Dr. Mang ... 52 A4
Stockwell Glen. Mang ... 52 A4
Stockwood Cres. Bris ... 63 F1
Stockwood Hill. Keyn ... 81 E4
Stockwood La. Bris ... 80 C3
Stockwood La. Whit ... 80 C3
Stockwood Rd. Bris ... 81 D4
Stodeigh Cl. W-S-M ... 89 D2
Stoke Bridge Ave. St Gif ... 36 B3
Stoke Hamlet. Bris ... 48 C3
Stoke Hill. Bris ... 48 C2
Stoke Hill. Ch St ... 112 B4
Stoke La. Bris ... 48 C3
Stoke La. Bris ... 50 C4
Stoke La. St Gif ... 36 B4
Stoke Mead. Li St ... 119 F4
Stoke Meadows. St Gif ... 24 B1

Stoke Paddock Rd. Bris ... 48 B3
Stoke Park Rd S. Bris ... 48 C2
Stoke Park Rd. Bris ... 48 C2
Stoke Rd. Bris ... 49 D1
Stoke Rd. Portis ... 45 E3
Stoke View Rd. Bris ... 50 C2
Stoke View. Bris ... 36 A2
Stokefield Cl. Thorn ... 8 A1
Stokeleigh Wlk. Bris ... 48 B3
Stokemead. St Gif ... 36 B4
Stokes Croft. Bris ... 63 F4
Stokes. Ct. Kingsw ... 66 A2
Stone La. Wint ... 37 F2
Stone's Cross. Mid No ... 132 A1
Stoneable Rd. Mid No ... 133 D2
Stoneage La. P St J ... 117 D1
Stoneberry Rd. Bris ... 80 A2
Stonebridge Park. Bris ... 50 C1
Stonebridge Rd. W-S-M ... 104 C2
Stonebridge. Cleve ... 57 E1
Stonechat Gdns. Bris ... 50 C3
Stonehenge La. Nail ... 59 F2
Stonehill. Kingsw ... 65 F2
Stonehouse Cl. Bath ... 102 A1
Stonehouse La. Bath ... 102 A1
Stoneleigh Cres. Bris ... 64 A1
Stoneleigh Rd. Bris ... 64 A1
Stoneleigh Wlk. Bris ... 64 A1
Stoneleigh. Ch Mag ... 96 A2
Stonewell Dr. Cong ... 91 E2
Stonewell Gr. Cong ... 91 E2
Stonewell La. Cong ... 91 E2
Stonewell Park Rd. Cong ... 91 E2
Stoney Steep. Wrax ... 60 A2
Stoney Stile Rd. Alve ... 15 D3
Stoneyard La. Litt ... 129 E1
Stoneyfield Cl. E in G ... 47 D3
Stoneyfields. E in G ... 47 D2
Stores Rd. Avon ... 33 E2
Stormont Cl. W-S-M ... 104 C2
Stothard Rd. Bris ... 50 A2
Stottbury Rd. Bris ... 50 A2
Stoulton Gr. Bris ... 35 D2
Stourden Cl. Bris ... 51 D4
Stourton Dr. Kingsw ... 65 F2
Stover Rd. Yate ... 27 D1
Stover Trading Est. Yate ... 27 D1
Stowel Hill Rd. Tim ... 16 A3
Stowey Bottom. Bi Sut ... 113 F3
Stowey Park. Yatt ... 91 E4
Stowey Rd. Yatt ... 91 E4
Stowick Cres. Bris ... 34 B1
Stradbrook Ave. Bris ... 65 D2
Stradling Ave. W-S-M ... 104 C3
Stradling Rd. Bris ... 34 B1
Straight St. Bris ... 63 F3
Straits Par. Bris ... 51 D3
Stratford Cl. Bris ... 79 F2
Stratford La. Co Mar ... 112 C1
Strathmore Rd. Bris ... 50 B3
Stratton Cl. St Gif ... 36 B4
Stratton Rd. Keyn ... 82 A3
Stratton St. Bris ... 63 F4
Strawberry Cl. Nail ... 59 E1
Strawberry Gdns. Nail ... 75 E4
Strawberry Hill. Cleve ... 57 F2
Strawberry La. Dun ... 78 C2
Strawbridge Rd. Bris ... 64 A4
Stream Cl. Bris ... 35 E2
Stream Side. Mang ... 51 F3
Stream The. Bris ... 37 D1
Streamcross. Yatt ... 74 C1
Streamleaze Ct. Thorn ... 15 D4
Streamleaze. Ch Mag ... 96 A2
Streamleaze. Thorn ... 15 E4
Streamside Rd. Ch Sod ... 28 A1
Streamside. Ch Mag ... 96 A2
Streamside. Cleve ... 57 F2
Street End La. Blag ... 110 B1
Street End. Blag ... 110 B1
Street The. Alve ... 15 D3
Street The. Bi Sut ... 113 F2
Street The. Ch St ... 112 B4
Street The. Chil ... 137 D2
Street The. Co Mar ... 111 E1
Street The. Co Mar ... 128 A3
Street The. Farm ... 115 F2
Street The. Luck ... 31 F2
Street The. N Nib ... 5 E2
Street The. Olve ... 14 A2
Street The. Rad ... 132 B1
Street The. Win ... 94 C1
Stretford Ave. Bris ... 64 B4
Stretford Rd. Bris ... 64 B4
Stride Cl. Piln ... 22 A3
Stride Comm. Alve ... 14 C3
Strode Gdns. Alve ... 14 C3
Strode Rd. Cleve ... 57 E1
Stroud Rd. Bris ... 47 F3
Stroud Rd. Bris ... 47 E4
Stuart Rd. W-S-M ... 105 D3
Stuart St. Bris ... 64 B4
Stumpwell La. N Nib ... 5 F1
Sturden La. Bris ... 37 F2
Sturdon Rd. Bris ... 63 D2
Sturmer Cl. Yate ... 27 F2
Sturminster Cl. Bris ... 80 B3

Sturminster Rd. Bris ... 80 B4
Sullivan Cl. Bris ... 79 E3
Sumerlin Dr. Cleve ... 57 F2
Summer Hill. Bris ... 64 A2
Summer La N. W-S-M ... 89 D1
Summer La. Ban ... 106 C2
Summer La. W-S-M ... 89 D2
Summer St. Bris ... 63 E2
Summerfield Rd. Bath ... 85 D1
Summerfield. W-S-M ... 89 D2
Summerhayes. Kingsw ... 66 B3
Summerhill Rd. Bath ... 85 D1
Summerhill Rd. Bris ... 64 C4
Summerhill Terr. Bris ... 64 C4
Summerhouse. Nail ... 59 E2
Summerlands Rd. W-S-M ... 105 D4
Summerlands. Back ... 76 A3
Summerlea. Pris ... 117 D3
Summerleaze. Bris ... 51 E2
Summerleaze. Keyn ... 81 F4
Summers Dr. Doyn ... 54 A1
Summers Mead. Yate ... 27 F2
Summers Rd. Bris ... 50 A1
Summers Terr. Bris ... 50 A1
Sundays Hill. Alm ... 24 A2
Sundayshill La. Falf ... 9 E4
Sundayshill La. Rock ... 9 E4
Sunderland Pl. Bris ... 63 D4
Sunderland St. Bath ... 102 A4
Sundridge Park. Yate ... 39 F4
Sunfield Rd. Lock ... 105 F2
Sunningdale Cl. Nail ... 60 A1
Sunningdale Dr. Kingsw ... 66 A3
Sunningdale Rd. W-S-M ... 88 C2
Sunningdale. Bris ... 63 D4
Sunningdale. Yate ... 39 F4
Sunny Bank. Bris ... 51 D1
Sunny Hill. Bris ... 48 B4
Sunny Wlk. Bris ... 51 D1
Sunnybank. Mang ... 51 F3
Sunnydene. Bris ... 64 B2
Sunnyhill Dr. Bris ... 47 F3
Sunnymead. Keyn ... 81 F2
Sunnymead. Mid No ... 131 F1
Sunnymeade Rd. Nail ... 59 E2
Sunnyside Cres. Cleve ... 57 E2
Sunnyside. Yate ... 27 E1
Sunnyside Rd N. W-S-M ... 104 C3
Sunnyside Rd. Cleve ... 57 E2
Sunnyside View. P St J ... 133 E4
Sunnyside. Bris ... 48 C3
Sunnyside. Clut ... 115 D2
Sunnyside. Fr Cot ... 38 A4
Sunridge Cl. Mid No ... 137 F4
Sunridge Park. Mid No ... 137 F4
Sunridge. Mang ... 51 E3
Sunrise Gr. Bris ... 64 B2
Surry Rd. Bris ... 49 F2
Surrey St. Bris ... 63 F4
Sussex Pl. Bris ... 49 F1
Sussex St. Bris ... 64 A3
Sutherland Ave. Mang ... 51 F4
Sutherland Ave. Yate ... 27 E2
Sutherland Dr. Lock ... 105 E1
Sutherland Pl. Bris ... 49 D1
Sutton Ave. Bris ... 64 B2
Sutton Hill Rd. Bi Sut ... 113 E2
Sutton La. Wring ... 93 F1
Sutton Park. Bi Sut ... 113 E2
Sutton St. Bath ... 102 A4
Swainswick Gdns. Bath ... 85 E1
Swainswick La. Bathe ... 85 E2
Swainswick. Bris ... 79 F3
Swaish Dr. Mang ... 66 A2
Swallow Cl. Rod ... 138 A4
Swallow Dr. Bris ... 35 F4
Swallow Gdns. W-S-M ... 105 F4
Swallow Park. Thorn ... 8 B2
Swallow St. Bath ... 102 A3
Swallows Ct. St Gif ... 36 C2
Swan Cl. W-S-M ... 105 F4
Swan La. Fr Cot ... 25 D1
Swan La. Wint ... 37 E4
Swancombe. Blag ... 110 C1
Swancombe. W in G ... 59 F4
Swane Rd. Bris ... 80 C3
Swangrove. Wint ... 37 F3
Swanley La. Newp ... 4 A3
Swanmoor Cres. Bris ... 35 D2
Sweets Cl. Kingsw ... 51 F1
Sweets Rd. Kingsw ... 51 F1
Swift Cl. W-S-M ... 88 C1
Swinhay La. N Nib ... 5 E1
Swiss Dr. Bris ... 62 C1
Swiss Rd. Bris ... 62 C1
Swiss Rd. W-S-M ... 104 C4
Sycamore Cl. Bris ... 50 C1
Sycamore Cl. Kingsw ... 65 D2
Sycamore Cl. Nail ... 59 D1
Sycamore Cl. Ship ... 125 F4
Sycamore Cl. W-S-M ... 105 D3
Sycamore Dr. Bris ... 35 F4

Sycamore Rd. Rad ... 133 D1
Sydenham Bldgs. Bath ... 101 F3
Sydenham Hill. Bris ... 49 F3
Sydenham La. Bris ... 49 F1
Sydenham Pl. Bris ... 49 F1
Sydenham Rd. Bath ... 101 F3
Sydenham Rd. Bris ... 49 E1
Sydenham Rd. Bris ... 64 A2
Sydenham Way. Kingsw ... 65 E2
Sydney Bldgs. Bath ... 102 A3
Sydney House. E in G ... 47 E2
Sydney Mews. Bath ... 102 A4
Sydney Pl. Bath ... 102 A4
Sydney Rd. Bath ... 102 A4
Sydney Row. Bris ... 63 D3
Sydney Wharf. Bath ... 102 A4
Sylvan Way. Bris ... 48 B4
Sylvia Ave. Bris ... 63 F2
Symes Ave. Bris ... 79 E2
Symington Rd. Bris ... 51 D3
Syston Way. Kingsw ... 51 E1

Tabernacle Rd. Kingsw ... 65 E3
Tackley Rd. Bris ... 50 A2
Tadwick La. Bathe ... 84 C4
Tailor's Ct. Bris ... 64 A4
Talbot Ave. Bris ... 51 E1
Talbot Rd. Bris ... 64 B1
Talgarth Rd. Bris ... 49 F2
Tallis Gr. Bris ... 79 E3
Tamar Cl. Thorn ... 15 E4
Tamar Dr. Keyn ... 82 A2
Tamar Rd. Bris ... 64 B3
Tamar Rd. W-S-M ... 89 D1
Tamblyn Cl. Mid No ... 133 D2
Tamsin Ct. Keyn ... 81 F3
Tamworth Rd. Keyn ... 81 F2
Tanhouse La. In Act ... 27 E4
Tanhouse La. Yate ... 27 E4
Tankard's Cl. Bris ... 63 E4
Tanner Cl. Kingsw ... 65 F3
Tanners Ct. Bris ... 37 D1
Tanners Ct. Thorn ... 15 E4
Tanners La. Marsh ... 69 F4
Tanorth Cl. Bris ... 80 A2
Tanorth Rd. Bris ... 79 F2
Tanyard The. Kingsw ... 66 A1
Tapsters. Kingsw ... 66 A2
Tarnock Ave. Bris ... 80 A4
Tarnwell. Pens ... 97 D1
Taunton Rd. W-S-M ... 89 D2
Taunton Wlk. Bris ... 50 A4
Taverners Ind Est. Nail ... 59 F2
Taverner Cl. Bris ... 79 E4
Tavistock Rd. Bris ... 63 F1
Tavistock Rd. W-S-M ... 89 D1
Tavistock Wlk. Bris ... 63 F1
Tawny Way. W-S-M ... 105 F4
Taylor Cl. Kingsw ... 66 B2
Taylor Ct. W-S-M ... 89 D2
Taylor Gdns. Bris ... 78 C2
Tayman Cl. Bris ... 49 F3
Tayman Ridge. Bit ... 82 B4
Taynton Cl. Kingsw ... 66 B1
Teal Cl. St Gif ... 24 B1
Teal Cl. W-S-M ... 88 C1
Teddington Cl. Bath ... 101 E2
Teesdale Cl. W-S-M ... 105 E4
Teewell Ave. Kingsw ... 51 F2
Teewell Cl. Kingsw ... 51 F2
Teewell Hill. Kingsw ... 51 F2
Teignmouth Rd. Bris ... 63 F1
Teignmouth Rd. W-S-M ... 105 E4
Telephone Ave. Bris ... 63 E3
Telford Wlk. Bris ... 51 D1
Tellisford La. N St P ... 135 F2
Templar Rd. Yate ... 27 F1
Temple Back. Bris ... 63 F3
Temple Gate. Bris ... 63 F3
Temple Rose St. Bris ... 63 F3
Temple St. Bris ... 63 F3
Temple St. Keyn ... 81 F3
Temple Way Underpass.
Bris ... 63 F3
Temple Way. Bris ... 63 F3
Templeland Rd. Bris ... 78 C3
Tenby Rd. Keyn ... 81 E2
Tenby St. Bris ... 64 A4
Tennessee Gr. Bris ... 49 E3
Tennis Court Ave. Paul ... 131 E3
Tennis Court Rd. Paul ... 131 E3
Tennis Rd. Bris ... 64 A1
Tenniscourt Rd. Kingsw ... 52 A1
Tennyson Ave. Cleve ... 57 D1
Tennyson Cl. Keyn ... 81 F4
Tennyson Rd. Bath ... 101 E4
Tennyson Rd. Bris ... 50 B1
Tennyson Rd. W-S-M ... 105 D2
Tenterk Cl. Blea ... 122 A4
Tenth Ave. Bris ... 36 A4
Tereslake Green. Bris ... 35 F2
Terrace Wlk. Bath ... 102 A3
Terrell Gdns. Bris ... 64 B4
Terrell St. Bris ... 63 E4
Terry Hill. Kilm ... 139 E4
Tetbury Cl. St Gif ... 36 B4
Tetbury Gdns. Nail ... 59 E1
Tetbury Rd. Bris ... 64 C3
Teviot Rd. Keyn ... 82 A2

Tewkesbury Rd. Bris ... 50 B1
Tewther Rd. Bris ... 79 E2
Teyfant Rd. Bris ... 79 F2
Teyfant Wlk. Bris ... 79 F2
Thackeray Ave. Cleve ... 57 F2
Thackeray Rd. Cleve ... 57 F2
Thackeray Wlk. Bris ... 50 A4
Thames Cl. Char ... 11 D2
Thanet Rd. Bris ... 63 D1
Thatcher Cl. Portis ... 45 E2
Thatchers Cl. Bris ... 65 D4
The Timbers. Rod ... 138 A4
The Triangle. Wring ... 92 B1
The Tyning. Hi Cha ... 120 A2
The Weal. Bath ... 84 B4
There-and-back-again La.
Bris ... 63 E4
Theresa Ave. Bris ... 49 F2
Theynes Croft. Lo Ash ... 62 A1
Thicket Ave. Bris ... 51 E2
Thicket Rd. Bris ... 51 E2
Thiery Rd. Bris ... 64 B1
Thingwall Park. Bris ... 50 C2
Third Ave. Bath ... 101 E3
Third Ave. Bris ... 36 A1
Third Ave. Rod ... 138 B4
Third Way. Avon ... 33 E1
Thirlmere Ct. Kingsw ... 66 B3
Thirlmere Rd. Bris ... 36 A4
Thirlmere Rd. W-S-M ... 105 D2
Thistle St. Bris ... 63 D2
Thomas Cl. Ban ... 107 D2
Thomas La. Bris ... 63 F3
Thomas Pring Wlk. Bris ... 51 D1
Thomas St N. Bris ... 49 E2
Thomas St. Bath ... 102 A4
Thomas St. Bris ... 63 F4
Thomas St. Bris ... 64 A4
Thompson Rd. Bris ... 80 C3
Thomson Rd. Bris ... 64 A4
Thorn Cl. Yate ... 27 E1
Thornbank Pl. Bath ... 101 F3
Thornbury Dr. W-S-M ... 104 B1
Thornbury Rd. W-S-M ... 104 B1
Thorndale Cl. W-S-M ... 104 C4
Thorndale. Bris ... 63 D4
Thornhayes Cl. Fr Cot ... 38 A4
Thornleigh Rd. Bris ... 49 F3
Thornmead Dr. Bris ... 35 D1
Thornycroft Cl. Bris ... 50 A4
Three Queens' La. Bris ... 63 F3
Three Wells Rd. Bris ... 78 C2
Throgmorton Rd. Bris ... 79 F2
Thrubwell La. But ... 94 A2
Thrush Cl. W-S-M ... 105 F4
Thurlestone. Bris ... 80 A3
Thurston's Barton. Bris ... 50 C2
Tibberton. Kingsw ... 66 A1
Tibbott Rd. Bris ... 80 B3
Tibbott Wlk. Bris ... 80 B3
Tichborne Rd. Bris ... 64 A4
Tichborne Rd. W-S-M ... 87 F1
Tickenham Hill. Nail ... 59 F3
Tickenham Rd. Cleve ... 58 A2
Tide Gr. Bris ... 48 A4
Tidenham Way. Bris ... 23 F1
Tiffany Ct. Bris ... 63 F2
Tiledown Cl. Clut ... 114 C1
Tiledown. Clut ... 114 C1
Tilley Cl. Farm ... 116 A3
Tilley Cl. Keyn ... 82 A3
Tilley La. Farm ... 115 F3
Tilling Rd. Bris ... 49 F4
Tilling Wlk. Bris ... 49 F4
Tilting Rd. Thorn ... 8 A1
Timber Dene. Bris ... 50 B2
Timbercombe Wlk. Bris ... 80 B3
Timsbury Rd. Bris ... 63 E1
Timsbury Rd. Paul ... 115 E1
Timsbury Wlk. Bris ... 63 E1
Tindell Ct. Kingsw ... 65 F2
Tinker's La. Co Mar ... 124 C2
Tinker's La. Hol ... 139 D1
Tintagel Cl. Keyn ... 81 E2
Tintern Ave. Bris ... 64 B4
Tintern Cl. Kingsw ... 66 B2
Tippetts Rd. Kingsw ... 65 E3
Titan Barrow. Bathf ... 86 B1
Tiverton Gdns. W-S-M ... 89 D1
Tiverton Rd. Cleve ... 57 D1
Tiverton Wlk. Bris ... 50 B3
Toll Down Way. Burt ... 43 D2
Toll Rd. W-S-M ... 121 F4
Tolland. W-S-M ... 105 D1

Rd. Bath 85 F2
Cleve 57 E1
ship 125 F4
-S-M 89 D1
Cres. Bele 34 C2
Rd. A Tur 42 C3
Rd. Marsh 56 A2
Marsh 70 A4
Rd. W-S-M 88 C2
Bris 63 E1
Rd. Bris 63 E1
Cl. Kingsw 66 B3
Rd. Keyn 82 A2
Ave. Bris 79 F4
Cres. W-S-M 89 D2
Rd. Bris 49 F3
-W-S-M 89 D1
Bris 79 F2
Bris 79 F2
wn La. W-S-M 105 D1
wn Rd. W-S-M 104 C2
End La. Marsh 69 F4
ne Ave. St Gif 36 C2
W-S-M 88 C2
Bris 63 E3
use La. Wrax 60 A2
Bris 63 F1
s. Bris 66 A3
k. Kingsw 66 A4
S. Kingsw 66 A3
Bris 51 E1
Portis 45 D2
Bris 63 F3
k. W-S-M 87 E1
Ban 107 E2
rton. N St P 135 F2
d. N St P 135 F2
d Cl. Bris 80 C3
La. Alm 24 A3
d Rd. Bris 80 C3
d Rd. W-S-M 89 D3
Alm 23 F2
d. E Harp 129 D3
Corm 10 A1
k. Bris 79 F4
Rd. Bath 84 A1
Bris 63 D1
rk. Bris 63 E1
Rd. Bris 64 B2
ne Ave. Bris 35 D2
e Gr. Bris 35 D2
a. Rock 2 B2
Bris 63 E3
St Gif 36 C3
Cl. W-S-M 88 A1
Rd. Bris 51 D2
aze. Yate 27 F1
ll Pl. Bris 50 A1
Rd. Cleve 57 E1
Rd. Bris 62 C1
Lock 89 E1
y Ave. Bris 64 B4
y Park. Bris 64 B3
ey Rd. Bris 49 E1
Mews. W-S-M 89 D2
.a. St Gif 36 C3
d Rd. Keyn 82 B2
t St. Bris 63 E3
wood Park. Bris 50 C3
wood Way. Nail 60 A1
h Dr. W-S-M 89 D1
. Thorn 15 D4
. Keyn 82 A2
St. Bris 51 E3
n Cl. St Gif 24 B1
n Rd. Bris 62 C1
an Rd. W-S-M 104 C4
an Wlk. Bris 34 C2
ows Wlk. Bris 34 B2
an Cl. Kingsw 65 E4
Gr. Bris 35 E2
na Cl. W-S-M 104 C4
na Park. W-S-M 104 C4
Gdns. Bris 79 F4
Centre The. Cleve 57 F2
E. Bath 101 E3
N. Bath 101 E3
s South. Bris 63 D4
The. Cleve 57 E2
W. Bath 101 E3
s West. Bris 63 D4
Cl. Mang 38 A1
dge. Bath 101 F3
Bris 63 E3
Rd. E in G 47 D2
Cl. Bath 101 F3
Ct. Nail 59 E1
Cl. W-S-M 87 E1
d. Bath 102 A1
ld. Bris 64 A3
Rd. Nail 59 E1
W-S-M 87 E1
St. Bath 101 F3
St. Bris 64 A4
Wlk. Bris 64 A4
Cnr. Yatt 91 E4

Troon Dr. Kingsw 66 A3
Troon. Yate 39 F4
Troopers Hill Rd. Bris 65 D4
Trossachs Dr. Bath 102 B4
Trowbridge Rd. Bris 35 E1
Trowbridge Wlk. Bris 35 E1
Truro Rd. Bris 63 D2
Truro Rd. Nail 60 A1
Trym Cross Rd. Bris 48 B3
Trym Side. Bris 48 B3
Trymleaze. Bris 48 B3
Trymwood Cl. Bris 34 C1
Tucker St. Bris 63 F4
Tucker's La. Co Mar 127 F4
Tuckett La. Bris 51 E4
Tuckingmill La. Co Dan 98 C3
Tuckmill. Cleve 57 D1
Tudor Cl. Kingsw 66 B2
Tudor Mews. W-S-M 104 C4
Tudor Rd. Bris 49 F4
Tudor Rd. Bris 50 B1
Tudor Rd. Kingsw 65 E3
Tudor Rd. Portis 45 F2
Tudor Rd. W-S-M 89 D2
Tuffley Rd. Bris 49 E4
Tugela Rd. Bris 78 C4
Tuggy's La. Hin Cha 119 F1
Tunbridge Cl. Ch Mag 96 A1
Tunbridge Rd. Ch Mag 96 A1
Tunley Hill. Tims 116 C1
Tunley Rd. Pris 117 E2
Tunnel La. Chil 137 F3
Tunstall Cl. Bris 48 C2
Turley Rd. Bris 50 B1
Turnberry Wlk. Bris 64 B1
Turnberry. Kingsw 66 A3
Turnbridge Rd. Bris 35 E2
Turnbury Ave. Nail 60 A1
Turnbury Cl. W-S-M 88 C2
Turnbury. Yate 39 F4
Turner Cl. Keyn 82 A3
Turner Cl. W-S-M 88 C2
Turner Gdns. Bris 50 A3
Turner Way. Cleve 57 D1
Turner's Terr. Faulk 134 A1
Turners Ct. Kingsw 65 F2
Turnpike Gate. Wickw 18 A3
Turnpike Rd. Co Bi 124 C2
Turnpike Rd. Ship 125 F4
Turtlegate Ave. Bris 78 C2
Turtlegate Wlk. Bris 78 C2
Turville Dr. Bris 50 A3
Tutton Way. Cleve 57 F1
Tweed Rd. Thorn 15 E4
Tweed Cl. Thorn 15 E4
Tweed Rd. Cleve 57 E1
Tweeny La. Kingsw 66 B3
Twenty Acres Rd. Bris 35 D1
Twerton Farm Cl. Bath 101 D3
Twickenham Rd. Bris 49 E4
Twinhoe La. Well 118 C1
Two Acres Rd. Bris 80 B4
Two Mile Ct. Bris 65 E4
Two Stones La. Ch Sod 40 B4
Two Trees. Priddy 126 C4
Twomile Hill Rd. Bris 65 D4
Twynings The. Kingsw 51 F1
Tyball Way. St Gif 36 C3
Tybalt Way. St Gif 36 C3
Tyler Cl. Kingsw 65 F3
Tyler Green. W-S-M 89 D2
Tyler St. Bris 64 A3
Tyler's La. Mang 51 E3
Tyndale Ave. Bris 51 E3
Tyndale Ave. Yate 27 E2
Tyndale Cl. N Nib 5 F2
Tyndale Rd. Kingsw 51 F1
Tyndale View. Thorn 15 E4
Tyndall Ave. Bris 63 E4
Tyndall Rd. Bris 64 A4
Tyndall's Park Mews. Bris 63 E4
Tyndall's Park Rd. Bris 63 E4
Tyne St. Bris 64 A4
Tyne St. Bris 50 A1
Tyning Cl. W-S-M 80 A4
Tyning La. Bath 27 F1
Tyning End. Bath 102 A3
Tyning Hill. Mid No 133 D2
Tyning La. Bath 85 D1
Tyning Pl. Bath 85 F1
Tyning Rd. Bath 102 B1
Tyning Rd. Bris 63 F2
Tyning Rd. Keyn 82 C3
Tyning Rd. P St J 133 E4
Tyning Rd. Winsl 120 C2
Tyning The. Bath 102 A3
Tynings The. Cleve 57 D1
Tynings Way. Clut 114 C2
Tynings Way. Westw 120 C2
Tynte Ave. Bris 79 D2
Tyntesfield Rd. Bris 79 D4
Tyrone Wlk. Bris 79 F4
Tyrrel Way. St Gif 36 C3
Tytherington Rd. Alve 16 A3

Ubley Dr. Priddy 127 D4
Ullswater Cl. Kingsw 66 B3
Ullswater Cl. Yate 27 F2
Ullswater Dr. Bath 85 D1

Ullswater Rd. Bris 35 E1
Uncombe Cl. Back 76 B4
Under La. Wring 93 E1
Underbanks. E in G 47 E2
Underhill Ave. Mid No 131 F1
Underhill Dr. W-S-M 104 B1
Underhill La. Mid No 131 F1
Underhill La. Ston E 131 F1
Underhill Rd. Char 11 D3
Underwood Ave. W-S-M 88 A4
Underwood Cl. Alve 15 D2
Underwood End. Wins 108 A2
Underwood Rd. Portis 45 E2
Union Pas. Bath 102 A3
Union Pl. W-S-M 104 B4
Union St. Bris 64 A3
Union St. Bath 102 A3
Union St. Bris 58 B3
Union St. Nail 59 E1
Union St. W-S-M 104 B4
Unity Rd. Keyn 82 A3
Unity Rd. Keyn 82 A3
Unity St. Bris 63 E3
Unity St. Bris 63 F4
Unity St. Bris 65 E4
University Cl. Bris 48 C2
University Rd. Bris 63 E4
University Wlk. Bris 63 E4
Uphill Dr. Bath 85 D1
Uphill Rd N. W-S-M 104 B1
Uphill Rd S. W-S-M 104 C1
Uphill Rd. Bris 49 F3
Uphill Way. W-S-M 104 B1
Upjohn Cres. Bris 79 E2
Uplands Cl. Li St 119 F4
Uplands Dr. Keyn 82 C1
Uplands Rd. Bris 51 E2
Uplands Rd. Keyn 82 C1
Uplands The. Nail 75 E4
Upper Bath Rd. Thorn 15 D4
Upper Belgrave Rd. Bris 49 D1
Upper Berkeley Pl. Bris 63 D4
Upper Bloomfield Rd. Bath 101 E1
Upper Borough Walls. Bath 101 F3
Upper Bristol Rd. Bath 101 E3
Upper Bristol Rd. Clut 114 B2
Upper Bristol Rd. W-S-M 88 A1
Upper Byron Pl. Bris 63 D4
Upper Chapel La. Fr Cot 38 A4
Upper Cheltenham Pl. Bris 49 F1
Upper Church La. Bris 63 E3
Upper Church La. Lock 105 E1
Upper Church Rd. W-S-M 87 E1
Upper Church St. Bath 101 F4
Upper Cranbrook Rd. Bris 49 D2
Upper East Hayes. Bath 85 D1
Upper Camden Pl. N St P 135 F2
Upper Hedgemead Rd. Bath 102 A4
Upper Lambridge St. Bath 85 E1
Upper Lansdown Mews. Bath 84 C1
Upper Maudlin St. Bris 63 E4
Upper Mount Pleasant. Hi Cha 120 A2
Upper Myrtle Hill. E in G 47 E2
Upper New Rd. Ched 125 E3
Upper Oldfield Park. Bath 101 F3
Upper Perry Hill. Bris 63 E3
Upper Pitching. Chil 137 E3
Upper Rd. Hin Ble 129 F3
Upper Sandhurst Rd. Bris 64 B2
Upper St. Bris 64 A4
Upper St. Dyrh 54 C2
Upper Stanton. Pens 97 D1
Upper Station Rd. Kingsw 51 F1
Upper Stone Cl. Fr Cot 38 B4
Upper Strode. Win 111 F4
Upper Sydney St. Bris 63 D2
Upper Tockington Rd. Olve 14 A1
Upper Town La. Win 94 B4
Upper Wells St. Bris 63 E4
Upper York St. Bris 63 F4
Upton La. Ch Mag 95 F4
Upton La. Dun 95 F4
Upton Rd. Bris 63 D2
Upton. W-S-M 105 D1
Urchinwood La. Cong 91 F2
Urfords Dr. Bris 51 E3

Vain Cl. W-S-M 88 C2
Valda Rd. W-S-M 88 B1
Vale Cres. Lock 89 E1
Vale End. Nail 59 E1
Vale La. Bris 79 E4
Vale St. Bris 64 A3
Vale The. Puck 52 C3
Vale View. Rad 133 D1
Vale View. Terr. Bathe 85 F2
Valentine Cl. Bris 80 A3
Valerian Cl. Bris 47 F3
Valetta Cl. W-S-M 104 C2

Valley Cl. Nail 59 F1
Valley Gdns. Mang 51 F4
Valley Gdns. Nail 59 F1
Valley Rd. Bris 79 D4
Valley Rd. Cleve 57 F3
Valley Rd. Kingsw 66 A4
Valley Rd. Lo Ash 62 B4
Valley Rd. Mang 52 A3
Valley Rd. Portis 44 C2
Valley Rd. W in G 45 D1
Valley View Cl. Bath 85 D2
Valley View Rd. Bath 85 E2
Valley View Rd. Paul 131 F3
Valley View. Clut 114 C2
Valley Way. Rd. Nail 59 F2
Valley Wlk. Mid No 132 A1
Valls The. St Gif 36 C3
Valma Rocks. Bris 65 D3
Van Diemen's La. Bath 84 C1
Vandyke Ave. Keyn 81 F3
Vane St. Bath 102 A4
Vassall Ct. Bris 51 D3
Vassall Rd. Bris 51 D3
Vattingstone La. Alve 14 C3
Vaughan Cl. Bris 34 C2
Vayre Cl. Ch Sod 28 A1
Veale The. Blea 122 B3
Vee La. Win 94 A4
Vellore La. Bath 102 A4
Ventnor Ave. Bris 64 C4
Ventnor Rd. Bris 36 A2
Ventnor Rd. Bris 50 C1
Venus La. Clut 114 C2
Venus St. Cong 91 F1
Vera Rd. Bris 50 C1
Verbena Way. W-S-M 89 D3
Vereland Rd. Lock 105 F2
Verlands. Cong 91 F3
Vernals La. N Nib 11 E4
Vernham Gr. Bath 101 E1
Vernon Cl. Keyn 82 B2
Vernon La. Co Bi 124 A2
Vernon Park. Bath 101 E3
Vernon St. Bris 63 F2
Vernon Terr. Bath 101 E3
Verrier Rd. Bris 64 A4
Verwood Dr. Kingsw 66 B1
Vicarage Cl. W-S-M 89 D2
Vicarage Cl. Kingsw 65 D3
Vicarage Gdns. P St J 133 D4
Vicarage La. Ba Gu 77 E3
Vicarage La. Co Bi 124 A2
Vicarage La. Co Dan 98 B3
Vicarage La. Hill 19 E4
Vicarage La. N St P 135 F2
Vicarage La. Olve 14 C3
Vicarage Rd. Bris 63 D2
Vicarage Rd. Bris 64 B4
Vicarage Rd. Bris 79 D3
Vicarage Rd. Fr Cot 38 B3
Vicarage Rd. Kingsw 66 A4
Vicarage Rd. Lo Ash 62 B3
Vicarage Rd. Pill 22 B4
Vicars Cl. Bris 51 D2
Victor St. Bris 64 A3
Victor St. Bris 64 B4
Victoria Ave. Bris 64 B4
Victoria Bldgs. Bath 101 E3
Victoria Bridge Rd. Bath 101 F3
Victoria Cl. Bath 101 E3
Victoria Cl. Portis 45 E3
Victoria Cl. Thorn 8 A2
Victoria Cotts. Sosto 118 C4
Victoria Cres. Pill 22 A3
Victoria P. W-S-M 104 B4
Victoria Pl. Bris 63 E3
Victoria Quadrant. W-S-M 104 C4
Victoria Rd. Avon 47 D3
Victoria Rd. Bath 101 E3
Victoria Rd. Bris 64 A3
Victoria Rd. Cleve 57 E2
Victoria Rd. Keyn 82 B2
Victoria Rd. Kingsw 65 D3
Victoria Rd. W-S-M 66 B3
Victoria Sq. Bris 63 D4
Victoria Sq. Portis 45 E3
Victoria Sq. W-S-M 104 B4
Victoria St. Bris 63 F3
Victoria St. Bris 64 B3
Victoria Terr. Bath 101 E1
Victoria Terr. Bath 102 A4
Victoria Terr. Bris 64 A3
Victoria Terr. Paul 131 F3
Victoria Wlk. Bris 49 E1
Vigor Rd. Bris 79 D3
Village Cl. Yate 27 E1
Villice La. Co Mar 128 A4
Villiers Rd. Bris 50 A1

Vilner La. Thorn 15 D4
Vimpany Cl. Bris 34 C2
Vimpennys La. Alm 22 C1
Vincent Cl. Bris 34 B1
Vine Gdns. W-S-M 89 D1
Viner's La. A Tur 43 D3
Vinery The. Wins 125 D4
Vineyard La. Kings 14 A4
Vining Wlk. Bris 64 A4
Vinney Ave. Mang 52 A4
Vinney La. Hort 28 C4
Vintery Leys. Bris 49 D4
Virginia Cl. Ch Sod 28 A1
Vivian St. Bris 63 E2
Vivien Ave. Mid No 132 A1
Vowell Cl. Bris 79 D2
Vynes Cl. Nail 60 A1
Vynes Way. Nail 60 A1
Vyvyan Rd. Bris 63 D4
Vyvyan Terr. Bris 63 D4

Wade Rd. Yate 27 D2
Wade St. Bris 63 F4
Wadehurst Ind Pk. Bris 64 A4
Wades Rd. Bris 36 A2
Wadham Dr. Bris 37 D1
Wadham St. W-S-M 104 B4
Wagtail Gdns. W-S-M 105 F4
Wainbridge Cres. Piln 22 B4
Wainbrook Dr. Bris 50 B1
Wains Cl. Cleve 57 E1
Wainwright Cl. W-S-M 89 D2
Waits Cl. Ban 106 C2
Wakedean Gdns. Yatt 74 A1
Wakeford Rd. Mang 52 A4
Walcot Gate. Bath 102 A4
Walcot St. Bath 102 A4
Waldegrave House. Bris 79 E2
Waldegrave Rd. Bath 84 C1
Waldegrave Terr. Mid No 133 D2
Walden Rd. Keyn 82 B2
Walford Ave. Lock 89 D2
Walk Mill La. Kings 11 F2
Walk The. Kings 11 F3
Walker Cl. Bris 64 A4
Walker Cl. Mang 52 A4
Walker St. Bris 63 E4
Walker Way. Thorn 15 D4
Wall Green. Axb 125 E1
Wallace La. E Harp 128 C2
Walled Bath. Bath 85 D1
Wallenge Cl. Paul 131 F3
Wallenge Dr. Paul 131 F3
Walley La. Ch Mag 113 D4
Wallingford Rd. Bris 79 E4
Walliscote Ave. Bris 49 E3
Walliscote Grove Rd. W-S-M 104 C4
Walliscote Rd S. W-S-M 104 B2
Walliscote Rd. Bris 49 E3
Walliscote Rd. W-S-M 104 B3
Wallscourt Rd S. Bris 36 A1
Wallscourt Rd. Bris 36 A1
Wallsend La. Tor 55 E3
Wallycourt Rd. Ch St 112 C4
Walnut Ave. Yate 28 A4
Walnut Bldgs. Mid No 133 D2
Walnut Cl. Axb 125 D1
Walnut Cl. E in G 47 D2
Walnut Cl. Keyn 81 E2
Walnut Cl. Nail 75 F4
Walnut Cl. W-S-M 89 D1
Walnut Cl. Kingsw 51 F1
Walnut Dr. Bath 101 F2
Walnut Dr. Col 70 C3
Walnut La. Kingsw 66 A4
Walnut Tree Cl. Alm 24 A3
Walnut Wlk. Bris 79 D3
Walnut Wlk. Keyn 81 E2
Walsh Ave. Bris 80 A4
Walsh Cl. W-S-M 105 D1
Walsh Ave. Ch Sod 28 B1
Walsingham Rd. Bris 49 F1
Walter St. Bris 63 D2
Walton Ave. Bris 64 B3
Walton Cl. Keyn 82 A4
Walton Cl. Kingsw 66 B1
Walton Rd. Bris 47 F3
Walton Rd. W-S-M 88 B3
Walton St. Bris 64 A4
Walton. W-S-M 105 D1
Walwyn Cl. Bath 101 D3
Walwyn Gdns. Bris 79 E2
Wansbeck Rd. Keyn 82 A2
Wansbrough Rd. W-S-M 89 D3
Wanscow Wlk. Bris 49 D3
Wansdyke Ct. Bris 80 A3
Wansdyke Rd. Bath 101 E3
Wapley Hill. West 39 F2
Wapley Rd. Dod 40 A2
Wapping Rd. Bris 63 E3
Warden Rd. Bris 63 E2
Wardour Rd. Bris 79 E4

Wareham Cl. Nail

Wareham Cl. Nail 59 E1
Warleigh Dr. Bathe 86 A2
Warleigh La. Bath 103 E3
Warleigh La. Mon Far 103 E3
Warman Cl. Bris 80 C3
Warman Rd. Bris 80 C3
Warmington Rd. Bris 80 B4
Warminster Rd. Bath 103 D3
Warminster Rd. Bris 80 A1
Warminster Rd. Hin Cha .. 119 F3
Warminster Rd. Li St 120 A4
Warne Park. W-S-M 105 D3
Warne Rd. W-S-M 105 D3
Warner Cl. Brock 92 A4
Warner Cl. Kingsw 65 F3
Warns The. Kingsw 66 A2
Warren Cl. Kingsw 105 E1
Warren Cl. Lock 105 E1
Warren Cl. St Gif 24 B2
Warren Croft. N Nib 5 F2
Warren Gdns. Bris 80 C3
Warren La. Lo Ash 61 F1
Warren Rd. Bris 36 A2
Warren Way. Yate 27 F2
Warrilow Cl. W-S-M 89 D3
Warrington Rd. Bris 64 B1
Warth La. W ST L 89 D4
Warwick Ave. Bris 50 A1
Warwick Cl. Kingsw 66 A1
Warwick Cl. Thorn 8 A1
Warwick Cl. W-S-M 105 E4
Warwick Gdns. Clut 114 B2
Warwick Rd. Bath 101 D4
Warwick Rd. Bris 49 D1
Warwick Rd. Keyn 50 A1
Warwick Rd. Keyn 81 E2
Washing Pound La. Nail ... 59 D2
Washing Pound La. Whit ... 80 A2
Washingpool Hill Rd. Olve . 14 B1
Washingpool La. Avon 33 F4
Washington Ave. Bris 50 B1
Washpool La. Engl 100 C1
Watch Elm Cl. St Gif 36 C3
Watchhouse Rd. E in G 47 E2
Watchill Ave. Bris 78 C3
Watchill Cl. Bris 78 C3
Water La. Bris 63 F2
Water La. Bris 64 B1
Water La. Bris 64 B1
Water La. E in G 47 E2
Water La. Kingsw 65 D1
Water La. Mid No 132 A2
Water St. E Harp 128 C2
Water's La. Bris 49 D4
Waterbridge Rd. Bris 78 C3
Watercress Rd. Bris 49 F2
Waterdale Cl. Bris 49 E4
Waterdale Gdns. Bris 49 E4
Waterford Cl. Thorn 15 E4
Waterford Park. Rad 132 C1
Waterford Rd. Bris 49 D3
Waterloo Bldgs. Bath 101 D3
Waterloo Pl. Bris 64 A4
Waterloo Rd. Bris 63 F4
Waterloo Rd. Rad 133 D1
Waterloo St. Bris 62 C4
Waterloo St. Bris 63 F4
Waterloo St. W-S-M 104 B4
Watermore Cl. Fr Cot 38 B4
Waters Rd. Bris 65 E4
Waters Rd. Kingsw 65 E4
Waterside Cres. Rad 132 B1
Waterside Dr. St Gif 24 A1
Waterside La. Kilm 138 C3
Waterside Park. Portis 44 B2
Waterside Rd. Rad 132 B1
Waterside Way. Rad 138 B4
Watery La. Bath 101 D3
Watery La. Chil 138 A2
Watery La. Doyn 68 A4
Watery La. Nail 59 E1
Watery La. Win 95 D2
Wathen Rd. Bris 49 E4
Watkins Yd. Bris 49 D4
Watley's End Rd. Wint 37 F4
Watling Way. Bris 47 F2
Watson Ave. Bris 64 B2
Watson's Rd. Kingsw 65 F2
Watters Cl. Fr Cot 38 B3
Wavell Cl. Yate 27 E2
Waveney Rd. Keyn 82 A2
Waverley Rd. Back 76 A4
Waverley Rd. Bris 47 F3
Waverley Rd. Bris 49 E1
Waverley Rd. Ir Act 27 E2
Waverley Rd. W-S-M 104 C2
Waverley St. Bris 50 A1
Wayacre Dro. Blea 121 E2
Wayfield Gdns. Bathe 85 F2
Wayford Cl. Keyn 82 A2
Wayland Rd. W-S-M 88 C2
Wayleaze. Fr Cot 38 B4
Wayside. Cl. Fr Cot 38 A4
Wayside Dr. Cleve 57 F3
Wayside. W-S-M 88 B1
Weare Cl. Bris 63 D3
Weatherley Ave. Bath ... 101 E1
Weavers Cl. Kings 11 F2
Webb St. Bris 64 A4

Webbington Rd. Co Bi ... 124 B2
Webbs Heath. Sist 66 C4
Webbs Wood Rd. St Gif .. 36 C3
Webbs Wood. St Gif 36 C4
Wedgewood Rd. Mang 37 E1
Wedgwood Cl. Bris 80 A3
Wedgwood Rd. Bath 101 D3
Wedmore Cl. Kingsw 65 F4
Wedmore Cl. W-S-M 104 C1
Wedmore Park. Bath 101 D2
Wedmore Rd. Cleve 57 D1
Wedmore Rd. Keyn 82 B2
Wedmore Rd. Nail 75 F4
Wedmore Vale. Bris 63 F1
Weedon Cl. Bris 50 A1
Weekesley La. Tims 116 B1
Weetwood Rd. Cong 91 F3
Weight Rd. Bris 64 B4
Weind The. W-S-M 88 B1
Weir La. Ab Lei 61 F3
Weir La. Marsh 69 F4
Weir Rd. Cong 91 F3
Well Cl. Lo Ash 62 A1
Well Cl. W-S-M 105 D1
Well Cl. Winns 125 D4
Well House Cl. Bris 48 C2
Well La. Yatt 91 E4
Well Park. Cong 91 F2
Welland Rd. Keyn 81 F2
Wellard Cl. W-S-M 89 D2
Wellgarth Rd. Bris 64 A1
Wellgarth Wlk. Bris 64 A1
Wellington Ave. Bris 49 F1
Wellington Bldgs. Bath ... 84 A1
Wellington Cres. Bris 49 F3
Wellington Dr. Bris 49 E3
Wellington Dr. Yate 27 D1
Wellington Hill W. Bris ... 49 E4
Wellington Hill. Bris 49 F3
Wellington La. Bris 49 F1
Wellington Mews. Bris ... 47 E3
Wellington Park. Bris 49 D1
Wellington Pl. Bris 37 D1
Wellington Pl. W-S-M ... 104 B4
Wellington Rd. Bris 63 F4
Wellington Rd. Kingsw ... 51 E1
Wellington Rd. Yate 27 F2
Wellington Terr. Cleve 57 E3
Wellington Wlk. Bris 49 E4
Wellow La. Hin Cha 119 E1
Wellow La. N St P 135 E3
Wellow La. P St J 133 E3
Wellow Mead. P St J 133 D4
Wellow Rd. Well 134 A4
Wellow Tyning. P St J ... 133 E4
Wells Cl. Bris 80 B3
Wells Cl. Nail 60 A1
Wells Rd. Bath 101 F3
Wells Rd. Bris 64 A1
Wells Rd. Bris 80 B4
Wells Rd. Ch Mag 95 F4
Wells Rd. Chil 137 F2
Wells Rd. Cleve 57 E1
Wells Rd. Dun 95 F4
Wells Rd. Mid No 132 B1
Wells Rd. N St P 135 E2
Wells Rd. Paul 131 D3
Wells Sq. Rad 132 B1
Wells St. Bris 63 D3
Wellsea Gr. W-S-M 105 D4
Wellshead Ave. Yate 27 E1
Wellsway. Bath 101 F1
Wellsway. Keyn 81 F2
Wellsway. W-S-M 104 C2
Welsford Ave. Bris 50 B2
Welsford Rd. Bris 50 B2
Welsh Back. Bris 63 E3
Welton Br. Mid No 132 A2
Welton Rd. Rad 132 C1
Welton Vale. Mid No 132 A1
Welton Wlk. Bris 51 E1
Wemberham Cres. Yatt .. 74 A1
Wemberham La. Yatt 90 C4
Wenmore Cl. Mang 37 E1
Wentforth Dr. Bris 51 E1
Wentwood Dr. W-S-M ... 105 D1
Wentworth Rd. Bris 49 E2
Wentworth. Kingsw 66 A3
Wentworth. Yate 27 F1
Wesley Ave. Kingsw 65 E3
Wesley Ave. Rad 132 B1
Wesley Cl. Kingsw 51 F2
Wesley Dr. W-S-M 89 D2
Wesley Hill. Kingsw 51 E1
Wesley La. Kingsw 66 A3
Wesley Pl. Bris 49 D1
Wesley Rd. Bris 49 F2
Wesley St. Bris 63 E2
Wessex Ave. Bris 49 F4
Wessex Rd. W-S-M 88 C2
West Ave. Bath 101 E3
West Broadway. Bris 49 E3
West Cl. Bath 101 D3
West Coombe. Bris 48 B3
West Croft. Bris 49 E4
West Croft. Cleve 57 D1
West Dene. Bris 48 B2
West Dundry La. Dun 78 C1
West End. Bris 63 E3

West End. Bris 63 E4
West Garston. Ban 107 D2
West Gr. Bris 49 F1
West Hay Rd. Wring 92 B2
West Hill Gdns. Portis ... 45 E3
West Hill Gdns. Rad 132 C1
West Hill. Portis 45 E3
West Hill. Wrax 60 A3
West La. Win 94 A4
West Lea Rd. Bath 84 A1
West Leaze Pl. St Gif 36 C3
West Links Cl. W-S-M 88 A2
West Littleton Rd. Marsh .. 55 F1
West Mall. Bris 62 C4
West Par. Bris 48 B4
West Park Rd. Mang 51 F3
West Park. Bris 63 D4
West Point Row. St Gif ... 24 B2
West Priory Cl. Bris 49 D4
West Rd. Lymp 122 A1
West Rd. Mid No 132 A2
West Rd. Yatt 91 D4
West Ridge. Fr Cot 38 B4
West Rocke Ave. Bris 48 B3
West Rolstone Rd. Ban ... 89 F1
West Shrubbery. Bris 49 D1
West St. Axb 125 D1
West St. Ban 107 D2
West St. Bris 63 E2
West St. Bris 63 F4
West St. Kingsw 65 E4
West St. Kingsw 66 B2
West St. Tyth 16 A3
West St. W-S-M 104 B4
West Town Ave. Bris 64 B1
West Town La. Bris 64 B1
West Town La. Bris 64 B1
West Town Park. Bris 80 B4
West Town Rd. Back 76 A3
West Town Rd. Bris 47 E4
West Tyning. Marks 99 D1
West View Rd. Bathe 86 A2
West View Rd. Bris 63 D2
West View Rd. Keyn 81 F3
West View. Alve 14 C2
West Way. Bris 35 F2
West Way. Cleve 57 E2
West Wlk. Lock 89 D1
West Wlk. Yate 27 F1
West. St Gif 24 A1
Westacre Cl. Bris 35 D1
Westaway Cl. Yatt 91 E4
Westaway Park. Yatt 91 E4
Westbourn Rd. Bris 64 A4
Westbourne Ave. Keyn ... 81 F3
Westbourne Cres. Cleve .. 57 D1
Westbourne Gr. Bris 63 E2
Westbourne Pl. Bris 63 D4
Westbourne Rd. Mang 51 F4
Westbourne Terr. Bris 51 D4
Westbrook Park. Charl ... 84 A1
Westbrook Rd. Bris 80 B4
Westbrook Rd. W-S-M ... 88 B1
Westbrooke Ct. Bris 63 D3
Westbury Court Rd. Bris .. 49 D1
Westbury Cres. W-S-M .. 104 C1
Westbury Ct. Bris 49 D4
Westbury Hill. Bris 49 D4
Westbury La. Bris 48 B4
Westbury Park. Bris 49 D2
Westbury Rd. Bris 49 D3
Westcourt Dr. Kingsw 66 A2
Westcroft. Blag 110 C1
Westend La. O-on-S 7 D3
Westend Rd. Wickw 17 F3
Westend. Yate 17 F3
Westering Cl. Mang 52 A3
Westerleigh Cl. Bris 51 F4
Westerleigh Rd. Mang 52 A4
Westerleigh Rd. Puck 53 E4
Westerleigh Rd. West 39 E2
Westerleigh Rd. Yate 39 E4
Western Ave. Fr Cot 26 A1
Western Ct. Cleve 57 E2
Western Dr. Bris 79 F3
Western La. E Harp 128 B2
Western La. Priddy 128 B2
Western Rd. Bris 49 F3
Westfield Cl. Back 76 A3
Westfield Cl. Bath 101 F2
Westfield Cl. Keyn 81 E3
Westfield Cl. W-S-M 104 B1
Westfield Cres. Ban 107 D2
Westfield Dr. Back 76 A3
Westfield Ind and Trading Est.
    Rad 138 B4
Westfield La. St Gif 36 C2
Westfield Park S. Bath .. 101 D4
Westfield Park. Bath 101 D4
Westfield Pl. Bris 62 C4
Westfield Rd. Back 76 A3
Westfield Rd. Ban 107 D2

Westfield Rd. Bris 49 D2
Westfield Rd. W-S-M 104 B1
Westfield Terr. Rad 132 B1
Westfield Way. St Gif 24 B1
Westfield. Cleve 73 E4
Westgate Bldgs. Bath ... 101 F3
Westgate St. Bath 101 F3
Westhall Rd. Bath 101 E4
Westland Ave. Kingsw 66 B2
Westleigh Cl. Yate 27 E1
Westleigh Park. Bris 80 A4
Westleigh Rd. Bris 35 E1
Westmarch Way. W-S-M .. 89 D2
Westmarsh La. O-on-S 7 D3
Westmarsh. O-on-S 7 D3
Westmead Gdns. Charl 84 A1
Westmead Rd. Bris 65 D4
Westminster Cl. Bris 49 D4
Westminster Rd. Bris 64 B4
Westmoreland Dr. Bath .. 101 F3
Westmoreland Rd. Bath .. 101 F3
Westmoreland Rd. Bris ... 49 D2
Westmoreland St. Bath .. 101 F3
Westmoreland Station Rd.
    Bath 101 F3
Westmorland Terr. Ch Sod . 41 E4
Weston Cl. Bris 48 B4
Weston Cres. Bris 49 F3
Weston Dro. W in G 58 C4
Weston Farm La. Bath 84 A1
Weston Ind Est. W-S-M . 105 D2
Weston La. Bath 84 A1
Weston Park Court. Bath .. 84 B1
Weston Park E. Bath 84 B1
Weston Park W. Bath 84 B1
Weston Park. Bath 84 B1
Weston Rd. Berr 121 D3
Weston Rd. Cong 91 D3
Weston Rd. Lo Ash 77 E4
Weston Rd. Wrax 62 A3
Weston Way. Lock 105 F1
Weston Wood Rd. Portis .. 45 D2
Westons Way. Kingsw 65 F4
Westover Cl. Bris 34 C1
Westover Dr. Bris 35 D1
Westover Gdns. Bris 48 C4
Westover Rd. Bris 35 D1
Westover Rise. Bris 35 D1
Westview Orchard. Hi Cha 120 A3
Westview. Paul 131 E3
Westward Cl. Wring 92 B1
Westward Dr. E in G 47 E2
Westward Gdns. Lo Ash ... 62 A1
Westward Rd. Bris 78 C4
Westway. Nail 59 F1
Westwood Ave. Paul 115 E1
Westwood Cl. W-S-M 88 C1
Westwood Cres. Bris 64 B3
Westwood Rd. Bris 80 B4
Westwoods. Bathe 86 A2
Wetherby. Mang 37 F1
Wetherell Pl. Bris 63 D4
Wetlands La. Portis 45 E2
Wexford Rd. Bris 79 E4
Weymouth Rd. Bris 63 F1
Weymouth St. Bath 102 A4
Wharf La. Porth 46 A3
Wharf Rd. Bris 50 C2
Wharfedale. Thorn 15 E4
Wharfside. Lymp 121 F2
Wharnecliffe Cl. Bris 80 A3
Wharnecliffe Gdns. Bris .. 80 A3
Whatley Rd. Bris 49 D1
Wheatfield Dr. St Gif 24 B1
Wheathill Cl. Keyn 81 E3
Wheelers Cl. Mid No 132 B1
Wheelers Dr. Mid No 132 B1
Wheelers Rd. Mid No ... 132 B1
Whinchat Gdns. Bris 50 C3
Whippington Ct. Bris 63 F4
Whistley La. E Harp 128 C3
Whitby Rd. Bris 64 B3
Whitchurch La. Bris 79 F3
Whitchurch La. Bris 80 A2
Whitchurch La. Dun 79 E1
Whitchurch La. Dun 79 E1
White Cross Gate. Paul . 130 C3
White Hill. E Harp 128 C2
White Horse Rd. Wind ... 120 C4
White House La. Badg ... 123 D2
White House Rd. Yatt 91 F4
White Lodge Park. Portis .. 45 E3
White Ox Mead La. Well .. 117 F1
White St. Bris 64 A4
White Tree Rd. Bris 49 D2
Whitebrook La. P St J ... 133 D4
Whitebrook La. Tims ... 132 C4
Whitecross Way. Kingsw .. 66 A4
Whitecross Ave. Bris 80 C3
Whitecross La. Ban 107 D2
Whitecross Rd. E Harp .. 128 C2
Whitecross Rd. W-S-M .. 104 C3
Whitefield Ave. Bris 51 D1
Whitefield Ave. Kingsw .. 65 E3

Willoughby Cl.

Whitefield Cl. Bathe
Whitefield Cl. Kingsw
Whitefield Rd. Bris
Whitefields. Ch Sod
Whitegate Cl. Blea
Whitegate Cl. Blea
Whitehall Ave. Bris
Whitehall Gdns. Bris
Whitehall Rd. Bris
Whitehall Trading Est. Bris . .
Whitehouse La. Bris
Whitehouse La. Litt 1
Whitehouse La. Wrax
Whitehouse Pl. Bris
Whitehouse Rd. Piln
Whitehouse Rd. W-S-M
Whitelands Hill. Mid No ... 1
Whiteleaze. Bris
Whiteladies Rd. Bris
Whitelands Hill. Mid No ... 1
Whiteleaze. Bris
Whiteoak Way. Nail
Whites Hill. Bris
Whitesfield Rd. Nail
Whiteway Cl. Bath 1
Whiteway Cl. Bris
Whiteway Ct. Bris
Whiteway Mead. St Gif
Whiteway Rd. Bath 1
Whiteway Rd. Bris
Whitewells Rd. Bath
Whitfield Cl. Bath
Whitfield Rd. Thorn
Whiting Rd. Bris
Whitland Ave. Bris
Whitland Rd. Bris
Whitley Cl. Yate
Whitley Mead. St Gif
Whitting St. Win
Whitmead Gdns. Bris
Whitmore Ave. Bris
Whitmore St. Bris
Whitson St. Bris
Whitting Rd. W-S-M 1
Whittington Dr. W-S-M 8
Whittington Rd. Bris
Whittock Rd. Bris
Whittock Sq. Bris
Whittucks Cl. Kingsw
Whittucks Rd. Kingsw
Whittucks Rd. Kingsw
Whitwell Rd. Bris 4
Whytes Cl. Bris
Wick Cres. Bris
Wick Ct. W-S-M
Wick House Cl. Keyn
Wick La. Bath 1
Wick La. Lymp 12
Wick La. Pens 12
Wick La. Tims 1
Wick Rd. Berr 6
Wick Rd. Bi Sut 11
Wick Rd. Bris
Wick Rd. Bris
Wick Rd. Lymp 12
Wick Rd. Piln 6
Wick St. Bris
Wick. Kingsw
WickCourtry La. Ba Gu 7
Wickcoundry La. Lo Ash 7
Wicket The. Bris
Wilder St. Bris
Willada Cl. Bris
William Daw Cl. Ban 10
William Mason Cl. Bris 6
William St. Bath 10
William St. Bath 10
William St. Bris
William St. Bris
William St. Bris
William St. Kingsw
Williamson Rd. Bris
Williamstowe. Bath 10
Willinton Rd. Bris
Willis Rd. Kingsw
Willis Rd. Kingsw
Willmott Cres. W-S-M 8
Willment Way. Avon
Willmott Cl. Bris
Willoughby Cl. Alve
Willoughby Cl. Bris 7

by Rd. Bris 49 F3
. Bris 35 F4
. Char 11 D2
Cleve 57 F2
Kingsw 66 B3
Lo Ash 61 F1
Lock 89 E1
Portis 45 E2
Rad 132 C1
W-S-M 104 C1
Wick 67 D3
r. Blea 122 B3
r. Lock 105 F1
r. Lock 105 F3
dns. Lock 89 E1
r. Bris 51 E1
reen. Bath 101 F2
ld. Kingsw 65 E2
Vay. Fr Cot 38 B3
Vlk. Bris 35 D2
Vlk. Keyn 81 E2
own. W-S-M 88 C2
ills The. Bath 85 F2
Shopping Centre The.
g 51 F3
The. Bris 37 D1
The. Nail 59 F2
The. St Gif 36 B4
The. Yate 27 E1
Bris 64 A4
ge Hill. Kingsw 66 A1
St. Bris 63 E2
St. Bris 63 F4
Ct. Kingsw 66 A3
Way. E in G 47 E2
House. E in G 47 E2
Pl. Bris 63 F4
St. Bris 63 F4
Cl. Bris 35 E1
dns. W-S-M 104 B4
Wring 92 B1
e Ave. Kingsw 65 E3
e Ave. Yate 28 A2
e Pl. Kingsw 51 F2
e Way. Bath 85 D1
y Ind Est. Bris 64 A1
don Rd. Bris 49 E3
stone Rd. Winsc 107 F1
ne Rd. Bris 63 E1
Cl. Bris 80 B4
ton Cl. Nail 60 A1
ombe Cl. Nail 76 A4
ombe Gr. Bris 47 F3
ombe Rd. Fr Cot 38 A4
ster Ave. Bris 64 B2
ster Rd. Bath 101 E3
ster Rd. Bris 64 B2
r Cl. Kingsw 66 B2
ff Cres. Bris 47 F4
mere Rd. Bris 36 A4
mere Way. Kingsw 66 B3
II Cl. Bris 63 F2
II Farm Bsns Cen.
II Hill. Bris 63 E2
II Hill. Lock 106 A1
II La. Bris 34 B2
ish Cl. Bath 100 C3
ish Cl. Thorn 15 E4
ish Green. Keyn 82 A2
ish Rd. Keyn 82 A2
r Ave. Bris 65 D3
r Ave. Keyn 81 F2
r Bridge Rd. Bath 101 E4
r Cl. Cleve 57 E1
r Cl. St Gif 36 C2
r Cres. Bris 34 B2
r Ct. Bath 101 E4
r Ct. Mang 51 F4
r Ct. Wick 67 E4
r Dr. Yate 27 E1
r Gr. Bris 63 F2
r Pl. Bris 62 C3
r Pl. Mang 52 A3
r Pl. Bris 49 F1
r Rd. Kingsw 65 F1
r Rd. W-S-M 88 B1
r Terr. Bris 62 C3
r Terr. Bris 63 F2
histle Circ. W-S-M 104 C2
histle La. W-S-M 104 C2
histle Rd. W-S-M 104 B2
St. Bath 102 A3
La. Dun 78 B4
rry Cl. Bris 50 B1
d Rd. Sist 66 B4
Ct. Portis 45 D3
d Gr. Bris 79 D4
d La. Dun 78 B4
rd Cl. Ch Mag 95 F2
rd Cl. W-S-M 104 B1
eld Rd. Bris 63 F3
nd's La. Bath 84 C1
orth Pl. Bris 49 F1
wing End. Wins 108 A2
ury Way. St Gif 24 B1
combe Cl. Keyn 81 E3

Winscombe Dro. Ship 125 E3
Winscombe Dro. Wins 125 E3
Winscombe Hill. Wins 124 C3
Winscombe Rd. W-S-M 105 D4
Winsford St. Bris 64 A4
Winsham Cl. Bris 80 A3
Winsley Hill. Winsl 120 A3
Winsley Rd. Bris 49 E1
Wint Hill. Ban 107 D1
Winterbourne Hill. Wint 37 E3
Winterbourne Rd. St Gif 36 C3
Winterfield Park. Paul 131 F2
Winterfield Rd. Paul 131 F3
Winterstoke Cl. Bris 63 D1
Winterstoke Rd. Bris 62 C2
Winterstoke Rd. W-S-M 105 D2
Winterstoke Underpass. Bris 62 C2
Winton St. Bris 63 F2
Wistaria Ave. Ch Sod 28 A1
Wisteria Ave. Lock 105 E1
Witch Hazel Rd. Bris 79 F2
Witchell Rd. Bris 64 B4
Witcombe Cl. Kingsw 51 F1
Witcombe. Yate 39 E4
Witherlies Rd. Bris 50 C3
Withey Cl E. Bris 48 C3
Withey Cl W. Bris 48 C3
Witheys The. Whit 80 B2
Withies La. Mid No 134 C2
Withies Park. Mid No 137 F4
Withington Cl. Kingsw 66 B1
Withleigh Rd. Bris 64 A2
Withydlich La. Pris 117 E2
Withymead Rd. Marsh 70 A4
Withypool Gdns. Bris 80 A3
Withywood Gdns. Bris 78 C2
Withywood Rd. Bris 78 C2
Witney Cl. Keyn 82 B2
Woburn Cl. Kingsw 65 F3
Woburn Rd. Bris 50 A2
Wolferton Rd. Bris 49 F1
Wolfridge Gdns. Bris 80 A4
Wolfridge La. Alve 14 C2
Wolfridge Ride. Alve 14 C2
Wolseley Rd. Bris 49 E2
Wolvers Hill Rd. Ban 106 C3
Wolvers Hill Rd. Lock 106 C3
Wolvershill Park. Ban 107 D2
Wood Hill. Cong 91 F3
Wood Kilns The. Yatt 74 A4
Wood La. Axb 125 E1
Wood La. Horb 13 D3
Wood La. W in G 59 F4
Wood La. W-S-M 87 F1
Wood Rd. Kingsw 65 E4
Wood St. Bath 101 F3
Wood St. Bath 101 F3
Wood St. Bris 50 A1
Woodbine Rd. Bris 64 B4
Woodborough Cres. Wins . 125 D4
Woodborough Dr. Wins 125 D4
Woodborough La. Mid No 133 D2
Woodborough Rd. Mid No 133 D2
Woodborough Rd. Wins 125 D4
Woodborough St. Bris 50 A1
Woodbridge Rd. Bris 64 A1
Woodbury La. Bris 49 D1
Woodchester Rd. Bris 49 E4
Woodchester. Kingsw 51 F2
Woodchester. Yate 39 F4
Woodcliff Ave. W-S-M 88 B1
Woodcliff Rd. W-S-M 88 B1
Woodcote Rd. Bris 51 D2
Woodcote Wlk. Bris 51 D1
Woodcote. Kingsw 65 E3
Woodcroft Ave. Bris 50 B3
Woodcroft Cl. Bris 64 C2
Woodcroft Rd. Bris 64 C2
Woodcroft. Bi Sut 113 E2
Woodend La. Rock 2 C1
Woodend Rd. Fr Cot 38 B4
Woodend. Kingsw 65 E3
Woodfield Rd. Bris 49 D1
Woodfinch Cres. Puck 53 E2
Woodford Cl. Nail 60 A1
Woodgrove Rd. Bris 34 B1
Woodhall Cl. Mang 51 F3
Woodhill Ave. Portis 45 E3
Woodhill Rd. Portis 45 D4
Woodhill Views. Nail 59 F2
Woodhouse Ave. Alve 24 B4
Woodhouse Cl. Alve 24 B4
Woodhouse Gr. Bris 49 F3
Woodhouse Rd. Bath 101 D3
Woodhurst Rd. W-S-M 105 D4
Woodington Ct. Kingsw 65 F2
Woodington Rd. Cleve 57 E1
Woodland Ave. Kingsw 51 E1
Woodland Cl. Wrax 61 D2
Woodland Ct. Bris 48 B3
Woodland Cotts Winsl 120 B3
Woodland Glade. Cleve 57 F3
Woodland Gr. Bath 102 C3
Woodland Gr. Bris 48 B3
Woodland Rd. Bris 63 E4
Woodland Rd. Crom 10 A2

Woodland Rd. Nail 59 F2
Woodland Rd. W-S-M 104 B2
Woodland Terr. Bris 49 D1
Woodland Terr. Kingsw 65 F4
Woodland Way. Bris 51 E1
Woodland Way. Wrax 61 D2
Woodlands Ct. St Gif 24 A2
Woodlands Dr. Winsl 120 A3
Woodlands La. Alve 24 C3
Woodlands La. St Gif 24 B2
Woodlands Park. Bath 85 E1
Woodlands Park. St Gif 24 B2
Woodlands Rd. Char 11 D2
Woodlands Rd. Cleve 57 E2
Woodlands Rd. Portis 45 F4
Woodlands Rd. Tyth 16 A3
Woodlands Rise. Mang 51 E3
Woodlands The. Pris 116 C2
Woodlands. Mang 51 F3
Woodlands. St Gif 24 B2
Woodlands. Tyth 16 A3
Woodleaze. Bris 48 A3
Woodleigh Gdns. Bris 80 B3
Woodleigh. Thorn 8 B1
Woodmancote Rd. Bris 49 F1
Woodmancote. Yate 39 E4
Woodmans Cl. Ch Sod 40 A4
Woodmans Vale. Ch Sod ... 40 A4
Woodmans Vale. Ch Sod 40 B4
Woodmarsh Cl. Bris 80 A2
Woodmead Gdns. Bris 79 E2
Woodmead La. Doyn 54 A1
Woodmill. Yatt 74 A1
Woodpecker Ave. Rod 138 A4
Woodpecker Dr. W-S-M ... 105 D1
Woods Hill. Li St 120 A4
Woodside Ave. W-S-M 105 D1
Woodside Gdns. Portis 44 C3
Woodside Gr. Bris 34 B2
Woodside Rd. Bris 64 C3
Woodside Rd. Cleve 57 F3
Woodside Rd. Fr Cot 38 B4
Woodside Rd. Kingsw 65 E4
Woodside Rd. Mang 51 E3
Woodside. Bris 48 B2
Woodside. Mid No 131 F1
Woodspring Ave. W-S-M ... 88 A4
Woodspring Cres. W-S-M . 88 A2
Woodstock Ave. Bris 49 E1
Woodstock Cl. Kingsw 65 F4
Woodstock Rd. Bris 49 E1
Woodstock Rd. Kingsw 65 F4
Woodstock Rd. W-S-M 105 D4
Woodview Cl. Bris 47 F4
Woodview Dr. Brock 92 A4
Woodview Terr. Nail 59 F1
Woodview Terr. W-S-M 105 D3
Woodview. Chil 137 F3
Woodview. Cleve 57 D1
Woodview. Paul 131 E3
Woodward Dr. Kingsw 65 F2
Woodwell Rd. Bris 47 F3
Woogyleaze Dr. Kingsw 65 E3
Wookey Cl. Nail 75 F4
Woolcot St. Bris 49 D1
Wooler Rd. W-S-M 104 C4
Woollard La. Pens 80 B1
Woollard La. Whit 80 C1
Woolley La. Char 85 D2
Woolley Rd. Bris 80 C3
Wootton Cres. Bris 64 C3
Wootton Pk. Bris 64 A1
Wootton Rd. Bris 64 C3
Worcester Bldgs. Bath 85 D1
Worcester Cl. Bris 51 D1
Worcester Cres. Bris 63 D4
Worcester Gdns. Nail 75 E4
Worcester Park. Bath 85 D1
Worcester Pl. Bath 85 D1
Worcester Rd. Bris 63 D4
Worcester Rd. Kingsw 51 E1
Worcester Terr. Bns 63 D4
Worcester Terr. Bath 85 D1
Wordsworth Rd. Bris 50 A4
Wordsworth Rd. Cleve 57 E1
Wordsworth Rd. W-S-M 105 D2
Workshop Rd. Avon 33 E2
World's End La. Keyn 82 B3
Worldsend La. Stone 2 C4
Worle Cl. W-S-M 88 C2
Worle Parkway. W-S-M 89 D1
Worlebury Cl. W-S-M 88 A2
Worlebury Hill Rd. W-S-M . 88 B2
Worlebury Park Rd. W-S-M . 88 A1
Wormcliffe La. Box 46 C4
Worrall Rd. Bris 49 D1
Worrel's La. Wint 37 E2
Worsley St. Bris 64 B4
Worth Cl. Kingsw 65 F3
Worthies The. Lymp 122 A1
Worthing Rd. Bris 35 F4
Worthy Cres. Lymp 122 A1
Worthy La. W-S-M 104 C4
Worthy Pl. W-S-M 104 B4
Worthy Rd. Avon 33 F4
Worthys The. St Gif 37 D3
Wotton Rd. Char 11 D3
Wotton Rd. Ir Act 26 C3

Wotton Rd. W-u-E 11 F3
Wotton Rd. Wickw 27 D4
Wrangle Farm Green. Cleve 57 F1
Wraxall Gr. Bris 79 D4
Wraxall Hill. Wrax 60 B3
Wraxall Rd. Kingsw 66 A3
Wren Cl. W-S-M 105 E4
Wren Dr. Bris 51 D3
Wrenbert Rd. Mang 51 E3
Wrington Cl. St Gif 36 B4
Wrington Cres. Bris 79 D4
Wrington Hill. Cong 92 C3
Wrington Hill. Wring 92 C3
Wrington La. Cong 91 F3
Wrington Mead. Cong 91 F3
Wrington Rd. Cong 91 F3
Wroughton Dr. Bris 79 E2
Wroughton Gdns. Bris 79 E2
Wroxham Dr. St Gif 36 B4
Wyatt Ave. Bris 78 C3
Wyatt Cl. Bris 78 C3
Wyatt's Cl. Nail 59 E1
Wychwood. Kingsw 65 F3
Wyck Beck Rd. Bris 35 D2
Wycliffe Rd. Bris 49 D4
Wycombe Gr. Bris 64 C1
Wye Croft Cl. Bris 35 E2
Wye Ct. Thorn 15 E4
Wyedale Ave. Bris 48 A4
Wykis Ct. Kingsw 65 F3
Wyllie Ct. W-S-M 89 D3
Wymbush Cres. Bris 79 E3
Wymbush Gdns. Bris 79 E3
Wyndham Cres. Bris 65 D2
Wyndham Cres. E in G 47 D2
Wyndham Way. Portis 45 F3
Wynstones The. Kingsw 65 E4
Wynter Cl. W-S-M 89 D2
Wytham Rd. Keyn 82 A2

Yadley Cl. Wins 125 D4
Yadley La. Wins 125 D3
Yadley Way. Wins 125 D4
Yanleigh Cl. Dun 78 B3
Yanley La. Lo Ash 78 B4
Yarbury Way. W-S-M 89 D1
Yate Rd. Ir Act 26 C2
Yate Rocks. Yate 27 F4
Yelverton Rd. Bris 64 C1
Yeo Bank La. K Sey 72 C1
Yeo Cl. W-S-M 105 D3
Yeo Cl. Cong 91 E2
Yeo La. Lo Ash 61 F1
Yeo Moor. Cleve 57 F1
Yeo Way. Cleve 57 D1
Yeolands Dr. Cleve 57 D1
Yeoman's Cl. Bris 48 B3
Yeomans Orch. Wring 92 C2
Yeomanside Cl. Bris 80 B3
Yeomead. Nail 59 F2
Yeomeads. Lo Ash 61 F1
Yeoward Rd. Cleve 57 F1
Yew Tree Cl. Bi Sut 113 E2
Yew Tree Cl. Blag 109 F3
Yew Tree Cl. Nail 59 E1
Yew Tree Dr. Kingsw 51 F2
Yew Tree Gdns. E in G 47 E2
Yew Tree Gdns. Nail 59 E1
Yew Tree Gdns. Wins 108 A2
Yew Tree La. Co Mar 128 A4
Yew Tree La. K Sey 73 D1
Yew Tree Park. Cong 91 E2
Yewcroft Cl. Bris 80 A2
Yewtree Batch. Buf 94 A1
Yomede Park. Bath 101 D4
York Ave. Bris 49 F2
York Cl. Mang 37 F1
York Cl. St Gif 36 B2
York Cl. W-S-M 89 D2
York Cl. Yate 27 D1
York Gdns. Bris 62 C3
York Gdns. Bris 63 D3
York Gdns. Wint 37 F4
York Pl. Bris 63 D4
York Pl. Bris 49 F1
York Rd. Bris 50 B1
York Rd. Bris 63 F2
York Rd. Kingsw 51 F2
York St. Bath 102 A3
York St. Bris 50 A1
York St. Bris 63 F4
York St. Bris 64 B4
York St. W-S-M 104 B4

Zetland Rd. Bris 49 E1
Zig Zag. Cleve 57 E2
Zinc Rd. Avon 33 E2
Zion Hill. Ston E 137 D4

STREET ATLASES ORDER FORM

PHILIP'S

COLOUR LOCAL ATLASES	PAPERBACK Quantity @ £3.50 each	£ Total
CANNOCK, LICHFIELD, RUGELEY	☐ 0 540 07625 2 ➤	☐
DERBY AND BELPER	☐ 0 540 07608 2 ➤	☐
NORTHWICH, WINSFORD, MIDDLEWICH	☐ 0 540 07589 2 ➤	☐
PEAK DISTRICT TOWNS	☐ 0 540 07609 0 ➤	☐
STAFFORD, STONE, UTTOXETER	☐ 0 540 07626 0 ➤	☐
WARRINGTON, WIDNES, RUNCORN	☐ 0 540 07588 4 ➤	☐

COLOUR REGIONAL ATLASES	HARDBACK	SPIRAL	POCKET	
	Quantity @ £10.99 each	Quantity @ £8.99 each	Quantity @ £4.99 each	£ Total
MERSEYSIDE	☐ 0 540 06480 7	☐ 0 540 06481 5	☐ 0 540 06482 3	☐
	Quantity @ £12.99 each	Quantity @ £8.99 each	Quantity @ £5.99 each	£ Total
BERKSHIRE	☐ 0 540 06170 0	☐ 0 540 06172 7	☐ 0 540 06173 5	☐
	Quantity @ £12.99 each	Quantity @ £9.99 each	Quantity @ £4.99 each	£ Total
DURHAM	☐ 0 540 06365 7	☐ 0 540 06366 5	☐ 0 540 06367 3	☐
	Quantity @ £12.99 each	Quantity @ £9.99 each	Quantity @ £5.50 each	£ Total
GREATER MANCHESTER	☐ 0 540 06485 8	☐ 0 540 06486 6	☐ 0 540 06487 4	➤ ☐
TYNE AND WEAR	☐ 0 540 06370 3	☐ 0 540 06371 1	☐ 0 540 06372 X	➤ ☐
	Quantity @ £12.99 each	Quantity @ £9.99 each	Quantity @ £5.99 each	£ Total
BEDFORDSHIRE	☐ 0 540 07801 8	☐ 0 540 07802 6	☐ 0 540 07803 4	➤ ☐
BIRMINGHAM & WEST MIDLANDS	☐ 0 540 07603 1	☐ 0 540 07604 X	☐ 0 540 07605 8	➤ ☐
BUCKINGHAMSHIRE	☐ 0 540 07466 7	☐ 0 540 07467 5	☐ 0 540 07468 3	➤ ☐
CHESHIRE	☐ 0 540 07507 8	☐ 0 540 07508 6	☐ 0 540 07509 4	➤ ☐
DERBYSHIRE	☐ 0 540 07531 0	☐ 0 540 07532 9	☐ 0 540 07533 7	➤ ☐
EDINBURGH & East Central Scotland	☐ 0 540 07653 8	☐ 0 540 07654 6	☐ 0 540 07656 2	➤ ☐
NORTH ESSEX	☐ 0 540 07289 3	☐ 0 540 07290 7	☐ 0 540 07292 3	➤ ☐
SOUTH ESSEX	☐ 0 540 07294 X	☐ 0 540 07295 8	☐ 0 540 07297 4	➤ ☐
GLASGOW & West Central Scotland	☐ 0 540 07648 1	☐ 0 540 07649 X	☐ 0 540 07651 1	➤ ☐
NORTH HAMPSHIRE	☐ 0 540 07471 3	☐ 0 540 07472 1	☐ 0 540 07473 X	➤ ☐